Preparing for the ACT English, Reading & Writing

Dr. Robert D. Postman

AMSCO

Amsco School Publications, Inc.,
a division of Perfection Learning®

Author

Robert Postman is a college professor who is an expert in test preparation and subject-matter study. Dr. Postman holds a doctorate from Columbia University, where he received a full fellowship to pursue his graduate study. He is the author of more than 30 books and is recognized for his work as a dean and department chair and for his faculty affiliation with Teachers College, Columbia University. An active participant in the community, he has served on various boards, including special education boards, and as an elected member of the Board of Education.

Reviewers

Christina Albers
English Teacher
Marshall Early College
High School, Louisiana

Lesley Babcock
English Department Head
Academy of Our Lady, Louisiana

Dana Convery
English Teacher
Prairie Central High School, Illinois

Candace Drake
English Teacher
Wekiva High School, Florida

Rona S. Gabin
Guidance Counselor
Bergen County Technical
High School, New Jersey

Ruth Getchius
English Teacher
Prairie Central High School, Illinois

Conni Hilston
English Teacher
Aurora High School, Ohio

Warren Jones
Educational Consultant
State of Illinois

Mary Mitchell
English Department
Weber High School, Illinois

Donna Underwood
Director
Learning TECH/Quest School,
Louisiana

Elise Womack
English Teacher
Zion-Benton Township
High School, Illinois

Composition: Sierra Graphics, Inc.
Cover and Text Design: Delgado and Company, Inc.

Please visit our Web sites at: *www.amscopub.com* and *www.perfectionlearning.com*

Preface

Preparing for the ACT: English, Reading & Writing shows you how to get your highest possible score on the English, Reading, and Writing sections of the ACT. The book includes a thorough subject review with extensive practice and effective test-taking strategies. This book will help you to win admission to the college of your choice and, once there, to get the most out of college that you can. It is a once-in-a-lifetime opportunity. I wish you well as you prepare to continue your education.

I am grateful to the teachers who reviewed the manuscript. I am also indebted to two doctoral students who contributed significantly to the development of this book: Lisa Preston, who received her undergraduate degree from Washington and Lee University and is finishing her doctoral work in English at George Washington University; and Jennifer Roberts, who completed her undergraduate work at Union College and is completing her doctoral work in English at the Catholic University of America.

The ACT Writing Test was first field tested in Montana, and I am grateful to Dr. Jan Clinard, the Director of Academic Initiatives for the Montana Commissioner of Higher Education, who organized that field test. Dr. Clinard's office sponsors Webwriters (**http://webwriters.msugf.edu/**), a Web site designed to help students with the ACT Writing Test. I am also grateful to Jonathan Moore and Robyn Wingo, holistic scorers trained for the ACT field test, who contributed scored essays to this book.

Special thanks go to those at ACT who were very helpful as I worked on this manuscript. It was wonderful to speak with people who are truly interested in the students who take their test.

My special regard goes to my wife, Betty Ann, who has been a constant source of support. I could not have completed this project without her. My children—Chad, Blaire, Ryan—and my grandson, Quinn, have been an inspiration as I have worked on this and other books over the years.

Robert D. Postman

Contents

Section I

Introduction
and Test Preparation

Introduction

The ACT Assessment

The ACT Assessment is a college-admissions test. Colleges use ACT scores to help determine which students will be admitted as freshmen or as transfer students. The ACT consists of four separate multiple-choice tests: English, Reading, Mathematics, and Science Reasoning. An optional writing test is also available.

Each test has a different number of items. The composite score is an average of the four reported scores. ACT score reports show the composite score, the score for each test, and subscores for groups of items that show achievement in particular areas.

You'll find more detailed information about these tests, scores, test preparation and test-taking strategies, subject reviews, and practice tests starting in the next chapter. This book will lead you through the preparation you need to get your absolute best ACT score.

Comparison of the ACT and the SAT

The two national college-admissions tests are the ACT from the American College Testing Program and the SAT from the College Board and the Educational Testing Service. There are good reasons to take the ACT whether or not you take the SAT. The ACT focuses more on achievement and is related to the high school curriculum. ACT test makers are very clear about the material covered on the test and about the number of test items devoted to each area. Since items on the ACT are related to the curriculum, you can effectively prepare for this test.

All the items on an ACT Assessment count toward your final score. On the SAT, one of the sections is experimental and does not count.

The ACT reports your scores quickly, which gives you plenty of time to decide about retaking the test. You can even decide which ACT scores will be reported to colleges after you have seen the scores.

The SAT penalizes you for incorrect answers. There is no incorrect answer penalty on the ACT, and you can—and should—guess whenever you can't determine the correct answer.

About as many students take the ACT as take the SAT. Every college accepts ACT scores, and more than 60 percent of students attending college in recent years have taken the ACT. Many colleges use subscores of the ACT as achievement scores and placement scores. So if you take the ACT, you may not have to take the SAT II Achievement Tests.

Registering for the ACT

Register in advance for the ACT. ACT registration packets should be available in your high school. Ask your guidance counselor, adviser, or teacher. You can also request a packet online or contact the ACT for a registration packet.

> ACT Registration Department
> P.O. Box 414
> Iowa City, IA 52243-0414
> **http://actstudent.org**
> (319) 337-1270 (Monday–Friday, 8:00 A.M.–8:00 P.M. central time)

Note:

If you plan to test at an international testing center, you must register for the ACT online. On the other hand, if you are requesting special accommodations, are younger than 13, or are paying by check or money order, you must use a paper packet to register.

The ACT's Web site (**http://actstudent.org**) has complete information about the test, including registration information, test dates, and test sites. You can also register and e-mail the ACT through links on the Web page, which is updated regularly. Log on to see what additional features or services have been added.

You can call ACT or use the Web site to check on a late or delayed admission ticket, or to change your test date or test center. Everyone at ACT wants to help you, and you should feel very comfortable about contacting them.

Regular ACT administrations occur on a Saturday in October, December, February, April, and June. Check the registration packets or Web site for test dates and registration deadlines. Registration ends a little over a month before the test date. Late registration, for an additional fee, ends about three weeks before the test date.

When and Where to Take the ACT

You have to make three important registration decisions: (1) where to take the test, (2) in which school year to take the test, and (3) when during the school year to take the test.

Note:

Make sure you check the fee required for standby registration. You should include the basic test fee and the additional standby registration fee. Remember to include the fee for the optional writing test if you plan to take it.

Take the ACT as close to home as possible. The test may even be given in your high school. The ACT is not given at every site on every test date. Check the registration packet or Web site to be sure the test is given at one of your preferred sites on the date you will take the test. If you register online, you can check availability at your preferred site instantly.

You should first take the ACT in your junior year. You can always take the test again in your senior year. Besides, application deadlines for many colleges and scholarship programs require you to take the ACT as a junior. Take the test toward the end of your junior year, probably on the April test date. Since the ACT is closely tied to course content, junior-year classes will probably help. If you are taking the test in your senior year, take it early so the test scores are available to colleges.

Forms of Identification

You must bring an acceptable form of identification to the test center. If you don't have an acceptable ID, you probably won't be able to take the test. Acceptable forms of identification include an up-to-date official photo ID or a picture from a school yearbook showing your first and last name (individual pictures only—no group photos). Unacceptable forms of identification include unofficial photo ID, learner's permit or license without a photograph, a birth certificate, or a social security card. If you are not sure whether you have an acceptable ID, the ACT has a special number for you to call: (319) 337-1510. You can also see a detailed list of acceptable and unacceptable forms of identification in the FAQs tab on the ACT Student Web site.

Standby Registration

You may be able to register as standby at an ACT test center. Needless to say, you should do everything you can to avoid standby registration. There is a good chance that there will be no room for you.

Show up at a center on test day with a valid ID, a completed registration packet (sealed inside the registration envelope with your payment), and some hope. All those registered at that center are seated first. If there's room, those registered at other centers are seated next. If there's still room, you will be seated to take the test.

Alternate Testing Arrangements

The ACT provides a wide variety of alternate testing arrangements. These arrangements can involve special test dates, special testing for those with a disability, or special accommodations for a disability on regular test dates.

Special test dates. You can arrange special test dates through the ACT Universal Testing Office. Call or write to them at the number and address below if you think you need or qualify for a special test date.

> ACT Arranged Testing
> 301 ACT Drive
> P.O. Box 4028
> Iowa City, IA 52243-4028
> (319) 337-1448

Sunday testing. If your religious beliefs prevent you from taking a Saturday test, you may take the ACT on the following Sunday. A limited number of sites offer Sunday testing. If you live within 50 miles of one of those sites, you must take a Sunday test there. Fill out a regular registration form and be sure to request a Sunday test date and site. If you live farther than 50 miles from a Sunday test site, write or call ACT Arranged Testing at the address or number above, or go to the Request Arranged Testing form in the Registration tab on the ACT Student Web site.

Homebound, hospitalized, incarcerated. If you are in one of these categories you may qualify for a special test date. Do not fill out a registration form. Contact ACT Arranged Testing for information.

Active military service. If you are on active military service, you may qualify for a special test date. Do not complete a registration form. Check with your base education office about testing on the base, or contact ACT Arranged Testing.

Testing outside the 50 states. You may be able to take the ACT outside the 50 United States. Do not complete a registration form. Contact ACT for information. You can also click on the "test at an international test center" link in the Registration tab on the ACT Student Web site.

Disabled and needing more than five hours or needing nonprint test materials. If you have a diagnosed disability and you need more than five hours to take the test

Note:
You will need to fill out the form to request arranged testing if you find yourself in one of the following situations:

- You are homebound or confined on all test dates.
- There is no test center within 50 miles of where you live.
- Your religion prohibits Saturday testing and there is no non-Saturday testing scheduled within 50 miles of where you live.

The form to request arranged testing is available in the Registration tab on the ACT Student Web site.

Note:
If you need to use the standby option for a Sunday or Monday test date, you must bring a letter from your religious leader or a notarized statement to verify your religious observance.

or you need Braille or nonprint test materials, you may qualify for special testing. If you qualify, the test will be administered on a special test date. Learning-disabled students must have been professionally evaluated during the past three years, or have a current IEP or Section 504 Plan on file. You or your counselor should contact ACT Special Testing at (319) 337-1701.

Special accommodations for a disability on regular test dates. Apply for a special accommodation if you can complete the test in five hours or less using regular print or large-type materials. Special accommodations at the test center can be arranged through the ACT Test Administration Office.

ACT Test Administration
301 ACT Drive
P.O. Box 168
Iowa City, IA 52243-0168
(319) 337-1510

Scoring

The maximum reported score for each test is 36, although each test has a different number of items. The composite score is an average of the four reported scores. The maximum composite score is 36. ACT score reports show the composite score, the score for each test, and subscores for groups of items that show achievement in particular areas. Many colleges use these subscores for placement.

The **raw score** on a test is the number correct. Charts on the following pages show you how to convert the raw score for each test to a scale score.

Scale scores are the scores reported to colleges. Because different ACTs have different difficulty levels, the same raw score does not always convert to the same scale score. The scale scores here are approximations and are given only to familiarize you with the process of converting scores. The scale scores for the practice tests in this book will almost certainly be different from the scale scores on the ACT you take.

Scoring the English Tests

Use the chart that follows to convert the raw score for each English Test to a scale score. The highest possible raw score is 75; the lowest is 0. The highest possible scale score is 36; the lowest is 1. In the chart, a raw score of 75 yields a scale score of 36. A raw score of 0 yields a scale score of 1.

English Scale Scores

Raw Score	Scale Score	Raw Score	Scale Score	Raw Score	Scale Score	Raw Score	Scale Score
75	36	68	31	61	26	54	23
74	35	67	30	60	26	53	22
73	34	66	29	59	25	52	22
72	34	65	28	58	25	51	21
71	33	64	28	57	24	50	21
70	32	63	27	56	24	49	20
69	32	62	27	55	23	48	20

Raw Score	Scale Score	Raw Score	Scale Score	Raw Score	Scale Score	Raw Score	Scale Score
47	20	35	15	23	11	11	7
46	19	34	15	22	11	10	6
45	19	33	15	21	11	9	6
44	18	32	15	20	10	8	5
43	18	31	14	19	10	7	5
42	18	30	14	18	10	6	4
41	17	29	13	17	9	5	4
40	17	28	13	16	9	4	4
39	17	27	13	15	9	3	3
38	16	26	12	14	8	2	2
37	16	25	12	13	8	1	1
36	16	24	12	12	7	0	1

Scoring the Reading Tests

The chart below shows the approximate raw score for each Reading Test scale score. The highest possible raw score is 40; the lowest is 0. The highest possible scale score is 36; the lowest is 1. In the chart below, a raw score of 40 yields a scale score of 36. A raw score of 0 yields a scale score of 1.

Reading Scale Scores							
Raw Score	Scale Score	Raw Score	Scale Score	Raw Score	Scale Score	Raw Score	Scale Score
40	36	29	25	19	16	9	7
39	35	28	24	18	15	8	6
38	34	27	23	17	14	7	5
37	33	26	22	16	14	6	4
36	32	25	21	15	13	5	4
35	31	24	20	14	12	4	3
34	30	23	19	13	11	3	2
33	29	22	18	12	10	2	2
32	28	21	18	11	9	1	1
31	27	20	17	10	8	0	1
30	26						

Detailed Reports

You can receive a copy of the test items, your scored answer sheet, and the correct answers if you take the test in December, April, or June. This scoring information can be a valuable diagnostic tool. You will get more information about how to use this scoring service as a part of the testing strategy later in this book. You can request this service on the registration form or you can apply for this service when you receive your test scores in the mail. However, you can request this service only up to three months after your test date. The test items, answers, and your answer sheet will be mailed to you eight to twelve weeks after the test date.

Note:
You will also receive national ranks on your score report. These ranks show you how many recent ACT test takers scored the same as you did or achieved lower scores than yours.

Score reporting. Those at the ACT treat your scores as though they were your property. That means you decide who sees your scores, which scores they see, and when they see them.

Colleges use ACT scores in different ways. Some colleges just take your highest composite score. Some colleges may use the highest score you earned on each individual test. But suppose you received a composite score of 23 for one administration and 27 on another administration. It is often better for a college admissions office to see only the higher score.

Automatic reporting. Your ACT scores are automatically sent to you. Copies are also sent to the high school and high school counselor you list on the registration form. If you do not want scores sent to the high school, do not list a high school code on your ACT registration form.

Scores are also automatically sent to state and regional scholarship programs. If you do not want scores reported to these agencies, write or call in the week following the test.

ACT Records
301 ACT Drive
P.O. Box 451
Iowa City, IA 52243-0451
(319) 337-1313.

Score recipients listed on the registration form. Your ACT scores are sent free of charge to up to four colleges and scholarship programs you list on the registration form. There is an extra charge for additional choices. You have the following options:

- Do not list the colleges for which you think a particular score is needed or required. Wait four weeks for ACT to report the scores to you. Then decide whether and where to send the scores. This is a good option if you know that a college requires a minimum score for admission. There is no sense confusing the admissions office with a lower score than you are capable of.
- List all the colleges to which scores should be sent. If you think you did poorly on the test, you can ask the ACT to cancel some or all of your college choices. Your answer sheet will still be scored. However, to cancel your score report, you must call (319) 337-1313 *by noon on the Thursday following the test date* and tell the person there which colleges should not be sent scores. Be careful. You may not have an accurate view of your performance on the test. However, if you ask the ACT office not to send the scores, and it turns out that you like them, you can have them sent out at a later date.
- Cancel your scores. You must make this request at the test center. There is not much reason for doing this unless you have to leave the test early because you are sick or for some other reason.

Additional score reports (ASRs). You can request the ACT to send out a score report for any of your test dates. There is a fee for each ASR, which includes the scores for just that one test date. For an additional fee you can have your report processed within one to two working days and usually delivered in three to four days.

ASRs can be requested by mail, by phone, or on the ACT Student Web site. The phone service entails a fee in addition to the ASR fee. Call (319) 337-1313. You must use a credit card for this service. A single report sent to one college could cost a total of $25 or more. However, it is worth the expense if you need to get a score report to a college within a day or two.

ACT Realities

You take the ACT because it is required for college admissions or because it will help you get admitted to a college of your choice.

Tests can be unfair. A lucky guesser may occasionally do very well on a multiple-choice test. Someone who knows the answers may get a lower score because he or she mismarks the answer sheet. Students who are sick the day of the test may do more poorly than they would have otherwise.

Some students may get a higher score than they have any right to expect; others may get a lower score than they need and deserve to receive. Students who know strategies for taking multiple-choice tests often do better than students who don't know these strategies. You've got to make the best of it and get your highest score. This book will show you how.

Chapter 1
Preparing for the ACT

The ACT consists of four separate tests: English, Mathematics, Reading, and Science Reasoning. There is also an optional Writing Test. The first four tests are always given in that order and they must be taken together. You have 2 hours and 55 minutes to answer the items on these tests. If you take the writing test, you have an additional 30 minutes to write the essay. On the typical test day you will check in at about 7:30 A.M., begin the tests at 8:00 A.M., and leave around 12:15 P.M. You get a short break after the first two tests, English and Mathematics. You will also get a short break before the Writing Test if you are taking it.

This book contains a complete subject and strategy review and four ACT English practice tests, four ACT Reading practice tests, and four ACT Writing practice tests. An overview of the English, Reading, and Writing tests is given on the following pages. A brief description of the Mathematics and Science Reasoning tests is also included.

English Test Overview

ACT English: 45 minutes—75 items

The English Test consists of 75 multiple-choice items. Each item is based on one of five prose passages. Each item has four answer choices, and most have NO CHANGE as one of the answer choices. You have 45 minutes to complete the test.

The test measures English skills in two broad areas, Usage/Mechanics and Rhetorical Skills. The number of test items in each of these broad areas is shown here. Following that is a list of the topics tested in each area and examples of ACT test items.

AREA	NUMBER OF ITEMS
Usage/Mechanics	40
Punctuation	10
Grammar and Usage	12
Sentence Structure	18

AREA	NUMBER OF ITEMS
Rhetorical Skills	35
Strategy	12
Organization	11
Style	12
Scores Reported:	Usage/Mechanics
	Rhetorical Skills
	Total Number Correct

Usage/Mechanics (40 Items)

The topics tested by the ten punctuation items are

commas	periods
colons and semicolons	question marks
parentheses	exclamation points
apostrophes	hyphens and dashes

The 12 grammar and usage items are

nouns	subject-verb agreement
use of appropriate pronouns	parallel form
verb formation	adjectives and adverbs
verb tense	comparatives and superlatives
tense shift	idioms

The 18 sentence-structure items cover

run-on sentences	misplaced modifiers
comma splices	shifts in construction
sentence fragments	

This book contains a thorough review of each of these topics. Following are sample ACT English passages, along with questions like those that will appear on the test. Correct answers are indicated with an asterisk; this, of course, would not be the case on the actual ACT.

EXAMPLE

Look at the item with the same number as the underlined portion of the passage. Pick the best replacement for the underlined portion. If the current portion is best, choose NO CHANGE.

Many people would benefit from investing in a book about etiquette. There is at least a few reasons for this. People
<u>1</u>
inevitably find themselves in complex situations when knowing how to act might make things easier. One instance

Sentence Structure

1. **A.** NO CHANGE
   *__**B.** are
   C. were
   D. will be

of this, <u>for example</u>, might be at a funeral; knowing the
₂
right words to say to someone who is grieving could
be very helpful. Wondering how to deal with this
<u>delicate situation. A person</u> may become awkward and
₃
stumble over words, instead of comforting someone
in mourning.

Grammar and Usage

2. F. NO CHANGE
   G. to give an example
   H. for instance
  * J. OMIT underlined phrase

Punctuation

3. A. NO CHANGE
   B. delicate situation? A person
   C. delicate situation a person
  *D. delicate situation, a person

Rhetorical Skills (35 items)

The topics tested in each Rhetorical Skills area are shown below. Look these over to familiarize yourself with the test. This book contains a thorough review of each of these topics, which will also be helpful to you if you decide to take the optional Writing Test.

Strategy. All 12 strategy items are one of these three types:

- Choose appropriate transitional, opening, and closing statements and sentences.
- Choose a sentence most appropriate to the passage's intended readers or to the author's purpose.
- Evaluate the impact of adding, deleting, and revising supporting material and details in the passage.

Organization. The 11 organization items ask you about the best order or placement of sentences or paragraphs. There are two primary types of organization items:

- Place a new sentence in a paragraph or in a passage.
- Reorder the sentences in a paragraph or the paragraphs in a passage.

Style. The 12 style items are about how well the passage communicates. There are different types of style items:

- Identify wordy or redundant sentences and clichés.
- Choose the correct word or words.
- Choose wording that ensures that pronouns correctly and clearly refer to their antecedents.
- Choose wording that maintains the level of style and tone of a passage.
- Choose wording that maintains the effectiveness of the sentence.

Look at the item with the same number as the underlined portion of the passage. Pick the best replacement for the underlined portion. If the current portion is best, choose NO CHANGE.

Strategy

Tyler wanted to change the look of his room. Nevertheless,
                                              ‾‾‾‾‾‾‾‾‾‾‾
                                                   1
he decided to have a painting party.

Organization

☐1 To organize the party, he first needed to get some

paint. ☐2 Luckily, they had some cans of returned paint in

just the right shade of blue. ☐3 Next, Tyler had to invite over

some friends. ☐4 He told each of them to come with a

paintbrush. ☐5 His parents said they would supply pizza.

☐6 Now Tyler just needed some good music.

Style

Before everyone came over, Tyler checked on the paint.

He noticed that the finish was high gloss (paint that would
                                          ‾‾‾‾‾‾‾‾‾‾‾‾‾‾
                                                  3
dry with a lot of shine to it).
‾‾‾‾‾‾‾‾‾‾‾‾‾‾‾‾‾‾‾‾‾‾‾‾‾‾‾‾‾

1. **A.** NO CHANGE
 * **B.** Therefore
    C. In spite of this
    D. But

2. The author wants to add this sentence.

    He didn't have much of a budget, so he talked to some clerks at the hardware store.

    The sentence should be added to the paragraph after sentence:

 * **F.** 1.
    G. 3.
    H. 5.
    J. 6.

3. * **A.** NO CHANGE
    B. (a lot of shine)
    C. (shine)
    D. OMIT the underlined portion.

Reading Test Overview

ACT Reading: 35 minutes—40 items

The ACT Reading Test consists of 40 multiple-choice items based on four passages. Each item has four answer choices. You have 35 minutes to complete the test. The passages are in four broad areas shown below, along with the number of test items in each of these areas.

AREA	NUMBER OF ITEMS
Prose Fiction	10
Humanities	10
Social Studies	10
Natural Sciences	10

Scores Reported: Arts/Literature (prose fiction and humanities)
Social Studies/Science (social studies and natural sciences)
Total Number Correct

A portion of a reading passage and several sample reading test items are shown here. The correct answers to the questions are indicated with an asterisk; this, of course, would not be the case on the actual ACT.

EXAMPLE

At the turn of the century, the Chinese film industry found itself enveloped by Western culture, which competed with traditional values. The industry responded with long-established, conventional stories. Early martial arts depictions were stage-bound affairs, with little
5 unarmed combat and a reliance on the supernatural. From the outset of their film production, the Chinese developed their *wu xia* stories, action genres known as "martial chivalry." The *wu xia* are one of China's principal central myths, much like the American Western, and combine elements of magic and the fantastic with martial arts-trained
10 warriors and monks fighting for any number of noble causes as they wander the land. These films eventually evolved into the unarmed combat cinema of the 1970s, exemplified by Bruce Lee's "Kung Fu" films. Training, dignity and identity were all themes associated with these films.

15 The Cantonese *Wong Fei* films, based on a real-life nineteenth-century character who employed his considerable fighting skills to defend the weak and uphold justice, constitute one of the longest series ever, 99 black-and-white films from 1949 to 1970. These films also rejected the stage aspects of earlier martial arts movies and con-
20 centrated on proper martial arts forms and genuine weapon conflict. Today, Hong Kong martial arts cinema has exerted its influence on action-thrillers, and well-known western directors such as Oliver Stone, Francis Ford Coppola and Quentin Tarantino have all indicated a certain keenness for the genre. Taiwanese director Ang Lee's
25 *Crouching Tiger, Hidden Dragon* (2000) is just one in a long line of *wu xia* films.

Though this style of film is popular in Asia, and with some audiences in the West, the realm of implausibility so readily accepted by Asian audiences limits mass appeal to American audiences, which are more into
30 "realism." Warriors who could flip up to the top of a fortress 30 feet high, or disappear in thin air, or catch knives with their hands and arrows between their teeth did not catch the fancy of the American viewer.

From these movies evolved a different type of martial arts film that was more suited to American tastes. The "American" martial arts film
35 featured a ritualized style of violence (such as karate, judo, kung-fu, keno or other forms of martial arts) to advance along a traditional narrative. The films emerged during the mid-70s, and mostly came from America, but productions from other countries like Australia, Canada, Hong Kong and South Africa are also included, so long as the film is
40 shot in the English language.

1. Which is NOT a characteristic of *wu xia* films?

   A. Magic
   B. A sense of identity
   C. Martial arts-trained warriors
   *D. Long series

2. What reason does the author give for American audiences' rejection of earlier martial arts films?

   *F. The audiences had a hard time suspending their disbelief.
   G. The audiences wanted to see Western characters and themes portrayed.
   H. Big-name American directors had not yet popularized the genre.
   J. American audiences were more accustomed to traditional, linear narratives.

3. Which BEST sums up the main idea of the passage as a whole?

   A. Chinese martial arts filmmakers used supernatural effects throughout their works.
   *B. American audiences influenced martial arts films to become more realistic.
   C. Martial arts films contain highly stylized scenes of violence.
   D. The popularity of martial arts movies is an international phenomenon.

Writing Test Overview

The optional ACT Writing Test gives you 30 minutes to write a persuasive essay in response to a prompt. The test gives the topic for your essay and asks you to convince someone or some group of your position on the topic. For example, you may write an essay about whether or not a school should have a dress code.

Two readers evaluate your essay holistically and assign a score from 1 to 6. Holistic scoring means a reader's evaluation is based on his or her informed impression of your writing. The readers do not go into detailed analysis. If the readers' scores differ by more than 1 point, a third reader evaluates the essay.

Here is an example of a writing prompt.

Prompt

Some parents asked the Town Council to impose a curfew requiring students under the age of 18 to be off the streets by 10:00 P.M. to reduce disciplinary problems and to help ensure children's safety. Other parents do not agree with a curfew. They believe that imposing a curfew will not necessarily ensure students' safety and it should be up to parents to decide what time their children should be off the streets. In your opinion, should the Town Council impose a curfew for students under the age of 18?

Take a position on the issue outlined in the prompt. Choose one of the two points of view given in the prompt, or you may present your own point of view on this issue. Be sure to support your position with specific reasons and details.

Mathematics and Science Reasoning Tests Overview

This section gives a brief overview of these tests. You can get Amsco's *Preparing for the ACT: Mathematics and Science Reasoning* for a thorough description with sample tests and explained answers.

Mathematics Test

The 60-minute Mathematics Test consists of 60 multiple-choice items, each with five answer choices. The Mathematics Test measures mathematical skills in six areas:

> Pre-Algebra (14 items), Elementary Algebra (10 items), Intermediate Algebra (9 items), Coordinate Geometry (9 items), Plane Geometry (14 Items), Trigonometry (4 items)

Science Reasoning Test

The 35-minute Science Reasoning Test consists of 40 multiple-choice items, each with four answer choices. The test focuses on your ability to read, understand, and interpret written material about biology, physical sciences, chemistry, and physics in three broad areas:

> Data Representation (15 items), Research Summaries (18 items), Conflicting Viewpoints (7 items)

Getting Ready to Take the Test

Complete the following steps in the order shown to take the test in April of your junior year. Follow these steps but adjust the time line to take the test on other dates. You will be following the same steps for the Mathematics and Science Reasoning tests. Make sure when you are building your schedule that you include enough time for all four tests.

September

- ❏ Review this chapter.
- ❏ Complete the English Topic Inventory on pages 25–31.
- ❏ Start work on the English section (pages 32–167).

October

- ❏ Continue work on the English section.

November

- ❏ Complete work on the English section.
- ❏ Take the Diagnostic English ACT on pages 168–180 under test conditions (work in a quiet place and time yourself).
- ❏ Use the Diagnostic English Checklist (pages 181–184) and review problem areas noted.

December

❏ Start work on the Writing section (page 355).
❏ Take the Diagnostic ACT Writing Test (page 371).
❏ Review the essay with your teacher.
❏ Start work on the Reading section (page 188).

January

❏ Continue work on the Reading section.
❏ Register for the April ACT. List only the colleges you want the scores sent to immediately after your test is scored. You may want to wait to send scores to colleges where you know that a particular minimum score is required for admission.

February

❏ Complete work on the Reading section.
❏ Take the Diagnostic Reading ACT on pages 229–237 under test conditions.
❏ Use the Diagnostic Reading Checklist and review problem areas noted on the Diagnostic Reading ACT (page 238).

March

❏ Review problem areas noted on the Diagnostic tests.
❏ Review the test-taking strategies on pages 21–22 and the general guidelines for writing on pages 358–360.

Seven weeks before the test

❏ Take Model English and Reading ACT I (pages 245–268) and ACT Writing Test I (page 378) under simulated test conditions.
❏ Score the tests. Review the answer explanations.

Six weeks before the test

❏ Review the problem areas noted on the Model ACTs and on the Writing Test.

Five weeks before the test

❏ Take Model English and Reading ACT II (pages 281–304) and ACT Writing Test II (page 385) under simulated test conditions.
❏ Score the tests.

Four weeks before the test

❏ Review the problem areas noted on the Model ACTs.
❏ Review the test-taking strategies on pages 21–22.

April
Two weeks before the April test date

❏ Take Model English and Reading ACT III (pages 316–339) under simulated test conditions.
❏ Score the tests.

Two weeks before the test

❏ Review the problem areas from the Model ACTs. Refer back to the review sections. Get up at the same time every day that you will on the morning of the test. Work for a half hour each morning on items from one of the Model ACTs.

Test Week

You may continue your review through Thursday, if you want.

Monday

❏ Make sure you have your registration ticket.

❏ Make sure you know where the test is given.

❏ Make sure you have valid forms of identification. If you are not sure whether you have a valid form of ID, call the ID Requirements Office at (319) 337-1510. They will help you.

Tuesday

❏ Visit the test site, if you haven't done it already. Be as thorough as possible, finding the actual room on a college campus, etc.

Wednesday

❏ Set aside some sharpened No. 2 pencils, a digital watch or clock, a good eraser, and the calculator you will use for the Mathematics Test.

Thursday

❏ Complete any forms you have to bring to the test.

Friday

❏ Relax. Your review is over.

❏ Get together any snacks or food for test breaks.

❏ Get a good night's sleep.

Saturday—TEST DAY

❏ Dress in comfortable clothes.

❏ Eat the same kind of breakfast you've eaten every morning. Don't overeat!

❏ Get together things to bring to the test, including registration ticket, identification forms, pencils, eraser, calculator, and snacks or food.

❏ Get to the test check-in site about 7:30 A.M.

❏ You're there and you're ready.

❏ Follow the test-taking strategies on pages 21–22 and the general guidelines for writing on pages 358–360.

After the Test

May

❑ You will receive your scores about four weeks after the test. Discuss the scores with your guidance counselor, adviser, or teacher. You need YES or NO answers to these two questions:

1. Should ACT send these scores to colleges I did not list on my registration form?

   NO—Wait until next time.

   YES—Arrange to have Additional Score Reports (ASRs) sent to those colleges. If there is no rush, write to the ACT requesting that an ASR be sent out. If you want a score sent out immediately, call the ACT at (319) 337-1313 for expedited service.

2. Should I take the test again?

   Lots of people take the ACT several times. If you have a bad day test day or you are sick, you might not do your best. You may just feel that you can improve your score through further review. Consider taking the ACT again if you believe you could improve your score enough to make a difference in college admissions.

   NO—You're finished with this book.

   YES—Decide if you want to take the test again in June or in the following October. A June test date gives you limited opportunity for further review, but the test scores can reach colleges by September. An October test date gives you time to get your scored answer sheet along with the test questions and correct answers, but test scores won't reach colleges before that November.

June Test Date. You have about a month to prepare. Be sure to register for the test. Go back to "Four weeks before the test" on this checklist (page 16) and follow the checklist from there.

October Test Date. Order the test questions and answers and your answer sheet from ACT. You will receive a copy of the test items, your scored answer sheet, and the correct answers. The booklet *Using Your ACT Test Scores* that arrived with your test scores has an order form for these services.

June or early July

The scoring information will arrive.

❑ Compare your answer sheet to the correct answers to make sure the sheet was marked correctly. Look also for any patterns that indicate that you may have mismarked your answer sheet.

❑ Check the answers and note the types of problems that were difficult for you.

August

❑ Register for the October ACT.

September

❑ Show the questions, correct answers, and your answers from your previous test to teachers or others who can explain the types of errors you made. Use the review sections of this book and help from teachers to review problem areas on the test.

Four weeks before the test

❑ Retake the actual ACT that was returned to you under simulated test conditions.

❑ Mark the test and review any remaining problem areas.

❑ Review the test-taking strategies on pages 21–22.

Two weeks before the test

❑ Go back to "Two weeks before the test" on this checklist (page 16) and follow it from there.

Test-Preparation Strategies

Use these strategies and the checklist on the preceding pages as you prepare to take the ACT. They take you right up to test day.

- **Start early.**

  If you are going to take the test in April or June, start preparing in September. Do some work each week rather than cramming just before the test.

- **Eliminate stress.**

  Stress reduces your effectiveness. Moderate exercise is the best way to reduce stress. Try to find some time each day to walk, run, jog, swim, or play a team sport. Remember to exercise within your limits.

- **Be realistic.**

  You are not going to answer all the items correctly. The composite score is the total score for the entire test, and the highest ACT composite score is 36. The national average ACT composite score is normally around 21.

  About 56 percent correct on the entire test will likely earn you an above-average score. The percent correct on each test shown below would earn a composite ACT score of about 21.

English	60 percent correct
Mathematics	45 percent correct
Reading	55 percent correct
Science Reasoning	60 percent correct

  Other combinations of test scores could also earn an above-average composite score. You can always take the ACT over again.

Test-Taking Strategies

Nothing is better than knowing the subject matter for the ACT, but these test-taking strategies can help you get a better score.

- **Relax.**

  Get a comfortable seat. Don't sit near anyone or anything that will distract you. If you don't like where you are sitting, move or ask for another seat. You have a right to favorable test conditions.

- **Accept that you're going to make mistakes.**

  You will get some answers wrong on this test. The people who wrote the test expect you to make mistakes. Remember, the average score for the ACT is about 55 percent correct, so don't let those really difficult questions throw you.

- **All that matters is which circle you fill in.**

  A machine will score the English and Reading sections of your test. The machine detects whether or not the correct place on the answer sheet is filled in. Concentrate on filling in the correct circle. The machine can't tell what you are thinking.

- **Save the hard items for last.**

  You're not supposed to get all the items correct, and some of them will be too difficult for you. Work through the items and answer the easy ones. Pass the other ones by. Do these items the second time through. If an item seems really hard, draw a circle around the item number in the test booklet. Save these items to the very end.

- **They try to trick you.**

  Test writers often include distracters. Distracters are traps—incorrect answers that look like correct answers. It might be an answer you're likely to get if you're doing something wrong. It might be a correct answer to a different item. It might just be an answer that catches your eye. Watch out for these trick answers.

- **Watch out for *except*, *not*, or *least*.**

  ACT items can contain these words. The answer to these items is the choice that does not fit in with the others.

- **Still don't have the answer? Eliminate and guess.**

  If you can't figure out the correct answer, eliminate the answers you're sure are incorrect. Cross them off in the test booklet. Guess the answer from those remaining choices.

  NEVER leave any item blank. Unlike on some other tests, there is no penalty for guessing on the ACT.

- **Do your work in the test booklet.**

  The test booklet is not scored. You can write anything in it you want. Use it for scrap paper and to mark up diagrams and tables in the booklet. You may want to do calculations, underline important words, or draw a figure. Do your work for an item near that item in the test booklet. You can also do work on the cover or wherever else suits you.

- **Write the letter for the answer choice in your test booklet.**

  Going back and forth from the test booklet to the answer sheet is difficult and can result in a mismarked answer sheet. To avoid mismarking the answer sheet, write the letter for the answer choice big next to the item number in the test booklet. In the example that follows, note how the test taker also eliminates some answer choices. When you have written the answer choice letters for each two-page spread, transfer the answer choices to the answer sheet.

EXAMPLE

Why do so many people think teenagers are lazy? This is just one myth about teens that <u>aren't</u> true. Other myths, <u>besides this</u> *B* <u>first one</u>, include that teens always disrespect authority and that all teens are on the verge of making bad life choices. While it's true that teens test <u>boundaries they</u> do also have *J* respect for their role models, who are often adults. Furthermore, teens are faced with difficult decisions, but with the right guidance they can make wise choices.

1. A̶. NO CHANGE
   B. isn't
   C. has been
   D̶. won't be

2. F. NO CHANGE
   G. other than this
   H. aside from this one
   J. OMIT the underlined portion.

3. A. NO CHANGE
   B̶. boundaries: they
   C̶. boundaries; they
   D. boundaries, they

D

Section II

English

Chapter 2
English Topic Inventory

Introduction

The ACT English Test consists of five passages with 13 to 17 questions about each passage, for a total of 75 questions. Each question refers to an underlined portion in the passage. You have 45 minutes to complete this test. That gives you about 30 seconds for each item.

The ACT tests specific English skills. This section of the book is organized to help you review and practice these skills as a part of your overall preparation for the test.

First take the English Topic Inventory on the following pages. Starting on page 27, you'll see the correct answers and a study chart, which will point you to the English skills you need to study. Chapters 2, 3, 4, 5, and 6 review the English skills tested on the ACT.

At the end of the section, you will have a chance to practice your English skills and test-taking strategies on a Diagnostic English ACT. The Diagnostic English ACT is just like the real thing. However, it is specially designed to detect and direct you to the English skills you should review further.

There are three model ACT English Tests in Section IV of this book. Take these under simulated test conditions according to the schedule on pages 16–20.

Begin with the English Topic Inventory. You'll find out what you need to study, and you'll begin to think about English.

Topic Inventory

Each numbered item contains a single error or no error at all. Correct each error. There may be more than one way to correct an error. Circle the number of each item that does not contain an error. Don't guess. If you are not sure, put a question mark (?) next to the item.

EXAMPLES

       had
A. The lake ~~was~~ been stocked with fish earlier in the year.

B. The lake is about two miles deep at the deepest point.

C. My mother made me a neurotic.

1. We decided to go ice skating, but it turned out that no one could get a ride to the rink.

2. I was just getting ready to ride over to a friend's house, I had to help my sister with some chores.

3. The runners were ready the stands were full the weather was beautiful.

4. The student driver was just getting comfortable. As the time for the lesson ran out.

5. To be good enough to play professional soccer. That was one of his great desires.

6. When I was younger I had a dog named Dirk, who learned tricks quickly.

7. Rachel helped a girl across a busy street who was blind.

8. While at the pool one day, it was sunny and windy.

9. The play was starting; who had to hold my little cousin so she would not talk or cry during the show.

10. Where all the mouse had gone was a mystery.

11. That pot is too small for eight potatos.

12. John's favorite saying is, "The sky's the limit."

13. Whom has the keys to the yearbook office?

14. Somebody took their textbook home by mistake.

15. Three boys volunteered to take the dirt bike to get it fixed.

16. The warm water feels.

17. The lonely cowboy dreams.

18. At the concert, the band played my favorite song.

19. Even though I was late coming back from lunch, I didn't miss anything because class begun just as I arrived.

20. Anthony sent the e-mail just as he notices a spelling mistake.

21. The crowd was restless as they wait for the year-end sale to begin.

22. Erin and Ryan decides to move west.

23. Whichever contestant has the most points win the game.

24. Why are everyone laughing?

25. Dancers sometimes seems to move their bodies in ways that defy nature and gravity.

26. Hikers often find their packs are too heavy and they have tight shoes.

27. The camper said she would rather take the train than go by car ride.

28. Matt walked very slow to school.

29. Harry and Ashley decorated their house very well.

30. David played golf badly.

31. Danny was the less experienced of the members of the softball team.

32. Compared to Julie, Rosalie was the most creative.

33. Tim concluded that his opinion was different than that of his parents.

34. Brandon was obsessed by space travel.

35. Well that certainly was an interesting experience.

36. I wiped the apple with a paper towel, before I took a bite out of it.

37. Either Olivia was going to give her mom a chaperone's phone number, or she wasn't going to the prom after-party.

38. I was ready to leave; but my friends still wanted to stay.

39. You should keep these things in the trunk of your car; jack, spare tire, and flares.

40. Learning to do an Ollie it's a skateboard trick was challenging but also lots of fun.

41. Its very likely that I will play softball this weekend.

42. The mens' restroom was closed for cleaning.

43. The question is, "Will it rain tomorrow"?

(Answers to the Topic Inventory, with explanations, appear on the following pages)

Topic Inventory Answers Explained

Compare your answers to the correct answers shown here. If your answer is incorrect, or you were not sure of the answer, circle the number for that item. Then turn to the Study Chart on page 31. Check the box for the study topic of each circled item. Carefully review each topic you check.

1. We decided to go ice skating, but it turned out that no one could get a ride to the rink.

[This sentence is correct.]

but

2. I was just getting ready to ride over to a friend's house, ∧ I had to help my sister with some chores.

[Add a conjunction that suggests a contrast after the comma to separate these two main clauses.]

;   **;**

3. The runners were ready ∧ the stands were full ∧ the weather was beautiful.

[Use semicolons to separate the independent clauses.]

as

4. The student driver was just getting comfortable. ~~As~~ the time for the lesson ran out.

[The second "sentence" is a sentence fragment—a phrase.]

, that

5. To be good enough to play professional soccer. ~~That~~ was one of his great desires.

[The first "sentence" is a sentence fragment—a dependent clause. Use a comma (or a dash) to separate the dependent clause from the independent clause. Or delete the comma and *that*, so the prepositional phrase is the subject of the sentence.]

6. When I was younger I had a dog named Dirk, who learned tricks quickly.

[This sentence is correct.]

who was blind

7. Rachel helped a girl ∧ across a busy street.

[The modifier *who was blind* is misplaced. Move it nearer to the word it modifies. In addition, the modifier is necessary. Rachel didn't help just any girl; she helped a girl who was blind. Therefore it would not be set off with commas.]

I was

8. While ∧ at the pool one day, it was sunny and windy.

[Insert words such as *I was* so that the words being modified by *at the pool* are in the sentence.]

9. The play was starting; ~~who~~ had to hold my little cousin so she would not talk or cry during the show.

[Replace *who* with the word that tells who had to hold the little cousin. The pronoun *I* is one possible solution. Another solution is to change the semicolon to a period, then add *I*.]

mice
10. Where all the ~~mouse~~ had gone was a mystery.

[Use the plural form.]

potatoes
11. That pot is too small for eight ~~potatos~~.

[Use the correct spelling for the plural form.]

12. John's favorite saying is, "The sky's the limit."

[This sentence is correct.]

Who
13. ~~Whom~~ has the keys to the yearbook office?

[Use the subjective form of the pronoun—use *who* when the person is the subject of the sentence, and use *whom* when the person is the object.]

his or her
14. Somebody took ~~their~~ textbook home by mistake.

[Use a singular pronoun to agree with the singular subject *Somebody*.]

15. Three boys volunteered to take the dirt bike to get it fixed.

[This sentence is correct.]

16. The warm water feels **nice (soothing**, etc.).

[*Feels* is a linking verb that must be linked to a word that describes the subject.]

17. The lonely cowboy dreams.

[This sentence is correct.]

18. At the concert, the band played my favorite song.

[This sentence is correct.]

19. Even though I was late coming back from lunch, I didn't miss anything because class ~~begun~~ just as I arrived.

had begun *or* began
[Use the past participle or the past tense.]

noticed
20. Anthony sent the e-mail just as he ~~notices~~ a spelling mistake.

[This is a tense shift. Use the past tense in the subordinate clause so that the verb tense stays consistent.]

waited
21. The crowd was restless as they ~~wait~~ for the year-end sale to begin.

[This is also a tense shift. Use the past tense in the subordinate clause.]

decide *or* **decided**
22. Erin and Ryan ~~decides~~ to move west.

[Use the plural form of the verb to agree with the plural subject *Erin and Ryan.* The past tense is also acceptable, depending on meaning.]

wins
23. Whichever contestant has the most points ~~win~~ the game.

[Use the singular form of the verb to agree with the singular subject *contestant.*]

is
24. Why ~~are~~ everyone laughing?

[Use the singular form of the verb to agree with the singular subject *everyone.*]

seem
25. Dancers sometimes ~~seems~~ to move their bodies in ways that defy nature and gravity.

[Use the plural form of the verb to agree with the plural subject *Dancers.*]

their shoes are too tight
26. Hikers often find their packs are too heavy and ~~they have tight shoes~~.

[Rewrite the sentence to maintain a parallel form.]

27. The camper said she would rather take the train than go by car ~~ride~~.

[*Take the train* and *go by car* are parallel.]

slowly
28. Matt walked very ~~slow~~ to school.

[Use the adverb *slowly*, not the adjective *slow*, since the word modifies a verb and not a noun.]

29. Harry and Ashley decorated their house very well.

[This sentence is correct.]

30. David played golf badly.

[This sentence is correct.]

least
31. Danny was the ~~less~~ experienced of the members of the softball team.

[Use the superlative form *least* in place of the comparative form *less* because the sentence describes more than two people.]

more
32. Compared to Julie, Rosalie was the ~~most~~ creative.

[Use the comparative form *most creative* in place of the superlative form *more creative*.]

from
33. Tim concluded that his opinion was different ~~than~~ that of his parents.

[The idiom is "different from."]

with

34. Brandon was obsessed ~~by~~ space travel.

[The correct idiom is "obsessed with."]

,

35. Well ∧ that certainly was an interesting experience.

[Set off the introductory phrase with a comma.]

towel before

36. I wiped the apple with a paper ~~towel, before~~ I took a bite out of it.

[Eliminate the comma. The phrase is not introductory.]

37. Either Olivia was going to give her mom a chaperone's phone number, or she wasn't going to the prom after-party.

[This sentence is correct.]

leave, but

38. I was ready to ~~leave; but~~ my friends still wanted to stay.

[Replace the semicolon before the conjunction with a comma.]

car:

39. You should keep these things in the trunk of your ~~car;~~ jack, spare tire, and flares.

[Use a colon, not a semicolon, to introduce a list.]

(it's a skateboard trick)

40. Learning to do an Ollie ~~it's a skateboard trick~~ was challenging but also lots of fun.

[Use parentheses to set off this parenthetical clause. You could also use dashes.]

It's

41. ~~Its~~ very likely that I will play softball this weekend.

[Use an apostrophe in the contraction for *It is*.]

men's

42. The ~~mens'~~ restroom was closed for cleaning.

[Use the plural possessive form. Since *men* is already plural, the apostrophe comes before the *s*.]

?"

43. The question is, "Will it rain tomorrow~~?"~~?

[Put the question mark inside the quotation marks. The question is contained entirely within the quotation marks; the entire sentence is not a question.]

Study Chart

Study Topic	Question Numbers	Pages to Study
Sentence Structure		
Sentences	Everyone should review this section.	32–34
Run-on sentences and comma splices	1, 2, 3	34–38
Sentence fragments	4, 5, 6	38–43
Misplaced modifiers and shifts in construction	7, 8, 9	43–47
Grammar and Usage		
Nouns	10, 11, 12	56–58
Pronouns	13, 14, 15	59–63
Verbs	16, 17	64–66
Verb tense	18, 19	67–72
Tense shift	20, 21	72–75
Subject-verb agreement	22, 23, 24, 25	76–79
Parallel form	26, 27	79–83
Adjectives and adverbs	28, 29, 30	84–87
Comparative and superlative adjectives and adverbs	31, 32	87–90
Idioms	33, 34	90–92
Punctuation		
Commas	35, 36, 37	103–108
Semicolons and colons	38, 39	108–111
Hyphens, dashes, and parentheses	40	111–118
Apostrophes	41, 42	118–120
Periods, question marks, exclamation points, and quotation marks	43	120–125
Rhetorical Skills		
Strategy	Everyone should review this section.	133–141
Organization	Everyone should review this section.	145–152
Style	Everyone should review this section.	156–160

Chapter 3
Sentence Structure

Sentences

A **sentence** is a group of words. However, it is also much more than just a group of words. For a sentence to be considered complete, it must meet three criteria:

1. It must have a subject.
2. It must have a predicate.
3. It must express a complete thought.

The **subject** of the sentence usually tells what the sentence is about. The **predicate** of a sentence tells about the subject or tells what the subject is doing. Here are examples of sentences showing the subject and predicate.

Subject	Predicate
The oversized, 18-wheel <u>truck</u>	wove dangerously across the highway.
ACT <u>scores</u>	can be improved through study and practice.
<u>Joshua</u>	is the captain of the varsity basketball team.
<u>She</u>	preferred a quiet day at the beach.

A sentence can be a statement, a question, or an exclamation. Sentences begin with a capitalized word and usually end with a period, a question mark, or an exclamation point. Good sentences convey a complete thought. Good sentences make sense.

Note:
There are 18 sentence-structure questions on the ACT.

Note:
Even very short sentences can be complete or independent. For example, Barry sings—this is a complete thought. In very long and complicated sentences, just be sure there is one main subject and one main verb; these will make up the independent clause, and the other clauses are dependent.

Phrases and Clauses

A **phrase** is part of a sentence that does not contain its own subject and predicate.

A **clause** is part of a sentence that contains its own subject and predicate. An **independent (main) clause** makes sense on its own (see the three criteria for sentences on the previous page).

A **dependent (subordinate) clause** is not a complete sentence; it does not make sense on its own. That's why it's called a *dependent clause*—it *depends* on other clauses in the sentence to complete the idea it is trying to convey.

EXAMPLES

After school, Larry studied this ACT book and took the practice tests.
   phrase   **independent clause**

After he finished studying, Larry went to baseball practice.
   dependent clause   **independent clause**

Larry felt a lot better after he studied for the test.
independent clause   **dependent clause**

Modifiers

Modifiers develop a sentence by giving further details about other words in the sentence. Modifiers can be either words, phrases, or clauses. Modifiers can come before or after the words they modify.

EXAMPLES

Basic sentence:	The sun rose.
Word modifier:	The warm sun rose.
	[The adjective *warm* modifies the noun *sun*.]
Word modifier:	The warm sun rose slowly.
	[The adverb *slowly* modifies the verb *rose*.]
Phrase modifier:	The warm sun rose slowly from the east.
	[The adverbial phrase *from the east* modifies the verb *rose*.]
Clause modifier:	The warm sun, which cast its rays on the river, rose slowly from the east.
	[The clause *which cast its rays on the river* modifies the noun *sun*.]

Notice how these modifiers help build the basic sentence into a more complete and descriptive sentence.

Practice

Underline and identify the phrases and clauses in each sentence below. Write P for phrase, IC for independent clause, and DC for dependent clause.

Example

<u>Before the ball game,</u> <u>Rob went home to study.</u>
       P   **IC**

1. The car screeched to a stop near the intersection.
2. Mark went to the store, and then he went to the movies.
3. Until she is able to drive, Lisa cannot get a part-time job.
4. The ACT exam will be easier after you finish the practice tests.
5. Wanda adopted a dog.
6. When he gets his new boat, Robert will take everyone water-skiing.
7. After school, Justin volunteers at the community clinic.
8. Laura will move to Oregon, but not until she graduates from college.
9. If it rains, the picnic will be canceled.
10. It is hot.

Identify the modifiers and the words they modify in the following sentences.

Example

The ballpark, <u>across the river,</u> will open <u>next</u> year.
          modifies *ballpark*   **modifies *year***

11. Mary came to school in a bright red car.
12. Mark has a shiny new bike.
13. The hiker, who has a blue backpack, climbs the mountain carefully.
14. Jane tried hard to run, but she only moved awkwardly in her knee brace.
15. The old man walked slowly down the road.

(*Answers on page 51*)

▬▬ Run-on Sentences and Comma Splices

Run-on Sentences

A **run-on sentence** consists of two or more independent clauses with no punctuation or connector between them. Run-on sentences must be corrected.

EXAMPLES

Run-on: We headed off to the game during the rain the rain stopped before we got there.

[This sentence expresses two complete ideas, so it should be separated into two independent sentences.]

Corrected: We headed off to the game during the rain. **It** stopped before we got there.

[Change the run-on sentence into two separate sentences.]

or

We headed off to the game during the rain, **but** it stopped before we got there.

[Use a comma and the connector *but* between the clauses.]

or

We headed off to the game during the rain; the rain stopped before we got there.

[Use a semicolon between the clauses.]

Note:
To see if a sentence is a run-on, read it backward. If you get to the middle of the sentence and the words you've read express a complete thought, those words are an independent clause. Keep reading. If the remaining words also express a complete thought—if they are an independent clause—then you have a run-on that needs to be fixed.

Comma Splices

A **comma splice** is like a run-on sentence, except that a comma separates the two clauses. Comma splices must be corrected.

EXAMPLE

Comma splice: The computer is an invaluable tool, it links together millions of people.

Corrected: The computer is an invaluable tool **because** it links together millions of people.

[Insert the connecting word *because* to replace the comma.]

or

The computer is an invaluable tool; it links together millions of people.

[Replace the comma with a semicolon.]

or

The computer is an invaluable tool. **It** links together millions of people.

[Make two separate sentences.]

Note:
To avoid comma splices, remember to use commas only when a coordinating conjunction joins two sentences, or when separating dependent clauses (like introductory clauses) from independent clauses.

Practice

Semicolon
Period

Correct the run-on sentences and comma splices. If a sentence is correct, mark it C.

1. I like to use my computer for research when I have to write a paper.
2. Referees in professional football use instant replays for close calls they also use them after the two-minute warning.
3. When I make cupcakes, I usually use a box of cake mix.
4. The officer turned on his siren, the car pulled over to the side of the road.
5. Running through the rain, the player headed toward the clubhouse.
6. I couldn't find my house keys I knew our neighbors had an extra set.
7. It will be a long time before I order takeout from that terrible place again.
8. My clothes are drenched, water is squishing out of my shoes.
9. I sent an "I'm sorry" card to my girlfriend, although I wasn't sure if she would accept my apology.
10. The doors closed the train started moving.
11. We all went off campus for lunch, we went to the deli.
12. The sun had set the park would be closing soon.
13. After they adopted a puppy, the family spent many hours training it.
14. I like pizza with pepperoni and sausage Rob hates mushrooms on his pizza.
15. In the fall I'll go to college, but this summer I'm working at a movie theater.

(Answers on page 51)

Model ACT Questions

These Model ACT Problems show how this topic might be tested on the real ACT. The answers and explanations immediately follow the problems. Try the problems and then review the answers and the explanations.

Mark and Laura rode their bikes into <u>town, they</u> <u>stopped at</u> the ice-cream store for a cone. <u>Then they rode to the zoo; they</u> did not go inside.

1. **A.** NO CHANGE
   B. town they stopped at
   C. town. They stopped at
   D. town they stopped. At

2. **F.** NO CHANGE
   G. Then they rode to the zoo they
   H. Then, they rode to the zoo they
   J. Then they rode to the zoo, they

Answers

1. The sentence is a comma splice. To correct it, separate the two independent clauses with either a period, a semicolon, or a conjunction. Choice B is a run-on sentence. In choice D, the words "At the ice-cream store for a cone" are not a sentence.

   C is the correct choice.

2. The sentence is correct as it is because the semicolon separates the two independent clauses. Choice G is a run-on sentence. The sentence in choice H is also a run-on because the two independent clauses are not separated. Choice J is a comma splice.

   F is the correct choice.

ACT-Type Questions

Look at the item that matches the number of the underlined part. Pick the best replacement for the underlined part. If the underlined part is the best, select NO CHANGE.

Teens often make mistakes <u>while driving it is a</u> ¹ new skill for them and they need practice. The mistakes are mostly <u>simple, they're</u> ² easily avoided. Talking to friends and listening to music can <u>distract drivers being in</u> ³ the car with an adult has been proved to be safer. After teens get more driving <u>experience, having</u> ⁴ friends in the car becomes safer. Another common mistake teen drivers make is going <u>too fast even driving</u> ⁵ five miles over the speed limit is wrong. Good drivers also slow down in difficult <u>conditions, these</u> ⁶ include traffic, bad weather, and construction areas. Along with driving at an appropriate speed <u>themselves. Teens</u> ⁷ need to be aware of how fast other drivers are moving. They should look both ways twice before proceeding through an <u>intersection. Another</u> ⁸

1. **A.** NO CHANGE
   B. while driving, it is
   C. while driving. It is
   D. while driving: it is

2. **F.** NO CHANGE
   G. simple; they're
   H. simple. Their
   J. simple they're

3. **A.** NO CHANGE
   B. distract drivers, being in
   C. distract, drivers being in
   D. distract drivers. Being in

4. **F.** NO CHANGE
   G. experience. Having
   H. experience; having
   J. experience! Having

5. **A.** NO CHANGE
   B. too fast, even driving
   C. too fast. Even driving
   D. too fast even. Driving

driver may be speeding through. To help avoid accidents like <u>these, teens</u> should learn to drive

_9_

defensively. This means they should try to anticipate what other drivers <u>might do they should</u>

_10_

scan the road ahead and around them as they drive.

6. **F.** NO CHANGE
   G. conditions these
   H. conditions, and these
   J. conditions! These

7. **A.** NO CHANGE
   B. themselves; teens
   C. themselves: teens
   D. themselves, teens

8. **F.** NO CHANGE
   G. intersection: another
   H. intersection, another
   J. intersection another

9. **A.** NO CHANGE
   B. these teens
   C. these; teens
   D. these. Teens

10. **F.** NO CHANGE
    G. might do, and they should
    H. might do, they should
    J. might do: they should

(*Answers on page 52*)

Sentence Fragments

A sentence must contain a subject and a predicate. It must also make sense on its own. A **sentence fragment** is a part of a sentence that is written as though it were a sentence but does not meet the three criteria for a complete sentence. Some sentence fragments may appear to be acceptable sentences. On the ACT, you will be asked to identify and correct sentence fragments.

Sentence-fragment errors as shown in the following section appear frequently on the ACT.

The Sentence Fragment Is a Dependent Clause

A dependent clause does not stand on its own. A single word may change an independent clause to a dependent clause. A dependent clause usually leaves you feeling up in the air, as though you were waiting for the rest of an idea or thought.

EXAMPLES

Independent clause: Ann went to the football game.

[This is a sentence. It has a subject and a predicate, and it stands on its own.]

Dependent clause: As Ann went to the football game.

[This clause is a sentence fragment. It does not stand on its own. We are left wondering what happened as Ann went to the football game, so the sentence does not express a complete thought.]

Fragment: The football game continued. <u>While the band played in the background.</u>

[The underlined portion is a sentence fragment. It has a subject and a predicate, but it does not stand on its own.]

Corrected: The football game continued, while the band played in the background.

[Make one sentence with a comma separating the clauses; join the two sentences together to make a complete thought.]

or

Corrected: The football game continued. The band played in the background.

[Remove the word *while* to change the sentence fragment to a sentence.]

> **Note:**
> Sometimes you can identify fragments by looking for dependent word markers: words that indicate that more information is needed to complete a thought. Examples of these are *as, while, if, because, since, after, when, so that, although, even though, though, whether, unless, which, who, before, whenever,* and *until.*
>
> If you see one of these words in a sentence, check to make sure the rest of the thought is completed. If it isn't, you have a dependent clause that must be corrected.

The Sentence Fragment Is a Verbal Phrase

A **verbal phrase** begins with words such as *to jump, to sleep, jumping, sleeping, jumped,* and *slept.* This phrase cannot be made into a sentence by just dropping a word or two.

EXAMPLES

Fragment: I have one goal for this month. <u>To score well on the ACT.</u>
[The underlined verbal phrase is a fragment. There is no subject.]

Corrected: I have one goal for this month, to score well on the ACT.
[Make one sentence with a comma separating the phrase from the clause.]

Fragment: Liz made a big mistake this weekend. <u>Sleeping on the beach.</u>
[The underlined verbal phrase is a fragment.]

Corrected: Liz made a big mistake this weekend. She fell asleep on the beach.
[Rewrite the fragment to form a sentence.]

The Sentence Fragment Is an Appositive

An **appositive** is a group of nouns, or words that describe a noun, that are not sentences.

Fragment: I'll go shopping anywhere if there's a good sale. <u>Malls, department stores, grocery stores, convenience stores.</u>

[The underlined appositive is a fragment.]

Corrected: I'll go shopping anywhere—malls, department stores, grocery stores, convenience stores—if there's a good sale.

[Make one sentence with commas or dashes separating the appositive from the clause.]

Fragment: My favorite gift was a small statue. <u>A figure that stood cheerily, unflinching, through the best and worst of times.</u>

[The underlined appositive is a fragment.]

Corrected: My favorite gift was a small statue, a figure that stood cheerily, unflinching, through the best and worst of times.

[Make one sentence with a comma separating the appositive from the clause.]

The Sentence Fragment Is Missing a Sentence Part or Parts

Many fragments are just lacking sentence parts. Remember, at first glance a fragment may appear to be a sentence.

EXAMPLES

Fragment: When I was young I had a favorite form of transportation. <u>A bus that traveled to the beach.</u>

[The underlined portion is a fragment. There is no predicate.]

Corrected: When I was young I had a favorite form of transportation, a bus that traveled to the beach.

[Make one sentence with a comma separating the phrase from the clause.]

Fragment: There were some great rides at the amusement park. <u>Was open from 9:00 A.M. to 11:00 P.M.</u>

[The underlined portion is a fragment. There is no subject.]

Corrected: There were some great rides at the amusement park, which was open from 9:00 A.M. to 11:00 P.M.

[Make one sentence with a comma and a connecting word separating the clause from the phrase.]

Practice

Correct the sentence fragments. If a sentence is correct, mark it C.

1. We went out for ice cream. Everybody got double scoops.
2. The wind swirling around me reminded me of something. An assignment on weather I had to complete.
3. Cars, trucks, and motorcycles. They whizzed by on the highway.
4. As I was standing by the entrance to the gym. My step-class instructor arrived with all her equipment.
5. The music took me back. I remembered listening to those songs when I was five years old.
6. This is my idea of fun. To ski as the sun is rising.
7. I saw people silhouetted against the spotlights. Like silent movie stars on a modern stage.
8. I was completely absorbed in the TV show. I didn't even hear my father come home and say hello to me.
9. To be at the beach right now. That is my deepest wish.
10. We got the campfire burning bright. Then we reached for the cookies, chocolate, and marshmallows.
11. I like fresh garden vegetables in the summer. Tomatoes, peppers, and carrots.
12. After a long day in the sun. I like to go swimming in the lake.
13. To finish my college application essay, that was my goal for the evening.
14. Standing on the roof, I saw the people down below. Like tiny ants in a maze.
15. As I woke up and stretched, I thought about what an important day this would be for me.

(*Answers on pages 52–53*)

Model ACT Questions

These Model ACT Questions show how this topic might be tested on the real ACT. The answers and explanations immediately follow the questions. Try the questions and then review the answers and the explanations.

Before going to <u>the party. Kate bought</u> a new
1
dress. It was a <u>spring dress. One with red</u>
2
polka dots.

1. **A.** NO CHANGE
   B. the party, Kate bought
   C. the party; Kate bought
   D. the party! Kate bought

2. **F.** NO CHANGE
   G. spring dress; One with red
   H. spring dress one with red
   J. spring dress, one with red

Answers

1. The dependent clause *Before going to the party* is a sentence fragment. It cannot stand on its own and leaves the reader wondering what happened before the party.

   B is the correct choice.

> **2.** *One with red polka dots* is an appositive fragment. It describes the dress but has no subject or verb of its own. It is corrected by joining it to the previous sentence, separated by a comma.
>
> **J** is the correct choice.

ACT-Type Questions

Look at the item that matches the number of the underlined part. Pick the best replacement for the underlined part. If the underlined part is the best, select NO CHANGE.

Growing up <u>in Idaho. I was used</u> to life in a small
1
town. Traffic jams, crime, and <u>deadlines. These</u>
2
things did not concern me. After <u>college, however.</u>
3
<u>I moved</u> to Seattle. While I had to deal with the
3
<u>problems. I also learned</u> good things about city
4
life. In a <u>large city, new</u> things can be experienced
5
every day. Trying <u>new restaurants. That's one</u> good
6
thing. Chinese, Thai, Ethiopian, <u>and Mexican,</u>
7
<u>these are all new foods</u> I've learned to like. I also
7
enjoy meeting all kinds <u>of people. They each</u> have
8
something different to contribute. While living in
the city has <u>its bad points. The good ones</u> can
9
outweigh them. For <u>me, however, I will</u> eventually
10
return to small-town life.

1. A. NO CHANGE
   B. in Idaho, I was used
   C. in Idaho! I was used
   D. in Idaho; I was used

2. F. NO CHANGE
   G. deadlines; these
   H. deadlines—these
   J. deadlines these

3. A. NO CHANGE
   B. college. However, I moved
   C. college, however? I moved
   D. college, however, I moved

4. F. NO CHANGE
   G. problems; I also learned
   H. problems I also learned
   J. problems, I also learned

5. A. NO CHANGE
   B. large city. New
   C. large city; new
   D. large city new

6. F. NO CHANGE
   G. new restaurants? That's one
   H. new restaurants, that's one
   J. new restaurants; that's one

7. **A.** NO CHANGE
   B. and Mexican. These are all
   new foods
   C. and Mexican? These are all
   new foods
   D. and Mexican: these are all
   new foods

8. **F.** NO CHANGE
   G. of people, they each
   H. of people they each
   J. of people they. Each

9. **A.** NO CHANGE
   B. its bad points, the good ones
   C. its bad points; the good ones
   D. its bad points the good ones

10. **F.** NO CHANGE
    G. me, however. I will
    H. me, however; I will
    J. me. However, I will

(*Answers on page 53*)

Misplaced Modifiers and Shifts in Construction

Adjectives, adverbs, and groups of words serving as modifiers should clearly refer to the word they modify. The ACT items for misplaced modifiers and construction shifts test the same material with slightly different question types. Be sure the placement of the modifier makes sense. To correct such errors, move the modifier closer to the word it modifies.

EXAMPLES

Misplaced: The driver brought a delivery to the store in a red container.

[The modifier is *in a red container.* It doesn't make sense for the store to be in a red container. These words must modify *delivery*, so move them close to *delivery*.]

Corrected: The driver brought a delivery in a red container to the store.

Misplaced: The driver shifted the van into first gear and firmly drove out of the parking lot.

[This example is a little trickier. The word *firmly* seems to place the modifier near the word it modifies: *drove.* But does it make sense to firmly drive a van? No. But it does make sense to shift gears firmly. The modifier *firmly* should be placed near the word it modifies: *shifted.*]

Corrected: The driver firmly shifted the van into first gear and drove out of the parking lot.

Be sure the word being modified is in the sentence. To correct such errors, include the word being modified in the sentence.

EXAMPLES

Misplaced: While on vacation in Iowa, a tornado alert was issued.

[The modifier is *While on vacation in Iowa.* However, the word it modifies is not in the sentence, and the sentence looks silly.]

Corrected: While **we** were on vacation in Iowa, a tornado alert was issued.

or

A tornado alert was issued while **we** were on vacation in Iowa.

[Any pronoun or noun could be added to the sentence.]

Misplaced: The wind was howling, which had to take cover under a highway overpass.

[The word *which* makes no sense here. Replace it with the word that tells what or who *had to take cover under a highway overpass.*]

Corrected: The wind was howling, **and we** had to take cover under a highway overpass.

[Replace *which* with *we.* Remember to include *, and* because the second part of the sentence changes from a phrase to a clause.]

Practice

Identify and correct the misplaced modifiers. If a sentence does not contain a misplaced modifier, mark it C.

1. I went to school to take the ACT in my mother's car.
2. The room was empty; who had to go to another room.
3. I was on the way to my house, which was about a mile away.

4. John drove a van into the night that had no lights.

5. Ron wore a jacket with pockets to the party.

6. It started to rain when on the way to Six Flags.

7. An emergency alert when a mudslide caused hazardous conditions was issued.

8. Lisa completed her speech and brought it to debate club with careful attention to detail.

9. Which bathing suit should I wear to the water park?

10. Leon turned his head, and his eyes looked slowly into the store window.

11. Ryan bought a bowl for his fish which was broken.

12. Ann has a room that is full of toys.

13. While still on the airport runway, a blizzard started.

14. The boy with two pieces missing has a jigsaw puzzle.

15. Sean rode his bike down the path which had no pedals.

(*Answers on page 53*)

Model ACT Questions

These model ACT Questions show how this topic might be tested on the real ACT. The answers and explanations immediately follow the questions. Try the questions and then review the answers and explanations.

Being cold on the <u>roof, put on</u> jackets. The boy

                        1   2

<u>dropped his ball off the building which bounced.</u>

                   2

1. **A.** NO CHANGE
   B. roof put on
   C. roof, people put on
   D. roof; put on

2. **F.** NO CHANGE
   G. The boy, which bounced, dropped his ball off the building.
   H. The boy which bounced dropped his ball off the building.
   J. The boy dropped his ball, which bounced, off the building.

Answers

1. In this sentence, *put on jackets* should modify the word *people*. In the original sentence, *put on jackets* modifies *roof*. The roof cannot put on a jacket. Choice B is incorrect because it does not change the sentence; it just drops the comma. Choice D is incorrect because changing the comma to a semicolon doesn't fix the dangling modifier, and it creates a fragment.

   C is the correct choice.

2. The phrase *which bounced* modifies the noun *ball*. Choice F is not correct because there, *bounced* modifies *building*. Choice G is incorrect because *bounced* incorrectly modifies *boy*. Choice H is incorrect for the same reason.

J is the correct choice.

ACT-Type Questions

Look at the item that matches the number of the underlined part. Pick the best replacement for the underlined part. If the underlined part is the best, select **NO CHANGE**.

<u>Sue looked out over the sea who was scared.</u>
　　　　　　　　　　　1

A <u>foghorn had sounded when on the way home.</u>
　　　　　　　　　2

She <u>knew the boat was missing with the green</u>
　　　　　　　　3

<u>paint.</u> Sue <u>knew her brother often used the</u>
　3　　　　　　　4

<u>boat, which was missing an oar.</u> <u>A radio</u>
　　　　　4　　　　　　　　　5

<u>announcement as the storm rose issued a</u>
　　　　　　　　5

<u>warning to all boats.</u> Just then, <u>a sharp knock</u>
　　　　　5　　　　　　　　　　6

<u>sounded at her door.</u> Sue <u>peered through the</u>
　　　6　　　　　　　　　　7

<u>peephole at the figure outside with one eye.</u>
　　　　　　　　　7

A man in a raincoat stood outside. <u>In a flash</u>
　　　　　　　8　　　　　　　　　9

<u>of lightning, she saw it was John, her brother.</u>
　　　　　　　　9

<u>Sue opened the door and let in her brother</u>
　　　　　　　　　10

<u>with a cry of delight.</u>
　　　10

1. **A.** NO CHANGE
   B. Sue looked out over the sea, who was scared.
   C. Sue, who was scared, looked out over the sea.
   D. Sue looked out, who was scared, over the sea.

2. **F.** NO CHANGE
   G. foghorn had sounded, when on the way home.
   H. foghorn, when on the way home, had sounded.
   J. foghorn had sounded when she was on the way home.

3. **A.** NO CHANGE
   B. knew the green paint was missing with the boat.
   C. knew the boat with the green paint was missing.
   D. knew with the green paint the boat was missing.

4. **F.** NO CHANGE
   G. knew her brother, which was missing an oar, often used the boat.
   H. which was missing an oar, knew her brother often used the boat.
   J. knew, which was missing an oar, her brother often used the boat.

5. **A.** NO CHANGE
   B. A radio announcement issued a warning as the storm rose to all boats.
   C. As the storm rose, a radio announcement issued a warning to all boats.
   D. A radio announcement issued as the storm rose a warning to all boats.

6. **F.** NO CHANGE
   G. then, sounded at her door a sharp knock.
   H. then, her door a sharp knock sounded.
   J. then, a sounded at her door sharp knock.

7. **A.** NO CHANGE
   B. peered with one eye through the peephole at the figure outside.
   C. peered through the peephole with one eye at the figure outside.
   D. through the peephole peered at the figure with one eye outside.

8. **F.** NO CHANGE
   G. A man stood outside in a raincoat.
   H. A man stood in a raincoat outside.
   J. In a raincoat a man stood outside.

9. **A.** NO CHANGE
   B. a flash of lightning her brother she saw it was John.
   C. she saw it was John in a flash of lightning, her brother.
   D. she saw it was John, her brother in a flash of lightning.

10. **F.** NO CHANGE
    G. With a cry of delight, Sue opened the door and let in her brother.
    H. Sue opened the door with a cry of delight and let in her brother.
    J. Sue opened the door and let in with a cry of delight her brother.

(*Answers on page 54*)

Sentence Structure Subtest

This Subtest has the type of sentence structure items found on the ACT. If you don't know an answer, eliminate the choices you know are incorrect, then guess. Circle the number of any guessed answer. Check pages 54–55 for answers and explanations.

INSTRUCTIONS: Certain words or phrases in the following passage are underlined and numbered. There is a corresponding item for each underlined portion. Each item offers three suggestions for changing the underlined portion to conform to standard written English or to make it understandable or consistent with the rest of the passage. If the underlined portion is not improved by one of the three suggested changes, mark NO CHANGE.

Choose the best answer to each question based on the passage. Then fill in the appropriate circle on the answer grid.

```
1 Ⓐ Ⓑ Ⓒ Ⓓ      7 Ⓐ Ⓑ Ⓒ Ⓓ      13 Ⓐ Ⓑ Ⓒ Ⓓ
2 Ⓕ Ⓖ Ⓗ Ⓙ      8 Ⓕ Ⓖ Ⓗ Ⓙ      14 Ⓕ Ⓖ Ⓗ Ⓙ
3 Ⓐ Ⓑ Ⓒ Ⓓ      9 Ⓐ Ⓑ Ⓒ Ⓓ      15 Ⓐ Ⓑ Ⓒ Ⓓ
4 Ⓕ Ⓖ Ⓗ Ⓙ      10 Ⓕ Ⓖ Ⓗ Ⓙ     16 Ⓕ Ⓖ Ⓗ Ⓙ
5 Ⓐ Ⓑ Ⓒ Ⓓ      11 Ⓐ Ⓑ Ⓒ Ⓓ     17 Ⓐ Ⓑ Ⓒ Ⓓ
6 Ⓕ Ⓖ Ⓗ Ⓙ      12 Ⓕ Ⓖ Ⓗ Ⓙ     18 Ⓕ Ⓖ Ⓗ Ⓙ
```

The Olympic Games are a major international event featuring summer and winter <u>sports</u>[1] <u>thousands</u>[1] of athletes participate in a variety of competitions. The Games are currently held every two years. <u>Summer and Winter Olympic Games.</u>[2] The ancient Olympic Games were held in <u>Olympia, Greece from</u>[3] the 8th century B.C. to the 5th <u>century A.D., in the</u>[4] late 19th century, <u>Olympic festivals were inspired by Pierre, Baron de Coubertin, to revive the Games.</u>[5] He founded the International Olympic Committee (IOC) <u>in 1894 two years</u>[6] later, the modern Olympic Games were established in Athens. The IOC has since become the governing body of the <u>Olympic Movement, whose structure</u>[7] is defined by the Olympic Charter.

1. **A.** NO CHANGE
   B. sports, thousands
   C. sports; thousands
   D. sports and thousands

2. **F.** NO CHANGE
   G. Summer, and Winter Olympic games.
   H. Summer and Winter Olympic games;
   J. There are Summer and Winter Olympic games.

3. **A.** NO CHANGE
   B. Olympia. Greece, from
   C. Olympia, Greece. From
   D. Olympia, Greece; from

4. **F.** NO CHANGE
   G. century A.D. In the
   H. century A.D. in the
   J. century A.D.: in the

The Olympic Movement looked at the world's
<u>changing circumstances with great caution.</u> There
                              8
had to be <u>adjustments, some</u> included the creation
                              9
of the Winter Games, the Paralympic Games for
athletes with physical <u>disabilities. The</u> Youth
                              10
Olympic Games for teenage athletes. The IOC
also had to accommodate the Games to the 20th
<u>century, and the</u> Games shifted from amateurism
       11
to the participation of professional athletes.

<u>The growing importance of the mass media</u>
                              12
<u>created the issue of corporate sponsorship.</u>
                              12
Observers knew <u>that the Games were changing their</u>
                              13
<u>spirit with their commercialism.</u>
       13

Although the Olympic Movement currently
comprises international sports federations <u>(ISFs).</u>
                              14
<u>There are committees for each Olympic Games.</u>
       14
<u>The IOC chooses the host city, which is then</u>
                              15
<u>responsible for organizing the Games.</u> There
                 15
are specific events contested at each
<u>Olympic Games; each event</u> is also determined
                 16
by the IOC. While the celebration of the
Games encompasses many <u>symbols. The real</u>
                              17
focus of the Games is on the athletes. More
than 13,000 athletes compete at the Summer
and Winter Games. <u>The awards are made to</u>
                              18
<u>the athletes as gold, silver, and bronze</u>
                 18
<u>medals at an awards ceremony.</u>
       18

5. **A.** NO CHANGE
   B. The Games were inspired by Pierre, Baron de Coubertin, to revive the Olympic festivals.
   C. Pierre, Baron de Coubertin, was inspired by Olympic festivals to revive the Games.
   D. To inspire the Games, Pierre, Baron de Coubertin, revived the Olympic festivals

6. **F.** NO CHANGE
   G. in 1894, two
   H. in 1894? Two
   J. in 1894. Two

7. **A.** NO CHANGE
   B. Olympic Movement. Whose
   C. Olympic Movement; whose
   D. Olympic Movement whose

8. **F.** NO CHANGE
   G. The world looked at the Olympic Movement's changing circumstances with great caution.
   H. The Olympic movement and the world's changing circumstances looked on with great caution.
   J. The Olympic Movement looked with great caution at the world's changing circumstances.

9. **A.** NO CHANGE
   B. adjustments; some
   C. adjustments some
   D. adjustments: some

10. **F.** NO CHANGE
    G. disabilities. As well as the
    H. disabilities, and the
    J. disabilities. Along with the

11. **A.** NO CHANGE
    B. century: and the
    C. century and the
    D. century, the

12. **F.** NO CHANGE
    G. The growing importance of the mass media, created the issue of corporate sponsorship.
    H. The growing importance of the mass media; created the issue of corporate sponsorship.
    J. The growing importance of the mass. Media created the issue of corporate sponsorship.

13. **A.** NO CHANGE
    B. the Games' spirit was changing their commercialism.
    C. the Games' commercialism was changing their spirit.
    D. the Games were changing their spirit and their commercialism.

14. **F.** NO CHANGE
    G. (ISFs); there
    H. (ISFs), there
    J. (ISFs)? There

15. **A.** NO CHANGE
    B. The IOC is chosen by the host city, which is then responsible for organizing the Games.
    C. The IOC chooses the host city which is then responsible for organizing the Games.
    D. The host chooses the IOC, which is then responsible for organizing the Games.

16. **F.** NO CHANGE
    G. Olympic Games, each event
    H. Olympic Games and each event
    J. Olympic. Games and each event

17. **A.** NO CHANGE
    B. symbols, the real
    C. symbols; the real
    D. symbols: the real

18. **F.** NO CHANGE
    G. The awards are made at an awards ceremony as gold, silver, and bronze medals to the athletes.
    H. The awards of gold, silver, and bronze medals are made to the athletes at an awards ceremony.
    J. The awards are made to the athletes at an awards ceremony of gold, silver, and bronze medals.

(*Answers on pages 54–55*)

ANSWERS

PRACTICE **Phrases, Clauses, and Modifiers**
(page 34)

1. The car screeched to a stop near the intersection.
   <u>IC</u>   **IC**   **P**

2. Mark went to the store,
   IC

   and then he went to the movies.
   IC

3. Until she is able to drive,
   DC

   Lisa cannot get a part-time job.
   IC

4. The ACT exam will be easier
   IC

   after you finish the practice tests.
   DC

5. Wanda adopted a dog.
   IC

6. When he gets his new boat,
   DC

   Robert will take everyone water-skiing.
   IC

7. After school,
   P

   Justin volunteers at the community clinic.
   IC

8. Laura will move to Oregon,
   IC

   but not until she graduates from college.
   DC

9. If it rains, the picnic will be canceled.
   DC   **IC**

10. It is hot.
    IC

11. Mary came to school in a bright red car
                modifies / modifies
                   red   *car*

12. Mark has a shiny new bike.
    modify *bike*

13. The hiker, who has a blue backpack,
             modifies *hiker*
    climbs the mountain carefully.
             modifies *climbs*

14. Jane tried hard to run, but she
             modifies *tried*
    only moved awkwardly in her knee brace.
    modify *moved*   **modifies** *brace*

15. The old man walked slowly down the road.
        modifies *man*   **modifies** *walked*

PRACTICE **Run-on Sentences and Comma Splices** (page 36)

1. No comma splice or run-on errors.

2. Referees in professional football use instant replays for close calls; they also use them after the two-minute warning.

[You could also create two sentences, or put a comma and a conjunction between the clauses.]

3. No comma splice or run-on errors.

4. The officer turned on his siren; the car pulled over to the side of the road.

[You could also create two sentences, or put a comma and a conjunction between the clauses.]

5. No comma splice or run-on errors.

6. I couldn't find my keys; I knew our neighbors had an extra set.

[You could also create two sentences, or put a comma and a conjunction between the clauses.]

7. No comma splice or run-on errors.

8. My clothes are drenched; water is squishing out of my shoes.

[You could also create two sentences, or put a comma and a conjunction between the clauses.]

9. No comma splice or run-on errors.

10. The doors closed; the train started moving.

[You could also create two sentences, or put a comma and a conjunction between the clauses.]

11. We all went off campus for lunch. **We** went to the deli.

[You could also separate the sentences with a semicolon or insert a coordinating conjunction after the comma.]

12. The sun had set, **and** the park would be closing soon.

[You could also create two sentences and separate them with either a period or a semicolon.]

13. No comma splice or run-on errors.

14. I like pizza with pepperoni and sausage. **Rob** hates mushrooms on his pizza.

[You could also separate the sentences with a semicolon or put a comma and a conjunction between the clauses.]

15. No comma splice or run-on errors.

ACT-TYPE QUESTIONS   Run-on Sentences and Comma Splices (pages 37–38)

1. C
There are two independent clauses—both able to stand on their own. Therefore, they must either be separated by a semicolon, a comma and a conjunction, or be made into two sentences. This correct choice separates them with a period.

2. G
There are two independent clauses—both able to stand on their own. Therefore, they must either be separated by a semicolon or a comma and a conjunction, or be made into two sentences. Choice H separates them into two sentences, but the contraction of *they are* is *they're*. It is correct to use a semicolon to separate the sentences because they contain closely related ideas.

3. D
There are two independent clauses—both able to stand on their own. Therefore, they must either be separated by a semicolon or a comma and a conjunction, or be made into two sentences. This correct choice separates them into two sentences.

4. F
No change. *After teens get more driving experience* is a dependent clause, so it should be set off with a comma.

5. C
The first independent clause, *Another common mistake teen drivers make is going too fast*, must be separated from the second by a period, making two sentences.

6. H
There are two independent clauses—both able to stand on their own. Therefore, they must either be separated by a semicolon or a comma and a conjunction, or be made into two sentences. This choice separates them with a comma and a conjunction. The first clause does not need special emphasis, so an exclamation point is incorrect.

7. D
Along with driving at an appropriate speed themselves is an introductory phrase, not an independent clause. Therefore, it is separated from the rest of the sentence by a comma.

8. F
Both the original sentences are independent clauses.

9. A
No change. *To help avoid accidents like these* is an introductory phrase, so it should be separated from the rest of the sentence by a comma.

10. G
There are two independent clauses—both able to stand on their own. Therefore, they must either be separated by a colon or a comma and a conjunction, or be made into two sentences. This choice separates them with a comma and a conjunction.

PRACTICE   Sentence Fragments (page 41)

1. No sentence-fragment errors.

2. The wind swirling around me reminded me of something, **an** assignment on weather I had to complete.
   or
   The wind swirling around me reminded me **of an assignment** on weather I had to complete.

3. Cars, trucks, and **motorcycles whizzed** by on the highway.

4. As I was standing by the entrance to the gym, **my** step-class instructor arrived with all her equipment.
   or
   My step-class instructor arrived with all her equipment as I was standing by the entrance to the gym.

5. No sentence-fragment errors.

6. To ski as the sun is **rising, this** is my idea of fun.
   or
   My idea of fun **is** to ski as the sun is rising.

7. I saw people silhouetted against the spotlights, **like** silent movie stars on a modern stage.

8. No sentence-fragment errors.

9. To be at the beach right **now is** my deepest wish.
   or
   To be at the beach right **now, that** is my deepest wish.
   or
   My deepest wish is to be at the beach right now.

10. No sentence-fragment errors.

11. I like fresh garden vegetables in the summer—**tomatoes**, peppers, and carrots.

12. After a long day in the sun, I like to go swimming in the lake.

13. No sentence-fragment errors, but you could change the sentence as follows:

    To finish my college application essay **was** my goal for the evening.

14. Standing on the roof, I saw the people down below, **like** tiny ants in a maze.

15. No sentence-fragment errors.

ACT-TYPE QUESTIONS   Sentence Fragments
(pages 42–43)

1. B
Growing up in Idaho is a sentence fragment.

2. H
The fragment *Traffic jams, crime, and deadlines* needs to be made part of the sentence, and it must be separated from the rest of the sentence by a dash or a comma.

3. D
The fragment must be connected to the sentence.

4. J
The fragment needs to be made part of the sentence and must be separated by a comma.

5. A
No change.

6. H
The fragment *Trying new restaurants* needs to be made part of the sentence and must be separated from the rest of the sentence by a comma.

7. A
No change. The introductory phrase is separated from the rest of the sentence by a comma.

8. F
No change. Both sentences are complete.

9. B
The fragment *While living in the city has its bad points* needs to be made part of the sentence and must be separated from the rest of the sentence by a comma.

10. F
No change.

PRACTICE   Misplaced Modifiers and Shifts in Construction (pages 44–45)

1. I went to school in my mother's car to take the ACT.

2. The room was empty; **we** had to go to another room.

3. No modifier errors.

4. John drove a van that had no lights into the night.

5. No modifier errors.

6. It started to rain when **we were** on the way to Six Flags.

[There are other possible substitutions for *we were.*]

7. An emergency alert was issued when a mudslide caused hazardous conditions.

8. Lisa completed her speech with careful attention to detail and brought it to debate club.

9. No modifier errors.

10. Leon slowly turned his head, and his eyes looked into the store window.

11. Ryan bought a bowl, which was broken, for his fish.

12. No modifier errors.

13. While **the plane was** still on the airport runway, a blizzard started.

14. The boy has a jigsaw puzzle with two pieces missing.

15. Sean rode his bike, which had no pedals, down the path.

ACT-TYPE QUESTIONS   Misplaced Modifiers and Shifts in Construction (pages 46–47)

1. C
Sue is the one who was scared, not the sea.

2. J
She was on the way home, not the foghorn.

3. C
The boat has green paint; the boat and the green paint are not two missing items.

4. F
No change.

5. C
The announcement issued the warning.

6. F
No change.

7. B
Sue is peering with one eye. Neither the peephole nor the figure has one eye.

8. F
No change.

9. A
No change.

10. G
Sue is crying with delight.

SENTENCE STRUCTURE SUBTEST (pages 48–50)

1. C
There are two independent clauses in this sentence. Choice C is correct because it separates these two independent clauses with a semicolon. Other correct choices are *sports. Thousands* or *sports, and thousands.* Choices B and D do not reflect any of these correct methods.

2. J
Summer and Winter Olympic Games is a sentence fragment that cannot stand on its own. J is the correct choice because it rewrites the sentence fragment as a sentence. G leaves the underlined text as a fragment. H is incorrect because a semicolon should be used to connect two independent clauses, not to connect a sentence fragment and an independent clause.

3. A
No change. The sentence is correct and expresses a complete thought. The other choices change the second part of the sentence into an incorrect sentence fragment.

4. G
Choice G correctly begins a new sentence with the words *In the . . .* The other choices all result in a run-on.

5. C
The modifier in the original sentence is misplaced. Choice C correctly rewrites the sentence to show that it was the festivals that inspired Baron de Coubertin. B is incorrect because it makes no sense that the Games were inspired to revive festivals. Choice D changes the intent of the original sentence by saying that the festivals were revived to inspire the games.

6. J
There are two independent clauses. Independent clauses must be joined by a semicolon, or by a comma and a conjunction, or rewritten as two separate sentences. Choice J solves the sentence structure problem by rewriting each clause as a separate sentence. Choice G is incorrect because a comma cannot be used to join two independent clauses. Choice H is incorrect because the first independent clause is a statement, not a question.

7. A
No change. In the original sentence, a comma correctly sets off the appositive phrase from the beginning of the sentence. Choice B creates a sentence fragment beginning with *Whose.* Choice C is incorrect because a semicolon is used to join two independent clauses, not to set off an introductory phrase. Choice D is incorrect because a comma is needed to set off the appositive.

8. J
The modifiers in the sentence are misplaced. Choice J is correct because it clarifies that it was the Olympic Movement that looked with great caution. Choice G incorrectly indicates that it was the world that looked on with great caution. Choice H incorrectly states that both the world and the Olympic Movement looked on with great caution.

9. B
There are two independent clauses. Choice B shows one correct way to separate these independent clauses—with a semicolon. Other correct methods include joining the independent clauses with a comma and a conjunction or rewriting the clauses as two separate sentences. Choices C and D are incorrect because neither one includes an appropriate way to write two independent clauses.

10. H

The original wording creates a sentence fragment. Among the choices given, only H changes the fragment into a sentence by joining it to the list of adjustments in the previous sentence. Choices G and J just create even longer sentence fragments.

11. A

No change. The two independent clauses are correctly separated by a comma and the conjunction *and*. Choice B is incorrect because a colon with a conjunction is not the appropriate way to join independent clauses. C is incorrect because a comma does not precede the conjunction *and*, as it must to join two independent clauses. Choice D is incorrect since there is no conjunction following the comma.

12. F

No change. The sentence consists of a single independent clause, so no further punctuation is required. Choice G is incorrect because a comma should not be used to break up a single independent clause. Choice H is incorrect because the semicolon is breaking up a single independent clause and creating a sentence fragment. J creates a sentence fragment, *The growing importance of the mass.*

13. C

The modifier is misplaced. The intent of the sentence is to show that the Games' commercialism was creating the change, not the spirit's commercialism. Choice C clarifies that point, moving *commercialism* next to the word *Games'*. Choices B and D incorrectly alter the meaning of the sentence.

14. H

The "sentence" beginning with *Although* is a fragment. Choice H shows one acceptable solution to that problem. It incorporates the fragment in the following sentence. Choice G is incorrect because a semicolon should not be used to join a fragment and an independent clause. Choice J does not correct the sentence fragment, and it uses a question mark after a statement.

15. A

The intent of the sentence is that the IOC chooses the host city, and the host city is responsible for organizing the games. The phrase *which is then responsible for organizing the Games* should modify *host city*. Choice A best makes this clear by placing *host city* before *which*. Choices B and D both incorrectly indicate that the IOC organizes the Games. Choice C is incorrect because the dependent clause *which is then responsible for organizing the Games* needs to be set off with a comma.

16. F

No change. Two independent clauses are correctly joined by a semicolon. Choice G is incorrect because it joins two independent clauses with a comma. Choice H is incorrect because *and* would have to be preceded by a comma to correctly join the two independent clauses. J creates a nonsensical sentence.

17. B

The "sentence" beginning with *While* is a dependent clause. It cannot stand on its own as a sentence. Choice B correctly incorporates the dependent clause in the following independent clause. Choice C is incorrect because a semicolon does not correctly join the dependent clause to the independent clause. Choice D is incorrect because a colon should not be used to join a dependent clause and an independent clause.

18. H

Gold, silver, and bronze refer to the medals, not to the athletes or the awards ceremony. Choice H rewrites the sentence to clarify that point. Choices G and J are incorrect because they do not put *gold, silver, and bronze* close to the word *awards*.

Chapter 4
Grammar and Usage

Nouns

Nouns name a person, place, thing, attribute, or idea. There is a noun to name everything you can think of. The subject of a sentence can contain nouns such as *dog*, *scores*, *Michelle*, *school*, and *beauty*.

Singular and Plural Nouns

Singular nouns name one thing. **Plural nouns** name more than one thing. Follow these rules for changing singular nouns to plural nouns.

> **Note:**
> There are 12 grammar and usage questions on the ACT.

Add *s* to most singular nouns.

Singular	Plural
student	students
computer	computers
monkey	monkeys
CD	CDs
television	televisions

Drop the *y* and add *ies* when the singular noun ends in *y* preceded by a consonant.

Singular	Plural
mystery	mysteries
sky	skies
fly	flies

Add *es* to singular nouns ending in *s*, *sh*, *ch*, *x*, or *z*.

Singular	Plural
glass	glasses
match	matches
lash	lashes
fox	foxes
waltz	waltzes

Some plurals are special cases. The plural may have a different form from the singular. The plural may be the same as the singular.

Singular	Plural
mouse	mice
zero	zeros
foot	feet
child	children
cactus	cacti
sheep	sheep
thief	thieves

Practice

Write the plural of each singular noun.

1. tree _____

2. echo _____

3. leaf _____

4. cry _____

5. church _____

6. lady _____

7. hippopotamus _____

8. deer _____

9. tooth _____

10. calf _____

11. goose _____

12. game _____

13. boy _____

14. couch _____

15. party _____

(*Answers on page 96*)

Model ACT Question

This Model ACT Question shows how this topic might be tested on the real ACT. The answer and explanation immediately follow the question. Try the question and then review the answer and the explanation.

There were a <u>dozen boxs</u> in the truck.

1

1. **A.** NO CHANGE
   B. dozen box
   C. dozen boxes
   D. dozen of boxes

Answer 1. Any word that ends in *x*, such as *box* or *fox*, has *es* added to it to make it plural. Since there are a dozen in the truck, the word must be plural.
   C is the correct choice.

ACT-Type Questions

Look at the item that matches the number of the underlined part. Pick the best replacement for the underlined part. If the underlined part is the best, select NO CHANGE.

All the <u>house</u> were decorated for parties. The cake's

1

candles were ablaze and there was a balloon on

each front <u>door</u>. The doorbell rang, and in walked some

2

<u>childs</u>. Each child held a gift <u>box</u> that was about

3   4

two <u>foot</u> long.

5

1. **A.** NO CHANGE
   B. hice
   C. houses
   D. houseses

2. **F.** NO CHANGE
   G. doors
   H. doorses
   J. doores

3. **A.** NO CHANGE
   B. child
   C. children
   D. childrens

4. **F.** NO CHANGE
   G. boxed
   H. boxes
   J. boxing

5. **A.** NO CHANGE
   B. feets
   C. feet
   D. foots

(*Answers on page 96*)

▰▰ Pronouns

Pronouns take the place of nouns. The noun that a pronoun replaces is called an **antecedent**. Pronouns include the words *I, we, she, him, them, my, their, whose.*

EXAMPLES

Liz drove her car to school. She parked it near the front door.

The pronouns *her* and *she* refer to the noun *Liz. Liz* is the antecedent of the pronouns *her* and *she.* The pronoun *it* refers to the noun *car. Car* is the antecedent of the pronoun *it.*

Clear Reference

A pronoun must clearly refer to its antecedent.

EXAMPLES

Unclear reference: Andy wanted Nathan to use his car.

[The pronoun *his* does not clearly refer to a particular noun.]

Clear reference: Andy wanted Nathan to use **his own** car.

or

Andy wanted Nathan to use **Andy's** car.

Unclear reference: Ann got them and handed them to Julia.

[The antecedent for the pronoun *them* is not stated.]

Clear reference: Ann got **the keys** and handed them to Julia.

Case

Pronouns can be in the subjective, objective, or possessive case.

Subjective pronouns are used as the subject of a sentence or a clause, or to refer to the subject.

EXAMPLE

Who is supposed to take the garbage out today? Liz announced it was she.

[The pronoun *she* refers to the subject *Liz.*]

Objective pronouns are the object of a verb or preposition.

EXAMPLES

Inga decided to help <u>her.</u>

I don't know if I should help <u>them.</u>

Possessive pronouns show possession.

EXAMPLES

It seemed to me that Inga and Liz could do <u>their</u> work.

I decided not to run the risk of spraining <u>my</u> back.

Number

Number refers to whether a pronoun is singular or plural. Here is a list of singular and plural pronouns in each case.

Singular			Plural		
Subjective	**Objective**	**Possessive**	**Subjective**	**Objective**	**Possessive**
I	me	my, mine	we	us	our, ours
he	him	his	you	you	your, yours
it	it	its	they	them	their, theirs
she	her	hers	who	whom	whose
you	you	your, yours			
who	whom	whose			

Indefinite pronouns, shown below, are always singular.

anyone	neither	everyone
each	anybody	no one
either	everybody	somebody

Gender

The **gender** of a pronoun refers to whether it indicates a female, a male, or a gender neutral antecedent. A singular pronoun referring to a third person may be masculine, feminine, or neuter. All other pronouns, including plural pronouns, are neuter.

EXAMPLES

The man got ready to leave for <u>his</u> vacation.

[The pronoun is masculine because it refers to the noun *man.*]

Mrs. James was driving her car.

[The pronoun is feminine because it refers to the noun phrase *Mrs. James*.]

Every dog has its day.

[The pronoun is neuter because animals are referred to as neuter unless the gender is known.]

I'm up to my old tricks.

[The pronoun is neuter—first-person pronouns are neuter.]

The two boys ran until they got to the school.

[The pronoun is neuter because all plural pronouns are neuter.]

Agreement

Each pronoun must **agree** in number (singular or plural) and gender (male, female, or neuter for the third-person singular) with the noun, noun phrase, or pronoun to which it refers.

EXAMPLES

Nonagreement in number: Everyone went home to get their raincoats.

[The plural *their* does not agree with the singular *Everyone*. Recall that indefinite pronouns such as *each* and *everyone* are singular.]

Agreement: Everyone went home to get his or her raincoat.

Nonagreement in gender: The girls took their car to get her brakes fixed.

[The feminine *her* does not agree with the noun *car*.]

Agreement: The girls took their car to get its brakes fixed.

Nonagreement in gender: The man on the platform made way for the woman to get off the train, which she had been waiting to board.

[The feminine *she* does not agree with *man*.]

Agreement: The man on the platform made way for the woman to get off the train, which he had been waiting to board.

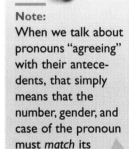

Note:
When we talk about pronouns "agreeing" with their antecedents, that simply means that the number, gender, and case of the pronoun must *match* its antecedent.

Practice

Correct the pronoun errors in these sentences. If a sentence is correct, mark it C.

1. Sarah and Jennifer wanted to take her nephew to the park.
2. Erica went to get them from the bakery.
3. Each car handles differently, depending on how it is pressed.

4. Paul's dog chased their tail.

5. The storms destroyed every house she hit.

Correct the case and number errors in these sentences. If a sentence is correct, mark it C.

6. After the meeting, everyone are going to Jan's house.

7. Send the computer instructions to we.

8. Them are a great relay team.

9. Did you ever meet him parents?

10. Whom lives closer to the stadium than you do?

Correct the agreement errors in these sentences. If a sentence is correct, mark it C.

11. Either of the girls can win if they are consistent.

12. The glass was cracked near his base.

13. I am responsible; the responsibility is ours.

14. He paid for children to get into the carnival because that's the kind of person he is.

15. Whichever of the six players hit the most home runs, they win the contest.

(*Answers on page 96*)

Model ACT Questions

These Model ACT Questions show how this topic might be tested on the real ACT. The answers and explanations immediately follow the questions. Try the questions and then review the answers and the explanations.

It was broken and wouldn't start. Mark took his
‾
1

car to the shop and discovered their battery was dead.
                                     ‾‾‾‾
                                       2

The mechanic replaced Mark's battery, and he was happy.
                                                 ‾
                                                 3

1. A. NO CHANGE
   B. They
   C. He
   D. The car

2. F. NO CHANGE
   G. her
   H. its
   J. your

3. A. NO CHANGE
   B. Mark
   C. it
   D. they

Answers　　**1.** *It* has no referent in the sentence. Therefore, it needs to be replaced with *The car*.

　　D is the correct choice.

2. The pronoun refers to the car, which is singular and neuter.

H is the correct choice.

3. Replace the pronoun with the noun *Mark*. The referent *he* is vague and could also refer to the mechanic. The pronoun *it* would indicate that the car is happy, not Mark. The pronoun *they* is plural, not singular. Both the mechanic and Mark could be happy, but the verb *was* is singular.

B is the correct choice.

ACT-Type Questions

Look at the item that matches the number of the underlined part. Pick the best replacement for the underlined part. If the underlined part is the best, select NO CHANGE.

One day, the circus came to town, and <u>he</u> set up a big
                                            1

tent at the fairgrounds. Many performers set up equipment

so <u>they</u> could practice their acts. Each person wanted to
   2

be sure <u>their</u> act was perfect for the big night. Before the
     3

circus started, Mary and Sharon went to see <u>her</u> favorite
                                       4

animal, the tiger. The girls also bet on which one of the

them would see the most clowns; <u>they</u> would win an
                                5

ice-cream cone.

1. **A.** NO CHANGE
   B. they
   C. she
   D. the manager

2. **F.** NO CHANGE
   G. he or she
   H. it
   J. their

3. **A.** NO CHANGE
   B. his or her
   C. its
   D. your

4. **F.** NO CHANGE
   G. his
   H. its
   J. their

5. **A.** NO CHANGE
   B. their
   C. she
   D. it

(Answers on page 97)

Verbs

Every predicate contains a **verb**, the word that tells what action is taking place. The main verb is underlined in each predicate below.

EXAMPLES

Subject	Predicate
The screeching bat	<u>flew</u> suddenly out of the cave.
ACT scores	can <u>be</u> improved through study and practice.
Ricky	<u>was</u> the best friend I ever had.
He	<u>preferred</u> warm weather.

Verbs are the heart of a sentence. The main verb provides the action in a sentence, or else it links the subject to a word or words that describe the subject. So there are two types of main verbs—action verbs and linking verbs.

Action Verbs and Linking Verbs

The ACT most likely will not ask you to identify a verb as an action verb or a linking verb, but it is very important to be able to spot these verbs in a passage.

Action verbs describe an action. That is, an action verb tells what the subject is doing.

EXAMPLES

The dog <u>ran</u>.

The student <u>studies</u> every night.

The actress <u>sang</u> upon the stage.

Linking verbs connect the subject to its complement. That is, a linking verb links the subject to a word that describes the subject. The most common linking verbs are *am*, *are*, *is*, *was*, and *were*. Verbs that may be linking verbs include *appear*, *feel*, *grow*, *look*, *smell*, and *taste*.

EXAMPLES

The baby <u>was</u> sleeping.

The student <u>is</u> studying.

Christina <u>appears</u> angry.

I <u>felt</u> dizzy.

Some words can be either action verbs or linking verbs, depending on the context.

Action	Linking
The vine <u>grew</u> up the building.	He <u>grew</u> tired of the extra work.
<u>Smell</u> the burning leaves in the fall air.	The pies <u>smell</u> wonderful.

Singular Verbs and Plural Verbs

Most singular third-person verbs end in *s*. Most plural verbs do not. Look at these examples:

Singular	Plural
runs	run
says	say
helps	help
thinks	think
passes	pass

Some singular verbs have special plural forms:

Singular	Plural
am, is	are
was	were

Practice

Underline the main verb. Write A for action or L for linking, S for singular or P for plural.

Example

The passenger <u>seems</u> tired.
            L S

1. Buses pass through my hometown every day.
2. The steps leading up to the bank are very narrow.
3. Some planes carry only cargo or mail, instead of passengers.
4. Hear the roar of the waterfalls up ahead.
5. Paramedics move accident victims very carefully.
6. I'll steer you to the waiting room.
7. Many species of birds fly south for the winter.
8. Occasionally my mom is late picking me up from school.
9. Keep on your 3D glasses throughout the movie.
10. The dispatcher radioed the firefighters on duty.
11. The helicopter circled above the parking lot.
12. The brokers were waiting for the closing bell.
13. Upon arrival, we all jumped excitedly out of our cramped, uncomfortable seats.
14. My new sneakers finally arrived in the mail today.
15. Finals are over now.

(*Answers on page 97*)

This Model ACT Question shows how this topic might be tested on the real ACT. The answer and explanation immediately follow the question. Try the question and then review the answer and the explanation.

The track star <u>run</u> very fast.
        1

1. **A.** NO CHANGE
   B. are running
   C. runs
   D. do run

Answer

1. The verb must be singular to agree with the noun *star*. Notice that *runs* is a regular third-person singular verb that ends in *s*.

C is the correct choice.

ACT-Type Questions

Look at the item that matches the number of the underlined part. Pick the best replacement for the underlined part. If the underlined part is the best, select NO CHANGE.

The <u>concert tomorrow sound like</u> a good idea.
       1
<u>Kevin and I plans to pick</u> you up at five. The
       2
<u>concert start</u> at eight. First, <u>we are going out</u>
   3   4
to dinner. Then, <u>Al and Maureen is joining</u> us.
         5

1. **A.** NO CHANGE
   B. concert tomorrow sounds like
   C. concert tomorrow was sounding like
   D. concert tomorrow sounded like

2. **F.** NO CHANGE
   G. Kevin and I is planning to pick
   H. Kevin and I plan to pick
   J. Kevin and I was planning to pick

3. **A.** NO CHANGE
   B. concert are starting at
   C. concert starts at
   D. concert were starting at

4. **F.** NO CHANGE
   G. we goes out
   H. we is going out
   J. we was going out

5. **A.** NO CHANGE
   B. Al and Maureen was joining
   C. Al and Maureen joins
   D. Al and Maureen are joining

(Answers on page 97)

Verb Tense

The **tense** of a verb tells what time—past, present, or future—an action occurs. The following explanations contain some special names for verbs, such as present participle, third-person singular, and past participle. The ACT will not test you on the names for verbs, but will ask if verbs are used correctly.

Present Tense

Use the **present tense** of a verb to refer to something that is occurring now, that is generally true, or that always occurs. The present tense is the basic form of the verb. Present tense verbs include *is*, *are*, *run*, *sing*, *stand*, etc.

EXAMPLES

> I <u>drop</u> the car keys.
> The team <u>runs</u> laps around the field
> Those trees <u>lose</u> their leaves in the fall.
> She <u>speaks</u> very loudly.

Third-Person Singular. The third-person singular is formed by adding *s* to the first-person form. Some third-person singular verbs have a special spelling.

Present Participle. The present participle also expresses present action. To form the present participle, add *-ing* to the present tense. Some present participles have special spellings. The present participle is always preceded by a helper verb, such as *are*, *am*, *be*, and *is*.

Present Tense		
First- and Second-Person and Plural	**Third-Person Singular**	**Present Participle**
stand	stands	standing
fix	fixes	fixing
save	saves	saving
run	runs	running

EXAMPLES

First- and Second-Person and Plural:	You <u>stand</u> still.
Third-person singular:	Joan <u>stands</u> still.
Present participle:	He <u>is standing</u> still.

First- and Second-Person and Plural:	You <u>fix</u> the tire.
Third-person singular:	She <u>fixes</u> the tire.
Present participle:	We <u>are fixing</u> the tire.
First- and Second-Person and Plural:	I <u>save</u> money when I use discount coupons.
Third-person singular:	Bob <u>saves</u> money when he uses discount coupons.
Present participle:	I <u>am saving</u> money when using discount coupons.
First- and Second-Person and Plural:	<u>Walk</u> three laps around the track.
Third-person singular:	Aaron <u>walks</u> three laps around the track.
Present participle:	I <u>am walking</u> three laps around the track.

Past Tense

Use the **past tense** of a verb to refer to something that has occurred in the past. To form the past tense of **regular** verbs, add *d*, *t*, or *ed*. The past tenses of **irregular** verbs often have special forms.

EXAMPLES

> You <u>dropped</u> the car keys.
>
> The wind <u>blew</u> leaves against the windshield.
>
> The trees <u>lost</u> their leaves in the fall.
>
> She <u>spoke</u> very loudly.

Past participle. You can use the past participle to express past action. For regular verbs, the past participle is the past tense form preceded by helper verbs such as *had*, *has*, and *have*. Irregular verbs have a special past-participle form preceded by helper verbs such as *had*, *has*, and *have*. A common error is to use the past participle form of an irregular verb without a helper verb ("We spoken to the dean").

Regular Verbs		
Present Tense	**Past Tense**	**Past Participle**
face	faced	(had, has, have) faced
pose	posed	(had, has, have) posed
mean	meant	(had, has, have) meant
hoist	hoisted	(had, has, have) hoisted
rent	rented	(had, has, have) rented
drop	dropped	(had, has, have) dropped

Irregular Verbs		
Present Tense	**Past Tense**	**Past Participle**
do	did	(had, has, have) done
know	knew	(had, has, have) known
speak	spoke	(had, has, have) spoken
fall	fell	(had, has, have) fallen
grow	grew	(had, has, have) grown

An extensive list of the principal parts of irregular verbs follows these examples.

EXAMPLES

Present:　　　　I <u>do</u> my best in class.

Past:　　　　　I <u>did</u> my best in class.

Past participle:　I <u>have done</u> my best in class.

　　　　　　　　　[*Incorrect:* I done my best in class.]

Present:　　　　Alicia <u>knows</u> how to get downtown.

Past:　　　　　Alicia <u>knew</u> how to get downtown.

Past participle:　Alicia <u>had known</u> how to get downtown.

　　　　　　　　　[*Incorrect:* Alicia <u>known</u> how to get downtown.]

Here is a list of the present, past, and past participle forms of some irregular verbs. Remember that the past participle of a verb *must* be preceded by one of these helping verbs: *had*, *has*, or *have*.

Irregular Verbs

Present Tense	Past Tense	Past Participle (preceded by *had*, *has*, or *have*)	Present Tense	Past Tense	Past Participle (preceded by *had*, *has*, or *have*)
am, is, are	was, were	been	go	went	gone
become	became	become	grow	grew	grown
begin	began	begun	know	knew	known
blow	blew	blown	lay	laid	laid
break	broke	broken	lie	lay	lain
bring	brought	brought	pay	paid	paid
catch	caught	caught	ride	rode	ridden
choose	chose	chosen	run	ran	run
come	came	come	see	saw	seen
do	did	done	speak	spoke	spoken
drink	drank	drunk	swim	swam	swum
drive	drove	driven	take	took	taken
eat	ate	eaten	teach	taught	taught
fall	fell	fallen	tear	tore	torn
freeze	froze	frozen	throw	threw	thrown
give	gave	given	wear	wore	worn
get	got	gotten	write	wrote	written

Future Tense

Use the **future tense** to refer to something that will occur in the future. To form the future tense, use the words *shall* or *will* before the present tense form of the verb.

EXAMPLES

You <u>will go</u> to college.

The wind <u>will blow</u> snow against the windshield.

The trees <u>shall lose</u> their leaves in the fall.

She <u>will speak</u> very loudly.

Practice

Correct the tense errors. If a sentence is correct, mark it C.

1. Eddie is sitting in the soft armchair in front of the TV.
2. Dawn begun to understand the reason she needed to give blood.
3. Did you ran around the track yesterday?
4. I shall spoken to my mother about this year's vacation.
5. My pet snake ate a live mouse the other day.
6. Harry had driven two hours to reach the specialty store.
7. Fixing cars is not my idea of fun.
8. I will visit the art studio yesterday.
9. Tim downloading a song to play at the party.
10. Joann will lost her bag if she leaves it in the store.
11. The cat was soaked if it stays out in the rain.
12. Tomorrow we will work on the decorations for the dance.
13. Dustin drives a used car if he can save up the money to buy one.
14. My dog will go to obedience school last year.
15. Emily and Megan left from the city airport yesterday.

(*Answers on pages 97–98*)

Model ACT Questions

These Model ACT Questions show how this topic might be tested on the real ACT. The answers and explanations immediately follow the questions. Try the questions and then review the answers and the explanations.

Long ago, people <u>are believing</u> the sun revolved
               1

around the earth. However, today, people

<u>did not think</u> that.
  2

1. **A.** NO CHANGE
    B. believe
    C. will believe
    D. believed

2. **F.** NO CHANGE
    G. do not think
    H. will not think
    J. had not thought

Answers

1. The sentence starts *Long ago*, setting the time and tense as past. Choices A and B are present tense; choice C is future tense.

    D is the correct choice.

2. The sentence is talking about today, now, which is present tense. Choice H is in future tense; choices F and J are in the past tense.

    G is the correct choice.

Look at the item that matches the number of the underlined part. Pick the best replacement for the underlined part. If the underlined part is the best, select NO CHANGE.

Last week, the mayor <u>decided</u> to close the park in order
1
to build a new office building. The people <u>will be</u> very
2
upset when they heard about it. The people <u>meet</u>
3
yesterday to discuss their options. Right now, they

<u>are talking</u> to the mayor about moving the mall to a
4
nearby vacant lot. If he won't agree, they <u>formed</u>
5
a picket line in front of his office tomorrow.

1. **A.** NO CHANGE
   B. decides
   C. will decide
   D. decide

2. **F.** NO CHANGE
   G. are
   H. was
   J. were

3. **A.** NO CHANGE
   B. met
   C. will meet
   D. meets

4. **F.** NO CHANGE
   G. talked
   H. will talk
   J. had talked

5. **A.** NO CHANGE
   B. form
   C. will form
   D. had formed

(*Answers on page 98*)

Tense Shift

Verbs in a sentence should reflect time sequence. If events represented by the verbs occurred at the same time, all verbs should have the same tense.

EXAMPLES

Correct: The rain <u>splattered</u> on the windshield as I <u>drove</u> to the store.
            past   **past**

Correct: As I <u>dig</u> the hole, I <u>throw</u> the dirt up onto a pile.
      present   **present**

Correct: I <u>will get</u> to the airport any way I can and then I <u>will board</u> the plane.
    future   **future**

Some tense shifts are acceptable. Mixing tenses is acceptable when the verbs represent events that happened at different times.

EXAMPLES

Correct: Jean <u>will march</u> in the parade tomorrow so she <u>is</u> practicing now.
       future   **present**

[Jean is practicing now (present tense) for something that will happen tomorrow (future tense).]

Correct: Ben <u>is</u> fixing the vase he <u>broke</u> last week.
     present   **past**

[Ben is fixing something now (present tense) that broke last week (past tense).]

Correct: I <u>will always</u> love dogs because of the years I <u>spent</u> with my poodle.
     future   **past**

[Something will occur (future tense) because of something that has already happened (past tense).]

Avoid faulty tense shifts. A faulty shift between present tense and past tense is a common error.

EXAMPLES

Incorrect: Her father <u>yelled</u> at her when she <u>come</u> home late.
       past   **present**

[This sentence describes something that happened in the past.]

Correct: Her father <u>yelled</u> at her when she <u>came</u> home late.

Incorrect: Dave <u>saves</u> money for the game, and he <u>saved</u> money for souvenirs.
       present   **past**

[These events both happened at the same time. It may be in the present or in the past.]

Correct: Dave <u>saves</u> money for the game, and he <u>saves</u> money for souvenirs.

or

Dave <u>saved</u> money for the game, and he <u>saved</u> money for souvenirs.

Incorrect: Just as Pam <u>was</u> putting away her book bag, her dog <u>runs</u> past her.
       past   **present**

[These events both happened at the same time. It may be in the present, or it may be in the past.]

Correct: Just as Pam <u>was</u> putting away her book bag, her dog <u>ran</u> past her.

or

Just as Pam <u>is</u> putting away her book bag, her dog <u>runs</u> past her.

Practice

Correct the tense shifts. If a sentence is correct, mark it C.

1. I liked to work with numbers, so I am thinking of becoming an accountant.
2. Michael wanted to be a great basketball player, so he practices every day.
3. Ava practices her routine every day for next week's dance contest.
4. Stephen will load his car because he left for a long trip.
5. Daniel raised his hand because he wants to answer the question.
6. I have to pay a fine because I will be speeding on the highway.
7. My cat rolls over and then purred very softly.
8. Jim headed out the door as he calls out a good-bye to his friends.
9. I already went to the store, but I am going there again.
10. The guard opens the roadblock as the soldier rode up to him.
11. At the carnival, Stephanie rode the Ferris wheel, and Bill is playing arcade games.
12. Tomorrow I will start football practice, and my sister was starting soccer practice.
13. I broke my leg two weeks ago, and the cast will come off next month.
14. Brittany ordered frozen yogurt with berries, but the store clerk gives her sliced mango.
15. After lunch I will turn in my fund-raising money, and then I will go to fifth-period ceramics.

(*Answers on page 98*)

Model ACT Questions

These Model ACT Questions show how this topic might be tested on the real ACT. The answers and explanations immediately follow the questions. Try the questions and then review the answers and the explanations.

Last year, Will <u>did extra jobs and saves</u> the money.
                            1

Now, <u>he is buying a car and planned</u> a trip.
                      2

1. **A.** NO CHANGE
   B. did extra jobs and saving
   C. did extra jobs and saved
   D. does extra jobs and will save

2. **F.** NO CHANGE
   G. he is buying a car and planning
   H. he bought a car and planning
   J. he bought a car and will plan

Answers

1. Both things, working and saving, happened *last year*, so the verbs should be in the past tense.

    C is the correct choice.

2. Both of these events are happening now. Therefore, both verbs should be in the present tense.

    G is the correct choice.

ACT-Type Questions

Look at the item that matches the number of the underlined part. Pick the best replacement for the underlined part. If the underlined part is the best, select NO CHANGE.

Last week, I start to prepare for the first day of school.
<u>   </u>
              1
To begin, I will go shopping for school clothes.
<u>   </u>
              2
Then, a couple of days ago, I bought my notebooks
                    <u>   </u>
                            3
and folders. Right now, I will be picking out my outfit
            <u>   </u>
                      4
for the first day. Tomorrow morning, I was getting
              <u>   </u>
                            5
up at six and caught the bus at seven.
<u>   </u>
        5

1. **A.** NO CHANGE
   B. Last week, I will start to
   C. Last week, I started to
   D. Last week, I am starting to

2. **F.** NO CHANGE
   G. To begin, I went shopping
   H. To begin, I am going shopping
   J. To begin, I will shop

3. **A.** NO CHANGE
   B. days ago, I will buy my
   C. days ago, I buy my
   D. days ago, I am buying my

4. **F.** NO CHANGE
   G. Right now, I am picking
   H. Right now, I picked
   J. Right now, I was picking

5. **A.** NO CHANGE
   B. Tomorrow morning, I was getting up at six and will catch the bus
   C. Tomorrow morning, I will get up at six and caught the bus
   D. Tomorrow morning, I will get up at six and catch the bus

(Answers on pages 98–99)

Subject-Verb Agreement

You have already read about singular and plural nouns, pronouns, and verbs. All this leads up to subject-verb agreement, a topic frequently tested on the ACT.

The **subject** of a sentence is the person or thing that performs the action. The **verb** is the action performed.

The subject and verb of a sentence must agree in number. Singular subjects take singular verbs. Plural subjects take plural verbs.

EXAMPLES

Singular: Lisa wants to go to the library after school.

Plural: Lisa and Terri want to go to the library after school.

Singular: The practice test helps me prepare for the ACT.

Plural: The practice tests help me prepare for the ACT.

Singular: The club meets every Saturday afternoon.

Plural: The club members meet every Saturday afternoon.

Some examples of incorrect and corrected subject-verb agreement are given below.

Incorrect: Emily want to get to the theater on time.

Corrected: Emily wants to get to the theater on time

[The singular noun *Emily* takes the singular verb *wants*.]

Incorrect: The players wants to do their best in the game.

Corrected: The players want to do their best in the game.

[The plural noun *players* takes the plural verb *want*.]

Incorrect: Deshaun and Micah judges the contest.

Corrected: Deshaun and Micah judge the contest.

[The plural subject *Deshaun and Micah* takes the plural verb *judge*.]

Incorrect: Everyone are at the door.

Corrected: Everyone is at the door.

[The singular subject *Everyone* takes the singular verb *is*. Indefinite pronouns such as *everyone* and *someone* are always singular.]

Locate the Subject and Verb

The subject and verb may come anywhere in a sentence. Remember, say the subject and verb to yourself. If it sounds right, it probably is right.

EXAMPLES

Find the subject and verb in the following sentence.

The ACT Practice Test, which Liz took on Saturday, prepared her for the actual test.

The verb is *prepared.* But what is the subject?

Saturday comes just before *prepared.* Say, "Saturday prepared her." That's not right. Saturday did not prepare her for the actual test. Try *Practice Test.* Say, "Practice Test prepared her." That's correct. The Practice Test prepared her for the actual test. *Practice Test* is the subject.

The person with the highest test scores wins an award.

Say, "test score wins an award." That's not correct. Test scores don't win awards. Say, "person wins an award." That makes sense. The person wins the award. *Person* is the subject, and *wins* is the verb.

What is your name?

Say, "Your name is what?" *Name* is the subject, and *is* is the verb.

Through the looking glass of life gazes the thoughtful mind.

Say, "Mind gazes." *Mind* is the subject, and *gazes* is the verb.

Note: To help you remember when to add an *s* to a verb, just think about how singular verbs need an *s* and plural verbs do not—you can remember that because *singular* starts with an *s*.

Practice

Correct any subject-verb agreement errors. If a sentence is correct, mark it C.

1. Everyone, including Renee and Louise, climb the mountain this morning.
2. Who do you think she were?
3. In Longfellow's ballad, Paul Revere use a lantern signal to find out if the British are marching.
4. Robert and Ryan skis as often as they can.
5. The tickets Dede bought gives her a reason for going out on Saturday night.
6. The principal will allow a day off from school as long as the class arrange the trip to the science center.
7. A pair of sneakers are all that reminds her of her basketball career.
8. The spray paint on the wall was removed with a power washer.
9. The 23 members of the soccer team practices each day at 4:00 P.M.
10. Each person who climbs the hundred steps mention the beautiful view.
11. James and Aiden both like to dance, but they dances to different music.
12. The stable were full of horses waiting for lunch.
13. Everyone at the table were ready to eat.
14. Andrew and Marcus were ready to go, but Karen was late.
15. Each person is allowed five minutes to speak.

(*Answers on page 99*)

Model ACT Questions

These Model ACT Questions show how this topic might be tested on the real ACT. The answers and explanations immediately follow the questions. Try the questions and then review the answers and the explanations.

Those are the horses Jan <u>are riding</u> this summer
                                1

at camp. Jan and her friends <u>rides</u> every day.
                              2

1. **A.** NO CHANGE
   B. is riding
   C. were riding
   D. are ridden

2. **F.** NO CHANGE
   G. is riding
   H. ride
   J. was riding

Answers

1. The subject of the sentence is not *horses*. Say, "the horses is riding"; that doesn't make sense. "Jan is riding the horses" does make sense. Since *Jan* is singular, the verb must also be singular.

   B is the correct choice.

2. The subject of the sentence, *Jan and her friends*, is plural. Therefore, the verb must also be plural.

   H is the correct choice.

ACT-Type Questions

Look at the item that matches the number of the underlined part. Pick the best replacement for the underlined part. If the underlined part is the best, select NO CHANGE.

<u>Chuck and Ann is trying</u> to go to Atlanta. While
          1

packing, <u>each of them lose something</u> important, such
                   2

as car keys and tickets. By the time they get to the

airport, <u>they are running</u>. Just as the gate is closing,
             3

<u>Chuck and Ann both makes the flight.</u> As they are
             4

sitting down, the pilot announces <u>the flight are delayed</u>
                              5

<u>an hour</u> due to bad weather.
  5

1. **A.** NO CHANGE
   B. Chuck and Ann are trying
   C. Chuck and Ann was trying
   D. Chuck and Ann has tried

2. **F.** NO CHANGE
   G. each of them are losing something
   H. each of them loses something
   J. each of them losed something

3. **A.** NO CHANGE
   B. they is running
   C. they was running
   D. they has been running

4. **F.** NO CHANGE
   G. Chuck and Ann both is making the flight
   H. Chuck and Ann both make the flight
   J. Chuck and Ann both made his flight

5. **A.** NO CHANGE
   B. the flight were delayed an hour
   C. the flight was delayed an hour
   D. the flight is delayed an hour

(*Answers on page 99*)

Parallel Form

Parallel form places sentence elements in the same or similar form to emphasize the equal importance of the elements.

EXAMPLES

I like to drive my car and to ride my bike.

I like driving my car and riding my bike.

There are several specific instances when you should use parallel form.

Phrases and Clauses Linked by a Coordinating Conjunction

Be sure to use parallel form when phrases or clauses in a sentence are linked by coordinating conjunctions. The coordinating conjunctions include *and, but, nor, or,* and *yet.*

EXAMPLES

Not parallel: Marge spent the afternoon taking a walk in the mall and finding bargains.

Parallel: Marge spent the afternoon walking in the mall and finding bargains.

Not parallel:	The teacher always threatens a detention yet does not ever give one.
Parallel:	The teacher always <u>threatens</u> a detention yet never <u>gives</u> one.
Not parallel:	Have you decided if you are skiing or going skating?
Parallel:	Have you decided if you are <u>going</u> skiing or <u>going</u> skating?

Phrases and Clauses Linked by Conjunctive Pairs

Use parallel form when the phrases and clauses in a sentence are linked by conjunctive pairs. The conjunctive pairs include *either . . . or, neither . . . nor,* and *not only . . . but also.*

EXAMPLES

Not parallel:	Neither local streets nor a trip on the highway seemed the best way to get home.
Parallel:	Neither <u>local streets</u> nor the <u>highway</u> seemed the best way to get home.
Not parallel:	She was not only an A student but also someone who was very responsible.
Parallel:	She was not only an <u>A student</u> but also a <u>very responsible person</u>.

Sentence Elements Compared and Parts of a List

When a sentence compares two or more items, or when it lists two or more items, use parallel form.

Note:
One section of the SAT will also ask you to look for errors in sentence construction, like parallel form. Learning how to identify and correct errors in grammar and usage will help you not only on the ACT English Test, but also on the SAT and on the ACT Writing Test.

EXAMPLES

Not parallel:	Gail would rather be a waitress in Colorado than to practice law in a big city.
Parallel:	Gail would rather be <u>a waitress</u> in Colorado than <u>a lawyer</u> in a big city.
Not parallel:	The dog preferred to eat the liver snaps than eating the beef snaps.
Parallel:	The dog preferred <u>the liver snaps</u> to <u>the beef snaps</u>.
Not parallel:	The mathematics test included arithmetic, algebra, and the study of geometry.
Parallel:	The mathematics test included <u>arithmetic</u>, <u>algebra</u>, and <u>geometry</u>.

Sentences with Subordinate Clauses

Do *not* use parallel form when one of the clauses or phrases is subordinated. **Subordinated** means that one sentence element is less important than another sentence element. The absence of parallel form emphasizes that one sentence element is subordinated to another sentence element.

The words *although, because, if . . . then, when, where, while, which, that,* and *who* signal subordinate sentence elements.

Subordinate: I need to go to sleep <u>because</u> I stayed up late last night studying.

[The conjunction *because* signals that *I stayed up late last night studying* is less important than *I need to go to sleep.* Notice that these two clauses are not in parallel form.]

Subordinate: I was studying <u>when</u> my favorite show was on television.

[The conjunction *when* subordinates *my favorite show* to *studying.*]

Subordinate: My favorite character on the show is the one <u>who</u> drives the bus.

[The pronoun *who* subordinates *drives the bus* to *My favorite character.*]

Practice

Correct any parallel-form errors. If a sentence is correct, mark it C.

1. I like to dive and to go swimming when I am at the lake.
2. Trains and airplanes are my favorite forms of transportation.
3. Neither the weather nor the condition of the roads will delay his trip.
4. Jim was trying to decide whether to be a newsman or someone who reports the weather.
5. Because VH1's reality shows are entertaining, I record them on my DVR.
6. The clouds are threatening, yet it seems unlikely that a rainy day will follow.
7. The band was ready; the crowd was cheering.
8. Although they were tired, the group kept working to get the Web site ready on time.
9. The barn that was old stood bravely against the wind, but the new house collapsed.
10. His belligerent attitude hid the more caring side of his personality.
11. On his trip, Andrew was biking in Seattle and then to visit relatives in Idaho.
12. Jamie's favorite summer activities are jet-skiing, fishing, and to swim.
13. At the clothing store, Benjamin bought sneakers, jeans, and T-shirts.
14. On rainy afternoons I often read a good book, but on sunny days I stay outdoors.
15. Al runs to the snack shop, and then he is coming to the beach.

(*Answers on pages 99–100*)

Model ACT Questions

These Model ACT Questions show how this topic might be tested on the real ACT. The answers and explanations immediately follow the questions. Try the questions and then review the answers and the explanations.

I like <u>riding horses and to hike</u> in the mountains.
₁
I enjoy being outdoors <u>not only when it is sunny but</u>
₂
<u>also in the rain or snow.</u> My favorite <u>place to go is</u>
₂ ₃
<u>the mountains, although I also spend a lot of time</u>
₃
on the beach.

1. **A.** NO CHANGE
   B. riding horses and hiking
   C. riding horses and to go on hikes
   D. to ride horses and hiking

2. **F.** NO CHANGE
   G. not only when it is sunny, but also when raining or snowing
   H. not only when it is sunny, but also when it is rainy or snowy
   J. not only in the sun, but also when it is raining or snowing

3. **A.** NO CHANGE
   B. place to go is the mountains, although also to spend a lot of time
   C. place is the mountains, although also spending a lot of time
   D. place to go is the mountains, although also spending a lot of time

Answers

1. The verbs must be in parallel form—*riding* and *hiking*. Choice C is not parallel, because the verbs are *riding* and *to go*. Choice D just reverses the order in the original sentence—*to ride* and *hiking* rather than *riding* and *to hike*.

   B is the correct choice.

2. The phrase *not only . . . but also* indicates coordinated elements and the need for parallel construction. Therefore, *it is sunny* must be parallel to *in the rain or snow.* Neither choice G nor J is in parallel form.

   H is the correct choice.

3. No change. The word *although* sets up the second phrase, *I also spend . . . ,* as subordinate to the phrase *My favorite place. . . .* Therefore, the phrases do not need to be parallel.

   A is the correct choice.

Look at the item that matches the number of the underlined part. Pick the best replacement for the underlined part. If the underlined part is the best, select NO CHANGE.

Debbie works in an office <u>typing letters, answering</u>
<u>phones, and she files documents</u>. Each morning.
1
she <u>walks to the corner and takes the bus</u> downtown.
2
In the evenings, Debbie likes <u>to cook dinner for her</u>
3
<u>children and walking the dog</u>. <u>Debbie lives a normal</u>
3   4
<u>life, although she is blind</u>. Debbie achieved her
4
independence through a <u>program that creates, sustains,</u>
5
<u>and is improving job opportunities</u> for people who
5
are blind.

1. **A.** NO CHANGE
   B. typing letters, answering phones, and to file documents.
   C. typing letters, answering phones, and filing documents.
   D. typing letters, to answer phones, and file documents.

2. **F.** NO CHANGE
   G. walks to the corner and to take the bus
   H. is walking to the corner and takes the bus
   J. walks to the corner and is taking the bus

3. **A.** NO CHANGE
   B. to cook dinner for her children and walks the dog.
   C. cooking dinner for her children and to walk the dog.
   D. cooking dinner for her children and walking the dog.

4. **F.** NO CHANGE
   G. Debbie is living a normal life, although she was blind
   H. Debbie lived a normal life, although she is blind
   J. Debbie is living a normal life, although she is blinding

5. **A.** NO CHANGE
   B. program that creates, sustains, and improves job opportunities
   C. program that is creating, sustaining, and improves job opportunities
   D. program that is creating, sustains, and improves job opportunities

(*Answers on page 100*)

Adjectives and Adverbs

Adjectives

Adjectives are used to modify nouns and pronouns. Adjectives add detail and describe nouns and pronouns in more depth. An adjective can modify a noun or pronoun directly, or it can be linked to the noun or pronoun by a linking verb.

Direct Modifier	Linking Verb
This is a helpful ACT book.	This ACT book is helpful.
Soccer is a popular game.	The game of soccer is popular.
They are beautiful animals.	The animals are beautiful.

Adverbs

Adverbs modify verbs, adjectives, and other adverbs. An adverb can also modify a phrase, a clause, or a sentence. Adverbs are often formed by adding *-ly* to an adjective (*quickly*, *happily*, etc.). However, not all adverbs end in *-ly* (*long*, *fast*, etc.), and some adjectives end in *-ly*.

EXAMPLES

Modify verbs: The hikers stepped carefully.
              The guards proceeded gingerly.

Modify adjectives: It was a bitterly cold winter.
                  It was an exceptionally dark night.

Modify adverbs: The diver very quickly used two air tanks.
                The parachutist will jump fairly soon.

Modify phrases: The firefighters arrived just in time.

clauses: I mailed the card; unfortunately, it did not arrive before my cousin's birthday.

sentences: Regrettably, the teacher is absent today.

Common Adjective and Adverb Errors to Avoid

Do not use an adjective in place of an adverb.

EXAMPLES

Incorrect: John traveled the course slow.

[The adjective *slow* is used instead of the adverb *slowly*.]

Corrected: John traveled the course **slowly**.

Incorrect: Chris walked up the path quick.

[The adjective *quick* is used instead of the adverb *quickly*.]

Corrected: Chris walked up the path **quickly**.

Do not confuse the adjectives *real* and *sure* with the adverbs *really* and *surely*.

EXAMPLES

Incorrect: Erin sang <u>real</u> well.

[The adjective *real* is used instead of the adverb *really*.]

Corrected: Erin sang **really** well.

[The adverb *really* modifies the adverb *well*.]

Incorrect: Ryan was <u>sure</u> playing less than his best.

[The adjective *sure* is used instead of the adverb *surely*.]

Corrected: Ryan was **surely** playing less than his best.

[The adverb *surely* modifies the verb *playing*.]

Do not confuse the adjectives *bad* and *good* with the adverbs *badly* and *well*.

EXAMPLES

Incorrect: Bob wanted to perform the dance <u>good</u>.

[The adjective *good* is used instead of the adverb *well*.]

Corrected: Bob wanted to perform the dance **well**.

Incorrect: Liz cooked <u>bad</u>.

[The adjective *bad* is used instead of the adverb *badly*.]

Corrected: Liz cooked **badly**.

Note:
Remember that although *feel* is an action verb—I feel the snow leaking into my shoes *or* You should feel how soft my cat is—it is also a linking verb. When it is a linking verb, it takes the adjective *bad* instead of the adverb *badly*. For example, I feel *bad* because I have a cold *or* Sue felt *bad* that she was not chosen for the school play.

Practice

Correct the adjective and adverb errors. If a sentence is correct, mark it C.

1. Wow, this is smoothly ice cream.
2. If you want my opinion, that lasagne is real great.
3. I think that Chris behaved very good today.
4. We were supposed to go go-kart racing, but because of the rain, we unfortunate had to cancel.
5. The understudy gave a truly exceptional performance.
6. The commentator conveniently forgot what she had said the previous night.
7. That's an extreme easy thing for you to say, but think about how somebody in that situation might feel.
8. That seems like a needless error, particularly since acting more careful would solve the problem.
9. I have my doubts about the company, but they made me a really large salary offer.
10. The motor behaved bad, so the trip did not go good.
11. Kevin learns very slow when it comes to computers.
12. The floors of my house creak, so I try to walk soft when Mom is sleeping.
13. Martin ran rapidly through the field to try to catch the wily gopher.

14. Advanced medical technology allows doctors to see inside human bodies in ways impossible previous.

15. The bodyguard involuntarily hiccupped, even though he was on camera behind the mayor at a press conference.

(*Answers on page 100*)

Model ACT Questions

These Model ACT Questions show how this topic might be tested on the real ACT. The answers and explanations immediately follow the questions. Try the questions and then review the answers and the explanations.

Angie put on her robe and <u>slipped downstairs quiet</u>.

                                  1

Then Angie <u>ran outside real quickly</u> to get the paper.

                      2

1. A. NO CHANGE
   B. slipped downstairs quietly
   C. slipped downstairs real quiet
   D. quiet slipped downstairs

2. F. NO CHANGE
   G. ran outside really quick
   H. ran outside real quick
   J. ran outside really quickly

Answers

1. *Quietly* is an adverb, while *quiet* is an adjective.

B is the correct choice.

2. Both *real* and *quick* must be in adverb form—*really quickly*.

J is the correct choice.

ACT-Type Questions

Look at the item that matches the number of the underlined part. Pick the best replacement for the underlined part. If the underlined part is the best, select NO CHANGE.

Yesterday, our boat <u>was smooth sailing</u> across the

                          1

lake, when the sky darkened. The wind picked up,

and we <u>thought our boat would surely be capsized</u>.

                      2

1. A. NO CHANGE
   B. was smooth sailingly
   C. were smoothly sailing
   D. was smoothly sailing

2. F. NO CHANGE
   G. thought our boat would sure be capsized
   H. thought our boat will surely be capsized
   J. thought our boat will sure be capsized

Quick turning for home, we tried to outrun the storm.
‾‾‾‾‾‾‾‾‾‾‾‾‾‾‾‾
        3

Then, just as sudden as it had started, the storm abated.
      ‾‾‾‾‾‾‾‾‾‾‾‾‾‾‾‾‾‾‾‾‾‾‾‾
              4

We decided not to test our well luck, however,
          ‾‾‾‾‾‾‾‾‾‾‾‾‾‾‾‾‾‾‾‾‾
                  5

and called it a day.

3. A. NO CHANGE
   B. Quickly turning for home
   C. Quick turningly for home
   D. Quickly turningly for home

4. F. NO CHANGE
   G. justly as sudden as it had started
   H. just as sudden as it will started
   J. just as suddenly as it had started

5. A. NO CHANGE
   B. not to test our goodly luck
   C. to not test our well luck
   D. not to test our good luck

(*Answers on page 100*)

Comparative and Superlative Adjectives and Adverbs

Adjectives and adverbs can show comparisons. Use the comparative form to compare two items. Use the superlative form to compare more than two items.

Comparative Form (Two Items)

The ending *-er* and the words *more* and *less* signal the **comparative form**. The comparative form includes words and phrases such as *warmer, colder, safer, higher, less industrious,* and *more fun.*

Incorrect	Correct
Fran is least creative than Liz.	Fran is less creative than Liz.
Alaska is cold than Florida.	Alaska is colder than Florida.
Ben is proudest than Warren.	Ben is prouder than Warren.
Ray is most happy than Jim.	Ray is happier than Jim.
Ann is most capable than Amelia.	Ann is more capable than Amelia.

Note:
Don't make the common mistake of using *less* when you should use *fewer.*

Use *fewer* when you are talking about items you can count:

An apple has **fewer** calories than a doughnut.

Fewer students take AP Art than AP English.

Use *less* when you can't count how much or how many:

I overslept this morning so I have **less** time to get ready for school.

Less than half of Marisol's classmates walk to school.

Superlative Form (More Than Two Items)

The ending -est and the words most and least signal the **superlative form**. The superlative form includes words and phrases such as *happiest, youngest, oldest, highest, least tired*, and *most interesting*. If you can't tell how many items there are, use the superlative form.

Note:

When you're using adjectives and adverbs for comparison, make sure that you're not "doubling up." In other words, if you've already added -er or -est, don't put *more* or *most* in front of the adjective or adverb, and vice versa.

Use *cutest* kitten, not *most cutest*.

Use *hotter* weather, not *more hotter* weather.

Incorrect	Correct
Ann has the <u>more experience</u> of any pilots flying to Europe.	Ann has the <u>most experience</u> of any pilots flying to Europe.
Julia was the <u>younger</u> student to enter the creative-writing contest.	Julia was the <u>youngest</u> student to enter the creative-writing contest.
Nathan was the <u>more energetic</u> student in kindergarten.	Nathan was the <u>most energetic</u> student in kindergarten.
Andy received the <u>higher</u> score on the law exam.	Andy received the <u>highest</u> score on the law exam.

Practice

Correct the sentences that do not correctly show the comparison. If a sentence is correct, mark it C.

1. Chad was the funnier member of the show's large writing team.
2. The red pair of shoes is larger than the black pair.
3. Of all the books in the library, the international bestseller was the more popular.
4. The cheetah is the fastest predator in Africa.
5. The taller of the five basketball players was on the bench.
6. She took the lightest of the two travel bags to the car.
7. That photograph was among the most creative in the exhibit.
8. Ron is the least able of the two drivers.
9. His shoe size is the smallest in his class.
10. She was the more capable of the two referees.
11. Cardinals are prettiest than blue jays.
12. Rick is the smaller of the two wrestlers who made the finals.
13. At the animal shelter, Douglas chose the cuter puppy of them all.
14. Tomorrow will be cloudier than today, but sunnier than yesterday.
15. Sometimes I think I'm the luckier person on Earth.

(Answers on pages 100–101)

Model ACT Questions

These Model ACT Questions show how this topic might be tested on the real ACT. The answers and explanations immediately follow the questions. Try the questions and then review the answers and the explanations.

Although <u>Anne is older than Michael</u>, she is
     ₁

<u>not the older in the class.</u>
     ₂

1. **A.** NO CHANGE
   B. Anne is oldest than Michael
   C. Anne is more oldest than Michael
   D. Anne is more older than Michael

2. **F.** NO CHANGE
   G. not the more older in the class
   H. not the oldest in the class
   J. not the most older in the class

Answers

1. Choices B and C use the superlative *oldest*, not the comparative *older*. Choice D is redundant; the word *more* is not needed.

   A is the correct choice.

2. The sentence is comparing more than two items—Anne to all the students in the class—so use the superlative. Choices G and J are incorrect because they use the comparative form and they are redundant.

   H is the correct choice.

ACT-Type Questions

Look at the item that matches the number of the underlined part. Pick the best replacement for the underlined part. If the underlined part is the best, select NO CHANGE.

This year's Halloween <u>party was the better ever</u>. The
                            ₁

costumes <u>were scariest than last</u> year's. I thought the
          ₂

decorations <u>were the most colorful</u> so far. The food was
              ₃

<u>even most delicious</u> than I had hoped. Plus, everyone
     ₄

said my <u>costume this year was better than Sheryl's</u>
          ₅

costume two years ago.

1. **A.** NO CHANGE
   B. party was the best ever
   C. party was the more good ever
   D. party was the most good ever

2. **F.** NO CHANGE
   G. were more scariest than last
   H. were most scary than last
   J. were scarier than last

3. **A.** NO CHANGE
   B. decorations were the more colorful
   C. decorations were the more color
   D. decorations were the colorest

4. **F.** NO CHANGE
   G. even deliciousest
   H. even more delicious
   J. even most deliciouser

5. **A.** NO CHANGE
   B. costume this year was more better than Sheryl's
   C. costume this year was most best than Sheryl's
   D. costume this year was more gooder than Sheryl's

(Answers on page 101)

▬▬▬ Idioms

Idioms do not follow the rules of standard English usage, but they effectively convey a complete thought. Incorrect idioms on the ACT usually use the incorrect preposition. The following are examples of incorrect and correct idioms.

Incorrect	**Correct**
angry <u>at</u> him	angry **with** him
detached <u>to</u> my parents	detached **from** my parents
differ <u>from</u> your view	differ **with** your view
differ <u>with</u> your appearance	differ **from** your appearance
in accordance <u>to</u> the rules	in accordance **with** the rules
independent <u>from</u> your effort	independent **of** your effort
just about the same <u>with</u>	just about the same **as**
occupied <u>with</u> my tenant	occupied **by** my tenant
occupied <u>by</u> my stamp collection	occupied **with** my stamp collection
prior <u>from</u> your visit	prior **to** your visit
wait <u>to</u> the airport	wait **at** the airport
wait <u>on</u> the teacher	wait **for** the teacher

Practice

Correct the idiom errors. If a sentence is correct, mark it C.

1. Whatever we accomplished was independent with her work.
2. I could spend endless days occupied with my books.
3. Notice how much the two men differ with each other in their speech patterns.
4. How much longer do you expect me to wait to the airport?
5. That person has just about the same appearance from you.
6. Although I expected to be free this afternoon, my time was occupied from my friend all day.
7. My opinion on that matter differs greatly from yours.
8. Our trip was delayed because we were waiting on Fred, who was late.
9. Carl is often occupied by his experiments.
10. Although she used to depend on him, Karen has broken with Chris.

(*Answers on page 101*)

Model ACT Question

This Model ACT Question shows how this topic might be tested on the real ACT. The answer and explanation immediately follow the question. Try the question and then review the answer and the explanation.

Someone cut in front of me as <u>I was standing by the line</u>

                                         1

for tickets.

1. **A.** NO CHANGE
   B. I was standing at the line
   C. I was standing in the line
   D. I was standing to the line

Answer

1. The correct idiomatic expression is "standing *in* the line."

C is the correct choice.

ACT-Type Questions

Look at the item that matches the number of the underlined part. Pick the best replacement for the underlined part. If the underlined part is the best, select NO CHANGE.

Prior from Mark's visit home, we got along well.
        1

However, he now seems to be very angry with me.
                  2

I don't know if something happened then, or if

the cause is independent from the trip itself. He asked
          3

me to wait on his arrival at the bus. However, when we
       4

drove home, he seemed detached from the conversation.
          5

1. A. NO CHANGE
    B. Prior at Mark's visit
    C. Prior to Mark's visit
    D. Prior of Mark's visit

2. F. NO CHANGE
    G. very angry to me
    H. very angry from me
    J. very angry in me

3. A. NO CHANGE
    B. cause is independent to the trip
    C. cause is independent at the trip
    D. cause is independent of the trip

4. F. NO CHANGE
    G. wait to
    H. wait for
    J. wait with

5. A. NO CHANGE
    B. detached with
    C. detached to
    D. detached by

(*Answers on page 101*)

Grammar and Usage Subtest

This Subtest has the type of grammar and usage items found on the ACT. If you don't know an answer, eliminate the choices you know are incorrect, then guess. Circle the number of any guessed answer. Check page 102 for answers and explanations.

INSTRUCTIONS: Each sentence is numbered in the passage that follows. There is a corresponding item for each numbered sentence. Each item offers three suggestions for changing the sentence to conform to standard written English or to make it understandable or consistent with the rest of the passage. If the numbered sentence is not improved by one of the three suggested changes, mark NO CHANGE.

Choose the best answer for each question based on the passage. Then fill in the appropriate circle on the answer grid.

```
1 Ⓐ Ⓑ Ⓒ Ⓓ      5 Ⓐ Ⓑ Ⓒ Ⓓ      9 Ⓐ Ⓑ Ⓒ Ⓓ
2 Ⓕ Ⓖ Ⓗ Ⓙ      6 Ⓕ Ⓖ Ⓗ Ⓙ     10 Ⓕ Ⓖ Ⓗ Ⓙ
3 Ⓐ Ⓑ Ⓒ Ⓓ      7 Ⓐ Ⓑ Ⓒ Ⓓ     11 Ⓐ Ⓑ Ⓒ Ⓓ
4 Ⓕ Ⓖ Ⓗ Ⓙ      8 Ⓕ Ⓖ Ⓗ Ⓙ     12 Ⓕ Ⓖ Ⓗ Ⓙ
```

---

[1] All of the computer in the lab are being used today.

1. A. NO CHANGE
B. All of the computers in the lab are being used today.
C. All of the computers in the lab were being used today.
D. All of the computer in the lab were being used today.

[2] Teachers are using some, groups of students are using others, and a handful are being repaired by the lab technician.

2. F. NO CHANGE
G. Teachers are using some, groups of students use others, and the lab technician repairs a handful.
H. Teachers are using some, groups of students are using others, and the lab technician is repairing a handful.
J. Teachers use some, groups of students are using others, and the lab technician is repairing a handful.

[3] Eric and Chelsea like to go there during lunch when he can.

3. A. NO CHANGE
B. Eric and Chelsea like to go there during lunch when she can.
C. Eric and Chelsea like to go there during lunch when they can.
D. Eric and Chelsea like to go there during lunch when we can.

4 Chelsea likes them best to go outside.

5 Eric has the most homework, though, so he tries to finish some of it during lunch.

6 He especially likes the colorfully scanner in the corner.

7 He uses it to quick copy pictures for AP art class.

8 Each picture is used as part of his collage project.

9 Right now, it seems Eric and Chelsea are waiting on a free computer.

10 The students should be finished soon, and then they were going out to lunch.

4. F. NO CHANGE
   G. Chelsea likes him most to go outside.
   H. Chelsea likes to go outside more good.
   J. Chelsea likes to go outside better.

5. A. NO CHANGE
   B. Eric has most homework, though, so he tries to finish some of it during lunch.
   C. Eric has the more homework, though, so he tries to finish some of it during lunch.
   D. Eric has more homework, though, so he tries to finish some of it during lunch.

6. F. NO CHANGE
   G. He especially likes the color scanner in the corner.
   H. He especially like the colorful scanner in the corner.
   J. He especially like the colorfully scanner in the corner.

7. A. NO CHANGE
   B. He use it to quick copy pictures for AP art class.
   C. He use it to quickly copy pictures for AP art class.
   D. He uses it to quickly copy pictures for AP art class.

8. F. NO CHANGE
   G. Each picture was used as part of his collage project.
   H. Each of the pictures are used as part of his collage project.
   J. Each picture is using as part of his collage project.

9. A. NO CHANGE
   B. Right now, it seems Eric and Chelsea is waiting for a free computer.
   C. Right now, it seems Eric and Chelsea was waiting on a free computer.
   D. Right now, it seems Eric and Chelsea are waiting for a free computer.

10. F. NO CHANGE
    G. The students should be finished soon, and then he was going out for lunch.
    H. The students should be finished soon, and then they was going out for lunch.
    J. The students should be finished soon, and then they will be going out for lunch.

11 After Eric gets on a computer, Chelsea will wait for another one to use.

11. **A.** NO CHANGE
    B. After Eric gets on a computer, Chelsea waits for another one to use.
    C. After getting on a computer, Chelsea will wait for another one to use.
    D. After Eric get on a computer, Chelsea will wait for another one to use.

12 When Chelsea gets a computer, they will just check her e-mail and play games.

12. **F.** NO CHANGE
    G. When Chelsea gets a computer, she will just check her e-mail and play games.
    H. When Chelsea gets a computer, he will just check her e-mail and play games.
    J. When Chelsea gets a computer, she will just check their e-mail and play games.

(*Answers on page 102*)

ANSWERS

PRACTICE   Nouns (page 57)

1. tree **trees**
2. echo **echoes**
3. leaf **leaves**
4. cry **cries**
5. church **churches**
6. lady **ladies**
7. hippopotamus **hippopotami**
8. deer **deer**
9. tooth **teeth**
10. calf **calves**
11. goose **geese**
12. game **games**
13. boy **boys**
14. couch **couches**
15. party **parties**

ACT-TYPE QUESTIONS   Nouns (page 58)

1. C
The word *All* tells us that there are multiple houses. Unlike *mouse*, which has the special plural form *mice*, *house* follows the standard rules for forming plurals: An *s* is added to the end.

2. F
No change. The word *door* should be singular because the sentence refers to *each*, one, door. The other three choices, plural words, are wrong. (The correctly spelled plural is *doors*.)

3. C
The correct plural form of *child* is *children*, as in choice C.

4. F
No change. This sentence uses the correct singular form of *box*. The article *a* tells us that each child held a single gift box.

5. C
This sentence should use the plural form of *foot* because the word *two* calls for the plural form. The correct plural is *feet*, as shown in choice C.

PRACTICE   Pronouns (pages 61–62)

1. Sarah and Jennifer wanted to take **Sarah's** nephew to the park.
   or
   Sarah and Jennifer wanted to take **Jennifer's** nephew to the park.
   or
   Sarah and Jennifer wanted to take **their** nephew to the park.

2. Erica went to get **the cupcakes** from the bakery.
[Other nouns that make sense in this context could be used in place of *the cupcakes*.]

3. Each car handles differently, depending on how **the gas pedal** is pressed.
[*Gas pedal* makes the most sense here, but *brake* or *clutch* might also be reasonable.]

4. Paul's dog chased **its** tail.
[The pronoun referring to *dog* should be singular and neuter.]

5. The storms destroyed every house **they** hit.
[The pronoun referring to *storms* should be plural and neuter.]

6. After the meeting, everyone **is** going to Jan's house.
[*Everyone* is an indefinite pronoun, so it takes a singular verb.]

7. Send the computer instructions to **us**.
[Use *we* for subjective and *us* for objective case.]

8. **They** are a great relay team.
[Use *they* for subjective and *them* for objective case.]

9. Did you ever meet **his** parents?
[Here the pronoun is possessive.]

10. **Who** lives closer to the stadium than you do?
[Use *who* for subjective case and *whom* for objective case.]

11. Either of the girls can win if **she is** consistent.
[*Either* calls for a singular pronoun, and *girls* calls for a feminine pronoun.]

12. The glass was cracked near **its** base.
[The pronoun referring to *glass* should be singular and neuter.]

13. I am responsible; the responsibility is **mine**.
[The first pronoun, *I*, is singular, so the second, in order to agree in number, should be singular too.]

14. No agreement errors.

15. Whichever of the six players **hits** the most home runs **wins** the contest.
[*Whichever* is singular, so all the verbs relating to it should be singular too.]

ACT-TYPE QUESTIONS Pronouns (page 63)

1. D

The manager set up. *He* is vague—no referent in the sentence.

2. F

No change.

3. B

Use *his* or *her*. *Each person* is singular.

4. J

Use the plural pronoun. The phrase *Mary and Sharon* is plural.

5. C

The words *which one* are singular, so use *she*.

PRACTICE Verbs (page 65)

1. Buses <u>pass</u> through my hometown every day.
    A P

2. The steps leading up to the bank <u>are</u> very narrow.   **L P**

3. Some planes <u>carry</u> only cargo or mail, instead
    A P
of passengers.

4. <u>Hear</u> the roar of the waterfalls up ahead.
  A S

5. Paramedics <u>move</u> accident victims very carefully.   **A P**

6. I'll <u>steer</u> you to the waiting room.
    A S

7. Many species of birds <u>fly</u> south for the winter.
    A P

8. Occasionally my mom <u>is</u> late picking me up from school.   **L S**

9. <u>Keep</u> on your 3D glasses throughout the movie.
  A S

10. The dispatcher <u>radioed</u> the firefighters on duty.
    A S

11. The helicopter <u>circled</u> above the parking lot.
    A S

12. The brokers <u>were</u> waiting for the closing bell.
    L P

13. Upon arrival, we all <u>jumped</u> excitedly out of
    A P
our cramped, uncomfortable seats.

14. My new sneakers finally <u>arrived</u> in the mail today.   **A P**

15. Finals <u>are</u> over now.
  L P

ACT-TYPE QUESTIONS Verbs (page 66)

1. B

The word *concert* is singular, so the verb must be singular also.

2. H

The subject is plural—*Kevin and I.* Therefore, the verb must be plural.

3. C

The word *concert* is singular, so it must take a singular verb.

4. F

No change.

5. D

Al and Maureen is a plural subject, and so the verb should also be plural.

PRACTICE Verb Tense (page 71)

1. No tense error.

    began
2. Dawn ~~begun~~ to understand the reason she needed to give blood.

    run
3. Did you ~~ran~~ around the track yesterday?

    speak
4. I shall ~~spoken~~ to my mother about this year's vacation.

5. No tense error—but if it is a continuing occurrence: My pet snake **eats** a live mouse every other day.

6. No tense error.

7. No tense error.

    visited
8. I ~~will visit~~ the art studio yesterday.

downloaded

9. Tim ~~downloading~~ a song to play at the party.

lose

10. Joann will ~~lost~~ her bag if she leaves it in the store.

will be

11. The cat ~~was~~ soaked if it stays out in the rain.

12. No tense error.

will drive

13. Dustin ~~drives~~ a used car if he can save up the money to buy one.

went

14. My dog ~~will go~~ to obedience school last year.

15. No tense error.

ACT-TYPE QUESTIONS Verb Tense (page 72)

1. A
No change.

2. J
The verb must be past tense, plural, because it refers to how people felt *when they heard* [past tense] about it.

3. B
The action happened yesterday, so the verb must be past tense.

4. F
The sentence is correct in the present tense.

5. C
The sentence is talking about action that will happen in the future since it depends on a decision that still has to be made, so the verb must be future tense.

PRACTICE Tense Shift (page 74)

like

1. I ~~liked~~ to work with numbers, so I am thinking of becoming an accountant.

wants

2. Michael ~~wanted~~ to be a great basketball player, so he practices every day.

or

Michael wanted to be a great basketball player so he ~~practices~~ every day.

practiced

3. No tense-shift errors.

---

loaded

4. Stephen ~~will load~~ his car because he left for a long trip.

wanted

5. Daniel raised his hand because he ~~wants~~ to answer the question.

was

6. I have to pay a fine because I ~~will be~~ speeding on the highway.

rolled

7. My cat ~~rolls~~ over and then purred very softly.

called

8. Jim headed out the door as he ~~calls~~ out a good-bye to his friends.

9. No tense-shift errors.

opened

10. The guard ~~opens~~ the roadblock as the soldier rode up to him.

is riding

11. At the carnival, Stephanie ~~rode~~ the Ferris wheel, and Bill is playing arcade games.

or

At the carnival, Stephanie rode the Ferris wheel, and Bill ~~is playing~~ arcade games.

played

12. Tomorrow I will start football practice, and my sister ~~was starting~~ soccer practice.

will start

13. No tense-shift errors.

14. Brittany ordered frozen yogurt with berries, but the store clerk ~~gives~~ her sliced mango.

gave

15. No tense-shift errors.

ACT-TYPE QUESTIONS Tense Shift (page 75)

1. C
Since the time frame is set in the past (last week), the verb must be past tense.

2. G
Preparations began *last week*, so the verb must be past tense.

3. A
No change.

4. G

The time is *now*, so the verb must be present tense.

5. D

The time is the future (tomorrow), so the verbs must be future tense.

PRACTICE Subject-Verb Agreement (page 77)

climbs *or* climbed

1. Everyone, including Renee and Louise, ~~climb~~ the mountain this morning.

is *or* was

2. Who do you think she ~~were~~?

uses

3. In Longfellow's ballad, Paul Revere ~~use~~ a lantern signal to find out if the British are marching.

ski

4. Robert and Ryan ~~skis~~ as often as they can.

give

5. The tickets Dede bought ~~gives~~ her a reason for going out on Saturday night.

6. The principal will allow a day off from school as long as the class ~~arrange~~ the trip to the science center.   **arranges**

is

7. A pair of sneakers ~~are~~ all that reminds her of her basketball career.

8. No agreement error.

practice

9. The 23 members of the soccer team ~~practices~~ each day at 4:00 P.M.

10. Each person who climbs the hundred steps ~~mention~~ the beautiful view.
    mentions

11. James and Aiden both like to dance, but they ~~dances~~ to different music.
    dance

was

12. The stable ~~were~~ full of horses waiting for lunch.

was

13. Everyone at the table ~~were~~ ready to eat.

14. No agreement error.

15. No agreement error.

ACT-TYPE QUESTIONS Subject-Verb Agreement (pages 78–79)

1. B

The subject, *Chuck and Ann*, is plural; therefore, the verb, *are*, must also be plural.

2. H

The subject, *each*, is singular, as in *each one*, and so the verb must be singular—*loses*.

3. A

No change.

4. H

The subject, *Chuck and Ann*, is plural and present tense so the verb must be as well.

5. D

The subject, *flight*, is singular and present tense, so the verb must be also.

PRACTICE Parallel Form (page 81)

swim

1. I like to dive and to ~~go swimming~~ when I am at the lake.

2. No parallel-form errors.

road conditions

3. Neither the weather nor the ~~condition of the roads~~ will delay his trip.

4. Jim was trying to decide whether to be a newsman or ~~someone who reports the weather~~.
   a weatherman

5. No parallel-form errors. The conjunction *Because* signals subordination.

6. The clouds are threatening, yet it seems unlikely that ~~a rainy day~~ will follow.
   rain

7. No parallel-form errors.

8. No parallel-form errors. The conjunction *Although* signals subordination.

old barn

9. The ~~barn that was old~~ stood bravely against the wind, but the new house collapsed.

his caring personality

10. His belligerent attitude hid ~~the more caring side of his personality~~.

11. On his trip, Andrew was biking in Seattle and then ~~to visit~~ relatives in Idaho.
    visiting

12. Jamie's favorite summer activities are jet-skiing, fishing, and ~~to swim~~.
    swimming

13. No parallel-form errors.

14. No parallel-form errors.

    is running
15. Al ~~runs~~ to the snack shop, and then he is coming to the beach.

ACT-TYPE QUESTIONS Parallel Form (page 83)

1. C.
Each verb ends in *ing*, creating a parallel form.

2. F.
No change. The verbs *walks* and *takes* are parallel.

3. D.
Each verb ends in *ing*, creating a parallel form.

4. F.
No change. The verbs have different tenses in choices G and H. Choice J makes no sense.

5. B.
The verbs *creates, sustains, and improves* create a parallel form.

PRACTICE Adjectives and Adverbs
(pages 85–86)

              smooth
1. Wow, this is ~~smoothly~~ ice cream.

                               really
2. If you want my opinion, that lasagne is ~~real~~ great.

                         well
3. I think that Chris behaved very ~~good~~ today.

4. We were supposed to go go-kart racing, but because of the rain, we ~~unfortunate~~ had to cancel.   **unfortunately**

5. No adjective or adverb errors.

6. No adjective or adverb errors.

           extremely
7. That's an ~~extreme~~ easy thing for you to say, but think about how somebody in that situation might feel.

8. That seems like a needless error, particularly since acting more ~~careful~~ would solve the problem.   **carefully**

9. No adjective or adverb errors.

                   badly
10. The motor behaved ~~bad~~, so the trip did not go ~~good~~.
    well

              slowly
11. Kevin learns very ~~slow~~ when it comes to computers.

12. The floors of my house creak, so I try to walk ~~soft~~ when Mom is sleeping.
    softly

13. No adjective or adverb errors.

14. Advanced medical technology allows doctors to see inside human bodies in ways impossible ~~previous~~.
    previously

15. No adjective or adverb errors.

ACT-TYPE QUESTIONS Adjectives and Adverbs (pages 86–87)

1. D
The verb *sailing* is modified by the adverb *smoothly*. Choice C is incorrect because the verb *were* is plural, not singular.

2. F
No change.

3. B
The adverb *quickly* modifies the verb *turning*.

4. J
Suddenly is an adverb and it should be used here because it modifies the verb *started*.

5. D
The word *well* is an adverb. *Good* is an adjective, which modifies the noun *luck*.

PRACTICE Comparative and Superlative Adjectives and Adverbs (page 88)

           funniest
1. Chad was the ~~funnier~~ member of the show's large writing team.

2. No comparison error.

3. Of all the books in the library, the international bestseller was the ~~more~~ popular.
  most

4. No comparison error.

  tallest
5. The ~~taller~~ of the five basketball players was on the bench.

  lighter
6. She took the ~~lightest~~ of the two travel bags to the car.

7. No comparison error.

  less
8. Ron is the ~~least~~ able of the two drivers.

9. No comparison error.

10. No comparison error.

  prettier
11. Cardinals are ~~prettiest~~ than blue jays.

12. No comparison error.

  cutest
13. At the animal shelter, Douglas chose the ~~cuter~~ puppy of them all.

14. No comparison error.

  luckiest
15. Sometimes I think I'm the ~~luckier~~ person on Earth.

ACT-TYPE QUESTIONS Comparative and Superlative Adjectives and Adverbs
(pages 89–90)

1. B
Use the superlative because this year's party is compared to all other parties.

2. J
Use the comparative because this year's costumes are compared to last year's costumes.

3. A
No change.

4. H
Use the comparative—the actual food is compared to the hoped-for food.

5. A
No change.

PRACTICE Idioms (page 91)

1. Whatever we accomplished was independent ~~with~~ her work.
  of

2. No idiom error.

  from
3. Notice how much the two men differ ~~with~~ each other in their speech patterns.

  at
4. How much longer do you expect me to wait ~~to~~ the airport?

5. That person has just about the same appearance ~~from~~ you.
  as

6. Although I expected to be free this afternoon, my time was occupied ~~from~~ my friend all day.
  by

  with
7. My opinion on that matter differs greatly ~~from~~ yours.

8. Our trip was delayed because we were waiting ~~on~~ Fred, who was late.
  for

  with
9. Carl is often occupied ~~by~~ his experiments.

10. No idiom error.

ACT-TYPE QUESTIONS Idioms (page 92)

1. C
The correct idiomatic form is *prior to.*

2. F
No change.

3. D
The correct idiomatic form is *independent of.*

4. H
The correct idiomatic form is *wait for.*

5. A
No change. The sentence already includes *detached from,* the correct idiomatic form.

GRAMMAR AND USAGE SUBTEST (pages 93–95)

1. B
Computers should be plural, and the verb should be present tense, as in sentence 2.

2. H
The list should contain parallel forms of the clauses.

3. C
The pronoun must be plural, third-person to match the subject, *Eric and Chelsea.*

4. J
Chelsea is comparing two items, going to the computer lab and going outside, so the comparative, not the superlative, should be used.

5. D
The comparative should be used since Eric's homework is compared to Chelsea's homework.

6. G
The word *color* should be used since it describes the type of scanner Eric uses.

7. D
The singular verb *uses* is correct, and the adverb *quickly* should modify the verb *copy.*

8. F
No change.

9. D
The present-tense, plural verb should be used, and the correct idiom is *waiting for.*

10. J
The future tense should be used because the students will go to lunch only after they finish. A plural pronoun should be used for the plural subject.

11. A
No change.

12. G
Singular, feminine pronouns and a singular verb should be used to match the noun *Chelsea.*

Chapter 5
Punctuation

Commas (,)

Use a Comma to Set Off Introductory Clauses or Phrases

Use commas as you see them used in the sentences that follow. The beginning clauses or phrases are **introductory**.

EXAMPLES

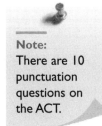

Note:
There are 10 punctuation questions on the ACT.

Incorrect: Before he began preparing for the ACT Joseph talked to his adviser.

Correct: Before he began preparing for the ACT, Joseph talked to his adviser.

Incorrect: Well I guess there is no way to tell when we can go swimming.

Correct: Well, I guess there is no way to tell when we can go swimming.

Incorrect: To get to the high school make a left on Hoight Street.

Correct: To get to the high school, make a left on Hoight Street.

Incorrect: Bob are you coming over?

Correct: Bob, are you coming over?

A comma is not required after a short introductory prepositional phrase if the meaning is clear.

Correct: In September I'll leave home for college.

Do not use commas in sentences like the following. The beginning clauses or phrases are not introductory. Instead, they explain an earlier independent clause.

EXAMPLES

Incorrect: Joseph talked to his adviser, before he began preparing for the ACT.

Correct: Joseph talked to his adviser before he began preparing for the ACT.

Incorrect: Make a left on Hoight Street, to get to the high school.

Correct: Make a left on Hoight Street to get to the high school.

Use a Comma Before a Conjunction That Begins an Independent Clause

Conjunctions are words that join together words or parts of sentences. Examples of conjunctions are *and, but, for, or, nor.*

EXAMPLES

Incorrect: I was in school on time but I was late for home room.

Correct: I was in school on time, but I was late for home room.

Correct: I was in school on time but was late for home room.

[In these examples, *but I was late for home room* is an independent clause, whereas *but was late for home room* is a dependent clause.]

Also use a comma in some sentences that include the **conjunctive word pairs** *either . . . or, neither . . . nor,* and *not only . . . but also.*

EXAMPLES

Correct: You can have <u>either</u> a sliced banana <u>or</u> strawberries on your cereal.

[No comma is needed because a dependent clause follows *or.*]

Correct: <u>Either</u> I will have a sliced banana on my cereal<u>, or</u> I will have straw-berries.

[The comma is correct because it separates two independent clauses.]

Correct: Sally visited <u>neither</u> the snake exhibit <u>nor</u> the insect museum.

Correct: <u>Neither</u> did Sally visit the snake exhibit<u>, nor</u> did she go to the insect museum.

Correct: Last winter I had <u>not only</u> the flu <u>but also</u> two colds.

Correct: Last winter I had <u>not only</u> the flu<u>, but</u> I <u>also</u> had two colds.

Use Commas to Set Off Parenthetical Expressions

A **parenthetical expression** (also called an appositive) does not provide essential information, and it interrupts the flow of a sentence. Use commas to set off this additional information.

Incorrect: My brother who loves to play soccer wants to be a teacher.

Correct: My brother, who loves to play soccer, wants to be a teacher.

Incorrect: Last summer when I turned 16 was especially humid.

Correct: Last summer, when I turned 16, was especially humid.

Often you can use parentheses or dashes instead of commas.

Do not use commas in the following examples. The information is essential to understanding the sentence or to identifying the subject, and so it should not be set off with commas.

EXAMPLES

Incorrect: The girls, who are on the dance team, will miss the last class.

Correct: The girls who are on the dance team will miss the last class.

[The words *who are on the dance team* provide essential information because they state exactly which girls will be missing the class.]

Incorrect: The shirt, that I wore to the wedding, needs to be cleaned.

Correct: The shirt that I wore to the wedding needs to be cleaned.

[The words *that I wore to the wedding* provide essential information about which specific shirt it is.]

Use a Comma to Separate Items in a List

Use commas in the same way they are used to separate items in a list in the examples that follow.

Note:

Do not use a comma to separate the adjectives in this example:

Incorrect: Ralph drove to the ACT test site in a bright, red convertible.

Correct: Ralph drove to the ACT test site in a bright red convertible.

The word *bright* describes the color red, not the convertible.

EXAMPLES

Incorrect: The plane entered a long slow spiral.

Correct: The plane entered a long, slow spiral.

Incorrect: Pat liked warm soft breezy nights.

Correct: Pat liked warm, soft, breezy nights.

Incorrect: Maria liked her eggs scrambled her toast buttered and her coffee black.

Correct: Maria liked her eggs scrambled, her toast buttered, and her coffee black.

Practice

Fix the sentences that do not correctly use commas. If a sentence is correct, mark it C.

C **1.** I had a sophomore slump, but I worked hard in my junior year.

2. Everybody, who is auditioning for the play, may leave 15 minutes early.

C **3.** After breakfast, we drove over to the horse stables.

4. The surprise party was a difficult, but exciting, secret to keep.

5. Make a left at the next corner but be sure to turn right at the second corner.

6. In the trunk of my car I found a spare tire, some candy wrappers, and sneakers.

7. Either clean up your room or you can't go out to the movies with your friends.

8. Because I had a cold, I kept blowing my nose, but it did not stop running.

9. Chad, Blaire, and Ryan attended graduation but left the car at home.

10. On weekdays, on holidays, and during the summer the fee to use the pool is higher.

11. When I scored low on my final exams my parents grounded me, took away my cell phone, and cut my allowance.

12. The girl in the newspaper photo, just got a sports scholarship.

13. You can go to the game, but come home as soon as it ends.

14. The captain, whose name was José, won MVP for the game.

15. When I'm hanging out with my friends, I hate it when my little sister tries to join in even though I usually think she's lots of fun.

(Answers on page 128)

Model ACT Questions

These Model ACT Questions show how this topic might be tested on the real ACT. The answers and explanations immediately follow the questions. Try the questions and then review the answers and the explanations.

<u>Nathan the guitarist with the short hair was</u> late for
₁
rehearsal. <u>Before he got to band practice, he stopped</u>
₂
to pick up snacks and then made two wrong turns.

We weren't angry, however, because <u>he brought</u>
₃
<u>sodas potato chips and minipizzas</u> with him.
₃

1. A. NO CHANGE
   B. Nathan the guitarist, with the short hair, was
   C. Nathan, the guitarist with the short hair, was
   D. Nathan the guitarist with the short, hair was

2. F. NO CHANGE
    G. Before he got to band
        practice he stopped
    H. Before he got, to band
        practice he stopped
    J. Before he got, to band
        practice, he stopped

3. A. NO CHANGE
    B. he brought sodas, potato
        chips, and minipizzas with
    C. he brought sodas potato
        chips, and minipizzas, with
    D. he brought, sodas potato
        chips and minipizzas, with

Answers

1. The phrase *the guitarist with the short hair* is a nonessential, parenthetical
    phrase, so it should be set off with commas. The sentence would make sense
    without the phrase—"Nathan was late for rehearsal." The parenthetical phrase
    gives the reader more information about Nathan.

    C is the correct choice.

2. No change. *Before he got to band practice* is an introductory phrase and must
    be separated by a comma.

    F is the correct choice.

3. The items in the list must be separated by commas.

    B is the correct choice.

ACT-Type Questions

**Look at the item that matches the number of the underlined part. Pick the best replacement
for the underlined part. If the underlined part is the best, select NO CHANGE.**

Comic book <u>fans who often own large collections</u> know
that the books need to be stored safely. Without proper

storage, the paper in the books can be damaged

<u>by its own acidic content moisture in the air and</u>

<u>changing light conditions.</u> <u>In addition, polluted air</u>

1. A. NO CHANGE
    B. fans, who often own large
        collections,
    C. fans who often own large
        collections,
    D. fans who often, own, large
        collections,

and dust can harm comic books. For the best preservation, comic books should be stored in <u>Mylar pockets and the pockets</u> should be changed
₄
every two to three years. The comics should be stored upright, <u>in acid-free, boxes.</u>
₅

2. **F.** NO CHANGE
   G. by its own acidic content moisture in the air, and changing light conditions.
   H. by its own, acidic content moisture in the air and changing light conditions.
   J. by its own acidic content, moisture in the air, and changing light conditions.

3. **A.** NO CHANGE
   B. In addition polluted air
   C. In addition polluted air.
   D. In addition polluted air,

4. **F.** NO CHANGE
   G. Mylar pockets, and the pockets,
   H. Mylar pockets, and the pockets
   J. Mylar, pockets, and the pockets

5. **A.** NO CHANGE
   B. in acid-free boxes.
   C. in, acid-free boxes.
   D. in acid, free boxes.

(*Answers on page 128*)

Semicolons and Colons

Semicolons (;)

Use a **semicolon** to connect independent clauses when the independent clauses are not connected by a conjunction and when their topics are closely related.

EXAMPLES

Incorrect: The detective took a DNA sample, it would be processed by the lab.
Correct: The detective took a DNA sample; it would be processed by the lab.

Incorrect: Some people like chocolate others do not.
Correct: Some people like chocolate; others do not.

Do not use a semicolon in the examples that follow, when a conjunction is used or when one of the clauses is dependent.

EXAMPLES

Incorrect: Taylor got a job at the shoe store; but she would have rather worked at the coffee shop.

Correct: Taylor got a job at the shoe store, but she would have rather worked at the coffee shop.

[These two independent clauses are connected by a conjunction.]

Incorrect: Before Chris left for college; he had a farewell party.

Correct: Before Chris left for college, he had a farewell party.

[*Before Chris left for college* is an introductory clause.]

Colons (:)

Use a **colon** after an independent clause to introduce a list or illustration.

EXAMPLES

Incorrect: Bring these items to the water park, a packed lunch, sunscreen, and a towel.

Correct: Bring these items to the water park: a packed lunch, sunscreen, and a towel.

Incorrect: The only personal trait you need is this, perseverance.

Correct: The only personal trait you need is this: perseverance.

> **Note:**
> A good trick to use when you're deciding whether to use a colon is to remember not to put a colon after a verb. A colon will normally follow a word like *these* or *this* that introduces a list, not a verb. If a list directly follows a verb, you do not need to use a colon. Look at these examples:
>
> Caleb had the following for breakfast: a protein bar, some yogurt, and fresh pineapple.
>
> For breakfast, Caleb had a protein bar, some yogurt, and fresh pineapple.

Do not use a colon in the following examples. The clause before the colon is dependent, and the clause after the colon forms part of the sentence to make it a complete thought.

EXAMPLES

Incorrect: You should bring: a packed lunch, sunscreen, and a towel.

Correct: You should bring a packed lunch, sunscreen, and a towel.

Incorrect: One necessary trait is: perseverance.

Correct: One necessary trait is perseverance.

Practice

Correct any semicolon or colon errors. If a sentence is correct, mark it C.

1. Put these things in your trunk; a jack, a spare tire, a flare, and a blanket.
2. To study all night, we would need: a large pot of coffee and some serious motivation.
3. There is only one thing on my shopping list; chocolate.

4. We went to play paintball; and the parking lot was filled with cars.

5. Alexis felt sick at the thought of speaking in front of the crowd, she hadn't thought so many people would come.

6. Although tomorrow is Saturday; we have to be at school for a test.

7. Left to pack were only two more things: firewood and batteries.

8. There were nearly 70,000 people at the stadium, they were all attending the playoff game.

9. Annie is my dog; she is a black Labrador.

10. Please do not bring to the barbeque: anything containing peanuts; some guests are highly allergic to them.

(Answers on pages 128–129)

Model ACT Questions

These Model ACT Questions show how this topic might be tested on the real ACT. The answers and explanations immediately follow the questions. Try the questions and then review the answers and the explanations.

Today I'm going to the beach, school starts
                      _____
                           1
again tomorrow. At the beach I can do many

different things: swim, play volleyball, jet-ski,
_____
                 2
or just relax.

1. **A.** NO CHANGE
   B. the beach school
   C. the beach; school
   D. the beach: school

2. **F.** NO CHANGE
   G. different things, swim, play, volleyball
   H. different things; swim, play volleyball
   J. different things swim, play volleyball

Answers

1. The two independent clauses need to be separated by either a semicolon or a period.

   C is the correct choice.

2. No change. The first part is an independent clause, followed by a list. A semi-colon cannot be used because the list cannot stand on its own as a sentence. A colon is the correct punctuation mark to use when introducing a list.

   F is the correct choice.

Look at the item that matches the number of the underlined part. Pick the best replacement for the underlined part. If the underlined part is the best, select NO CHANGE.

Winnie-the-Pooh is my favorite <u>children's book,</u>
1

<u>I like the</u> personalities of the animals. The book is
1

full of <u>great characters; Pooh, Piglet, Tigger,</u> and
2

Eeyore. Eeyore is <u>my favorite; he's so gloomy</u>
3

and depressed. However, I also like the

<u>philosophy of Pooh; and the energy</u> of Tigger.
4

The best thing about the <u>book is this: it's still great</u>
5

reading when you're an adult.

1. **A.** NO CHANGE
   B. children's book I like the
   C. children's book; I like the
   D. children's book: I like the

2. **F.** NO CHANGE
   G. great characters, Pooh, Piglet, Tigger
   H. great characters: Pooh Piglet Tigger
   J. great characters: Pooh, Piglet, Tigger

3. **A.** NO CHANGE
   B. my favorite, he's so gloomy
   C. my favorite he's so gloomy
   D. my favorite: he's so gloomy

4. **F.** NO CHANGE
   G. philosophy of Pooh, and the energy
   H. philosophy of Pooh and the energy
   J. philosophy of Pooh: and the energy

5. **A.** NO CHANGE
   B. book is this; it's still great
   C. book is this it's still great
   D. book is this, it's still great

(Answers on page 129)

Hyphens and Dashes

Hyphens (-)

A **hyphen** is a single short line (-). Use a hyphen to connect two (or more) distinct words to form a single word with a distinct meaning. This is especially true when you are joining two words to form an adjective. Look at the examples that follow for a better idea of how this works.

EXAMPLES

Incorrect: At the year end sale, everything was 50 percent off.

Correct: At the year-end sale, everything was 50 percent off.

Incorrect: The ACT consists of multiple choice questions.

Correct: The ACT consists of multiple-choice questions.

Incorrect: Antonio broke his leg in a water skiing accident.

Correct: Antonio broke his leg in a water-skiing accident.

Note that in the example sentences, the compound modifiers come before the nouns they modify. If they come after the nouns, they are not hyphenated.

EXAMPLES

The ACT consists of questions that are multiple choice.

Antonio broke his leg in an accident when he was water skiing.

Do not hyphenate words with the following prefixes and suffixes: *un-, non-, in-, co-, dis-, pre-, post-, re-, over-, semi-; -able/-ible, -ful, -less, -ment, -ness, -tion, -ist, -ance, -ence, -er/-or, -like, -ity*.

EXAMPLES

unimportant	gleeful
nonviolent	worthless
insincere	commitment
coauthor	sadness
disorganized	aviation
prewar	violinist
postgraduate	confidence
renew	adviser
overenthusiastic	childlike
semicolon	intensity

Do hyphenate words with these prefixes and suffixes: *self-, ex-, -full, -free*.

EXAMPLES

self-confidence

ex-husband

full-length

toll-free

Compound modifiers that contain adverbs ending in *-ly* are never hyphenated.

EXAMPLES

highly spiced chili
badly damaged car
happily married couple

Dashes (—)

A **dash** is two consecutive hyphens (—). Use a dash to set apart parenthetical comments. Remember that parenthetical information is not essential to the meaning of a sentence. Do not set off essential information.

EXAMPLES

Incorrect: The polar bears—in the park—were just as dangerous as in the wild.

Correct: The polar bears in the park were just as dangerous as in the wild.

[Do not use dashes. The phrase *in the park* is a necessary part of the sentence.]

Incorrect: Two of my friends Nicholas and Jordan got summer jobs as lifeguards.

Correct: Two of my friends—Nicholas and Jordan—got summer jobs as lifeguards.

[Use dashes. The names of the friends are not essential to understanding the sentence.]

Incorrect: I had a long wait for the doctor the office had overbooked patients.

Correct: I had a long wait for the doctor—the office had overbooked patients.

Note:
Here is an easy—and fool-proof—way to know if you have put dashes in the correct places in a sentence. Read the words before and after the dashes. This should be a complete sentence. If it isn't, one or both of the dashes are in the wrong place.

Practice

Correct hyphen and dash errors. If a sentence is correct, mark it C.

1. Jim is quite fond of his mother-in-law.
2. I knew Samantha very well we had been friends since elementary school so I was sad when she moved away.
3. She was a top notch teacher.
4. It seemed that everyone on the team worked nonstop.
5. Three cars in the parking lot were about to be towed.

6. Lisa was helped by a recently-discovered drug.

7. The writer was a self admitted workaholic.

8. Three cars—two red and one blue—were next in line for an oil change.

9. Bob had to admit that he is high-maintenance.

10. The light—in the bathroom—had been left on overnight.

(*Answers on page 129*)

Model ACT Questions

These Model ACT Questions show how this topic might be tested on the real ACT. The answers and explanations immediately follow the questions. Try the questions and then review the answers and explanations.

The circus ringmaster made a <u>carefully-timed</u>
                                       1
entrance to the center ring. Immediately after that,

<u>the next act—a trapeze artist—entered</u> the ring.
                 2

1. **A.** NO CHANGE
   B. —carefully—timed
   C. carefully timed
   D. —carefully timed—

2. **F.** NO CHANGE
   G. the next act entered a trapeze artist
   H. the next act—a trapeze artist entered
   J. the next act-a trapeze artist-

Answers

1. Do not use a hyphen to join adverbs ending in -*ly* to other words. The information about the timing is essential to understanding the sentence and should not be set off by dashes. The word *carefully* should also not be set off from the rest of the sentence.

   C is the correct choice.

2. The information about the trapeze artist entering the ring is not essential to understanding the question. The information should be set off with dashes, not hyphens.

   F is the correct choice.

ACT-Type Questions

Look at the item that matches the number of the underlined part. Pick the best replacement for the underlined part. If the underlined part is the best, select NO CHANGE.

The <u>hot-buttered popcorn machine</u> was running <u>non-stop</u>

near the carnival rides. The Ferris wheel attendant was

the <u>self-appointed</u> guardian of the soda machine. The

crowds <u>with every manner of person</u> were pushing into

the seats. This—<u>first-rate</u>—show was ready to begin.

1. **A.** NO CHANGE
   B. hot buttered-popcorn-machine
   C. hot-buttered-popcorn machine
   D. hot buttered popcorn machine

2. **F.** NO CHANGE
   G. nonstop
   H. —nonstop—
   J. non-stopping

3. **A.** NO CHANGE
   B. selfappointed
   C. self appointed
   D. self-apointed

4. **F.** NO CHANGE
   G. (with every manner of person)
   H. —with every manner of person—
   J. —with every manner of people—

5. **A.** NO CHANGE
   B. —first rate—
   C. first rate
   D. first-rate

(Answers on page 129)

Parentheses ( )

Use **parentheses** to set off explanations or definitions, as in the examples that follow.

EXAMPLES

Incorrect: The atmosphere on Venus the planet is not habitable is not like the atmosphere here on Earth.

Correct: The atmosphere on Venus (the planet is not habitable) is not like the atmosphere here on Earth.

[The words *the planet is not habitable* explain something about Venus.]

Incorrect: There is a paucity, scarcity, of information about the most distant parts of the galaxy.

Correct: There is a paucity (scarcity) of information about the most distant parts of the galaxy.

[The word *scarcity* defines *paucity*.]

Note:
Sometimes you can use commas instead of parentheses to set off additional explanatory information. Use commas if the parentheses interrupt the flow of the sentence too much. However, always use parentheses if the clause with the extra information is independent. You can use this trick for dashes too, since they also work to set off parenthetical information.

Practice

Correct parentheses errors. If a sentence is correct, mark it C.

1. The three animals (including two cows) grazed in the field.
2. Pluto, Disney created this doglike character, is one of my favorite cartoons.
3. Diction (using the correct word) is often confused with pronunciation.
4. Following a short delay caused by a rain shower, the game began.
5. One Earth year is about 365 days and six hours long.
6. Most working-age people who are blind nearly 74 percent are unemployed.
7. After the dance (we walked to the ice-cream store).
8. Most banks now have ATMs (automated teller machines) in many convenient locations.
9. Personification means giving something inanimate (like a tree) human characteristics.
10. I often use coriander a spice made from cilantro in my cooking.

(*Answers on pages 129–130*)

Model ACT Question

This Model ACT Question shows how this topic might be tested on the real ACT. The answer and explanation immediately follow the question. Try the question and then review the answer and the explanation.

My little brother and I waited for our order at the

coffeehouse he had ordered chocolate milk while
                         1

our mother ran to the bank across the street.

1. **A.** NO CHANGE
   B. coffeehouse (he had ordered chocolate milk while
   C. coffeehouse (he had ordered chocolate milk,) while
   D. coffeehouse (he had ordered chocolate milk) while

Answer

1. The explanation of the little brother's order should be enclosed in parentheses. Both an opening and a closing parenthesis must appear. There should not be a comma before the closing parenthesis.

   D is the correct choice.

ACT-Type Questions

Look at the item that matches the number of the underlined part. Pick the best replacement for the underlined part. If the underlined part is the best, select NO CHANGE.

Joan lives on Tipperary Hill named for the county in
                                  1

Ireland in Syracuse. At one intersection, there is
        1

an upside-down traffic light (the green is on top).
                 2

I expected my plane ticket to go see her to cost

four hundred dollars $400, but the airline
        3   4

(Azores Express) charged less because the airline
        4

(sold more tickets than there were seats) overbooked.
            5

1. **A.** NO CHANGE
   B. Tipperary Hill, named for the county in Ireland in Syracuse
   C. Tipperary Hill (named for the county in Ireland) in Syracuse
   D. Tipperary Hill named for the county in Ireland (in Syracuse)

2. **F.** NO CHANGE
   G. upside-down traffic light the green is on top
   H. upside-down traffic light, the green is on top
   J. upside-down (traffic light) the green is on top

3. **A.** NO CHANGE.
   B. four hundred dollars ($400)
   C. (four hundred dollars) $400
   D. (four hundred dollars $400)

4. **F.** NO CHANGE
   G. (the airline) Azores Express
   H. the airline Azores Express
   J. (the airline Azores Express)

5. **A.** NO CHANGE
   B. sold more tickets than there were seats (overbooked).
   C. (sold more tickets) than there were seats overbooked.
   D. sold more airlines (than there were seats) overbooked.

(*Answers on page 130*)

Apostrophes (')

An **apostrophe** indicates a missing letter or letters in a contraction.

Incorrect	Correct
wont	won't (will not)
dont	don't (do not)
isnt	isn't (is not)
lets	let's (let us)
its	it's (it is)

Do not confuse *it's* (the contraction of *it is* or *it has*) for the possessive pronoun *its*.

Use an apostrophe and the letter *s* after a singular noun to form the possessive unless the *'s* makes pronunciation too cumbersome. If you are in doubt, adding an *'s* to a noun ending in *s* is technically correct.

Incorrect	Correct
Bens father	Ben's father
Carls' cat	Carl's cat
Louis' car	Louis's car

Use an apostrophe after a regular plural noun to form the possessive.

Incorrect	Correct
animal's rights	animals' rights
driver's education	drivers' education
colonies's products	colonies' products

Use an apostrophe to form the possessive of indefinite pronouns but *not* personal pronouns.

Incorrect	Correct
everyones' shoes	everyone's shoes
anyones guess	anyone's guess
it's history	its history
her's shoes	her shoes

Practice

Correct apostrophe errors. If a sentence is correct, mark it C.

1. It's true, but it's hard to believe.
2. Her pitching style could never be confused with anothers' pitching style.
3. Would'nt you like to go to a game this afternoon?
4. The women's softball team had a great pitcher.
5. Wes' glove ended up in the coaches' locker room.
6. Do'nt go to Mel's store today.
7. Everyones' tickets for the play were lost.
8. In the forest, all of the trees' branches were covered in ice.
9. The childrens' matinee was canceled today.
10. The car's door was stuck, and it's brakes squeaked.

(*Answers on page 130*)

Model ACT Question

This Model ACT Question shows how this topic might be tested on the real ACT. The answer and explanation immediately follow the question. Try the question and then review the answer and the explanation.

The <u>Caribbean Island's</u> climate makes them popular
　　　　　　1
vacation spots.

1. **A.** NO CHANGE
   B. The Caribbean Islands'
   C. The Caribbean Islands's
   D. The Caribbean Islands

Answer *Islands* is a plural possessive noun in this sentence. The word should include an apostrophe to show possession, and the apostrophe should come after the *s*.

B is the correct choice.

Look at the item that matches the number of the underlined part. Pick the best replacement for the underlined part. If the underlined part is the best, select NO CHANGE.

Yesterdays' Little League game was rained out. Instead,
 1

each of the ballplayers went to his' or her's house
 2

to rest. The game will still take place—its been
 3

postponed until next week. The change won't affect

next weeks schedule since there weren't any other
 4

game's scheduled for then.
 5

1. **A.** NO CHANGE
   B. Yesterdays Little
   C. Yesterday's Little
   D. Yesterday Little

2. **F.** NO CHANGE
   G. his or her's house
   H. his' or hers' house
   J. his or her house

3. **A.** NO CHANGE
   B. it's
   C. its'
   D. it

4. **F.** NO CHANGE
   G. week's schedule
   H. weeks' schedule
   J. weeks's schedule

5. **A.** NO CHANGE
   B. games's
   C. games'
   D. games

(*Answers on page 130*)

Periods, Question Marks, and Exclamation Points

Periods (.)

Use a **period** to end a sentence unless the sentence is a question, a short interjection, or a command.

EXAMPLES

That was a fun night.
Never leave the answer blank for an ACT question.
You shouldn't send e-mails when you're angry.

Question Marks (?)

Use a **question mark** after a direct question.

EXAMPLES

What do you mean by that?

What time is it?

"Are you going to the prom?" he asked.

Exclamation Points (!)

Use an **exclamation point** at the end of a short interjection or a strong command.

EXAMPLES

Clean up that mess right now!

Stop!

Note:
Exclamation points are notoriously overused by writers, especially beginners. Be sure to use an exclamation point only when it is absolutely necessary. For example, an exclamation point is not necessary in this sentence:

That show was fantastic!

Or even in this sentence:

Brad Pitt just passed me on the street corner!

The speakers in these sentences are showing strong emotion, but they are not shouting or issuing a command, which is really what an exclamation point indicates.

Practice

Correct period, question mark, or exclamation point errors. If a sentence is correct, mark it C.

1. I was so tired at the end of the day!
2. Fire.
3. Where did you hear that!
4. Duck. The baseball is heading for us.
5. Do you sell any paintbrushes larger than these.
6. I need to get a ride home on Friday?
7. What is her name.
8. "Run!" she yelled.
9. Today is supposed to be a beautiful day!
10. Help.

(*Answers on pages 130–131*)

Model ACT Question

This Model ACT Question shows how this topic might be tested on the real ACT. The answer and explanation immediately follow the question. Try the question and then review the answer and the explanation.

Kayla shrilly <u>screamed, "It wasn't me."</u> She was tired
               <u>1</u>

of defending herself.

1. **A.** NO CHANGE
   B. screamed! "It wasn't me."
   C. screamed, "It wasn't me?"
   D. screamed, "It wasn't me!"

Answer   The quote should be introduced with a comma after *screamed*. Kayla's words are an emphatic statement, a scream, so they should end with an exclamation point, not a question mark.

        D is the correct choice.

ACT-Type Questions

Look at the item that matches the number of the underlined part. Pick the best replacement for the underlined part. If the underlined part is the best, select NO CHANGE.

<u>Oops.</u> Tomorrow is the big test. Do you think I can
 <u>1</u>

<u>pass without studying!</u>
     <u>2</u>

So here is the question for <u>you?</u> Do you think it will
                <u>3</u>

be <u>luck?</u> We should have worked <u>harder! Then</u> we would
  <u>4</u>   <u>5</u>

deserve to pass.

1. **A.** NO CHANGE
   B. Oops?
   C. Oops,
   D. Oops!

2. **F.** NO CHANGE
   G. pass without studying.
   H. pass without studying?
   J. pass without studying;

3. **A.** NO CHANGE
   B. you.
   C. you
   D. you!

4. **F.** NO CHANGE
   G. luck.
   H. luck
   J. luck!

5. **A.** NO CHANGE
   B. harder? Then
   C. harder. Then
   D. harder, then

(*Answers on page 131*)

Quotation Marks (" ")

Place double **quotation marks** around direct quotations.

Place single quotation marks around quotations within quotations.

Indirect quotations describe what has been said but not the speaker's exact words. Do not place quotation marks around indirect quotations.

EXAMPLES

Incorrect: The senator turned to the assembly and said, Let's talk about health care.

Correct: The senator turned to the assembly and said, "Let's talk about health care."

[Enclose direct quotes in quotation marks.]

Incorrect: She asked, "Who said, "sarcasm is the lowest form of wit"?"

Correct: She asked, "Who said, 'sarcasm is the lowest form of wit'?"

[Quoted words inside another quote are enclosed by single quotation marks.]

Incorrect: Matthew said that "he would rather spend spring break lounging at the beach than hiking in the mountains."

Correct: Matthew said that he would rather spend spring break lounging at the beach than hiking in the mountains.

[Remove the quotation marks from the indirect quote.]

Place periods and commas following a quotation inside the quotation marks.

Place semicolons and colons outside quotation marks.

Place question marks and exclamation points inside quotation marks if they belong to the quotation.

EXAMPLES

Incorrect: "Let's meet back here in an hour", said the tour guide.

Correct: "Let's meet back here in an hour," said the tour guide.

[Place the comma within the quotation marks.]

Incorrect: One passenger on the boat said, "It was an absolute thrill ride;" another passenger said, "I was afraid I wouldn't make it out alive."

Correct: One passenger on the boat said, "It was an absolute thrill ride"; another passenger said, "I was afraid I wouldn't make it out alive."

[Place the semicolon after the quotation marks.]

Incorrect: When did Roosevelt say, "The only thing we have to fear is fear itself?"

Correct: When did Roosevelt say, "The only thing we have to fear is fear itself"?

[The question mark is not part of the quote. Place it outside the quotation marks.]

Practice

Correct quotation mark errors. If a sentence is correct, mark it C.

1. "Turn left at the light to get downtown," said the police officer.
2. The instructor told us to "do our work carefully."
3. The student asked the question, "Who started the civil war"?
4. "It's time to go home", said the coach.
5. "I am going to Jenn's house," said Lisa. Then I am going home.
6. "Work at a steady pace on the ACT," the teacher said. The teacher did not want "any silly mistakes."
7. The basketball team had an unusual cheer, Boo Boo Choo Choo.
8. Chicken Little cried out, "The sky is falling"!
9. Did I hear the coach say that "there will be a double practice tomorrow."
10. I am tired of hearing about the "mistakes I made during the game."

(Answers on page 131)

Model ACT Question

This Model ACT Question shows how this topic might be tested on the real ACT. The answer and explanation immediately follow the question. Try the question and then review the answer and the explanation.

Sophocles writes in *Antigone* "How dreadful it is
                                          1
when the right judge judges wrong."
          1

1. **A.** NO CHANGE
    B. *Antigone*; "How dreadful it is when the right judge judges wrong."
    C. *Antigone*, "How dreadful it is when the right judge judges wrong."
    D. *Antigone*, "How dreadful it is when the right judge judges wrong".

Answer   The clause that introduces the quotation is dependent; therefore, it should be followed by a comma, not a semicolon. The period at the end of the sentence should be placed inside the quotation marks.

C is the correct choice.

Look at the item that matches the number of the underlined part. Pick the best replacement for the underlined part. If the underlined part is the best, select NO CHANGE.

"I am thinking of going to the movies", said Indira. Marcy
                                    1
wondered if they would "have time to go home first".
                      2
She asked Indira what time the movie started.
            3

I'm pretty sure it starts at 5:20, answered Indira.
4
She thought they were going to have to hurry.
                  5

1. **A.** NO CHANGE
   B. to the movies" said,
   C. to the movies," said
   D. to the movies" said

2. **F.** NO CHANGE
   G. would, "have time to go
        home first."
   H. would "have time to go
        home first."
   J. would have time to go home
        first.

3. **A.** NO CHANGE
   B. Indira: "what time the movie
        started."
   C. Indira "what time the movie
        started."
   D. Indira, "what time the movie
        started."

4. **F.** NO CHANGE
   G. "I'm pretty sure it starts at
        5:20" answered
   H. "I'm pretty sure it starts at
        5:20," answered
   J. 'I'm pretty sure it starts at
        5:20,' answered

5. **A.** NO CHANGE
   B. "were going to have to
        hurry."
   C. 'were going to have to
        hurry.'
   D. "were 'going to have' to
        hurry."

(*Answers on page 131*)

Punctuation Subtest

This Subtest has the type of punctuation items found on the ACT. If you don't know an answer, eliminate the choices you know are incorrect, then guess. Circle the number of any guessed answer. Check page 132 for answers and explanations.

INSTRUCTIONS: Certain words or phrases in the following passage are underlined and numbered. There is a corresponding item for each underlined portion. Each item offers three suggestions for changing the underlined portion to conform to standard written English or to make it understandable or consistent with the rest of the passage. If the underlined portion is not improved by one of the three suggested changes, mark NO CHANGE.

Choose the best answer for each question based on the passage. Then fill in the appropriate circle on the answer grid.

1 Ⓐ Ⓑ Ⓒ Ⓓ	5 Ⓐ Ⓑ Ⓒ Ⓓ	9 Ⓐ Ⓑ Ⓒ Ⓓ
2 Ⓕ Ⓖ Ⓗ Ⓙ	6 Ⓕ Ⓖ Ⓗ Ⓙ	10 Ⓕ Ⓖ Ⓗ Ⓙ
3 Ⓐ Ⓑ Ⓒ Ⓓ	7 Ⓐ Ⓑ Ⓒ Ⓓ	
4 Ⓕ Ⓖ Ⓗ Ⓙ	8 Ⓕ Ⓖ Ⓗ Ⓙ	

<u>It was cold dark and rainy</u> as we set off on our
₁
journey. Our plan was to make it to the mountains

<u>by sunrise we would rest there</u> a day before
₂
setting out across the plains. We brought with

<u>us only: a few clothes some money and food</u>
₃
for a week. In order to make it to <u>the ship on time;</u>
₄
<u>we needed to</u> be at the coast by Saturday. <u>Then as</u>
₄   ₅
<u>we neared the mountains we</u> heard something.
₅

1. **A.** NO CHANGE
   B. It was cold, dark, and rainy
   C. It was: cold dark and rainy
   D. It was: cold, dark, and rainy

2. **F.** NO CHANGE
   G. by sunrise, we would rest there
   H. by sunrise: we would rest there
   J. by sunrise; we would rest there

3. **A.** NO CHANGE
   B. us only: a few clothes, some money, and food
   C. us only a few clothes some money and food
   D. us only a few clothes, some money, and food

4. **F.** NO CHANGE
   G. the ship on time: we needed to
   H. the ship on time, we needed to
   J. the ship on time we needed to

5. **A.** NO CHANGE
   B. Then, as we neared the mountains, we
   C. Then! As we neared the mountains we
   D. Then as we neared the mountains, we

Boom? A loud echo rolled across the sky.
       6

"What is that?" we asked each other. We saw
       7

a horse (we could see no rider) galloping along
       8

the path. The horse slowed it's pace as it drew
       9

near. Then we saw the rider lying low along the
       10

horses' neck, urging him onward.
  10

6. **F.** NO CHANGE
   G. Boom. A loud
   H. Boom! A loud
   J. Boom, a loud

7. **A.** NO CHANGE
   B. "What is that" we asked
   C. "What is that!" we asked
   D. "What is that." we asked

8. **F.** NO CHANGE
   G. a horse we could see no rider galloping
   H. a horse we could see no (rider galloping)
   J. a horse, we could see no rider galloping

9. **A.** NO CHANGE
   B. slowed its' pace
   C. slowed its pace
   D. slowed its's pace

10. **F.** NO CHANGE
   G. the rider lying low along the horses' neck
   H. the rider lying low along the horse's neck,
   J. the rider: lying low along the horse's neck

(*Answers on page 132*)

ANSWERS

PRACTICE Commas (page 106)

1. No comma errors.

   Everybody who   play may
2. ~~Everybody, who~~ is auditioning for the ~~play, may~~ leave fifteen minutes early.

   breakfast we
3. After ~~breakfast, we~~ drove over to the horse stables.

4. No comma errors.

   corner, but
5. Make a left at the next ~~corner but~~ be sure to turn right at the second corner.

6. No comma errors.

   room, or
7. Either clean up your ~~room or~~ you can't go out to the movies with your friends.

8. No comma errors.

9. No comma errors.

10. On weekends, on holidays, and during the ~~summer the~~ fee to use the pool is higher.
    summer, the

    exams, my
11. When I scored low on my final ~~exams my~~ parents grounded me, took away my cell phone, and cut my allowance.

    girl in   photo just
12. The ~~girl, in~~ the newspaper ~~photo, just~~ got a sports scholarship.

13. No comma errors.

    captain, whose   José, won
14. The ~~captain whose~~ name was ~~José won~~ MVP for the game.

    in, even
15. When I'm hanging out with my friends, I hate it when my little sister tries to join ~~in even~~ though I usually think she's lots of fun.

ACT-TYPE QUESTIONS Commas (pages 107–108)

1. B
The phrase *who often own large collections* is a non-essential, parenthetical phrase.

2. J
These items are a list.

3. A
No change. Only the introductory phrase should be set off with a comma. Inserting a period creates a sentence fragment.

4. H
Insert a comma before the conjunction that joins two independent clauses.

5. B
The adjective *acid-free* modifies *boxes*.

PRACTICE Semicolons and Colons
(pages 109–110)

   trunk:
1. Put these things in your ~~trunk;~~ a jack, a spare tire, a flare, and a blanket.

   need a
2. To study all night we would ~~need: a~~ large pot of coffee and some serious motivation.

   list: chocolate
3. There is only one thing on my shopping ~~list;~~ ~~chocolate.~~

   paintball,
4. We went to play ~~paintball;~~ and the parking lot was filled with cars.

5. Alexis felt sick at the thought of speaking in front of the ~~crowd,~~ she hadn't thought so many people would come.
   crowd;

   Saturday, we
6. Although tomorrow is ~~Saturday; we~~ have to be at school for a test.

7. No error—colon is correct.

8. There were nearly 70,000 people at the ~~stadium, they~~ were all attending the playoff game.
   stadium; they

9. No error—semicolon is correct.

barbeque anything

10. Please do not bring to the ~~barbeque: anything~~ containing peanuts; some guests are highly allergic to them.

ACT-TYPE QUESTIONS   Semicolons and Colons (page 111)

1. C

Choices A and B are run-on sentences, and choice D uses a colon incorrectly. A semicolon should be used to separate the two independent clauses.

2. J

The sentence is not made up of two independent clauses, so a semicolon can't be used. Choice G is incorrect because the list should be introduced by a colon, and choice H is incorrect because the items in the list are not separated by commas.

3. A

No change.

4. H

No punctuation is needed between the two elements of the compound object.

5. A

No change.

PRACTICE   Hyphens and Dashes (pages 113–114)

1. No hyphen or dash errors.

well—we

2. I knew Samantha very ~~well we~~ had been friends since elementary ~~school so~~ I was sad when she moved away.

school—so

top-notch

3. She was a ~~top notch~~ teacher.

4. No hyphen or dash errors.

5. No hyphen or dash errors.

recently discovered

6. Lisa was helped by a ~~recently-discovered~~ drug.

self-admitted

7. The writer was a ~~self admitted~~ workaholic.

8. No hyphen or dash errors.

9. No hyphen or dash errors.

light in the bathroom had

10. The ~~light—in the bathroom—had~~ been left on overnight.

ACT-TYPE QUESTIONS   Hyphens and Dashes (page 115)

1. C

It is not a popcorn machine that is hot buttered, so choice A is not correct. It is not a buttered popcorn machine that is hot, so choice B is incorrect. It is a machine that makes hot-buttered popcorn, so C is the correct choice. Note that a compound modifier can contain more than two words.

2. G

Nonstop is one word, not hyphenated. Dashes are not needed, since the fact that the machine is running continually is essential information. Choice J makes no sense.

3. A

The prefix *self-* is always hyphenated. Therefore choices B and C are incorrect. Choice D misspells *appointed*.

4. H

The phrase *with every manner of person* gives extra information; it is helpful but not essential, so it should be separated with dashes. Choice G does separate the phrase, but parentheses are more intrusive than dashes. Although choice J correctly uses dashes, *every manner of people* is ungrammatical.

5. D

The adjective *first-rate* is essential information, so choices A and B are incorrect. The sentence should not include dashes. Since *first-rate* comes before the noun *show*, the hyphen is correct.

PRACTICE   Parentheses (page 116)

, including two cows,

1. The three animals ~~(including two cows)~~ grazed in the field.

[Replace the parentheses with commas or else the parentheses interrupt the sentence too abruptly.]

(Disney created this doglike character)

2. Pluto~~, Disney created this doglike character,~~ is one of my favorite cartoons.

3. No errors.

4. No errors.

5. No errors.

(nearly 74 percent)

6. Most working-age people who are blind ~~nearly 74 percent~~ are unemployed.

dance, we walked to the ice cream store.

7. After the ~~dance (we walked to the ice-cream store)~~.

8. No errors.

9. No errors.

(a spice made from cilantro)

10. I often use coriander ~~a spice made from cilantro~~ in my cooking.

ACT-TYPE QUESTIONS Parentheses
(pages 117–118)

1. C

In the other choices, it sounds like Ireland is in Syracuse.

2. F

No change.

3. B

This sentence incorrectly omits the parentheses around *$400*. Change *$400* to *($400)* because *($400)* clarifies the meaning of *four hundred dollars.*

4. F

No change. The sentence correctly places parentheses around *Azores Express* because *(Azores Express)* clarifies the meaning *the airline.*

5. B

This sentence incorrectly omits the parentheses around *overbooked*. Change *overbooked* to *(overbooked)* because *(overbooked)* explains *sold more tickets than there were seats.*

PRACTICE Apostrophes (page 119)

1. No apostrophe error.

2. Her pitching style could never be confused with ~~anothers'~~ pitching style.
another's

Wouldn't

3. ~~Would'nt~~ you like to go to a game this afternoon?

4. No apostrophe error.

Wes's

5. ~~Wes'~~ glove ended up in the coaches' locker room.

Don't

6. ~~Do'nt~~ go to Mel's store today.

Everyone's

7. ~~Everyones'~~ tickets for the play were lost.

8. No apostrophe error.

children's

9. The ~~childrens'~~ matinee was canceled today.

its

10. The car's door was stuck, and ~~it's~~ brakes squeaked.

ACT-TYPE QUESTIONS Apostrophes (page 120)

1. C

Yesterday is singular, so the apostrophe to make it possessive should come before the *s.*

2. J

No apostrophe is necessary for the possessive form of the pronouns *his* and *her.*

3. B

The word *it's* is a contraction for *it has,* so it should contain an apostrophe to replace the missing letters.

4. G

The schedule is that for the following week, so *week's* should be singular and possessive.

5. D

No apostrophe is necessary because the word does not form a possessive.

PRACTICE Periods, Question Marks, and Exclamation Points (page 121)

day.

1. I was so tired at the end of the ~~day!~~

Fire!

2. ~~Fire.~~

that?

3. Where did you hear ~~that!~~

Duck!

4. ~~Duck.~~ The baseball is heading for us.

these?

5. Do you sell any paintbrushes larger than ~~these.~~

Friday.
6. I need to get a ride home on ~~Friday?~~

name?
7. What is her ~~name.~~

8. No punctuation error.

day.
9. Today is supposed to be a beautiful ~~day!~~

Help!
10. ~~Help.~~

ACT-TYPE QUESTIONS Periods, Question Marks, and Exclamation Points (page 122)

1. D

Oops implies that the speaker is making an emphatic statement, and the second sentence reinforces this.

2. H

The sentence is a question. Placing a semicolon at the end of the sentence is incorrect since the semicolon should be followed by another independent clause. Since the speaker is not exclaiming or issuing a strong command, an exclamation point is also incorrect.

3. B

So here is a question for you is not actually a question. It is not an exclamation or a command either. A period is the correct ending punctuation for this sentence.

4. F

No change. The second sentence asks a question, so it ends with a question mark.

5. C

The first sentence is not an exclamation or a command, so it should not end with an exclamation point. It is also not a question, so it should not end with a question mark. Using a comma to separate the sentences creates a run-on. Using a period to separate these two sentences is the correct option.

PRACTICE Quotation Marks (page 124)

1. No quotation mark errors.

do our work carefully.
2. The instructor told us to "~~do our work carefully.~~"

3. The student asked the question, "Who started the civil ~~war"?~~
war?"

home,"
4. "It's time to go ~~home",~~ said the coach.

"Then I am going home."
5. "I am going to Jenn's house," said Lisa. ~~Then I am going home.~~

6. "Work at a steady pace on the ACT," the teacher said. The teacher did not want ~~"any silly mistakes."~~
any silly mistakes.

"Boo Boo Choo Choo."
7. The basketball team had an unusual cheer, ~~Boo Boo Choo Choo.~~

[Put quotation marks around "Boo Boo Choo Choo." It is a direct quote.]

falling!"
8. Chicken Little cried out, "The sky is ~~falling"!~~

there will be a double practice tomorrow?
9. Did I hear the coach say that "~~there will be a double practice tomorrow?"~~

[No quotation marks. This is something an unattributed source thought he or she heard.]

mistakes I made during the game.
10. I am tired of hearing about the "~~mistakes I made during the game."~~

ACT-TYPE QUESTIONS Quotation Marks (page 125)

1. C

The comma should come inside the quotation marks.

2. J

There is no quote, so quotation marks are not needed.

3. A

No change. The sentence does not need to contain any quotation marks because nothing in the sentence is directly spoken.

4. H

The words that are spoken should be enclosed in double quotation marks and there should be a comma before the second set of quotation marks.

5. A

No change. The sentence does not contain any spoken or quoted words, so no quotation marks are necessary.

PUNCTUATION SUBTEST (pages 126–127)

1. B
The items in the series need to be separated by commas.

2. J
The two independent clauses should be separated by a semicolon.

3. D
The series needs to be separated by commas but not set off by a colon.

4. H
The introductory phrase should be separated from the second part of the sentence by a comma.

5. B
The phrase *as we neared the mountains* is nonessential and so should be set off with commas.

6. H
Boom! is an exclamation.

7. A
No change.

8. F
No change.

9. C
The possessive form *its* has no apostrophe.

10. H
The first independent clause should be separated from the second clause by a comma; *horse* is singular, so its possessive form is *horse's*.

Chapter 6
Rhetorical Skills

Rhetorical Skills items are unique to the ACT. These items are not based on rules of grammar or punctuation. They ask you about writing and about how you might or might not edit a passage to make it more understandable. These questions are often based on your informed sense of what written English should sound like or in which order ideas should occur in a passage.

These items are not really harder than the sentence structure, grammar, and punctuation items discussed so far, but they are different. Luckily, rhetorical skills items follow very specific formats. Pay close attention to those formats to perform effectively on the ACT.

There are 35 rhetorical-skills questions on the ACT. The questions are divided among strategy, organization, and style.

Strategy	12 items
Organization	11 items
Style	12 items

Strategy

The word **strategy** sounds very substantial. You might even get the idea that you have to detect some detailed or complex strategy in the passage. However, answering strategy questions is simple. Strategy questions on the ACT are one of these two types: transitions and appropriate use.

Transitions

This is the most common type of strategy question, and these are the easiest rhetorical-skills items on the ACT. A **transition** may occur at any point in the passage as the writer uses words to connect thoughts or ideas. It is usually easy to spot transition items because the answer choices consist of transition words or phrases. The transition words usually appear at the beginning of a sentence or a clause, and they frequently connect two clauses.

Following are six categories of transition words and phrases. The first three categories of words occur most frequently. Familiarize yourself with these words and phrases.

Transition Words That Establish a Cause-and-Effect Relationship			
therefore	and so	as a result of	hence
because of	finally	consequently	thus

Transition Words That Show a Continuation			
and	in addition	also	similarly
further	furthermore	then	in other words
that is	by the same token		

Transition Words That Point Out Contrasts and Contradictions			
however	although	but	to the contrary
despite	rather	yet	as opposed to
unlike	nevertheless	not	in contrast to
conversely	on the other hand		

Transition Words That Signal an Explanation		
for example	for instance	that is

Transition Words That Suggest Elements Are Being Ordered			
then	last	next	primarily
before	after	finally	first, second, etc.

Transition Words That Point Out Similarities			
alike	in common	similar to	same

Note:
"Say" the sentence quietly to yourself to help determine whether a transition word is appropriate. Then figure out from the choices provided which word is best.

Here are correct and incorrect examples of sentences with transition words.

EXAMPLES

Correct: Jean's ACT score was high <u>because</u> she studied this book.

[The transition word *because* establishes a cause-and-effect relationship between studying this book and receiving a high score.]

Correct: There are 35 rhetorical-skills items, <u>and</u> they are very different from the other ACT English items.

[The transition word *and* shows a continuation in the discussion of rhetorical-skills items.]

Correct: Transition items are supposed to be the easiest; <u>however</u>, you can't take them for granted.

[The transition word *however* correctly points out a contrast. The transition questions are supposed to be the easiest, but you can't take them for granted.]

Incorrect: The school play was a success; <u>however</u>, there was loud applause from the audience.

[The word *however* is not an effective transition between a successful play and loud audience applause. *However* shows a contrast where none exists.]

Corrected: The school play was a success; <u>furthermore</u>, there was loud applause from the audience.

[The transition word *furthermore* continues the statement about the play's success with a statement about the audience's reaction.]

Corrected: The school play was a success; <u>therefore</u>, there was loud applause from the audience.

[The transition word *therefore* shows a cause-and-effect relationship between the play's success and the audience's reaction.]

Sometimes we have to rely on information that is not in the passage to decide if a transition word is effective. Look at the following example.

EXAMPLE

Correct: The play was a success <u>despite</u> the efforts of the stage crew.

[This sentence shows a contrast between the play's success and the efforts of the stage crew. The sentence implies that the stage crew's efforts did not contribute to the play's success. We don't know if this statement is true, but the transition word *despite* is used appropriately here.]

Correct: The play was a success <u>because</u> of the efforts of the stage crew.

[We don't know if this statement is true, but the transition word *because* does correctly show a cause-and-effect relationship between the efforts of the stage crew and the success of the play.]

Let's add some information and see how that changes the transition words. Remember, we were not at the play. We have to rely on the words in the passage.

EXAMPLE

Incorrect: The stage crew did a fantastic job. <u>As a result</u>, the play was not a success.

[It makes no sense to use the transition phrase *as a result*; there is no cause-and-effect relationship between a fantastic job by the stage crew and an unsuccessful play.]

Correct: The stage crew did a fantastic job. <u>Yet</u>, the play was not a success.

[It does make sense to use the transitional word *yet* to show a contrast between a fantastic job by the stage crew and an unsuccessful play.]

Correct: The stage crew did a fantastic job. *As a result*, the play was a success. [It does make sense to draw a cause-and-effect relationship between the fantastic work of the stage crew and the success of the play.]

The best way to practice ACT transition items is in the ACT format. Start out with model questions and follow up with ACT practice items.

Model ACT Questions

These Model ACT Questions show how this topic might be tested on the real ACT. The answers and explanations immediately follow the questions. Try the questions and then review the answers and the explanations.

It was a beautiful, warm fall day. <u>In spite of this,</u>
                                        1
the walkers wore shorts and short-sleeve shirts.

<u>And yet</u> for a skier, it may not have been the
    2
most beautiful day.

1. **A.** NO CHANGE
   B. Therefore,
   C. Nevertheless,
   D. But, — *same*

   same = wrong

2. **F.** NO CHANGE
   G. Therefore,
   H. And —
   J. Moreover,

Answers

1. This is a classic transition item. The first sentence tells us it's a warm day. The second sentence tells us the walkers wore shorts and short-sleeve shirts. The phrase *In spite of this* connects the first sentence to the second and also implies a contrast. Because of this transition phrase, we would expect the second sentence not to flow naturally from the first. And yet it does. The phrase *In spite of this* cannot be correct. Choices C and D also imply a contrast.

   B is the correct choice.

2. The original wording is correct. This sentence shows a contrast to the previous sentence. Choices G, H, and J imply that there is no contrast between this sentence and the previous sentence.

   F is the correct choice.

Look at the item that matches the number of the underlined part. Pick the best replacement for the underlined part. If the underlined part is the best, select NO CHANGE.

Investment involves many areas of the economy, and it includes business management and finance for households, firms, or governments. That is, an
<u>1</u>
investment involves the choice to place or lend money. An investment or asset, <u>on the other hand,</u>
<u>2</u>
provides the possibility of generating returns.

<u>Nevertheless,</u> investment comes with the risk of
<u>3</u>
the loss of the principal sum. The owner of an investment can assume high risks, and the possibility of losing money is not within his or her control. That is called liability.

As time passes, both prices and interest rates change; <u>consequently,</u> the values of the asset and
<u>4</u>
liability also change. A deposit made in a bank, <u>furthermore,</u> is assured of gaining a future return
<u>5</u>
or interest.

(Answers on page 163)

1. **A.** NO CHANGE
   B. therefore
   C. consequently
   D. by contrast

2. **F.** NO CHANGE
   G. consequently
   H. by the same token
   J. in other words

3. **A.** NO CHANGE
   B. As a result of
   C. And so
   D. Therefore

4. **F.** NO CHANGE
   G. in contrast
   H. although
   J. in other words

5. **A.** NO CHANGE
   B. by contrast
   C. although
   D. rather

Appropriate Use

These are the less common of the strategy questions on the ACT. **Appropriate use** questions ask you whether and how to revise or add content to a passage based on a specific set of criteria. Read the item and the answers carefully to be sure you are providing exactly what the item is asking for. There are no hard-and-fast rules for answering the questions, but there is always only one correct answer.

The first question type asks you to choose a sentence that will be most helpful to the intended reader. The second question type asks you to decide where to add or delete a particular sentence.

These question types make complete sense only in an ACT format, but let's think about these question types a little bit before we get to the actual ACT questions.

EXAMPLES

1. Let's say that you were asked to add a sentence to a passage that gave investment advice. Which one of these four sentences would be acceptable?
   A. Investing in stocks can be a very risky business.
   B. If you invest in stocks, diversify your portfolio.
   C. The major averages such as the DOW and the S&P 500 give important clues to the market's movement.
   D. ETFs (exchange traded funds) are baskets of stock, usually with a single theme.

All four sentences are true. But only B gives actual advice. This is the correct choice.

2. Consider this question: Should the sentence below be added to the passage that follows?

> A stock is an example of an asset and a loan is an example of a liability.

Passage:

As time passes, both prices and interest rates change; consequently, the values of the asset and liability also change. A deposit made in a bank, by contrast, is assured of gaining a future return or interest. Investment is an example of putting things (money or other claims to resources) into others' pockets.

Which choice BEST explains if the author should or should not add the sentence?
   F. No, don't add the sentence because there are other types of liabilities and assets.
   G. Yes, do add the sentence because it clarifies the meanings of *asset* and *liability.*
   H. No, don't add the sentence because the reader should already know this information.
   J. Yes, do add the sentence because more information is always better.

Consider each in turn.
   F. This is true, but that list would be too long to include in this brief paragraph.
   G. This is true, and the argument is sound. It's good to clarify terms.
   H. We don't know if this is true or not because we don't know who the reader is.
   J. This seems false. More information can't *always* be better.

G is the best choice, and the writer should add the sentence to clarify the meanings of the important terms in the passage.

Model ACT Questions

These Model ACT Questions show how this topic might be tested on the real ACT. The answers and explanations immediately follow the questions. Try the questions and then review the answers and the explanations.

1 Understanding bond yields can be difficult. **2** You have to consider both the price of the bond and the interest rate. **3** When the interest rate on the bond goes up, the price of the bond goes down.

1. Suppose that the author of this passage wanted to give an example of the statement about a bond's interest rate and price found in sentence 3. Which sentence would BEST meet the writer's purpose?
   A. This means that interest rate increases can actually lead to a loss.
   B. To determine yields on common stock, you usually have to determine only the gain or loss.
   C. Recently the interest rate on a bond went up 0.1 percent, and the price went down $0.90.
   D. Risky bonds can have an interest rate as high as 18 percent, while safer bonds can have an interest rate as low as 5 percent.

   Answer   Consider each item in turn: Choice A is not an example. It describes the consequences of a rate increase. Choice B has nothing to do with bonds. Choice C is an example. It describes a specific situation in which the interest rate of a bond went up while the price came down. Choice D gives an example but of the interest rates of risky and safe bonds.

   C is the correct choice.

Coin collectors place a significant premium on the quality of a coin. Coins in mint condition command the highest prices, followed by coins that have never been circulated. The value of a coin with even minor defects can drop by as much as 50 percent.

2. The author of this passage is considering including this sentence after the first sentence:

   Quality is also important for art collectors.

   Should the author add the sentence?
   F. Yes, because the sentence emphasizes the importance of quality for collectors.
   G. No, because quality is not as important in artwork since old paintings sell for high prices.
   H. Yes, because the sentence presents an interesting comparison between two types of collecting.
   J. No, because the sentence interrupts the flow of the passage.

   Answer   This item asks you to evaluate the wisdom of adding a sentence. You have to indicate whether the answer should be yes or no, as well as a reason for your choice.

   The sentence "Quality is also important for art collectors" doesn't have much to do with coin collecting. Consider the choices:

   Choices F and H give arguments for including the sentence. Choices G and J give plausible arguments for not including the sentence. Your choice is between G and J. Choice J is correct because a sentence about art collectors does not belong in this paragraph. The sentence interrupts the flow of the passage.

   J is the correct choice.

Pick the best answer for each of the following questions.

1. New England winters are cold, so Dr. James Naismith, a physical education professor at what is now Springfield College in Massachusetts, had a hard time keeping his students active in winter gym classes. He thought of some ideas for what activities he could do in an indoor gym, but nothing seemed to work quite well enough. Then he wrote some rules for a new game and attached an old peach basket to an elevated track in the gym. Unlike today's basketball nets, though, the peach basket was closed at the bottom. That meant the ball would have to be taken out by one of the players each time a point was scored.

Which sentence explains what happened after a basket was scored?

A. A new ball was used in the game.
B. The team scoring the basket won the game.
C. The bottom of the basket was removed.
D. The ball was manually removed from the basket.

2. If somebody got the ball in the basket, that person's team got a point. Whichever team scored the most baskets was the winner. At first, the baskets were attached to gym balconies. However, spectators started interfering with the baskets during games, so a backboard was added. Adding the backboard also allowed for rebound shots. If the ball bounced off the backboard, another player could swoop in and try for another shot.

Which of the following sentences most likely contains specific advice about scoring a rebound shot and can be added to the end of this second paragraph?

F. Players would simply try to get the ball in the basket and score points as often as possible.
G. Players would have to wait until there were no spectators to interfere with their shots.
H. The best strategy for players would be to shoot the ball toward the basket and wait underneath the basket for a rebound off the backboard.
J. Players would try to angle their shots so the ball would go in the basket.

3. [1] Naismith kept handwritten diaries, which were discovered by his granddaughter. [2] In them, he writes that he was nervous about the new game he had invented. [3] Some of his rules were borrowed from a children's game called Duck on a Rock, but he called the new game Basket Ball. [4] The first official game ended with a score of 1–0.

The author is considering adding this sentence following sentence 4.

> The shot was made from 25 feet from the basket.

Should the author add the sentence?

A. No, because the amount of detail does not match the detail in the remainder of the passage.
B. Yes, because the sentence adds historical information to the account of the first game.
C. No, because the author was obviously just guessing at the distance from the basket.
D. Yes, because the sentence shows the accurate records were kept even at the earliest games.

4. Senda Berenson, a physical education teacher at Smith College, is credited with starting women's basketball when she modified Naismith's rules for women. She met with him to get more details about the game when she was teaching at Smith College. She thought the game could teach good values. She soon organized the first women's collegiate game, in which her freshmen and sophomores played against each other. Eventually, her rules for women's basketball were published when she became the editor of A. G. Spalding's first *Official Basketball Guide for Women*.

Which of the following adds specific information about early rules for women's basketball?

F. Rules called for points that are scored by getting the ball in the basket.
G. Rules called for 6 to 9 players per team and for 11 officials.
H. Rules called for games to be played between players from the same school.
J. Rules called for players to follow the guidelines from A. G. Spalding's first *Official Basketball Guide for Women*.

5. [1] Dr. James Naismith was central to building college basketball as we know it today. [2] He coached at the University of Kansas for six years and then gave the position to renowned coach Forrest "Phog" Allen. [3] Amos Alonzo Stagg, a protégé of Naismith's, introduced the University of Chicago to basketball, and one of his students became a famous coach at the University of Kentucky.

The author is considering adding the sentence below after sentence 3.

> Soon, the standard became five players on a team, but all over America today, two-on-two and three-on-three "street" pickup basketball games are still common.

Should the author add the sentence?

A. Yes, because the sentence shows that basketball rules became standardized.
B. No, because the sentence does not fit into the context of the paragraph.
C. Yes, because the information in the sentence has important historical significance.
D. No, because once the standard was set at five players per team, no other size team should be discussed.

(Answers on pages 163–164)

Strategy Subtest

This Subtest has the same number and type of strategy items found on the ACT. If you don't know an answer, eliminate the choices you know are incorrect, then guess. Circle the number of any guessed answer. Check pages 164–165 for answers and explanations.

INSTRUCTIONS: Certain words or phrases in the following passage are underlined and numbered. There is a corresponding item for each underlined portion. Each item offers three suggestions for changing the underlined portion to conform to standard written English or to make it understandable or consistent with the rest of the passage. If the underlined portion is not improved by one of the three suggested changes, mark NO CHANGE.

You will also find questions about a section of the passage as a whole. These questions do not refer to an underlined portion of the passage, but rather are identified by a number in a box.

Choose the best answer for each question based on the passage. Then fill in the appropriate circle on the answer grid.

```
1 Ⓐ Ⓑ Ⓒ Ⓓ     5 Ⓐ Ⓑ Ⓒ Ⓓ     9 Ⓐ Ⓑ Ⓒ Ⓓ
2 Ⓕ Ⓖ Ⓗ Ⓙ     6 Ⓕ Ⓖ Ⓗ Ⓙ     10 Ⓕ Ⓖ Ⓗ Ⓙ
3 Ⓐ Ⓑ Ⓒ Ⓓ     7 Ⓐ Ⓑ Ⓒ Ⓓ     11 Ⓐ Ⓑ Ⓒ Ⓓ
4 Ⓕ Ⓖ Ⓗ Ⓙ     8 Ⓕ Ⓖ Ⓗ Ⓙ     12 Ⓕ Ⓖ Ⓗ Ⓙ
```

[1]

Arthur Conan Doyle's great sleuth, Sherlock Holmes, was superrational, <u>and</u> the famous author [1] himself was the world's best-known advocate of spiritualism, the belief that human personality survives death and that the living can communicate with the dead. <u>Nevertheless,</u> spiritualism was [3] all the rage around the turn of the twentieth century. Séances, rapping, table turning, automatic writing, and other occult methods of contacting the spirit world attracted thousands. Doyle was the antithesis of a man who would try communicating with the dead; <u>and</u> after converting to Spiritualism, [4] he set about trying to convert others. ⬚5

1. **A.** NO CHANGE
   B. since
   C. that is
   D. but

2. The author deleted the following sentence, which was originally placed after the first sentence.

   Even today, people look to psychics for help and advice from other worlds and past lives.

   Was deleting the sentence a good decision?

   F. No, because it connects the spiritualism of the past to today's reader.
   G. No, because it elaborates on spiritualism.
   H. Yes, because the information is not relevant to the point and interrupts the flow of the passage.
   J. Yes, because people then didn't use psychics.

[2]

Eventually Doyle's obsession seriously
——————
6
compromised his reputation and strained his

friendships, most notably with the escape artist

Harry Houdini, who had been a fake medium since
——————
7
whose training in the "artifices of conjuring" led

him to approach spiritualism with great skepticism.

8 Although the most damaging blow to Doyle's
   ————————
   9
good name resulted from his outspoken advocacy

of the existence of fairies, a matter somewhat

fancifully retold in the film *Fairytale—A True*

Story, starring Peter O'Toole as Doyle, which was

released by Paramount Pictures in 1997.

[3]

In 1917, two girls from the Yorkshire village of
———————
10
Cottingley made fake photographs of themselves

cavorting with fairies. Few took the pictures

seriously, therefore Doyle did. He wrote a book
          ————————
          11
defending their authenticity. 12

3. **A.** NO CHANGE
   B. And yet
   C. In spite of this
   D. Delete *Nevertheless* and correct the capitalization.

4. **F.** NO CHANGE
   G. so
   H. however,
   J. therefore,

5. The author wants to give an example of Doyle's conversion here. Which sentence or sentences would BEST meet his needs?

   A. As the creator of Sherlock Holmes, Doyle relied upon facts and proof to support his ideas and theories. However, once he felt he had accumulated the "proof" of spiritualism, Doyle began to share this proof with others.
   B. Although Doyle created Sherlock Holmes, a man who relied on facts and clues, Doyle himself did not feel he needed proof of communication with the dead. Therefore, throughout his life, Doyle sought to convince others that his belief was right.
   C. When Doyle created Sherlock Holmes, he described him as a man who believed in spiritualism. Once that belief became outdated, however, Doyle edited those passages out of his books.
   D. Doyle used to believe in spiritualism. Then he did not, but he convinced others to believe in it.

6. **F.** NO CHANGE
   G. In spite of this,
   H. Therefore,
   J. However,

7. **A.** NO CHANGE
   B. and
   C. but
   D. nevertheless

8. The author considers adding the following sentence before sentence 2:

Houdini's skepticism of Doyle, since he was a friend of Doyle's and a man of renown himself, led to disbelief from other people as well.

Should he?

   F. Yes, because it shows that Houdini was a friend of Doyle's.
   G. Yes, because it links the disbelief of one person, Houdini, to that of others.
   H. No, because the sentence does not logically flow from the sentence before it.
   J. No, because Houdini did believe in Doyle's fairy stories.

9. **A.** NO CHANGE
   B. Since
   C. Perhaps
   D. In spite of this

10. **F.** NO CHANGE
   G. Throughout the year of 1917
   H. In the nineteenth century
   J. Until 1917

11. **A.** NO CHANGE
   B. as a result
   C. hence
   D. but

12. The author wishes to add a conclusion to the passage. Which sentence fits BEST?

   F. Today, no one really believes in fairies.
   G. Since the girls did not confess their hoax until 1983, Doyle died in 1930, still a believer.
   H. In the movie, Peter O'Toole does a great acting job as Doyle.
   J. Houdini never believed in fairies.

(Answers on pages 164–165)

Organization

Organization items are also unique to the ACT. On the ACT, **organization** items are of two main types.

- Reorder sentences in a paragraph or paragraphs in a passage. This is the most common type of reordering question.
- Place a new sentence in a paragraph or in a passage.

Paragraph Organization

The topic sentence should be the first sentence in a paragraph. The **topic sentence** conveys the main idea of the paragraph. The other sentences in a paragraph should contain details or examples that support the main idea.

The sentences should build on one another in some logical way. They are usually arranged according to one of the following organizational schemes.

Chronological. The sentences appear in time order, usually from earliest to latest.

Sentences in a passage about the Civil War would usually be arranged chronologically, from earlier battles to later battles.

Importance. The sentences present ideas from the most important to the least important.

Sentences in a passage about disease prevention would usually be arranged in order of importance, from the most important practice to the least important practice.

Spatial. Elements in sentences that are arranged spatially are usually arranged from the closest to the farthest.

The sentences in a paragraph about planets in the solar system would usually be arranged spatially, according to the planet's distance from the sun.

Classification. The sentences are arranged according to the classification of things or ideas.

The sentences in a paragraph about healthy eating might be arranged according to the different food groups. The sentences in a paragraph about scientists might be arranged according to whether they are chemists, biologists, and so on.

Compare and contrast. Sentences are arranged to compare or contrast things or ideas.

Sentences in a paragraph about oil drilling might begin with arguments for drilling and then arguments against the idea. A paragraph about the Founding Fathers might alternate sentences about each figure to compare and contrast their views about particular topics.

The last sentence in a paragraph may summarize the paragraph or provide a transition to the ideas that will appear in the next paragraph.

The passages on the ACT will always reveal the paragraph's organization. Reordering, replacing, or adding sentences will always maintain that organization.

Your first focus should be on the topic sentence. This sentence that describes what the passage is about should come first.

Let's look at some examples.

Consider this short paragraph.

1 *Lad, a Dog* was Terhune's most famous book. **2** Albert Payson Terhune is best known for his books about dogs. **3** He wrote another book titled *Wolf.* **4** The book about Lad is still widely read.

First find the topic sentence. You can tell this paragraph needs some reordering because the topic sentence does not appear first. Sentence 2 is the topic sentence, which tells what the paragraph is about. Sentence 2 should come first.

The sentences in a paragraph like this are usually arranged in order of importance. If sentence 2 is the topic sentence, what's the next important sentence? It is sentence 1, which mentions Terhune's most famous book.

Which sentence should come next? It is sentence 4, which gives more information about *Lad, a Dog.* That leaves sentence 3 as the final sentence in the paragraph.

The correct order of the sentences is 2, 1, 4, 3.

Here is another paragraph:

1 Martian meteorites that have landed on Earth have also been used to date material. **2** Rocks from the moon provide quite precise age dates. **3** That is because the moon has not undergone plate tectonics and has no atmosphere. **4** Lunar rock samples can also provide dating by direct electron microscope examination.

The sentences are not in the correct order. Suppose the ACT question asks you to correctly order the sentences. There would only be four choices—NO CHANGE, and then three other suggested sentence arrangements.

It looks like the sentences in this paragraph are listed in order of importance.

Find the topic sentence. Most of the information in this paragraph is about the dating of rocks and other material from the moon. That makes sentence 2 the topic sentence. It tells what the entire paragraph is about.

Which sentence should come after sentence 2? The best choice is sentence 3, which explains why the moon provides quite precise age measurements.

Which sentence should come after sentence 3? Only sentences 1 and 4 remain as choices. Sentence 4 is the better choice because it continues the main theme of discussing the dating of lunar samples. That leaves sentence 1 as the correct sentence to conclude the paragraph.

The correct order of the sentences in this paragraph is 2, 3, 4, 1.

Passage Organization

Paragraphs in passages are organized in much the same way that sentences are organized in paragraphs. Passages, however, are much larger structures, and it might help to briefly summarize a passage to better understand the appropriate paragraph order.

Remember that the actual ACT questions give you four choices: NO CHANGE, and then three choices for reordering the passage. This makes reordering passages easier than if you didn't have the answer choices.

Here is one example:

[1]

The interior of Earth is divided into five important layers: the crust, upper mantle, lower mantle, outer core, and inner core.

[2]

Seismic measurements show that the core is divided into two parts, a solid inner core and a liquid outer core extending beyond it to a radius of approximately 3,400 km. The solid inner core was discovered in 1936 and is generally believed to be composed primarily of iron and some nickel. The liquid outer core surrounds the inner core and is believed to be composed of iron mixed with nickel and trace amounts of lighter elements.

[3]

Earth's mantle is the thickest layer. The mantle is composed of silicate rocks that are rich in iron and magnesium relative to the overlying crust. Although the mantle is solid, its high temperatures cause the silicate material to flow on very long timescales. As there is intense and increasing pressure as one travels deeper into the mantle, the lower part of the mantle flows less easily than does the upper mantle.

[4]

The crust is the outermost layer. The thin parts are the oceanic crust, which underlie the ocean basins and are composed of silicate rocks, like basalt. The thicker crust is continental crust, which is less dense and composed of sodium-potassium-aluminum-silicate rocks, like granite.

[5]

The uppermost mantle together with the crust constitutes the lithosphere. The lithosphere is the hard, rigid outer layer of Earth.

Quickly summarize the paragraphs.

1. Mentions five important layers including two core layers, two mantle layers, and the crust.
2. Discusses core.
3. Discusses mantle.
4. Discusses crust.
5. Discusses lithosphere.

The paragraphs are arranged spatially from the inner part of Earth to the outer part.

Paragraph 5 is out of place. It mentions that the lithosphere combines the mantle with the crust, but this is not mentioned in the first paragraph as one of Earth's parts. The best place for this paragraph is after paragraph 1, as extra information. It does not belong between paragraphs 2 and 3 or paragraphs 3 and 4.

Adding Sentences to a Passage

This is the second type of ACT ordering question.

Reading a passage that needs sentences added to it will leave you with the feeling that something is missing. Look back at the passage about dating lunar rocks on page 146. The passage talks about dating rocks, but it never actually tells you anything about the dating. The author of the paragraph might want to add some more specific information.

Suppose an ACT question asks where a sentence should be added. The choice NO CHANGE does not appear for this type of question.

Here is a sentence an ACT question might ask you to add to the lunar rocks passage:

The meteorites have been dated to around 4.5 billion years.

This sentence must refer to the meteorites mentioned in sentence 1. The correct answer to a question about where this sentence should be added would be after sentence 1.

Following is another sentence. After which sentence in the lunar rocks paragraph does it belong?

By electron microscopic examination, lunar rocks have been reliably dated at a maximum of around 4.4 and 4.5 billion years old.

This sentence would come after sentence 4, which discusses electron microscope dating.

Model ACT Questions

These Model ACT Questions show how this topic might be tested on the real ACT. The answers and explanations immediately follow the questions. Try the questions and then review the answers and the explanations.

[1]

[1] Cloudwatching can often tell you what type of front is moving through. [2] For example, a cold front begins with high cirrus clouds. [3] A person can remember the order of convective rain clouds in a front with the mnemonic word CANS. [4] Once you have seen the CANS clouds move through, the front has passed, and the air will probably grow colder. [5] Next come altostratus clouds, nimbostratus (low rain clouds), and finally very low stratus clouds.

[2]

[1] Some clouds are caused by convection. [2] If you've ever been at the beach, you may have seen puffy clouds early in the day. [3] As the day wore on, these puffy clouds may have grown into convective rain clouds. [4] Later in the afternoon there may have been a rain shower or a thunderstorm.

1. Which of the following arrangements of sentences will make paragraph 1 most sensible?

   A. NO CHANGE
   B. 1, 4, 3, 2, 5
   C. 1, 3, 2, 5, 4
   D. 3, 2, 4, 5, 1

2. The author is considering adding this sentence to paragraph 2:

   (These convective rain clouds are called cumulonimbus clouds.)

   The sentence should be added to the paragraph after sentence:

   F. 1.
   G. 2.
   H. 3.
   J. 4.

Answers

1. This question asks for the most sensible arrangement of the sentences from among the choices given. Remember that you are asked to pick only from the choices given. There are 120 possible arrangements of the five sentences, so work backward from the answers and be flexible.

   It doesn't make sense to begin with sentence 3, so eliminate choice D.

   Sentence 3 is obviously out of place in the passage, so eliminate choice A. The remaining choices begin with sentence 1, so the question is which sentence should come next—sentence 3 or 4?

   Sentence 3 should come next and then sentences 2 and 5 since they give additional information. Sentence 4 clearly sums up the rest of the paragraph, so it should come last.

   C is the correct choice.

2. Question 2 asks you to place a new sentence somewhere in paragraph 2. The sentence is in parentheses, so we know that it is either a definition or an explanation. It is a definition.

The sentence defines cumulonimbus clouds as convective rain clouds. Look for one of these terms in the passage. *Convective rain clouds* appears in sentence 3. The definition of convective rain clouds should come right after sentence 3.

H is the correct choice.

ACT-Type Questions

Each paragraph and each sentence is numbered in the passage that follows. Use the numbers to help guide you as you answer each question to the right of the passage.

[1]

[1] When Superman became widely successful in the 1930s, the comic book division of National Publications (they would become DC Comics) asked for more superhero stories. [2] Bill Finger—who collaborated on Batman—remembers, "Kane said he had an idea for a character, and he'd like me to see the drawings. [3] In response, Bob Kane created the Bat-Man. [4] I went over to Kane's, and he had drawn a character who looked very much like Superman." [5] The character wore a sort of red-colored tights and a domino mask, but he had no gloves or gauntlets. [6] He had two large wings that made him look like a bat, and the drawing was labeled "BATMAN."

[2]

[1] In a 1988 comic, "Batman: A Death in the Family," the Joker kills Robin. [2] Batman works alone until the end of the eighties, and then Tim Drake becomes the

1. What is the BEST order of the first five sentences in paragraph 1?

  A. NO CHANGE
  B. 1, 2, 3, 6, 4, 5
  C. 1, 3, 2, 4, 5, 6
  D. 1, 2, 3, 5, 6, 4

2. The author wants to delete a sentence from paragraph 1. The BEST sentence to delete is:

  F. sentence 2.
  G. sentence 3.
  H. sentence 5.
  J. sentence 6.

3. What is the BEST order of the sentences in paragraph 2?

  A. NO CHANGE
  B. 1, 3, 2, 4
  C. 1, 3, 4, 2
  D. 1, 4, 3, 2

new Robin. [3] As a result, Batman's approach to fighting crime becomes overblown and quite dangerous. [4] This behavior is his reaction to the loss of Robin.

[3]

[1] In the long run, Batman's relationship with Gotham City's Police Department seriously deteriorates. [2] Batman has had Commissioner Gordon and Harvey Bullock on his side, but they are run out of the department. [3] Batman himself becomes a wanted criminal after one of his plans to fight Gotham City's criminals goes seriously awry. [4] His plan starts a gang war, which ends with the Black Mask ruling all the city's gangs.

[4]

[1] One writer, Grant Morrison, wrote a story line in 2008 called "Batman: R.I.P." in which Batman is broken down by Black Glove. [2] Originally, Batman was not supposed to die, and the story was supposed to continue with DC Comics's *Final Crisis*. [3] The story line was said to end with Batman's (Bruce Wayne's) death. [4] To explain the change, writers created "Last Rites" to show Batman survived to be summoned to the Hall of Justice by the JLA. [5] Batman visits the Hall of Justice and is then kidnapped in the later *Final Crisis*.

[5]

[1] After *Final Crisis*, the comic retraces Batman's experiences when he left Gotham City to "rebuild Batman." [2] After a year being away, Batman comes back with Robin. [3] Later, readers see Batman going through a profound meditation practice. [4] The

4. The author wants to add this sentence to the passage.

   The modern story of Batman continues quite a few years later.

   Where in the passage should the sentence go?

   F. Before paragraph 1
   G. Before paragraph 2
   H. Before paragraph 3
   J. Before paragraph 5

5. What is the BEST order of the sentences in paragraph 3?

   A. NO CHANGE
   B. 2, 1, 3, 4
   C. 1, 3, 2, 4
   D. 2, 3, 1, 4

6. What is the BEST order of the sentences in paragraph 4?

   F. NO CHANGE
   G. 1, 2, 3, 5, 4
   H. 1, 3, 2, 5, 4
   J. 1, 3, 2, 4, 5

7. What is the BEST order of the sentences in paragraph 5?

   A. NO CHANGE
   B. 2, 1, 3, 4, 5
   C. 2, 1, 3, 5, 4
   D. 2, 1, 5, 4, 3

8. The author wishes to add this sentence in paragraph 5.

   Part of this absence shows Batman fighting his fears.

   Which is the BEST placement for this sentence?

   F. After sentence 2
   G. After sentence 3
   H. After sentence 4
   J. After sentence 5

meditation practice becomes key to the Batman series. **5** It shows how Batman became a better superhero because he was able to eradicate any remaining fear from his mind.

9. The author wishes to delete a sentence in paragraph 5. Which is the BEST one to delete?

   A. Sentence 2
   B. Sentence 3
   C. Sentence 4
   D. Sentence 5

10. Which is the BEST order of the paragraphs in this passage?

   F. NO CHANGE
   G. 1, 2, 3, 5, 4
   H. 1, 3, 2, 5, 4
   J. 1, 3, 2, 4, 5

(*Answers on page 165*)

Organization Subtest

This Subtest has the same number and type of organization items found on the ACT. If you don't know an answer, eliminate the choices you know are incorrect, then guess. Circle the number of any guessed answer. Check pages 165–166 for answers and explanations.

INSTRUCTIONS: Each paragraph and each sentence is numbered in the passage that follows. There is a corresponding item for each boxed number, offering three suggestions for changing the paragraph to make it understandable or consistent with the rest of the passage. If the paragraph is not improved by one of the three suggested changes, mark NO CHANGE.

Choose the best answer for each question based on the passage. Then fill in the appropriate circle on the answer grid.

```
1 Ⓐ Ⓑ Ⓒ Ⓓ      5 Ⓐ Ⓑ Ⓒ Ⓓ      9 Ⓐ Ⓑ Ⓒ Ⓓ
2 Ⓕ Ⓖ Ⓗ Ⓙ      6 Ⓕ Ⓖ Ⓗ Ⓙ     10 Ⓕ Ⓖ Ⓗ Ⓙ
3 Ⓐ Ⓑ Ⓒ Ⓓ      7 Ⓐ Ⓑ Ⓒ Ⓓ     11 Ⓐ Ⓑ Ⓒ Ⓓ
4 Ⓕ Ⓖ Ⓗ Ⓙ      8 Ⓕ Ⓖ Ⓗ Ⓙ
```

[1]

1 As the curtain of darkness falls over the land, an entire universe is revealed. **2** Of course, understanding what we see is the goal of all of us who spend hours gazing up at a dark sky. **3** Stars pop out of the velvet darkness, and planets gleam, hiding a deeper truth than a simple telescope can reveal. |1| |2|

[2]

1 It took many years before Christiaan Huygens, the 17th-century Dutch astronomer who discovered Saturn's moon, Titan, figured out what he was seeing while observing Saturn. **2** In 1659 he realized that a set of rings surrounded the solar system's second largest planet, a conclusion that had initially escaped Galileo, who first observed the peculiar appendages

1. What is the BEST order of sentences in paragraph 1?

   A. NO CHANGE
   B. 1, 3, 2
   C. 3, 1, 2
   D. 2, 3, 1

2. The author wants to add this sentence to paragraph 1.

   The sun is setting over the earth, and the night begins.

   Where should it be placed?

   F. After sentence 2
   G. After sentence 3
   H. After sentence 1
   J. Before sentence 1

3. The BEST order of sentences for paragraph 2 is:

   A. NO CHANGE
   B. 1, 3, 2.
   C. 2, 1, 3.
   D. 3, 1, 2.

in 1610. **3** Galileo's later observations indicate that he had some ideas about the rings' true nature, but he never stated them. [3] [4]

[3]

1 Try it on your neighbors this fall. **2** Today, even the smallest telescope is powerful enough to reveal the delicate structure of the rings. **3** On first sight through a telescope, Saturn makes most people gasp with surprise. [5] [6] [7]

[4]

1 Saturn swims among the stars of Pisces the Fish, below the line of dim stars that forms the southern fish. **2** A nearly full moon glides half a degree north of Saturn on October 15. **3** For people in central Africa, Saudi Arabia, and much of Asia (including India, China, and Japan), the moon passes in front of Saturn on this night, occulting it from view. **4** By the end of October, Saturn is clear of the eastern horizon by nightfall and the only bright "star" in that area of sky. [8] [9]

4. The author wants to add this sentence to paragraph 2.

   In fact, Galileo reported to Johannes Kepler that "Saturn consists of three stars in contact with one another."

   It would BEST fit:

   F. before sentence 1.
   G. after sentence 3.
   H. after sentence 2.
   J. after sentence 1.

5. The BEST order for the sentences in paragraph 3 is:

   A. NO CHANGE
   B. 1, 3, 2.
   C. 3, 2, 1.
   D. 2, 3, 1.

6. The author wants to delete a sentence (or sentences) in paragraph 3. The BEST one(s) to delete is (are):

   F. 1
   G. 2 and 3
   H. 3
   J. 1 and 2

7. The author then wants to replace the deleted sentence(s) with this one:

   Although Saturn is 780 million miles away, it is astounding owing to its radiance.

   Where in the passage should it go?

   A. At the beginning of paragraph 3
   B. At the end of paragraph 3
   C. In the middle of paragraph 3
   D. At the end of paragraph 2

8. The BEST order for sentences in paragraph 4 is:

   F. NO CHANGE
   G. 1, 4, 3, 2.
   H. 4, 1, 2, 3.
   J. 4, 3, 1, 2.

9. The author wishes to delete one of the sentences in paragraph 4. Which is BEST?

A. Sentence 4
B. Sentence 3
C. Sentence 2 and change "this night" in sentence 3 to "October 15"
D. Sentence 1

Questions 10 and 11 ask about the passage as a whole.

10. What is the BEST order of paragraphs in this passage?

F. NO CHANGE
G. 4, 2, 3, 1
H. 2, 4, 1, 3
J. 3, 4, 2, 1

11. The author wants to add the following paragraph.

Despite its great distance, Saturn has been known since ancient times because it glows so brightly. Bright clouds cover every square inch of its huge surface, reflecting 47 percent of the sunlight striking them. This copious amount of reflected sunlight, compared with the mere 12 percent reflectivity of our moon, gives Saturn much of its radiance.

It should be placed:

A. at the beginning of the essay.
B. at the end of the essay.
C. between paragraphs 1 and 2.
D. between paragraphs 3 and 4.

(*Answers on pages 165–166*)

Style

Style questions are about how a passage communicates. Like the other rhetorical skills questions, style does not refer to a particular writing style or to the general idea of writing style. Rather, it refers to a limited number of very specific question types found on the ACT. ACT questions will ask you to correct one of three things:

- Redundancy
- Wordiness
- Clichés

Correct redundant or wordy sentences and replace clichés.

ACT testwriters want to know if you can identify parts of passages that are redundant or wordy, or that contain clichés. Let's consider these one at a time.

Redundancy

Redundant parts of a passage repeat information which is not necessary or not essential. This is often referred to as saying the same thing twice. Most often, repeated or reiterated information is redundant. However, there are some times when the extra information is not redundant because it adds meaning to a sentence.

Consider this sentence:

> The sign was shaped like a four-sided square.

This sentence contains redundant information. It is enough to say the sign was shaped like a square. All squares have four sides, so *like a four-sided* is redundant and should be removed.

> The corrected sentence should read like this:

> The sign was shaped like a square.

It is incorrect to rewrite the sentence like this:

> The sign has four sides.

This sentence conveys a different meaning from the original. There are many four-sided shapes, and this sentence does not tell us that the four-sided shape was a square.

Consider another sentence:

> Two old cars, a convertible and a hardtop, were on view at the car show.

This sentence is correct. The phrase *a convertible and a hardtop* does refer to the two cars, but it adds new information about the cars.

This sentence could not be rewritten like this:

> Two old cars were on view at the car show.

The construction above deprives us of information about the cars.

The sentence could not be rewritten this way either:

> A convertible and a hardtop were on view at the car show.

This construction leaves out the information that these were old cars.
Following are some more examples.

EXAMPLES

Incorrect: The invention was a new innovation.

[The word *new* is redundant because an innovation is new.]

Corrected: The invention was an innovation.

Incorrect: Where are they at?

[The word *at* is redundant because it adds nothing to the sentence.]

Corrected: Where are they?

Incorrect: The flu virus was widespread and extensive.

[The words *widespread* and *extensive* are synonyms and including both of the words adds no extra meaning to the sentence. These words are redundant.]

Corrected: The flu virus was widespread.

or

The flu virus was extensive.

Incorrect: It was an hour after sunset, at night, when the train arrived at the station.

[The words *at night* are redundant because it is always night "an hour after sunset."]

Corrected: It was an hour after sunset when the train arrived at the station.

Wordiness

Wordy sentences use more words than are necessary to express an idea. One of the most commonly abused wordy phrases is *the fact that.* Another commonly used wordy phrase is *the way in which.*

Consider this sentence:

The fact that he was late created scheduling problems.

This sentence should be rewritten. Here is one possibility:

His lateness created scheduling problems.

Consider this sentence, which has a similar problem:

He was late due to the fact that there was a traffic jam on Main Street.

This sentence also needs to be rewritten. Here is one possibility:

He was late because of a traffic jam on Main Street.

EXAMPLES

Wordy: The way in which the Egyptian pyramids were built is still unknown.

Corrected: The way the Egyptian pyramids were built is still unknown.

Wordy: I love the way in which Ling arranges flowers.
Corrected: I love the way Ling arranges flowers.

Here is a partial list of wordy phrases with possible replacements.

Wordy	Corrected
all the more	even more, more
as a matter of fact	in fact, actually
in order to	to
in terms of	in, by, for
know for certain	know, sure
methodology	method, why
once in a while	occasionally
take a look	look
past experience	experience
personal friend	friend

Clichés

A **cliché** is a trite expression, usually referring to everyday events, which has been used so often that it is stale and out of date. Clichés, some of which are shown below, should always be replaced on the ACT.

Cliché	Meaning
between a rock and a hard place	encountering two equally undesirable choices
beyond the shadow of a doubt	thoroughly proved
dyed-in-the-wool	unable to be changed
easier said than done	easier to talk about than to accomplish
needle in a haystack	difficult to locate
on a silver platter	received without work or effort
sneaking suspicion	assumption without evidence
stubborn as a mule	unwilling or unable to heed advice and change
tried and true	tested and proved to be worthy

Model ACT Questions

These Model ACT questions show how this topic might be tested on the real ACT. The answers and explanations immediately follow the questions. Try the questions and then review the answers and the explanations.

Speaking of the weather, have you ever been outside during sleet (rain that freezes as it falls to earth)? Sleet and freezing rain are different depending on conditions as they strike the earth. Hail is formed—created—when water droplets are blown again and again into high altitudes, where the droplets freeze over and over.

1. **A.** NO CHANGE
   B. (freezes as it falls to earth)
   C. (rain)
   D. OMIT the underlined portion.

2. **F.** NO CHANGE
   G. —molded—
   H. —structured—
   J. OMIT the underlined portion.

Answers

1. Item 1 is a classic redundancy and wordiness question. Notice that choice D is to omit the entire underlined portion, but the words in parentheses are not redundant. They give a useful definition of sleet.

   A is the correct choice.

2. Item 2 is another redundancy/wordiness question, and there is a redundancy. The word *created* is just another way of saying *formed*. It has to be removed. Choices G and H are also synonyms for *formed*.

   J is the correct choice.

ACT-Type Questions

Look at the item that matches the number of the underlined part. Pick the best replacement for the underlined part. If the underlined part is the best, select NO CHANGE.

Mars Exploration Rover Mission (MER) is an ongoing and continuing robotic space mission involving two rovers, Spirit and Opportunity, exploring the planet Mars. It began in 2003 with the sending of the two rovers—MER-A Spirit and

- 1. **A.** NO CHANGE
   B. and repeating
   C. and recycling
   D. OMIT the underlined portion.

MER-B Opportunity—to explore the Martian surface and geology—easier said than done. The mission's
<u>3</u>
scientific objective was to search for the wide range of <u>varied</u> rocks and soils that hold clues to <u>past</u> water
<u>4</u>   <u>5</u>
activity on Mars. The mission was part of NASA's Mars Exploration Program, which includes three previous landers: the two Viking program landers in 1976 and the Mars Pathfinder probe in 1997. The total cost of building, launching, landing, and operating the rovers on the surface for the initial 90-Martian-day (sol) primary mission was $820 million. Since the rovers have continued to function <u>above and beyond</u> their
<u>6</u>
initial 90-sol primary mission, they have each received five mission extensions. The fifth and final mission extension was granted in October 2007 and ran to the end of 2009. In July 2007, during the fourth mission extension, <u>dust storms on the surface of the planet</u>
<u>7</u>
<u>of Mars</u> blocked sunlight to the rovers and threatened
<u>7</u>
the ability of the craft to gather energy through their solar panels <u>because of the dust</u>. This caused engineers
<u>8</u>
to fear that one or both of them might be permanently disabled. However, <u>they lifted</u>, allowing scientists to
<u>9</u>
resume operations <u>and forge ahead</u>.
<u>10</u>

2. F. NO CHANGE
   G. with hopeful names
   H. named after positive human traits
   J. OMIT the underlined portion.

3. A. NO CHANGE
   B. —a difficult task
   C. —often spoken about but seldom accomplished
   D. OMIT the underlined portion.

4. F. NO CHANGE
   G. varying
   H. various
   J. OMIT the underlined portion.

5. A. NO CHANGE
   B. current
   C. subsequent
   D. OMIT the underlined portion.

6. F. NO CHANGE
   G. beyond the call of duty of
   H. beyond
   J. OMIT the underlined portion.

7. A. NO CHANGE
   B. Martian dust storms
   C. storms
   D. OMIT the underlined portion.

8. F. NO CHANGE
   G. because of the obstruction
   H. because of the wind
   J. OMIT the underlined portion.

9. A. NO CHANGE
   B. it lifted
   C. the storms lifted
   D. the rovers lifted

10. F. NO CHANGE
    G. abort the mission
    H. resume the mission
    J. OMIT the underlined portion.

(Answers on pages 166–167)

Style Subtest

This Subtest has the same number and type of style items found on the ACT. If you don't know an answer, eliminate the choices you know are incorrect, then guess. Circle the number of any guessed answer. Check page 167 for answers and explanations.

INSTRUCTIONS: Certain words or phrases in the following passage are underlined and numbered. There is a corresponding item for each underlined portion. Each item offers three suggestions for changing the underlined portion to conform to standard written English or to make it understandable or consistent with the rest of the passage. If the underlined portion is not improved by one of the three suggested changes, mark NO CHANGE.

Choose the best answer for each question based on the passage. Then fill in the appropriate circle on the answer grid.

1 Ⓐ Ⓑ Ⓒ Ⓓ	5 Ⓐ Ⓑ Ⓒ Ⓓ	9 Ⓐ Ⓑ Ⓒ Ⓓ
2 Ⓕ Ⓖ Ⓗ Ⓙ	6 Ⓕ Ⓖ Ⓗ Ⓙ	10 Ⓕ Ⓖ Ⓗ Ⓙ
3 Ⓐ Ⓑ Ⓒ Ⓓ	7 Ⓐ Ⓑ Ⓒ Ⓓ	11 Ⓐ Ⓑ Ⓒ Ⓓ
4 Ⓕ Ⓖ Ⓗ Ⓙ	8 Ⓕ Ⓖ Ⓗ Ⓙ	12 Ⓕ Ⓖ Ⓗ Ⓙ

The beauty of some words is <u>natural</u>. Consider
₁
these, found near the end of aviatrix Beryl Markham's
West With the Night: "Like all oceans, the Indian
Ocean seems never to end, and the ships that sail on it
are small and slow. <u>They have</u> no speed, nor any
₂
sense of urgency; they do not cross the water, they
live on <u>it until</u> the land comes home."
₃

It's a <u>satisfying</u> irony that when a reader goes
₄
looking for thrills in the literature of adventure, what
he or she often finds—perhaps next to a description
of a narrow escape—is an otherworldly passage like
the one from Markham's book.

1. The author wishes to describe some words as unreal or mysterious. Which works BEST for this purpose?

   A. NO CHANGE
   B. pedantic
   C. unearthly
   D. normal

2. F. NO CHANGE
   G. It has
   H. They has
   J. The ships have

3. A. NO CHANGE
   B. the ocean until
   C. them until
   D. that until

4. F. NO CHANGE
   G. unnatural
   H. complete
   J. verbal

Authentic adventure, as surely as a sentence of

hanging, can concentrate the mind, <u>pacifying</u> <u>it</u> to
                                        5   6
deeper truth, higher purpose. When starting any of the

adventure books mentioned here, prepare yourself for

the <u>certainty</u> that you'll discover descriptions you
      7
never bargained for.

If you're looking for <u>boring</u> stories of adventure,
                        8
the literature of the polar regions is a good place to

start. Mankind in small parties has been venturing

into this geography of <u>beautiful desolation</u> for at least
                          9
a thousand years, and often <u>him</u> on the trip had
                              10
decided to take notes. <u>How</u> the enduring interest in
                          11
the polar regions? For openers, there's the literary

<u>gawk</u> factor— readers are drawn to accounts of
  12
people who have put themselves at risk, and risk is

commonplace in the Arctic and Antarctic. One

misstep there and the cold can kill you.

5. **A.** NO CHANGE
   B. pleasing
   C. provoking
   D. angering

6. **F.** NO CHANGE
   G. the mind
   H. the adventure
   J. them

7. **A.** NO CHANGE
   B. possibility
   C. unlikelihood
   D. remote chance

8. **F.** NO CHANGE
   G. uninteresting
   H. vapid
   J. compelling

9. **A.** NO CHANGE
   B. ugly chaos
   C. beautiful chaos
   D. remote desolation

10. **F.** NO CHANGE
    G. somebody
    H. she
    J. he

11. **A.** NO CHANGE
    B. What
    C. When
    D. Why

12. **F.** NO CHANGE
    G. close-mindedness
    H. staring
    J. ogling

(*Answers on page 167*)

ANSWERS

1. A

No change. The passage correctly uses the transition term *That is* to signal a continuation and to indicate that an explanation follows. The second sentence in the passage gives an example of an investment.

2. G

The passage incorrectly uses *on the other hand* to suggest a contrast between an investment and what the investment provides. But there is a cause-and-effect relationship between an investment and what it provides. Choice G appropriately expresses that relationship.

3. A

No change. The passage correctly uses *Nevertheless* to express a contrast between the potential for returns and the dangers of a loss. None of the other choices reflects this contrast.

4. F

No change. The passage correctly uses *consequently* to point out the cause-and-effect relationship between the change in interest rates and the value of the investment.

5. B

The passage incorrectly uses the word *furthermore* to suggest that the second sentence agrees with and elaborates on the first sentence. But in fact there is a contrast between the risks of an investment and the safety of a bank deposit.

ACT-TYPE QUESTIONS   Appropriate Use
(pages 140–141)

1. Consider the answers in turn
   A. Incorrect. It makes no sense to use a new ball since there might not be room for a new ball in the basket.
   B. Incorrect. There is nothing in the passage to indicate that the game ended after one basket.
   C. Incorrect. It makes no sense to remove the bottom of the basket during a game, although the bottoms of the baskets were eventually removed before the game began.

D. Correct. This answer makes the most sense. The ball was stuck in the basket after a score and someone had to manually remove the ball.

The correct answer is **D**.

2. Consider each answer in turn. Remember, the item asks for "specific advice" about scoring a rebound shot.
   F. Incorrect. This may be the best overall strategy, but it has nothing to do with scoring a rebound shot.
   G. Incorrect. The backboard already prevented the spectators from interfering.
   H. Correct. This is the only choice that deals specifically with getting a rebound shot.
   J. Incorrect. Whether the ball was rebounding or not, players would try to angle it in order to make a shot.

The correct answer is **H**.

3. Consider the answers in turn.
   A. Correct. This may be an interesting point, but it is more detailed than other information in the paragraph.
   B. Incorrect. It is interesting information, but it does not belong in this paragraph.
   C. Incorrect. Actually, it seems this was an accurate measurement and not a guess.
   D. Incorrect. Information about the accuracy of records does not belong in this paragraph.

The correct answer is **A**.

4. Consider each answer in turn. The important words in the item are "adds specific information about early rules."
   F. Incorrect. Information about scoring points is not added information.
   G. Correct. This is new information about official rules needed to establish the game.
   H. Incorrect. This is not new information about rules; it just reiterates the description in the paragraph.
   J. Incorrect. This is a tempting answer, but it adds no actual information about the rules.

The correct answer is **G**.

5. Consider the answers in turn.

    A. Incorrect. This sentence about team size does not belong in the middle of a historic account of famous coaches.

    B. Correct. The sentence does not fit in the context of the paragraph.

    C. Incorrect for the same reason that choice A is incorrect.

    D. Incorrect. Other historical information involving different team sizes may have been appropriate for this paragraph.

The correct answer is **B**.

STRATEGY SUBTEST (pages 142–144)

1. D

The fact that Doyle was an advocate of spiritualism seems to be the opposite of something his superrational detective, Holmes, would believe. Therefore, the correct linking word is *but* because it implies that the two (Holmes and Doyle) are not the same. The word *since* is incorrect because it states that Doyle's spiritualism was caused by Holmes's superrationalism, which is not proved in the paragraphs following. The words *that is* would indicate that the author is elaborating on a previous point, which is not the case.

2. H

While the topic of the deleted sentence makes sense with the rest of the paragraph, the time frame does not. The other sentences refer to Doyle's time, while the deleted sentence refers to our time. Therefore, it makes sense to delete the sentence. J cannot be the correct answer, however, because the following sentences show that people at that time did believe in psychics and spiritualism.

3. D

The word *nevertheless* would mean that although Doyle believed in séances, others did not. Since the next sentence shows that others also believed in séances, A cannot be the right answer. The words *and yet* and *in spite of this* imply the same meaning as *nevertheless*, so they are incorrect also.

4. H

Using the word *however* completes the thought that although Doyle wasn't the type to believe in spiritualism, once he did believe, he tried to convert others. The word *and* simply connects the two thoughts, as if they belonged together, which they don't. It does not make sense that if he weren't the type he would convert others; therefore, an explanatory word like *however* is needed. The words *so* and *therefore* both imply that he converted others because he was not the type to believe.

5. A

This sentence elaborates on the one before it, showing that he accumulated the "proof" of spiritualism. Sentence B merely summarizes the paragraph without giving an example. There is nothing in the passage to support the idea that Holmes ever believed in spiritualism, and the last choice, D, is the opposite of what the passage states.

6. F

Choices G and J imply that the strain on his relationship caused by his obsession was not related to that obsession and his attempt to convert others. Since this is not the case, they can be ruled out. Choice H implies that his conversion attempts caused his obsession to compromise his friendships. This may be partly true, but other factors, like time, seem to have played a part.

7. B

The word *since* does not make sense. The words *but* and *nevertheless* are also incorrect. They imply that knowing mediums to be fake (as Houdini did) would lead him to believe in spiritualism rather than be skeptical.

8. G

The sentence flows logically from the sentence before it, which already states that Houdini was a friend of Doyle's who did not believe in fairies. Sentence 1 in the paragraph deals with Houdini's skepticism, and sentence 2 has to do with others' disbelief. Therefore, the only logical answer is that it helps show how his obsession compromised many friendships.

9. C

Using either *Although* or *Since* as the opening word makes this sentence a fragment. There is no second half to that thought (such as "although the most damaging blow was this, another factor was . . ."). The phrase *In spite of this* implies that his strained friendship with Houdini was not a damaging blow, which it was.

10. F

The two girls made their photographs at one point in time in the year 1917, which is in the twentieth century. They did not make them all throughout the year, nor did they make any up until that year.

11. D

The words *therefore*, *hence*, and *as a result* imply that Doyle believed the pictures because others did not and no causal link for this is explained. The word *but* merely states that although others didn't believe the pictures, Doyle did.

12. G

The paragraph offers no proof that people today don't believe in fairies or that Houdini never believed in fairies. It is also not concerned with reviewing the movie starring Peter O'Toole. Since the passage gives a brief chronological look at Doyle's belief in spiritualism and fairies, choice G gives the best conclusion to the essay.

ACT-TYPE QUESTIONS Organization
(pages 150–152)

1. C

Sentences 2 and 3 should be switched. Sentence 3 logically follows sentence 1, which states that the comics needed another superhero. Sentence 3 says that Batman was created. Then sentence 2 describes an invitation to come over to see the new creation. The remaining sentences are in the correct order.

2. H

Sentence 5 should be deleted. Sentence 2 is important because it describes a discussion about Batman's creation. Sentence 3 is important because it mentions who created Batman. Sentences 5 and 6 each provide details, but which detail is more important? The mention of the wings in sentence 6 makes it more important because these are a Batman trademark. Sentence 5 is the best candidate for deletion.

3. C

Sentence 3 must follow sentence 1 because it explains Batman's reaction to Robin's death. Sentence 4 must follow sentence 3 because it explains that Batman's reaction is the result of losing Robin. That leaves sentence 2 for the last sentence in the paragraph, which is the logical placement because it describes the next Robin to work with Batman.

4. G

The author is telling a story about the fictional character Batman. The longest break of 70 years in the story is between paragraphs 1 and 2. The beginning of paragraph 2 is the most logical place, of the choices given, to put a sentence that points out that time has passed.

5. A

No change. The sentences in this paragraph follow a clear chronological order. Moving the sentences as suggested in the other choices disrupts this order.

6. J

Sentence 1 must come first. Sentence 3 must follow sentence 1. Sentence 3 refers directly to the proposed conclusion to the story line mentioned in sentence 1. Sentence 2 must follow sentence 3 because sentence 2 explains how the story line was to be changed. Sentences 4 and 5 are in the correct order because paragraph 5 mentions that it follows *Final Crisis*, which is mentioned in sentence 5.

7. A

No change. Sentence 1 must come first because it follows naturally after the last sentence of paragraph 4. The last sentence in paragraph 4 and the first sentence in paragraph 5 both mention the *Final Crisis*. Any choice that does not include sentence 1 as the first sentence must be incorrect.

8. F

This sentence proposed for insertion refers directly to the absence mentioned in sentence 2 and describes what happened during this absence. The added sentence comes naturally after sentence 2.

9. C

Sentence 4 refers to information not included in the paragraph. What is more, the passage is just as effective with sentence 5 following sentence 3.

10. F

The current ordering of the passages shows a continuing chronological development from one paragraph to the next. Moving one of the paragraphs would interfere with that chronological development.

ORGANIZATION SUBTEST (pages 153–155)

1. B

The third sentence, "Stars pop out . . . ," makes the most sense if it follows the opening sentence. It is a continuation of the description that begins in that sentence. Then the second sentence adds to the idea of the deeper truth mentioned in sentence 3.

2. J

The additional sentence describes an event that occurs before the current sentence 1. By placing it first, the sentence "As the curtain of darkness . . ." elaborates on the idea that the sun is setting and night begins.

3. A

These sentences make sense as they are now. The second sentence cannot be first because then the reader would not know who the "he" is that realizing something in 1659. Also, the sentence about Galileo cannot go before the opening sentence because then it has no reference—his observations that were later than what?

4. H

This sentence needs to fall between the first mention of Galileo and the final sentence about Galileo's later observations. The *In fact* means that this follows an initial statement about Galileo's findings. However, we know the report he gave to Kepler does not mention rings, and therefore it is not one of his "later observations."

5. D

By moving Sentence 1 to the end of the paragraph, the word *it* makes sense. People gasp with surprise when they look at Saturn through a telescope. So try it on your friends; make them look through the telescope at Saturn.

6. F

This initial sentence makes no sense in paragraph 3 as it stands. The word *it* in the first sentence has no reference—what should the reader try on his or her friends? The other two sentences, however, follow directly from the discussion of Saturn's rings in the preceding paragraph.

7. B

This sentence explains why people gasp in surprise—because it is so far away yet so astounding. Therefore, it should go after sentence 3.

8. F

The paragraph makes the most sense as it is. The first sentence sets up where Saturn is in the sky. Sentences 2 and 4 explain in chronological order what happens to Saturn in October—the moon passes north of it, and by the end of the month it is the only bright star. Sentence 3 elaborates on sentence 2, giving more information about it.

9. D

Deleting sentence 1 would not affect the overall message of the paragraph. The other three sentences all describe Saturn's movement in the sky and the movement of other stars or moons in relation to it. Sentence 1 talks about astrology and could, therefore, be deleted.

10. F

The paragraphs make sense as they are. Paragraph 1 describes nightfall and the idea of looking at stars through a telescope. The second paragraph explains a specific instance of observation in relation to a telescope—this one about Saturn. Paragraph 3 elaborates on what we know about Saturn today, and the last tells where to look for Saturn in October.

11. D

This paragraph tells us more about Saturn in general and therefore should fall after paragraph 3 and before paragraph 4 because the last paragraph is much more specific about finding Saturn in the sky.

ACT-TYPE QUESTIONS   Style (pages 159–160)

1. D

Continuing and *ongoing* are synonyms, which makes the sentence redundant. Omit *and continuing* to remove the redundancy. Inserting *and repeating* or *and recycling* changes the meaning of the sentence, so neither is correct.

2. F

No change. *Spirit and Opportunity* repeat the meaning of *two rovers*, but this information adds useful detail and is not redundant.

3. B

The original wording *easier said than done* is a cliché meaning "difficult." Replace the cliché.

4. J

The phrase *wide range* and the word *varied* convey the same meaning in the sentence. Omit *varied* (and don't use its other word forms presented in the remaining choices) to eliminate the redundancy.

5. A

No change. The word *past* tells us about the time period of the water activity under study. There is no redundancy. Using any of the other word choices changes the meaning of the sentence.

6. H

The rover operated beyond, past, the primary mission time. Saying *above and beyond* or *beyond the call of duty of* is both wordy and cliché. Omitting the phrase completely makes the sentence nonsensical.

7. B

The underlined portion is wordy, but it contains important information, so it cannot be omitted entirely.

Saying just *storms* does not provide enough information, so *Martian dust storms* is the best answer.

8. J

The passage mentioned earlier that dust storms created the problem. It is redundant to state it again. Omit *because of the dust*. The phrase *because of the obstruction* is also redundant, and *because of the wind* does not make sense in the context of the passage.

9. C

The passage presents an unclear pronoun reference: *they*. Choice C makes clear that *they* refers to the storms.

10. J

The phrase *and forge ahead* means the same thing as *resume operations*, and this represents a redundancy. The underlined phrase is also a cliché. Omit *and forge ahead* to remove the redundancy/cliché and do not replace it with the other choices.

STYLE SUBTEST (pages 161–162)

1. C

The word *unearthly* describes something not of this earth, which is, therefore, often unreal. The word *natural* describes something belonging to nature or this earth, which would be very real. The word *pedantic* characterizes someone who is obsessed with conforming to rules, which something mysterious or unreal would not do. Finally, the word *normal* obviously does not mean "mysterious."

2. F

The sentence is correct the way it is. *It has*, with the singular subject, would have to refer to "the Indian Ocean," but saying the ocean has no speed doesn't make sense. *They has* is ungrammatical. *The ships have* is not incorrect, but it is unnecessary—the previous sentence says that the ships are "slow," so they are the only thing that could have "no speed."

3. B

The referent *it* could be vague if not spelled out as the ocean, which is what the boats live on.

4. F

Looking for thrills and adventure in a book is ironic because reading is a safe and nonadventurous task. However, the irony is satisfying in that the reader finds that adventure.

5. C

The adventure spurs the mind on to a deeper understanding, or provokes it. *Pleasing* means the same as *pacifying*—this would not urge the mind on but calm it into apathy. Also, the mind is not angered over this higher truth, so D cannot be correct.

6. F

The referent is not vague here; the word *it* clearly refers to the mind mentioned in the previous phrase. Therefore, the sentence does not need to be changed.

7. B

It is not proved that every reader will find descriptions that excite him or her. Also, the word *possibility* relates back to the idea that adventure can concentrate the mind—not will concentrate the mind. Obviously, if there is a possibility of excitement, the choices *unlikelihood* and *remote chance* cannot be correct.

8. J

The author is trying to promote stories of adventure and, therefore, would not refer to them as *boring*, *vapid*, or *uninteresting*. Instead, they are *compelling*, pushing the reader on to deeper truths.

9. A

The landscape of the polar regions is vast and empty—therefore, the word *chaos* would not work here. Also, chaos promotes a negative feeling, which the author is not trying to promote. Choice D won't work because it is redundant—most desolate places are also remote.

10. G

The words *he*, *she*, and *him* don't refer to anyone mentioned in the sentence. Therefore, the correct answer must be *somebody*.

11. D

The only question that makes sense here is *Why*, which refers to cause. *What* refers to place; *when* refers to time; *how* refers to the way something is done.

12. F

The words *ogling* and *staring* don't work because they are not adjectives. *Gawk* gives the same impression in a more descriptive and accurate way. The word *closed-mindedness* would convey a meaning opposite to what the author is most likely trying to say in this paragraph.

Diagnostic English ACT

Take this Diagnostic English ACT after you complete the English review. This Diagnostic English ACT is just like a real ACT, and it is the first of four English ACTs in this book. This Diagnostic English ACT is different from the English ACT Practice Tests because it is specially designed to help you decide which parts of the English section to review in more detail.

Take the Diagnostic English ACT under simulated test conditions. Allow 45 minutes to answer the 75 test questions. Use the Answer Sheet on the following page to mark your answers. Use a pencil to mark the answer sheet, and answer the questions in the Test 1 (English) section.

Review the answer explanations on pages 185–190. After you mark the test, complete the Diagnostic Checklist on pages 181–184. The Checklist directs you to the English skills you should review in more detail.

The test scoring chart on pages 6–7 shows you how to convert the number of correct answers to an ACT scale score. The chart on pages 181–184 shows you how to find the Usage/Mechanics and Rhetorical Skills Subscores.

DO NOT leave any answers blank. There is no penalty for guessing on the ACT. Remember that the test is yours. You may mark up, write on, or draw on the test.

When you are ready, note the time and turn to the Diagnostic English ACT. Stop in exactly 45 minutes.

ANSWER SHEET

The ACT answer sheet looks something like this one. Use a No. 2 pencil to completely fill the circle corresponding to the correct answer. If you erase, erase completely;
incomplete erasures may be read as answers.

TEST 1—English

1 Ⓐ Ⓑ Ⓒ Ⓓ	11 Ⓐ Ⓑ Ⓒ Ⓓ	21 Ⓐ Ⓑ Ⓒ Ⓓ	31 Ⓐ Ⓑ Ⓒ Ⓓ	41 Ⓐ Ⓑ Ⓒ Ⓓ	51 Ⓐ Ⓑ Ⓒ Ⓓ	61 Ⓐ Ⓑ Ⓒ Ⓓ	71 Ⓐ Ⓑ Ⓒ Ⓓ
2 Ⓕ Ⓖ Ⓗ Ⓙ	12 Ⓕ Ⓖ Ⓗ Ⓙ	22 Ⓕ Ⓖ Ⓗ Ⓙ	32 Ⓕ Ⓖ Ⓗ Ⓙ	42 Ⓕ Ⓖ Ⓗ Ⓙ	52 Ⓕ Ⓖ Ⓗ Ⓙ	62 Ⓕ Ⓖ Ⓗ Ⓙ	72 Ⓕ Ⓖ Ⓗ Ⓙ
3 Ⓐ Ⓑ Ⓒ Ⓓ	13 Ⓐ Ⓑ Ⓒ Ⓓ	23 Ⓐ Ⓑ Ⓒ Ⓓ	33 Ⓐ Ⓑ Ⓒ Ⓓ	43 Ⓐ Ⓑ Ⓒ Ⓓ	53 Ⓐ Ⓑ Ⓒ Ⓓ	63 Ⓐ Ⓑ Ⓒ Ⓓ	73 Ⓐ Ⓑ Ⓒ Ⓓ
4 Ⓕ Ⓖ Ⓗ Ⓙ	14 Ⓕ Ⓖ Ⓗ Ⓙ	24 Ⓕ Ⓖ Ⓗ Ⓙ	34 Ⓕ Ⓖ Ⓗ Ⓙ	44 Ⓕ Ⓖ Ⓗ Ⓙ	54 Ⓕ Ⓖ Ⓗ Ⓙ	64 Ⓕ Ⓖ Ⓗ Ⓙ	74 Ⓕ Ⓖ Ⓗ Ⓙ
5 Ⓐ Ⓑ Ⓒ Ⓓ	15 Ⓐ Ⓑ Ⓒ Ⓓ	25 Ⓐ Ⓑ Ⓒ Ⓓ	35 Ⓐ Ⓑ Ⓒ Ⓓ	45 Ⓐ Ⓑ Ⓒ Ⓓ	55 Ⓐ Ⓑ Ⓒ Ⓓ	65 Ⓐ Ⓑ Ⓒ Ⓓ	75 Ⓐ Ⓑ Ⓒ Ⓓ
6 Ⓕ Ⓖ Ⓗ Ⓙ	16 Ⓕ Ⓖ Ⓗ Ⓙ	26 Ⓕ Ⓖ Ⓗ Ⓙ	36 Ⓕ Ⓖ Ⓗ Ⓙ	46 Ⓕ Ⓖ Ⓗ Ⓙ	56 Ⓕ Ⓖ Ⓗ Ⓙ	66 Ⓕ Ⓖ Ⓗ Ⓙ	
7 Ⓐ Ⓑ Ⓒ Ⓓ	17 Ⓐ Ⓑ Ⓒ Ⓓ	27 Ⓐ Ⓑ Ⓒ Ⓓ	37 Ⓐ Ⓑ Ⓒ Ⓓ	47 Ⓐ Ⓑ Ⓒ Ⓓ	57 Ⓐ Ⓑ Ⓒ Ⓓ	67 Ⓐ Ⓑ Ⓒ Ⓓ	
8 Ⓕ Ⓖ Ⓗ Ⓙ	18 Ⓕ Ⓖ Ⓗ Ⓙ	28 Ⓕ Ⓖ Ⓗ Ⓙ	38 Ⓕ Ⓖ Ⓗ Ⓙ	48 Ⓕ Ⓖ Ⓗ Ⓙ	58 Ⓕ Ⓖ Ⓗ Ⓙ	68 Ⓕ Ⓖ Ⓗ Ⓙ	
9 Ⓐ Ⓑ Ⓒ Ⓓ	19 Ⓐ Ⓑ Ⓒ Ⓓ	29 Ⓐ Ⓑ Ⓒ Ⓓ	39 Ⓐ Ⓑ Ⓒ Ⓓ	49 Ⓐ Ⓑ Ⓒ Ⓓ	59 Ⓐ Ⓑ Ⓒ Ⓓ	69 Ⓐ Ⓑ Ⓒ Ⓓ	
10 Ⓕ Ⓖ Ⓗ Ⓙ	20 Ⓕ Ⓖ Ⓗ Ⓙ	30 Ⓕ Ⓖ Ⓗ Ⓙ	40 Ⓕ Ⓖ Ⓗ Ⓙ	50 Ⓕ Ⓖ Ⓗ Ⓙ	60 Ⓕ Ⓖ Ⓗ Ⓙ	70 Ⓕ Ⓖ Ⓗ Ⓙ	

TEST 2—Mathematics

1 Ⓐ Ⓑ Ⓒ Ⓓ Ⓔ	9 Ⓐ Ⓑ Ⓒ Ⓓ Ⓔ	17 Ⓐ Ⓑ Ⓒ Ⓓ Ⓔ	25 Ⓐ Ⓑ Ⓒ Ⓓ Ⓔ	33 Ⓐ Ⓑ Ⓒ Ⓓ Ⓔ	41 Ⓐ Ⓑ Ⓒ Ⓓ Ⓔ	49 Ⓐ Ⓑ Ⓒ Ⓓ Ⓔ	57 Ⓐ Ⓑ Ⓒ Ⓓ Ⓔ
2 Ⓕ Ⓖ Ⓗ Ⓙ Ⓚ	10 Ⓕ Ⓖ Ⓗ Ⓙ Ⓚ	18 Ⓕ Ⓖ Ⓗ Ⓙ Ⓚ	26 Ⓕ Ⓖ Ⓗ Ⓙ Ⓚ	34 Ⓕ Ⓖ Ⓗ Ⓙ Ⓚ	42 Ⓕ Ⓖ Ⓗ Ⓙ Ⓚ	50 Ⓕ Ⓖ Ⓗ Ⓙ Ⓚ	58 Ⓕ Ⓖ Ⓗ Ⓙ Ⓚ
3 Ⓐ Ⓑ Ⓒ Ⓓ Ⓔ	11 Ⓐ Ⓑ Ⓒ Ⓓ Ⓔ	19 Ⓐ Ⓑ Ⓒ Ⓓ Ⓔ	27 Ⓐ Ⓑ Ⓒ Ⓓ Ⓔ	35 Ⓐ Ⓑ Ⓒ Ⓓ Ⓔ	43 Ⓐ Ⓑ Ⓒ Ⓓ Ⓔ	51 Ⓐ Ⓑ Ⓒ Ⓓ Ⓔ	59 Ⓐ Ⓑ Ⓒ Ⓓ Ⓔ
4 Ⓕ Ⓖ Ⓗ Ⓙ Ⓚ	12 Ⓕ Ⓖ Ⓗ Ⓙ Ⓚ	20 Ⓕ Ⓖ Ⓗ Ⓙ Ⓚ	28 Ⓕ Ⓖ Ⓗ Ⓙ Ⓚ	36 Ⓕ Ⓖ Ⓗ Ⓙ Ⓚ	44 Ⓕ Ⓖ Ⓗ Ⓙ Ⓚ	52 Ⓕ Ⓖ Ⓗ Ⓙ Ⓚ	60 Ⓕ Ⓖ Ⓗ Ⓙ Ⓚ
5 Ⓐ Ⓑ Ⓒ Ⓓ Ⓔ	13 Ⓐ Ⓑ Ⓒ Ⓓ Ⓔ	21 Ⓐ Ⓑ Ⓒ Ⓓ Ⓔ	29 Ⓐ Ⓑ Ⓒ Ⓓ Ⓔ	37 Ⓐ Ⓑ Ⓒ Ⓓ Ⓔ	45 Ⓐ Ⓑ Ⓒ Ⓓ Ⓔ	53 Ⓐ Ⓑ Ⓒ Ⓓ Ⓔ	
6 Ⓕ Ⓖ Ⓗ Ⓙ Ⓚ	14 Ⓕ Ⓖ Ⓗ Ⓙ Ⓚ	22 Ⓕ Ⓖ Ⓗ Ⓙ Ⓚ	30 Ⓕ Ⓖ Ⓗ Ⓙ Ⓚ	38 Ⓕ Ⓖ Ⓗ Ⓙ Ⓚ	46 Ⓕ Ⓖ Ⓗ Ⓙ Ⓚ	54 Ⓕ Ⓖ Ⓗ Ⓙ Ⓚ	
7 Ⓐ Ⓑ Ⓒ Ⓓ Ⓔ	15 Ⓐ Ⓑ Ⓒ Ⓓ Ⓔ	23 Ⓐ Ⓑ Ⓒ Ⓓ Ⓔ	31 Ⓐ Ⓑ Ⓒ Ⓓ Ⓔ	39 Ⓐ Ⓑ Ⓒ Ⓓ Ⓔ	47 Ⓐ Ⓑ Ⓒ Ⓓ Ⓔ	55 Ⓐ Ⓑ Ⓒ Ⓓ Ⓔ	
8 Ⓕ Ⓖ Ⓗ Ⓙ Ⓚ	16 Ⓕ Ⓖ Ⓗ Ⓙ Ⓚ	24 Ⓕ Ⓖ Ⓗ Ⓙ Ⓚ	32 Ⓕ Ⓖ Ⓗ Ⓙ Ⓚ	40 Ⓕ Ⓖ Ⓗ Ⓙ Ⓚ	48 Ⓕ Ⓖ Ⓗ Ⓙ Ⓚ	56 Ⓕ Ⓖ Ⓗ Ⓙ Ⓚ	

TEST 3—Reading

1 Ⓐ Ⓑ Ⓒ Ⓓ	6 Ⓕ Ⓖ Ⓗ Ⓙ	11 Ⓐ Ⓑ Ⓒ Ⓓ	16 Ⓕ Ⓖ Ⓗ Ⓙ	21 Ⓐ Ⓑ Ⓒ Ⓓ	26 Ⓕ Ⓖ Ⓗ Ⓙ	31 Ⓐ Ⓑ Ⓒ Ⓓ	36 Ⓕ Ⓖ Ⓗ Ⓙ
2 Ⓕ Ⓖ Ⓗ Ⓙ	7 Ⓐ Ⓑ Ⓒ Ⓓ	12 Ⓕ Ⓖ Ⓗ Ⓙ	17 Ⓐ Ⓑ Ⓒ Ⓓ	22 Ⓕ Ⓖ Ⓗ Ⓙ	27 Ⓐ Ⓑ Ⓒ Ⓓ	32 Ⓕ Ⓖ Ⓗ Ⓙ	37 Ⓐ Ⓑ Ⓒ Ⓓ
3 Ⓐ Ⓑ Ⓒ Ⓓ	8 Ⓕ Ⓖ Ⓗ Ⓙ	13 Ⓐ Ⓑ Ⓒ Ⓓ	18 Ⓕ Ⓖ Ⓗ Ⓙ	23 Ⓐ Ⓑ Ⓒ Ⓓ	28 Ⓕ Ⓖ Ⓗ Ⓙ	33 Ⓐ Ⓑ Ⓒ Ⓓ	38 Ⓕ Ⓖ Ⓗ Ⓙ
4 Ⓕ Ⓖ Ⓗ Ⓙ	9 Ⓐ Ⓑ Ⓒ Ⓓ	14 Ⓕ Ⓖ Ⓗ Ⓙ	19 Ⓐ Ⓑ Ⓒ Ⓓ	24 Ⓕ Ⓖ Ⓗ Ⓙ	29 Ⓐ Ⓑ Ⓒ Ⓓ	34 Ⓕ Ⓖ Ⓗ Ⓙ	39 Ⓐ Ⓑ Ⓒ Ⓓ
5 Ⓐ Ⓑ Ⓒ Ⓓ	10 Ⓕ Ⓖ Ⓗ Ⓙ	15 Ⓐ Ⓑ Ⓒ Ⓓ	20 Ⓕ Ⓖ Ⓗ Ⓙ	25 Ⓐ Ⓑ Ⓒ Ⓓ	30 Ⓕ Ⓖ Ⓗ Ⓙ	35 Ⓐ Ⓑ Ⓒ Ⓓ	40 Ⓕ Ⓖ Ⓗ Ⓙ

TEST 4—Science Reasoning

1 Ⓐ Ⓑ Ⓒ Ⓓ	6 Ⓕ Ⓖ Ⓗ Ⓙ	11 Ⓐ Ⓑ Ⓒ Ⓓ	16 Ⓕ Ⓖ Ⓗ Ⓙ	21 Ⓐ Ⓑ Ⓒ Ⓓ	26 Ⓕ Ⓖ Ⓗ Ⓙ	31 Ⓐ Ⓑ Ⓒ Ⓓ	36 Ⓕ Ⓖ Ⓗ Ⓙ
2 Ⓕ Ⓖ Ⓗ Ⓙ	7 Ⓐ Ⓑ Ⓒ Ⓓ	12 Ⓕ Ⓖ Ⓗ Ⓙ	17 Ⓐ Ⓑ Ⓒ Ⓓ	22 Ⓕ Ⓖ Ⓗ Ⓙ	27 Ⓐ Ⓑ Ⓒ Ⓓ	32 Ⓕ Ⓖ Ⓗ Ⓙ	37 Ⓐ Ⓑ Ⓒ Ⓓ
3 Ⓐ Ⓑ Ⓒ Ⓓ	8 Ⓕ Ⓖ Ⓗ Ⓙ	13 Ⓐ Ⓑ Ⓒ Ⓓ	18 Ⓕ Ⓖ Ⓗ Ⓙ	23 Ⓐ Ⓑ Ⓒ Ⓓ	28 Ⓕ Ⓖ Ⓗ Ⓙ	33 Ⓐ Ⓑ Ⓒ Ⓓ	38 Ⓕ Ⓖ Ⓗ Ⓙ
4 Ⓕ Ⓖ Ⓗ Ⓙ	9 Ⓐ Ⓑ Ⓒ Ⓓ	14 Ⓕ Ⓖ Ⓗ Ⓙ	19 Ⓐ Ⓑ Ⓒ Ⓓ	24 Ⓕ Ⓖ Ⓗ Ⓙ	29 Ⓐ Ⓑ Ⓒ Ⓓ	34 Ⓕ Ⓖ Ⓗ Ⓙ	39 Ⓐ Ⓑ Ⓒ Ⓓ
5 Ⓐ Ⓑ Ⓒ Ⓓ	10 Ⓕ Ⓖ Ⓗ Ⓙ	15 Ⓐ Ⓑ Ⓒ Ⓓ	20 Ⓕ Ⓖ Ⓗ Ⓙ	25 Ⓐ Ⓑ Ⓒ Ⓓ	30 Ⓕ Ⓖ Ⓗ Ⓙ	35 Ⓐ Ⓑ Ⓒ Ⓓ	40 Ⓕ Ⓖ Ⓗ Ⓙ

Diagnostic English ACT

75 Questions—45 Minutes

INSTRUCTIONS: Certain words or phrases in the following five passages are underlined and numbered. There is a corresponding item for each underlined portion. Each item offers three suggestions for changing the underlined portion to conform to standard written English or to make it more understandable or consistent with the rest of the passage. If the underlined portion is not improved by one of the three suggested changes, mark NO CHANGE. Some items are about the entire passage, and the numbers for these items come at the end of the passage.

Choose the best answer for each question based on the passage. Then fill in the appropriate circle on the answer sheet.

Check pages 181–190 for answers and explanations.

PASSAGE I

The paragraphs in this passage may or may not be in the most appropriate order. The number of each paragraph is in brackets above the paragraph. The last item for this passage asks for the correct order of paragraphs to make the passage most sensible.

[1]

Juvenile delinquency is nothing <u>new, however,</u>
                          1
Aristotle, writing over 2,000 years ago, <u>complains</u>
                               2
that Greek youth "<u>are in character prone to desire and</u>
                          3
<u>ready to carry any desire they may have formed into</u>
                         3
<u>action."</u>
3

[2]

Headlines like these have become <u>commonplace:</u>
                         4
<u>JUVENILES</u> VANDALIZE LOCAL SCHOOL. TWO
4
TEENAGERS KILLED IN DRIVE-BY GANG

SHOOTING. YOUNG THIEF MUGS PREGNANT

1. **A.** NO CHANGE
   B. new however
   C. new. However,
   D. new, however.

2. **F.** NO CHANGE
   G. complained
   H. complaining
   J. is complaining

3. Which choice BEST explains why the authors put this clause in quotations?
   A. To show that these words were actually written by Aristotle himself
   B. To give special emphasis to this idea
   C. To show that Aristotle was in favor of juvenile delinquency
   D. To indicate that this is the title of a book

MOTHER OF THREE. The youthful lawbreakers
featured in these reports, are often called *delinquents*:
                  5   6
those who violate laws, disobeyed authority, or
                        7
behave in ways that endanger the safety or morals of
the community, like a dog that runs around the
                 8
neighborhood biting people.
8

[3]

Psychologists believe that many delinquency
                             9
grows out of the adolescent need to rebel against the
restrictions of the adult world. Such rebellion in
earlier times usually took the form of pranks. Such as
                                          10
tipping over outhouses or hoisting a cow to the
courthouse roof. Then, as now, some kids simply ran
                                       11
away from home.

[4]

Alarming is—muggings, burglaries, rape, car
             12
theft, vandalism, and assault with deadly weapons;
                  12
the increase in more serious teenage crimes. Because
                12
they commit such heinous crimes, many adults now
                                    13
feel that the courts should punish youthful criminals
                                 13
with the same sentences given adult offenders.
                    13

4. F. NO CHANGE
    G. commonplace JUVENILES
    H. commonplace. JUVENILES
    J. commonplace! JUVENILES

5. A. NO CHANGE
    B. reports. Are
    C. reports are
    D. reports—are

6. Why would the author italicize
    delinquents in this sentence?

    F. The word is from another language.
    G. The author wanted to emphasize the
        word.
    H. The word is a key term, followed by a
        definition.
    J. The word marks a change in the
        sentence.

7. A. NO CHANGE
    B. disobeying
    C. disobedient
    D. disobey

8. F. NO CHANGE
    G. like a mean-spirited dog who bites
        people.
    H. like a tiger that has escaped from the
        zoo.
    J. OMIT phrase entirely.

9. A. NO CHANGE
    B. much
    C. much,
    D. too many

10. F. NO CHANGE
    G. pranks! Such
    H. pranks, such
    J. pranks? Such

11. A. NO CHANGE
    B. young people
    C. kids,
    D. adults

12. Which choice presents the MOST logical order of information in this sentence?

   F. NO CHANGE
   G. The increase in more serious teenage crimes—muggings, burglaries, rape, car theft, vandalism, and assault with deadly weapons—is alarming.
   H. Muggings, burglaries, rape, car theft, vandalism, and assault with deadly weapons—the increase in more serious teenage crimes is alarming.
   J. The increase—muggings, burglaries, rape, car theft, vandalism, and assault with deadly weapons—in more serious teenage crime is alarming.

13. A. NO CHANGE
   B. the courts are now giving youthful criminals the same sentences that they give to adult offenders.
   C. youthful criminals now feel that adults should be given the same sentences as other offenders.
   D. youthful criminals are sometimes punished with the same sentences given to adult offenders.

Questions 14 and 15 ask about the entire passage.

---

14. Which option BEST describes the authors' purpose in writing this article?

   F. To make a plea for lighter sentencing for youthful criminals
   G. To explain the concept of juvenile delinquency to a person unfamiliar with the concept
   H. To show that older pranks, such as putting a cow on the courthouse roof, were a lot of fun
   J. To blame society for the corruption of American youth

15. Which sequence of paragraphs will make the essay MOST logical?

   A. NO CHANGE
   B. 1, 3, 2, 4
   C. 2, 1, 3, 4
   D. 4, 3, 2, 1

PASSAGE II

Why did the world heap such fame and glory upon Amelia Earhart after her flight across America? There was at least two reasons. A year earlier, in 1927, Charles Lindbergh had made the first daring solo flight across the Atlantic Ocean. Taking off from New York City. He had landed in Paris, France. The public went wild over this handsome young American pilot. "Lindy" became the greatest hero of his time. Now the public was ready for another hero. But a heroine, a woman as brave as "Lindy," would be even best.

Earhart was tall and slim, almost boyish looking her blond hair was cut short in an easy, natural style. She was outgoing and friendly, therefore this young woman was also modest and soft-spoken. Some people felt that Earhart even looked like Charles Lindbergh. Newspapers called her "Lady Lindy." Earhart wrote two popular books about her life and her flight from one coast to the other across the Atlantic. She became the aviation editor of Cosmopolitan magazine. Over a million American women read her articles about flying. She also urged women to try other careers.

In 1931, she married a book publisher George Putnam. He understood his wifes' desire to fly. As a result, they each enjoyed their chosen careers in

16. **F.** NO CHANGE
    G. were
    H. has been
    J. will be

17. **A.** NO CHANGE
    B. A year faster
    C. A year later
    D. OMIT the underlined phrase, and begin the sentence with *In 1927.*

18. **F.** NO CHANGE
    G. New York City? He had
    H. New York City he had
    J. New York City, he had

19. **A.** NO CHANGE
    B. worse
    C. more best
    D. better

20. **F.** NO CHANGE
    G. almost boyish looking, her
    H. almost boyish looking. Her
    J. almost boyish looking? Her

21. **A.** NO CHANGE
    B. thus
    C. yet
    D. because

22. **F.** NO CHANGE
    G. over the ocean
    H. from America to France
    J. OMIT the underlined portion.

23. **A.** NO CHANGE
    B. "Cosmopolitan"
    C. Cosmopolitan
    D. *"Cosmopolitan"*

24. **F.** NO CHANGE
    G. publisher, George
    H. publisher? George
    J. publisher. George

25. **A.** NO CHANGE
    B. wives'
    C. wife's
    D. wifes

publishing and aviation. They had a happy marriage.
It seemed as if Earhart's fame and good fortune
would never end. As one reporter described her, she
was "a girl who has everything — youth, intelligently,
                                                  26
beauty, personality, and a promising future." What
more could anyone want.
                    27

Yet all these honors made her strangely uneasy.
Talking about her first transatlantic flight, where they
                                                      28
had been only a passenger, she said, "I was just
baggage, like a sack of potatoes." To deserve her
fame, she felt that she must make the same flight
alone. While Earhart had another important reason to
      29
fly solo over the Atlantic, as Lindbergh had done.
Too she wanted to prove that whatever men could do,
30
women could do.

26. **F.** NO CHANGE
    G. intelligence,
    H. intelligent,
    J. intelligence

27. **A.** NO CHANGE
    B. want!
    C. want."
    D. want?

28. **F.** NO CHANGE
    G. he
    H. she
    J. their

29. **A.** NO CHANGE
    B. (Begin new paragraph) Earhart
    C. (Begin new paragraph) While Earhart
    D. (Do not begin new paragraph) Earthart

30. **F.** NO CHANGE
    G. (Place after *wanted*, between two commas)
    H. (Place after *men*, between two commas)
    J. (Place after the second *do*, following a comma)

PASSAGE III

[1]

In architecture, romanticism took the form of a return
to medieval styles and was known as the Gothic
Revival. The trend was especially strong in
England. Where it began in the mid-eighteenth
        31
century. 32

[2]

The Gothic Revival was inspired by literary
romantics, which found drama and mystery in the
           33
Middle Ages. Probably the writer Horace Walpole
                34

31. **A.** NO CHANGE
    B. England: where
    C. England; where
    D. England, where

32. In this first paragraph, the writer is assuming that the readers of the passage are:

    F. male.
    G. over the age of 30.
    H. familiar with the term *romanticism*.
    J. architects.

33. **A.** NO CHANGE
    B. who found
    C. that found
    D. they found

was an early figure of the most importance in the
<u>movement.</u> In the mid-1800s he acquired a country
estate, Strawberry Hill, which he soon began
converting into a sort of a Gothic castle. Actually its
basic design was <u>sort of</u> neoclassical, but it had such
medieval details as pointed arches and gargoyles.

[3]

Soon castlelike homes sprang up all over <u>England</u>
<u>the</u> <u>most unusual</u> was Fonthill Abbey, built for a rich
and eccentric author named William Beckford.
<u>He urged his builder to work with such haste that the</u>
<u>central tower collapsed soon after it was built.</u> The
whole building was in ruins in a few years.

[4]

In truth, ruins <u>that were left from broken-down</u>
<u>buildings</u> were all that some people wanted. Several
firms specialized in the "built ruin," a crumbling
fantasy of walls and towers that could lend a
picturesque air to any estate, <u>however new. In time,</u> as
scholars showed serious interest in the Middle Ages,
the Gothic Revival became less frivolous. Architects
studied castles and cathedrals and <u>buildings were</u>
<u>designed</u> that captured the essence of Gothic
architecture. Among their finest achievements were
the <u>British Houses of Parliament.</u> After the old ones
had burned down in 1834 (an event commemorated in
a painting by J.W.M. Turner), they were rebuilt in
Gothic style.

34. Which version of this sentence flows BEST in the paragraph as a whole?
   F. NO CHANGE
   G. Horace Walpole was a writer of probably most importance as an early figure of this movement.
   H. Probably the most important early figure of the movement was the writer Horace Walpole.
   J. Probably, the most important writer was an early figure of this movement, Horace Walpole.

35. A. NO CHANGE
   B. sorta
   C. kind of
   D. OMIT the underlined portion.

36. F. NO CHANGE
   G. England! The
   H. England, the
   J. England. The

37. A. NO CHANGE
   B. more unusual
   C. unusualest
   D. least usual

38. Which of these sentences flows MOST smoothly with the rest of the paragraph?
   F. NO CHANGE
   G. Soon after it was built, William Beckford urged his builder to work with such haste that the central tower collapsed.
   H. Beckford's builder, at William Beckford's urging, built the central tower with such haste that it collapsed.
   J. The central tower, soon after it was built, collapsed because William Beckford urged his builder to work in haste.

39. A. NO CHANGE
   B. from broken-down buildings
   C. from broken-down castles
   D. OMIT the underlined portion.

40. F. NO CHANGE
   G. however new, in time
   H. however new. (*New paragraph*) In time
   J. however new; in time

The Gothic Revival had relatively little impact on the continent. 43 Medieval architecture was praised by Chateaubriand in France and by Goethe in Germany, but there was less interest in recreating it. The style did take hold in America, where people with a short national history felt the need for old and established styles. In the United States its grandest monuments were churches, including Grace Church and St. Patrick's Cathedral in New York City.

41. A. NO CHANGE
    B. buildings have been designed
    C. designed buildings
    D. design buildings

42. F. NO CHANGE
    G. British, houses of parliament
    H. British: houses of parliament
    J. British. Houses of Parliament

43. To what does the author refer when he writes that the Gothic Revival had relatively little impact on the continent?
    A. North America
    B. The mainland of Europe
    C. The physical effects that the building of new structures may have had on the soil where they were built.
    D. Gothic Revival architecture is relative to other styles of architecture found on other continents.

Questions 44 and 45 ask about the entire passage.

44. Suppose the author was assigned to write an article focusing on the effects of European architecture on the United States. Does he fulfill this assignment?
    F. Yes, because the final paragraph explains how the Gothic Revival took hold in America.
    G. No, because the focus of this article is on the Gothic Revival in England.
    H. No, because this article mentions France and Germany.
    J. Yes, because America used to be a British colony.

45. This passage would best be supplemented by:
    A. a glossary of architectural terms.
    B. the life history of Horace Walpole.
    C. photographs and descriptions of J.W.M. Turner's art.
    D. a description of the fire that burned down the original British Parliament buildings.

PASSAGE IV

The paragraphs in this passage may or may not be in the most appropriate order. The number of each paragraph is in brackets above the paragraph. The last item for this passage asks for the correct order of paragraphs to make the passage most sensible.

[1]

It was disquieting to discover that an inert
                     46
material that can do all kinds of stuff—it serves as
         47
the working fluid in refrigerators and air conditioners,

as well as propellant for deodorants and other

products in aerosol cans and as lightweight foamy

packaging for fast foods, to name only a few can pose
                                          48
a danger to life on Earth. Who would have figured it?

[2]

This increased ultraviolet intensity ushers in a

ghastly procession of potential consequences

involving not just skin cancer but also the weakening

of the human immune system and, most dangerous of

all, agriculture and photosynthetic microorganisms
         49
are destroyed at the base of the food chain on which
49
most life on Earth depends.

[3]

The materials are called in question
                          50
chlorofluorocarbons (CFCs). They are extremely

chemically inert, which means they are

invulnerable—until they find themselves up in

46. F. NO CHANGE
    G. discovers
    H. discovered
    J. being discovered

47. A. NO CHANGE
    B. that can do all sorts of stuff
    C. that can fulfill many practical functions
    D. OMIT the underlined portion.

48. F. NO CHANGE
    G. few, can
    H. few; can
    J. few—can

49. A. NO CHANGE
    B. the destruction of agriculture and photosynthetic microorganisms
    C. agriculture and photosynthetic microorganisms destroyed
    D. the destruction by agriculture and photosynthesis microorganisms

50. F. NO CHANGE
    G. (Place after *materials*)
    H. (Place before *The*)
    J. [Place after *(CFCs)*]

51. A. NO CHANGE
    B. sunlight, the
    C. sunlight? The
    D. sunlight the

52. F. NO CHANGE
    G. of Earth
    H. where I live
    J. OMIT the underlined portion.

53. Why does the author set this information aside in parentheses?
    A. To give important information special emphasis
    B. As a way of including interesting yet nonessential information
    C. Because he is discussing a brand name
    D. To present secret information

54. F. NO CHANGE
    G. denying
    H. accepting
    J. destroying

the ozone layer, where they are dissociated by sunlight. The chlorine atoms thus liberated deplete
<u>51</u>
the ozone and let more ultraviolet light from the sun reach the ground <u>I walk on</u>.
<u>52</u>

[4]

The principal manufacturer of this material, the Dupont company <u>(which gave it the brand name</u>
<u>53</u>
<u>Freon)</u>, after years of <u>blowing off</u> the concern of
<u>53</u>   <u>54</u>
environmentalists—taking out full-page ads in newspapers and scientific magazines claiming that they all came from wild extrapolations from inadequate data, and that nobody had actually demonstrated any peril—announced that it would rapidly phase out all its CFC production. The precipitating event seems to have been the discovery in 1986 by British scientists of a hole in the Antarctic ozone <u>layer?</u> There is now <u>well</u> evidence of thinning
<u>55</u>   <u>56</u>
of the ozone layer at other latitudes as well. 57

55. **A.** NO CHANGE
B. layer
C. layer!
D. layer.

56. **F.** NO CHANGE
G. very well
H. good
J. gooder

57. Based on the language of this paragraph, how does the author feel about the early denial of the dangers of CFCs?
A. Frustrated that people who should have been concerned were ignoring the facts about CFCs
B. Confident Dupont had logical proof that CFCs were not harmful
C. Angry that environmentalists thought CFCs were good for Earth
D. Angry that so-called scientists would have invented such "wild extrapolations" from inadequate data

Questions 58, 59, and 60 ask about the entire passage.

58. What is the MOST logical order for the paragraphs in this essay?
F. NO CHANGE
G. 4, 3, 2, 1
H. 1, 4, 3, 2
J. 1, 3, 2, 4

59. Which choice is the MOST likely audience for this essay?
A. A new Dupont employee
B. Scientists studying the thinning of the ozone layer
C. Young children
D. Teens and adults with only a general knowledge of science

60. What information would provide the BEST conclusion for this essay?
F. An explanation of how CFCs caused the hole in the ozone layer
G. A description of lawsuits against Dupont for producing Freon
H. A description of what constitutes CFCs
J. An explanation of Earth's food chain

[1]

I could not wait. I was about to be like lots of my friends and get my first car. I thought I would never be able to <u>owned</u> one. Working at the pizza shop and
61
getting a contribution from my parents, who are not completely happy that I would have wheels, changed all of <u>that. Blaire's</u> first car was going to be a good
62
one. By the way, my name is Blaire. I wanted a new car, but I had to settle for an older Ford model. I did some research and found that <u>good cars drove safer</u>
63
<u>and sold for less money by Ford.</u> That should mean I
63
can get a car for a lower price than asked by other car dealers <u>in turn.</u>
64

[2]

My friends tell me that having a <u>car. Changed</u>
65
their lives completely. Sure, you can go to school by <u>car;</u> train, or bus. A car is definitely better. I can't
66
wait to drive <u>my friends. Friends' houses all</u>
67
<u>around where I live.</u>
67

[3]

[1] I think having a car will make a big difference in my life. [2] The <u>"Blaire has a car" message will</u>
68
<u>soon have spread all around.</u> [3] I hope everyone in
68
school finds out that I have wheels. [4] I hope they

61. **A.** NO CHANGE
    B. owning
    C. own
    D. owns

62. **F.** NO CHANGE
    G. that Blaire's
    H. that, Blaire's
    J. that? Blaire's

63. **A.** NO CHANGE
    B. Ford produces good cars that are safer and cheaper.
    C. good cars that are safer and sold for less money by Ford than by other car manufacturers.
    D. other car manufacturers could not produce cars that are safer or less expensive than Ford could.

64. **F.** NO CHANGE
    G. Place after *mean* and set off with commas
    H. Place after *price* and set off with commas
    J. Place before *That*, making the *i* uppercase and the *t* lowercase and adding a comma

65. **A.** NO CHANGE
    B. car, changed
    C. car changed
    D. car? Changed

66. **F.** NO CHANGE
    G. car
    H. car,
    J. car'

67. **A.** NO CHANGE
    B. my friends' houses. All around where I live.
    C. my friends' houses all around where I live.
    D. my friend's houses all around where I live.

make me a lot more popular. [5] I would not only
make me become better known, but they would also
probably get me invited to a lot more parties in other
neighborhoods.
70

[4]

[1] I can't wait to drive my car to parties. [2] My
friend Ashley and I will be a big hit. [3] I would also
like to safely drive people home after parties. [4] I
know that being a responsible driver is very
important. [73]

68. To make this paragraph flow MOST
logically, where does sentence 2 belong?
  F. NO CHANGE
  G. Before sentence 1
  H. After sentence 3
  J. After sentence 5

69. A. NO CHANGE
  B. They
  C. She
  D. We

70. F. NO CHANGE
  G. neighborhood's
  H. neighborhoods's
  J. neighborhoods'

71. A. NO CHANGE
  B. parties: my
  C. parties! my
  D. parties, my

72. F. NO CHANGE
  G. friend Ashley, and I
  H. friend, Ashley and I
  J. friend Ashley and me

73. For sentence 3 to make the MOST sense,
where does it belong in the paragraph?
  A. NO CHANGE
  B. Before sentence 1
  C. After sentence 1
  D. After sentence 4

Questions 74 and 75 are about the entire
passage.

74. What, if any, supporting information is
needed for this passage?
  F. A list of all the recent models of cars
Blaire considered
  G. The location of the friends' homes
Blaire wants to visit
  H. More information about Blaire's
friend Ashley
  J. No information is necessary.

75. Which sequence of paragraphs will make
the essay MOST logical?
  A. NO CHANGE
  B. 4, 3, 2, 1
  C. 2, 3, 1, 4
  D. 2 ,1, 3, 4

Diagnostic English Checklist

Answer	Check if missed	Usage/ Mechanics	Rhetorical Skills	Review this section	Pages
1. D	❑	❑		Run-on Sentences and Comma Splices	34–38
2. G	❑	❑		Verbs; Verb Tense; Subject-Verb Agreement	64–66, 67–75, 76–79
3. A	❑	❑		Quotation Marks	123–125
4. F	❑	❑		Semicolons and Colons	108–111
5. C	❑	❑		Commas	103–108
6. H	❑		❑	Style	156–160
7. D	❑	❑		Verbs; Verb Tense; Parallel Form	64–66, 67–75, 79–83
8. J	❑		❑	Style	156–160
9. B	❑	❑		Adjectives and Adverbs	84–87
10. H	❑	❑		Sentence Fragments; Commas	38–43, 103–108
11. B	❑		❑	Style	156–160
12. G	❑	❑		Hyphens and Dashes	111–115
13. D	❑	❑		Modifiers; Pronouns	33–34, 59–63
14. G	❑		❑	Strategy	133–141
15. C	❑		❑	Organization	145–152
16. G	❑	❑		Verbs; Verb Tense	64–66, 67–75
17. D	❑		❑	Strategy	133–141
18. J	❑	❑		Sentence Fragments; Commas	38–43, 103–108
19. D	❑	❑		Comparative and Superlative Adjectives and Adverbs	87–90
20. H	❑	❑		Run-on Sentences and Comma Splices; Commas; Periods, Question Marks, and Exclamation Points	34–38, 103–108, 120–122

Answer	Check if missed	Usage/Mechanics	Rhetorical Skills	Review this section	Pages
21. C	❑		❑	Strategy	133–141
22. J	❑		❑	Strategy	133–141
23. A	❑	❑		Nouns	56–58
24. G	❑	❑		Commas	103–108
25. C	❑	❑		Nouns; Apostrophes	56–58, 118–120
26. G	❑	❑		Parallel Form; Commas	79–83, 103–108
27. D	❑	❑		Periods, Question Marks, and Exclamation Points; Quotation Marks	120–122, 123–125
28. H	❑	❑		Pronouns	59–63
29. B	❑		❑	Strategy; Organization	133–141, 145–152
30. J	❑		❑	Strategy; Organization	133–143, 145–152
31. D	❑	❑		Sentence Fragments; Commas; Semicolons and Colons	38–43, 103–108, 108–111
32. H	❑		❑	Style	156–160
33. B	❑	❑		Pronouns	59–63
34. H	❑		❑	Strategy	133–141
35. D	❑		❑	Style	156–160
36. J	❑	❑		Run-on Sentences and Comma Splices; Periods, Question Marks, and Exclamation Points	34–38, 120–122
37. A	❑	❑		Comparative and Superlative Adjectives and Adverbs	87–90
38. F	❑		❑	Strategy	133–141
39. D	❑		❑	Style	156–160
40. H	❑		❑	Organization	145–152
41. C	❑	❑		Verbs; Verb Tense	64–66, 67–75
42. F	❑	❑		Commas; Semicolons and Colons; Periods, Question Marks, and Exclamation Points	103–108, 108–111, 120–122

Answer	Check if missed	Usage/ Mechanics	Rhetorical Skills	Review this section	Pages
43. B	❑		❑	Style	156–160
44. G	❑		❑	Strategy	133–141
45. A	❑		❑	Strategy	133–141
46. F	❑	❑		Verbs	64–66
47. C	❑		❑	Strategy; Style	133–141, 156–160
48. J	❑	❑		Hyphens and Dashes	111–115
49. B	❑	❑		Parallel Form	79–83
50. G	❑		❑	Organization	145–152
51. A	❑	❑		Run-on Sentences and Comma Splices; Periods, Question Marks, and Exclamation Points	34–38, 120–122
52. J	❑		❑	Strategy; Style	133–141, 156–160
53. B	❑		❑	Parentheses; Strategy	116–118, 133–141
54. G	❑		❑	Strategy	133–141
55. D	❑	❑		Periods, Question Marks, and Exclamation Points	120–122
56. H	❑	❑		Adjectives and Adverbs	84–87
57. A	❑		❑	Strategy	133–141
58. J	❑		❑	Organization	145–152
59. D	❑		❑	Strategy	133–141
60. F	❑		❑	Strategy	133–141
61. C	❑	❑		Verbs; Verb Tense; Subject-Verb Agreement	64–66, 67–75, 76–79
62. F	❑	❑		Run-on Sentences and Comma Splices; Periods, Question Marks, and Exclamation Points	34–38, 120–122
63. B	❑	❑		Modifiers	33–34
64. J	❑		❑	Strategy	133–141
65. C	❑	❑		Run-on Sentences and Comma Splices; Sentence Fragments; Periods, Question Marks, and Exclamation Points	34–38, 38–43, 120–122

Answer	Check if missed	Usage/ Mechanics	Rhetorical Skills	Review this section	Pages
66. H	❑	❑		Commas	103–108
67. C	❑	❑		Sentence Fragments	38–43
68. J	❑		❑	Organization	145–152
69. B	❑	❑		Pronouns	59–63
70. F	❑	❑		Apostrophes	118–120
71. A	❑	❑		Periods, Question Marks, and Exclamation Points	120–122
72. F	❑	❑		Commas	103–108
73. D	❑		❑	Organization	145–152
74. J	❑		❑	Strategy	133–141
75. A	❑		❑	Organization	145–152

Number Correct:

Usage/Mechanics _____

Rhetorical Skills _____

Total _____

Diagnostic English ACT Answers Explained

PASSAGE I

1. D

However refers to delinquency not being new, not to Aristotle. So it needs to be followed by a period. *However* is a transition word, which should be separated by a comma.

2. G

The preceding clause states that Aristotle lived and wrote more than 2,000 years ago. Therefore, the verb must be in the past tense. Both *complaining* and *is complaining* are present-tense verb forms.

3. A

The word that would precede this quotation, *complained*, indicates that the following words are Aristotle's actual complaint. The authors intend to demonstrate that these words are directly attributable (though translated) to Aristotle. There is nothing in this passage to indicate that the authors want to emphasize Aristotle's idea above any other ideas in the passage or that he was in favor of juvenile delinquency. Quotation marks can be used to set off titles of shorter works such as essays and short stories, but the verb *complained* shows us that the following phrase is most likely not a title.

4. F

A colon is used to introduce a list or series, linking the words before the colon to the words that come after it. For a colon to be used before a list, the introductory phrase must be an independent clause, as it is here. The words *like these* help us look ahead to the list that follows. If no punctuation is used, the initial sentence becomes a run-on. If a period or exclamation point were used instead, the headlines would not be well connected to the introductory idea.

5. C

The subject and the verb of a sentence should not be separated by punctuation, unless the verb comes later in the sentence after an introductory phrase or clause. Inserting a comma breaks up the flow of the sentence. By inserting a period or a dash, the independent clause is broken into sentence fragments.

6. H

The word *delinquents* does not mark a change in the sentence, and while italics are sometimes used for foreign words or to indicate emphasis, neither is the case here. The word is a key term and it is clearly followed by a definition.

7. D

Disobeyed is one verb in a series, including the verbs *violate* and *behave*, both of which are in the present tense. In order to maintain parallel construction in this sentence, the present tense form must be used here. *Disobedient* is not a verb but an adjective.

8. J

All of these items endanger the safety of society. However, these are inappropriate comparisons for they all refer to animals, who are incapable of reason, as opposed to humans, who make conscious decisions to act in delinquent ways. Animals would not be considered delinquents. Additionally, while these animals can endanger the safety of society, they cannot be connected to any of the other parts of the definition of *delinquents*. Finally, the clause is unnecessary.

9. B

The word *many* refers to plural items (people, dogs, shoes, etc.), while *much* refers to singular items or items that cannot be counted in individual parts. Here, *delinquency* is an abstract term and cannot be counted, so *much* must be used. No comma is needed to separate this single adjective from the subject it describes.

10. H

A comma connects the initial independent clause with the dependent clause that follows. By placing a period, question mark, or exclamation point here, the dependent clause becomes a sentence fragment.

11. B

Because this is a formal article discussing juvenile delinquency, the most appropriate choice is *young people*. Though *kids* means the same thing, it is inappropriately informal for this article. Since the article is focused on delinquency by minors, the choice *adults* does not fit here.

12. G

Choice G introduces the subject of more serious teenage crime, sets off a list of examples of these types of crimes in dashes, then returns to the sentence to comment on them. The list, which is interesting, is nonessential information because it does not change the meaning of the sentence. To begin or end the sentence with this list places undue emphasis on this nonessential information and detracts from the impact of the sentence. In choice H, the list comes before we know why the author is presenting it; the reader has difficulty following the awkward sentence and determining its meaning. Using a semicolon, as in choice F, splits the sentence into fragments.

13. D
Because the opening adverbial clause refers to *they*, the subject immediately following this clause should indicate who *they* is. Clearly, it is the *youthful criminals* committing crimes, not the courts or the adults who want them to get stricter sentences. While choice C begins with *youthful criminals*, the remainder of the sentence does not fit in with the rest of the article, for it refers to adults rather than juvenile delinquents.

14. G
Because this passage contains the definition of delinquency and talks about juvenile delinquency in very broad terms, the article seems to be written to explain the concept to someone who has little or no knowledge of the subject. In no way do the authors make any statements or use any language to indicate that society is to blame or that youths should be treated with any special leniency. Though the authors mention the older pranks, there is no indication that mentioning these pranks is the authors' main purpose.

15. C
The subject of delinquency is introduced and defined in paragraph 2. Since the other paragraphs expand on the information presented in this paragraph, it should begin the article. Paragraph 1 clearly does not belong up front because the opening sentence, ending with *however*, clearly shows that the topic should already have been introduced elsewhere. Paragraphs 3 and 4 provide additional information about and examples of juvenile delinquency, and they can be placed in chronological order, starting with older pranks and ending with contemporary concerns.

PASSAGE II

16. G
This form of the verb agrees with the plural subject of the sentence, *two reasons*. In choices F and H, a plural subject is matched with a singular verb. The use of the future tense in choice J would indicate that these reasons will be created in the future, but we know that the reasons have already been created because they appear in paragraph 2.

17. D
The phrase *In 1927* places the first sentence in time. Choice A leaves uncertain the time of Earhart's fame and glory. The adverbs *faster*, *earlier*, and *later* don't make sense in the context of the first two sentences.

18. J
Choice F makes the dependent clause *Taking off from New York City* a sentence fragment. Choice G does not make sense because the first part of the sentence is not a question. Choice H does not have the comma necessary to separate this long introductory clause from the independent clause that follows.

19. D
Only two people are being compared, so the comparative form should be used. Using *worse*, while grammatically correct, indicates that having a heroine would be negative, which does not fit in with the positive tone of the earlier sentences. Saying *more* and *best* is not only redundant but also uses the superlative instead of the comparative form.

20. H
Choice F is a run-on sentence. Choice G is a comma splice, separating two independent clauses with a comma. Though the sentences are properly separated in choice J, the first sentence does not ask a question; therefore, the appropriate punctuation is a period, not a question mark.

21. C
Choices A, B, and D indicate a cause-and-effect relationship between being *outgoing and friendly* and being *modest and soft-spoken*, characteristics that are generally unconnected. Only C correctly indicates that it is unusual for someone to be outgoing and soft-spoken at the same time.

22. J
Choice F is incorrect because Amelia Earhart's 1928 flight was from coast to coast over America, not over the Atlantic. For the same reason, choice G is incorrect. Choice H describes Lindbergh's flight, not Earhart's.

23. A
The title of a longer work, such as a book or a magazine, is always italicized or underlined. If the title is italicized or underlined, it should not be placed within quotation marks as well.

24. G
A comma is needed to separate the nonessential element (the name George Putnam) from the rest of the

sentence. Though this element contributes to the meaning of the sentence, it is not essential to its meaning. Choices H and J make the name George Putnam a sentence fragment.

25. C

Because the writer is describing Earhart's desire to fly, the apostrophe is necessary to form the possessive of *wife*. Choice A is an incorrect spelling but also indicates a plural for *wife*, which does not make sense in the context of this sentence. Since Earhart is Putnam's only wife, choice B cannot be correct. Choice D contains no apostrophe and so does not indicate possession.

26. G

Choice F uses an adverb instead of a noun to describe one of Earhart's traits. Choice H uses an adjective to name this trait. While choice J uses the noun *intelligence*, it is not followed by the comma necessary when there is a list of three or more nouns.

27. D

Since this final sentence asks a question, it must end with a question mark.

28. H

Since this sentence speaks only of Earhart, the pronoun that refers to her must be singular and feminine.

29. B

Since this sentence expresses a new thought, it should begin a new paragraph. However, the word *While* in choices A and C sets the reader up for a contradiction that does not occur. The word *While* should be omitted, and the new paragraph should begin with *Earhart*.

30. J

Though the word *too* can be placed in many locations in the sentence, it most logically fits after the statement that "whatever men could do, women could do." When placed at the beginning of the sentence, *too* appears to be a transition word, leading into the sentence. This is inappropriate here because the sentence gives the reason why Earhart wants to fly, rather than another statement parallel to the previous sentence. The same problem occurs when *too* comes after *wanted*—it connects this sentence incorrectly to the previous sentence. Placing *too* after *men* does not make sense.

PASSAGE III

31. D

Choices A and C make the second half of this sentence a fragment. A colon is also inappropriate, for it is not being used to introduce a list or explanatory material. A comma should be used to set off this parenthetical phrase from the rest of the sentence.

32. H

There is no language in this passage directed toward people of a certain age or gender. The writer does assume that the readers have a general familiarity with terms like *romanticism*, but the material would be too general for someone who already knows a great deal about architecture.

33. B

Because this pronoun refers to people (*literary romantics*), rather than things, the pronoun *who* should be used.

34. H

This sentence focuses on Horace Walpole's importance to the Gothic Revival movement. The fact that he is a writer is of secondary importance, so it is mentioned later. Choice F questions Horace Walpole's importance instead of asserting it. Choice J doesn't make sense because the commas set off information essential to the meaning of the sentence.

35. D

All of the suggested phrases are too casual for the more formal tone of this essay. Additionally, the information is not necessary to the meaning of the sentence, which already indicates that the style is a combination of neoclassical and Gothic elements.

36. J

This sentence as it stands is a run-on. By adding the comma, the sentence becomes a comma splice. Since the first clause of this sentence does not need greater emphasis, an exclamation point is inappropriate. Therefore, a period should separate the two independent clauses.

37. A

Fonthill Abbey was one of many castlelikes homes, so the superlative is needed. *Unusualest* is not a word. There is no reason why the author would describe a house that was not special.

38. F

Because the sentence before this discusses the eccentric William Beckford, this sentence should begin by focusing on him, rather than his central tower or his builder.

39. D

Choices A, B, and C are all redundant because they express the same idea that is reflected by the word *ruins* in this sentence.

40. H

The words *In time* introduce a new line of thought. Therefore, a new paragraph should begin at this point.

41. C

The first clause of this sentence refers to actions of the architects; therefore, the second clause, in order to maintain parallel construction, should also refer to the actions of the architects. Choices A and B shift the focus of the sentence from the architects to the buildings. Choice D is in the present tense, while the first part of the sentence is past tense.

42. F

In this case, *British* is an adjective describing the phrase *Houses of Parliament.* Therefore, no comma is necessary. No other punctuation should come between the adjective and the words it describes.

43. B

England is on an island, although it is part of Europe. When the author refers to Germany and France, he refers to other European countries that are on the mainland continent of Europe. These are clues in the context of the passage to help the reader understand *continent* as the European mainland.

44. G

Though the article mentions the effects of one particular architectural movement in the United States, the focus of the article is on this specific movement in England.

45. A

The author assumes that the reader is familiar with terms such as *romanticism, Gothic, gargoyle,* etc. A glossary would help the less informed reader to understand what has been written. All the other choices are related to supporting details in the article and not to the main idea.

PASSAGE IV

46. F

The infinitive phrase functions here as a noun. The sentence could be reworded as *To discover . . . was disquieting.* None of the other verb forms listed can function as subjects of a sentence. Therefore, choice F is the only acceptable answer.

47. C

The language in choices A and B is too informal. The word *stuff* is inappropriate in a scientific essay. However, some lead-in to the many functions is necessary, so C is the best choice because it is formal but provides a connection to the list that follows.

48. J

When illustrating material is inserted into the middle of a larger sentence, dashes are used to set this material off from the rest of the sentence. Because a dash is used to begin the list of uses for this product, a dash must also be used to end the list and bring the reader back to the remainder of the sentence.

49. B

Choices A and C offer alternatives that are not parallel in construction with the other items listed (which are the noun phrases *skin cancer* and *the weakening of the human immune system*). The noun phrase beginning with *the destruction* would follow correctly in this pattern. Choice D is parallel, but the word *by* changes the meaning of the sentence element.

50. G

Choices F and H make the sentence sound as if the author is questioning the CFCs about their behavior. Since they are not living, speaking beings, this is illogical. Choice H also does not make sense. By using the expression *the materials in question*, the author states that he is referring to specific materials that have already been mentioned in this article.

51. A

As it stands, these sentences are both logically and grammatically correct. A question mark cannot be substituted for the period because the first sentence is not a question. By substituting a comma or by taking out punctuation altogether, the sentence becomes a run-on.

52. J

The entire essay is written in third-person point of view. Choices F and H unnecessarily introduce the first-person voice of the author into the passage. Choice G does not add any new information to the passage; based on the other information we've already read, we know the author is discussing the effect of these rays on Earth.

53. B

If this information were removed, it would not alter the main focus of the sentence. This information presents an interesting yet relatively unimportant fact. Brand names are neither secret nor set apart by parentheses in typical circumstances.

54. G

Choice F reflects language that is too casual for the formal, scientific tone of this essay. Choice J makes no sense; the Dupont people did not have any information that would completely destroy the environmentalists' concerns. Choice H is grammatically correct, but it makes no sense in the context of the sentence, because Dupont was disregarding the claims of environmentalists.

55. D

This sentence is not asking a question or making an emphatic statement. However, it does need end punctuation. Therefore, a simple period is the appropriate choice.

56. H

The word *good* is an adjective and therefore used to describe a noun. *Well* generally functions as an adverb; when it does function as an adjective, it is used to describe a state of feeling. In this instance, the word must be an adjective describing the noun *evidence*. Evidence generally cannot feel, so the adjective form of *well* does not apply. *Gooder* is an incorrect form.

57. A

The language of the text indicates that the author is frustrated because chemical companies continued to market dangerous materials for profits. Clearly, the author does not believe that Dupont had proof that CFCs were not harmful (they are) or that environmentalists thought that CFCs were actually good for the planet. Since the scientists produced data that showed CFCs were bad, the author is frustrated with everyone who ignored this data, not at the scientists who produced it.

58. J

The end of paragraph 3 discusses how the depleted ozone layer allows more ultraviolet rays through to Earth. Paragraph 2 discusses the effect of these ultraviolet rays on Earth's life-forms. It makes sense that the author would introduce the topic of ultraviolet rays before discussing their effects.

59. D

Most likely, this essay would be too general for an audience of scientists. While new Dupont employees might find this information interesting, it would probably not help their job performance. The vocabulary used by this author, including words such as *invulnerable* and *precipitating*, would be too difficult for a child to understand. Additionally, some language of this essay (*photosynthetic microorganisms*, for example) would require that the reader have some familiarity with basic scientific terms.

60. F

The final paragraph provided indicates that there is a connection between CFCs and the thinning of the ozone layer. However, without a specific explanation, the reader cannot be confident that there is this connection. While the other choices provide information that might be interesting, none of them offers a proper conclusion to this essay.

PASSAGE V

61. C

The subject is first person singular. That means that the only verb from the choices given that would be correct is *own*.

62. F

These sentences are fine as they are written. The opening sentence is a statement, which should not be followed by a question mark. Removing the period or inserting a comma would create a single run-on sentence.

63. B

In a previous sentence, *Blaire's first car* refers to a Ford, not the other car manufacturers or the cars themselves. Unless the subject to which the modifier refers directly follows the modifying statement, the modifier is misleading. The descriptions at the end of the sentence should also both be adjectives to maintain parallel structure.

64. J

The phrase *in turn* is used to lead from the previous sentence into this sentence. In this instance, *in turn* means "therefore" or "as a result." If you remove this phrase from the opening of the sentence, the phrase no longer functions as a transition. In the other options listed, the phrase simply distracts the reader from the actual meaning of the sentence.

65. C

The period in the passage creates two sentence fragments. Remove the period to join these two fragments to form a sentence. A question mark in Choice D presents the same grammatical problem and is further complicated because the first sentence is not a question.

66. H
Because *car* is the first item in a list of three nouns, it must be followed by a comma.

67. C
The original sentence includes a fragment that describes the location of the houses. The fragment should be joined to the preceding sentence, and the first *friends* should be removed since the possessive *friends'* refers to the houses. The possessive is plural, so the apostrophe should come after the *s*.

68. J
Sentences 3, 4 and 5 introduce and discuss Blaire's thoughts about what will result from having a car. Sentence 2 is the culminating thought about how her life will be different. It does not belong early in the paragraph; it does belong after sentence 5.

69. B
The correct pronoun for the subject of this sentence is *They*, referring to her "wheels." This is emphasized later in the sentence when the author refers to *they* again. The use of *he* or *she* would indicate that the author was referring to Blaire herself or to one of the students at the school. Since the article is entirely in the first person singular, the use of *we* is inappropriate.

70. F
The apostrophe here is unnecessary because the author is not referring to anything belonging to the neighborhoods; the author is referring to the neighborhoods themselves. Therefore, the word in the paragraph is correct.

71. A
As they stand, these two sentences are logically and grammatically correct. Both are independent clauses.

Substituting a comma for the period creates a run-on sentence. A colon would indicate that the second independent clause defined or directly expanded on the first clause, which is not the case. An exclamation point is not logically correct, because the sentence does not require any special emphasis.

72. F
Blaire has more than one friend, so mentioning Ashley tells which friend she is talking about. If Ashley were Blaire's only friend, then her name would be set off with commas: *My friend, Ashley, and I.* Choices G and H have only one comma, which is incorrect no matter how many friends Blaire has. *Ashley and me* is not grammatical.

73. D
Because the word *also* is in this sentence, it is clear that this sentence must build upon similar information presented in another sentence. Since the only other sentence presenting this type of information is 4, this sentence must come after sentence 4.

74. J
While the options listed might provide interesting information, they would not contribute significantly to the general thesis of the passage.

75. A
These paragraphs are already in the appropriate order. The first paragraph refers to Blaire's choice of cars. The second paragraph refers to reasons having the car is a good idea. The third paragraph relates some of the benefits Blaire hopes to gain from having a car. The fourth paragraph refers to the actual driving she will do. The logic of the passage flows along these lines.

Section III

Reading

Chapter 7
Vocabulary and Context Clues

The ACT Reading Test can include questions about vocabulary, but there will be only a question or two at most. There are no particular words that frequently occur on the ACT. Most of the vocabulary in ACT readings is not extremely difficult, and technical terms are usually explained in the reading. However, you will come across some unfamiliar words that you may need to know to answer a question or to understand the passage. This chapter shows you how to figure out word meanings from context clues.

Context Clues

You can often determine the meaning of a word from its **context**—that is, from the way the word is used in a sentence. You normally don't have to know the word's precise meaning. You just have to figure out enough to understand the meaning in the sentence.

EXAMPLE

Christian hoped his boss would assent to his request for a day off so that he could attend his grandmother's birthday party.

1. The word <u>assent</u> in this sentence most nearly means:

   A. raise.
   B. agree.
   C. force.
   D. help.

The sentence mentions that Christian requested a day off. This is the context clue we need. If his boss gives him the day off, or agrees to his request, then Christian can go to the party. The word *assent* must mean "agree."

Determine Meaning from Context Alone

You may be able to determine word meaning from context alone.

EXAMPLES

1. Jim's long nights in Greenland inured him to the cold.

   What does <u>inured</u> mean in the sentence above? The context tells us that Jim's long nights in Greenland had some impact on his reaction to cold. Nights in Greenland are cold. Someone who had spent long nights in Greenland would be accustomed to cold. Rethink the sentence:

   Jim's long nights in Greenland <u>accustomed him to (prepared him for, hardened him to)</u> the cold.

2. Weights worn by divers enabled them to explore the benthic region of the ocean.

   What does <u>benthic</u> mean in the sentence above? The context tells us that *benthic* refers to a particular region of the ocean. Weights take divers deeper. So the benthic region is probably at or near the bottom of the ocean. Rethink the sentence:

   Weights enabled the divers to explore the region <u>at the bottom</u> of the ocean.

3. Bob's very limited budget requires that he take a parsimonious approach to gift expenditures.

   What does <u>parsimonious</u> mean in the sentence above? The context tells us that it describes an approach to gift expenditures. A very limited budget means very limited expenditures. *Parsimonious* must mean something like very economical. Rethink the sentence:

   Bob's very limited budget requires that he take a <u>very economical</u> approach to gift expenditures.

Note:

While the ACT does not ask questions about vocabulary in the same way the SAT does, you may be taking both tests, and the words you study for the SAT might end up helping you on the ACT as well. Increasing your vocabulary will also help improve your general reading comprehension of ACT passages, as well as your performance on the Writing Test, if you choose to take it.

Determine Meaning from Synonyms

Synonyms can help you determine the meanings of words. Remember that a **synonym** is a word that has the same or almost the same meaning as another word. Sometimes authors use synonyms that can help reveal the meanings of other words in a sentence.

EXAMPLES

1. Doug's presentations always seemed very haphazard, but Lynn's talks were less desultory.

   What does <u>desultory</u> mean in the sentence above? The context tells us it describes Lynn's talks. We can tell from the context that *desultory* and *haphazard* have very similar meanings. Replace the word *desultory* with a word that means the same as *haphazard*. Rethink the sentence:

Doug's presentations always seemed very haphazard, but Lynn's talks were less <u>disorganized</u>.

2. It took years before a complicated piscatory treaty was signed by representatives of the two countries. As for me, I just like fishing.

What does <u>piscatory</u> mean in the first sentence above? The context tells us that it describes a treaty. We can tell from the context that *piscatory* and *fishing* have very similar meanings. Replace the word *piscatory* with the synonym *fishing*. Rethink the sentence:

It took years before a complicated <u>fishing</u> treaty was signed by representatives of the two countries. As for me, I just like fishing.

Determine Meaning from Antonyms

Antonyms may help you determine the meanings of words. **Antonyms** are words that mean the opposite of each other. Authors may set up a contrast between words or ideas. You can use these contrasts and your knowledge of antonyms to figure out the meanings of unfamiliar words.

EXAMPLES

1. I wish I could get someone to tell me the truth. All the stories I hear about Scott's nomination are apocryphal.

What does <u>apocryphal</u> mean in the sentence above? The context tells us that it describes the stories about Scott's nomination. We can tell from the context that *truth* and *apocryphal* have opposite meanings. Replace *apocryphal* with the opposite of *truthful*. Rethink the sentence:

I wish I could get someone to tell me the truth. All the stories I hear about Scott's nomination are <u>untruthful</u>.

2. The movie made Tyneesha lachrymose, but I remained dry-eyed.

What does <u>lachrymose</u> mean in the sentence above? We can tell from the context that it means the opposite of *dry-eyed*. Replace *lachrymose* with a word that has to do with crying. Rethink the sentence:

The movie made Tyneesha <u>teary</u>, but I remained dry-eyed.

Practice

Use context clues to figure out the meanings of the underlined words in the following sentences. Write the meaning of the word in the space provided.

1. After a series of arguments, the coach stepped in to restore <u>comity</u> among team members.

    To bring back peace

2. Her parents thought Heather should go on a game show because she remembered all kinds of obscure information. Her mind was filled with <u>recondite</u> facts and figures.

Random

3. How dare you question my <u>veracity</u>! I'm no liar.

Honesty

4. His first job required long hours of hard work. His current job was just the opposite, a veritable <u>sinecure</u>.

Easy

5. The drill sergeant was tired of disciplining the <u>refractory</u> recruit.

Clumsy

6. It seemed that the jury would find the defendant guilty until a witness gave <u>exculpatory</u> testimony.

Shocking

7. After years of a <u>peripatetic</u> existence, Joan finally had a chance to settle down.

Hecktic, crazy

8. In the recipe, you can replace molasses with maple syrup, but salt and pepper are not <u>fungible</u>.

Doesn't work

9. Charitable contributions increase during the holidays when people are in more of an <u>eleemosynary</u> mood.

cheerful

10. At the beginning of his clarinet lessons, Bob's playing was jarring to the ear, but after several years of lessons, his playing had acquired a <u>euphonious</u> sound.

pleasent

(Answers on page 199)

Model ACT Questions

These Model ACT questions show how this topic might be tested on the real ACT. The answers and explanations immediately follow the questions. Try the questions and then review the answers and explanations.

The floor shook violently with the <u>impetuousness</u>
                                        1

of a spoiled child. It was indeed a <u>macroseism</u>,
                                      2

and more than a <u>paroxysm</u>.
                  3

1. In the context of the passage, <u>impetuousness</u> most nearly means:

   A. suddenness.
   B. gentleness.
   C. loudness.
   D. impishness.

2. In the context of the passage, <u>macroseism</u> most nearly means:

   F. minor earthquake.
   G. major earthquake.
   H. train collision.
   J. violent seizure.

3. In the context of the passage, <u>paroxysm</u> most nearly means:

   A. a major earthquake.
   B. a sudden stop.
   C. slight twitch.
   D. tremor.

Answers

1. Context clues help determine the meaning of *impetuousness*. The choice that best refers to both the actions of a spoiled child and an earthquake is *suddenness*. The other choices are not associated with an earthquake.

   A is the correct choice.

2. The word *macroseism* describes the shaking of the ground, which is almost certainly an earthquake. The prefix *macro-* is a further clue that it must be a major earthquake. *Microseism* would describe a minor earthquake.

   G is the correct choice.

3. The passage indicates that the *macroseism*, a major earthquake, is more than a *paroxysm*. That context clue indicates that *paroxysm* must be a tremor, which is a shaking of the earth but less destructive than an earthquake.

   D is the correct choice.

Look at the item that matches the number of the underlined word.

It was a prehistoric time, when dinosaurs roamed Earth. It was a world of <u>poikilothermic</u> creatures.
₁

The <u>Apatosaurus</u> was a large herbivore and unlike
₂

the <u>Theropods</u>. The dinosaurs may have seen <u>tuff</u>,
₃   ₄

which was ejected into the air from volcanic craters.

The creatures at that time were more <u>ferine</u> compared
₅

to the gentler creatures of the modern world.

1. In the context of the passage, <u>poikilothermic</u> most likely means:

   A. very large.
   B. cold-blooded.
   C. four-legged.
   D. lived on land.

2. In the context of the passage, <u>Apatosaurus</u> most likely means:

   F. lived in water.
   G. ate plants.
   H. lived on land.
   J. ate other animals.

3. In the context of the passage, <u>Theropods</u> most likely means:

   A. lived in water.
   B. ate plants.
   C. lived on land.
   D. ate other animals.

4. In the context of the passage, <u>tuff</u> most likely means:

   F. streams.
   G. bacteria.
   H. ash.
   J. hardened plant matter.

5. In the context of the passage, <u>ferine</u> most likely means:

   A. menacing.
   B. tame.
   C. catlike.
   D. mammalian.

(*Answers on page 199*)

ANSWERS

1. **comity:** courtesy, civility

   The coach had to restore friendliness because the team had been arguing so much.

2. **recondite:** obscure

   The context reveals that *obscure* and *recondite* have similar meanings.

3. **veracity:** truthfulness

   The context reveals that *liar* and *veracity* have opposite meanings.

4. **sinecure:** job with almost no work

   The context reveals that *sinecure* and *job required long hours of hard work* have opposite meanings.

5. **refractory:** disobedient

   Drill sergeants spend time disciplining disobedient recruits.

6. **exculpatory:** clears from guilt

   The context reveals that *exculpatory* and *find . . . guilty* have opposite meanings.

7. **peripatetic:** moving from place to place

   The context reveals that *peripatetic* and *settle down* have opposite meanings.

8. **fungible:** interchangeable

   The context reveals that *replace* and *fungible* have similar meanings.

9. **eleemosynary:** generous

   The context reveals that *charitable* and *eleemosynary* have similar meanings.

10. **euphonious:** pleasing to hear

    The context reveals that *euphonious* and *jarring to the ear* have opposite meanings.

1. B
The context clue is that the creatures who roamed Earth were dinosaurs. The suffix *–therm* has to do with temperature. The only choice that makes sense is that *poikilothermic* means cold-blooded.

2. G
The clue is *herbivore*, which means plant-eating (notice the root *herb*). In the context of this sentence, that means *Apatosaurus* most likely ate plants.

3. D
The passage states that the Apatosaurus was unlike the Theropods, meaning the Apatorsaurus did not eat the same food as the Theropods. Apatosaurus ate plants, so it follows from the context that Theropods likely ate other animals.

4. H
The passage indicates that *tuff* was ejected into the air from craters. This happens during a volcanic eruption. Among the choices given, only ash would have been thrown into the air during an eruption.

5. A
Think about what you know about dinosaurs. They were (mostly) very big. They used their sharp teeth and claws to kill one another. Choice A, *menacing*, does describe dinosaurs, but consider the other choices to be sure this is the best answer. *Menacing* and *tame* are antonyms, so you can eliminate choice B. Dinosaurs didn't look like cats, so choice C is incorrect. You learned in science that a mammal is an animal that gives live birth. Dinosaurs laid eggs, so choice D is incorrect.

Chapter 8
Reading Effectively and Efficiently

The ACT Reading Test has two important parts—the passages to read and the items to respond to. This section shows you how to read passages efficiently. Efficient reading is effective reading. Efficient reading means picking out the important points in a passage.

The following sections show you how to identify the topic, main idea, and important details in a paragraph. The terms *topic*, *main idea*, and *details* are not important in themselves, nor should they be interpreted rigidly. The purpose here is to show you how to quickly find the answer to a question.

Find the Main Idea of Each Paragraph

The **main idea** of a paragraph is the most important thing the writer has to say about that idea. The answers to many ACT test items are based on the main idea of a paragraph or a passage. Some ACT questions ask directly for the main idea.

The first step is to read the passage once. As you read, think about the main idea of each paragraph. Once you know the main idea, you know where to look for information about a specific topic. If there is a test item about a particular topic, you can then go directly to the appropriate paragraph. The main idea of a paragraph is usually in the first or last sentence, so look there if you're having a hard time figuring out a paragraph's main idea.

Once you know the main idea, write it next to the paragraph in your test booklet. Then read the questions one at a time and return to the passage to find the answer. Having labeled your paragraphs will make it much easier to find answers to the questions.

Note:
If you are running out of time, or if you read very slowly, do not read everything in a passage; read efficiently. You are not responsible for knowing about an entire passage. You just have to know enough to answer the questions.

EXAMPLES

Shapes of plant leaves

1. Plant leaves come in various shapes. Among the most distinctive leaf shapes are the fanlike, tooth-edged foliage of the Fatsia japonica and the deeply lobed leaves of the ubiquitous Philodendron selloum. But among the most popular of contemporary plants are the Dracaena marginata, whose long sword-shaped leaves are edged with a reddish tinge.

What is this paragraph about? The first sentence mentions plant leaf shapes. The next two sentences give specific examples of plants and the shape of their leaves.

Main idea: shapes of plant leaves. If a test question asked about plant leaf shapes, you would turn first to this paragraph for an answer.

Leaf arrangements and plants

2. Plant leaves come in various shapes, but sometimes a plant is distinguished by the arrangement of its leaves on the stem rather than by their shape. The oval leaflets of the Brassaia actinophylla radiate out from one point on the stem, whereas the leaves of the Pleomele reflexa break out from the center head in a rosettelike effect.

What is the paragraph about? This paragraph seems very similar to the paragraph in the first example, but the main ideas are different. The first sentence in example 2 mentions plant shapes and leaf arrangements, and the last sentence gives specific examples of leaf arrangements.

Main idea: leaf arrangements and plants. If a test question asked about leaf arrangements in plants, you would first look to this paragraph for an answer.

Stated Main Idea

A **stated main idea** can be found among the words in the paragraph. The sentence containing the main idea is called the **topic sentence**. The following example shows the main idea and the topic sentence.

EXAMPLE

Work and energy are related

The most important concept in all nature is energy. It represents a fundamental entity common to all forms of matter in all parts of the physical world. Closely associated with energy is work. To a layperson, work describes the expenditure of one's physical or mental energy. In science, work is a quantity that is the product of force times the distance through which the force acts. In other words, work is done when force moves an object. Work and energy are related because energy is the ability to do work.

A good main idea, *work and energy are related*, is found in the last sentence. The details about how and why work and energy are related are too specific to be the main idea, but these details may help you answer a question. Note, also, how you would write the main idea next to the paragraph so that you could easily find answers to questions about work and energy.

Unstated Main Idea

The main idea of a paragraph may not be stated. If the main idea is **unstated**, there will be no topic sentence. This type of paragraph may contain details related to the topic. The main idea will summarize or bind together these details. Unstated main ideas are found most frequently in prose-fiction passages. The unstated main idea of a prose-fiction passage may be a description of a character or a scene, or it may convey some other aspect of the story.

EXAMPLE

Many factors developed trade in the eastern colonies

Fertile, level land and a favorable climate encouraged family-size farms, which produced surplus grain (wheat, corn, and oats) for export to the other colonies. Long, navigable rivers, such as the Hudson, Susquehanna, and Delaware, promoted trade with the Indians for furs. First-class harbors, such as New York and Philadelphia, stimulated trade with other colonies, England, and the European continent.

The main idea is that favorable growing conditions, navigable rivers, good relations with Native Americans, and first-class harbors helped develop trade in the eastern colonies.

The main idea for this paragraph is not stated. You need to read the paragraph and piece together the details, think about what they all have in common, to get to the main idea.

Practice

Read each paragraph. Write the main idea or topic of the paragraph next to it, as you would on the ACT.

1. I went to the woods because I wished to live deliberately, to confront only the essential facts of life, and see if I could not learn what it had to teach, and not, when I came to die, discover that I had not lived. I did not wish to live what was not life, living is so dear, nor did I want to practice resignation, unless it was quite necessary. I wanted to live deep and suck out all the marrow of life, to live so sturdily and Spartan-like as to put to rout all that was not life, to cut a broad swath and shave close, to drive life into a corner, and reduce it to its lowest terms, and, if proved to be mean, why then to get the whole and genuine meanness of it, and publish its meanness to the world; or if it were sublime, to know by experience, and be able to give a true account of it in my next excursion.

2. An early humanist writer was Francesco Petrarch (1304–1374). He wrote poems called sonnets in Latin and Italian. Many of the sonnets express his love for a woman named Laura. Another well-known humanist was Giovanni Boccaccio (1313–1375). He wrote a book called *The Decameron*. It was created during the time of the terrible Black Death plague in Italy. The stories are told by a group of ten young men and women. They live in an isolated house in the country to escape the plague. The group amuses itself by making fun of many customs of the Middle Ages.

3. Possibly the greatest of all composers, Beethoven wrote romantic music: sonatas, concertos, an opera, and nine symphonies. His works marked the transition of music from the court and aristocracy to the concert hall and general public. About the Third (Eroica) Symphony, it is said that Beethoven tore up the dedication to Napoleon upon hearing that Napoleon had taken the title of emperor. The Fifth Symphony, perhaps best known of all symphonies, opens with four notes that Beethoven likened to fate knocking at the door. Beethoven combined orchestra and chorus, which sings Schiller's "Ode to Joy," as the final movement in the Ninth (Choral) Symphony.

4. The composition of a mixture may vary. Thus, different quantities of iron filings and powdered sulfur can form a variety of mixtures. Recall that the composition of a compound does not vary and that the compound is referred to as homogeneous matter. This means that the composition of the

compound is the same throughout the compound. On the other hand, the composition of a mixture may not be the same throughout the mixture—it may vary—and the mixture is referred to as unhomogeneous matter.

5. In the 1860s and 1870s, a completely different style of painting began in France. It was called *Impressionism*. Impressionists wanted to show the effect of light on their subjects. They generally used much brighter colors than the Romanticists and Realists. In creating their scenes of natural views of everyday life, they used small dabs of color side by side. The eye blended the colors and "saw" the objects the artist had painted. Leading Impressionists were Claude Monet (1840–1926), Pierre Renoir (1841–1919), and Edgar Degas (1834–1917).

6. About fifteen miles below Monterey, on the wild coast, the Torres family had their farm, a few sloping acres above the cliff that dropped to the brown reefs and to the hissing white waters of the ocean. Behind the farm the stone mountains stood up against the sky. The farm buildings huddled like clinging aphids on the mountain skirts, crouched low to the ground as though the wind might blow them into the sea. The little shack, the rattling, rotting barn were grey-bitten with sea salt, beaten by the damp wind until they had taken on the color of the granite hills. Two horses, a red cow and a red calf, half a dozen pigs and a flock of lean, multicolored chickens stocked the place. A little corn was raised on the sterile slope, and it grew short and thick under the wind, and all the cobs formed on landward sides of the stalks.

7. We came from the place where the sun is hid at night, over the great plains where the buffaloes live, until we reached the big river. There we fought the Alligewi, till the ground was red with their blood. From the banks of the big river to the shores of the salt lake, there was none to meet us. The Maquas followed at a distance. We said the country should be ours from the place where the river runs up no longer on this stream to a river twenty suns' journey toward the summer. The land we had taken like warriors we kept like men. We drove the Maquas into the woods with the bears. They only tasted salt at the licks; they drew no fish from the great lake; we threw them the bones.

8. The [boat] pranced and reared, and plunged like an animal. As each wave came, and she rose for it, she seemed like a horse making at a fence outrageously high. The manner of her scramble over these walls of water is a mystic thing, and, moreover, at the top of them were ordinarily these problems in white water, the foam racing down from the summit of each wave, requiring a new leap, and a leap from the air. Then, after scornfully bumping a crest, she would slide and race and splash down a long incline, and arrive bobbing and nodding in front of the next menace.

9. In the brick-wall family, the building blocks—the bricks—that are cemented together to make the family are a concern with order, control, obedience, adherence to rules, and a strict hierarchy of power. Kids are controlled, manipulated, and made to mind. Their feelings are often ignored, ridiculed, or negated. Parents direct, supervise, minilecture, order, threaten, remind, and worry over the kids. The brick-wall family is in essence a dictatorship, perhaps a benevolent one, but a dictatorship nevertheless. Power in a brick-wall family equals control, and all of it comes from the top. It can be a great training ground for the child who would become a bully or the proving ground for the bullied child to affirm her own lack of worth, lack of ability, and lack of personal resources to fend off the bully.

10. Before the concept of a "first 100 days" entered the popular imagination, there was George Washington, the original precedent setter for the American presidency. He took over the reins of government as the nation's first chief executive in an atmosphere of enormous uncertainty because many Americans wondered if the new nation could survive. And while Washington's agenda wasn't nearly as extensive as modern presidents', his first 100 days were important because everything he did set a standard for his successors and for the country at large.

(Answers on page 206)

Model ACT Question

This Model ACT Question shows how this topic might be tested on the real ACT. The answer and explanation immediately follow the question. Try the question and then review the answer and the explanation.

1. When we think about memory on an intuitive level, it often seems as though our memories just fade away with the passage of time. It is as though some physical or chemical trace of an experience decays or degenerates as time progresses. The decay interpretation of memory is an old one and is perhaps the most widely believed by the general public. But the idea that memories fade with the passage of time has not been supported by experimental research. Somewhat surprisingly, there is no direct evidence to support the decay interpretation. Although the idea is a simple one, it has not led to fruitful experimentation and must, at present, be taken as nothing more than an interesting possibility.

What is the author's intended message in this paragraph?

A. Memory loss occurs when memories fade away.
B. The brain steadily decays as humans age.
C. Fruitful experiments have been conducted in the field of memory loss.
D. The theory of memory decay is not adequate.

Answer This question asks you to identify the main idea by pointing to the "author's intended message." None of the first three choices is correct because they identify only details in the paragraph, not the main idea, and they actually contradict what the passage states. You can see this by reading the final sentences, which say that the memory decay theory is not supported by direct evidence and is "nothing more than an interesting possibility."

D is the correct choice.

ACT-Type Questions

Read each paragraph and answer the question that follows.

1. The task of classifying emotions, once a popular academic pastime, has fallen on hard times. There are just too many shades and variations among emotions to allow clear-cut, satisfactory definitions of them all. Modern psychology therefore limits identifying a few major emotions and classifying most emotions as either pleasant or unpleasant. (If you think about it, there just don't seem to be many neutral emotions.) In addition to the pleasant-unpleasant distinction, modern psychology tends to view emotions along a dimension from weak to strong.

Which BEST reflects the main idea of this paragraph?

A. Classifying emotions
B. Emotions
C. Strong emotions
D. Weak to strong emotions

2. Final goods are goods and services purchased by all sectors for final consumption, not for additional processing or resale. Intermediate goods are goods and services that undergo additional processing or are resold. Final goods, thus, are the result of the nation's productive effort, while intermediate goods are

all the goods and services that will be processed further to make final goods. The distinction between final and intermediate goods is not necessarily the same as that between finished products and raw materials. For example, polyethylene is an intermediate good when it is used by water-bed manufacturers to make products for households. If the polyethylene is sold directly to households, it becomes a final good. A product may be either a final good or an intermediate one, depending on who buys it and for what purpose.

Which BEST states the main idea of this paragraph?

F. There is a strong distinction between final goods that customers buy and intermediate goods.
G. One example of an intermediate good is polyethylene, which is used in water beds.
H. Final goods are used by consumers, but intermediate goods still need to be processed or resold.
J. Intermediate goods can significantly drive up the costs of final goods.

3. It was fortunate for me that, owing to its peculiar cause—indigestion—the irritability and consequent nervousness of Nippers were mainly observable in the morning, while in the afternoon he was comparatively mild. So that, Turkey's paroxysms only coming on about twelve o'clock, I never had to do with their [my employees'] eccentricities at one time. Their fits relieved each other, like guards. When Nippers' was on, Turkey's was off; and vice versa. This was a good natural arrangement, under the circumstances.

Which BEST summarizes the primary message in this paragraph?

A. The two employees each had problems, although they expressed them at different times of day.
B. The employer is plagued by workers who are unable to function for much of the day.
C. Employers believe that their employees try to find ways to get out of doing a full day's work.

D. There is no time of day during which this employer can expect both his clerks to be working.

4. The occupations of the criminals convicted between 1794 and 1800 attest to their poverty. Of the convicts whose occupations were noted, 27 percent were laborers. The next highest group, mariners, accounted for only 7.9 percent of the total. Equally significant, the mayor's court convicted few people whose occupations indicated possibly high income.

Which reflects the main point the author makes in this paragraph?

F. Only poor people were convicted of crimes in the eighteenth century.
G. People who earned higher incomes in the late 1700s could afford better lawyers.
H. In the late 1700s, a person's job might have biased court decisions against him or her.
J. Most of the people convicted of crimes in the eighteenth century were employed.

5. Some people seem to thrive on adrenaline. They deliberately seek out thrills, from small adventures—like riding roller coasters—to more elaborate blood-chilling behaviors—like jumping out of airplanes. Some scientists believe that this behavior is genetically determined. They say that a variant in genetic makeup causes some people to respond to dopamine, a neurotransmitter that is released by the brain during thrilling moments. People with this genetic variant have a specific brain reaction to dopamine, different from the reaction others may have.

With which of these statements would the author MOST likely agree?

A. People looking for a thrilling experience should try skydiving.
B. Genetic mutations have caused an increased release of adrenaline in a large group of people.
C. Variants in genetic makeup cause specific responses in all situations.
D. A genetically determined response to dopamine might be responsible for thrill-seeking behavior.

(Answers on pages 206–207)

ANSWERS

PRACTICE   Main Idea (pages 202–203)

1. *I went to the woods to learn what life really is* is a good topic for this paragraph. The first sentence states as much and gives many of the reasons.

2. *Humanist writers* is a good topic for this paragraph. The first sentence mentions one humanist writer, and the fourth sentence mentions another humanist writer.

3. *Beethoven's compositions (works, music)* is a good topic for this paragraph. The first sentence outlines Beethoven's works. *Beethoven* alone would not be a good topic for this paragraph. You would turn to this paragraph to answer a question about his music, but not to answer a question about his private life.

4. The main idea is that *the composition of a mixture may be unhomogeneous (vary throughout the mixture)*. The first and last sentences confirm that this paragraph is about the composition of a mixture. This is a better topic than just *mixture*. If a test question asked about the composition of a mixture, you would want to come right to this paragraph, and a topic of *mixture* might not lead you directly here. The last sentence of the paragraph provides the main idea. This paragraph contains information about compounds. The homogeneity of compounds is mentioned to help explain the possible unhomogeneity of a mixture.

5. The main idea is that *Impressionist painting founded in France in the 1860s and 1870s used dots of color.* The next-to-last sentence and the italic type provide the topic. The names of the painters and the comparison with other painting styles are not a part of the main idea.

6. The main idea is that *the small, dilapidated Torres farm stands in contrast to the majesty of the sea and mountains around it.*

7. The main idea is that *the tribe traveled over the plains from the great river (Mississippi?) to the sea, and vanquished their enemies.* Recognizing this main idea requires understanding the clues provided by the Native American speaker. The first line, "We came from a place where the sun is hid at night," gives a further clue about where this tribe may have originated—farther north, where the sun shines day and night during the summer.

8. The main idea is that *riding in this boat is like riding a bucking horse.* The first sentence compares the boat to an animal, and the second sentence mentions a horse. All the details suggest that the boat is like a bucking horse.

9. The main idea here is that *the brick-wall family is characterized by strict authority of parents over children, and this could lead to children becoming victims of bullying or bullies themselves.*

10. *George Washington set the standard for the first 100 days of American presidents' terms* is the main idea of this paragraph.

ACT-TYPE QUESTIONS   Main Idea (pages 204–205)

1. A

Classifying emotions is the best choice for this paragraph. If there was a question about classifying emotions, you would be likely to find the answer in this paragraph. *Emotions* is too general. *Strong emotions* and *weak to strong emotions* refer to ways of classifying emotions, so they are too specific to include the major idea of the paragraph.

2. H

Final goods are bought for final use while intermediate goods are bought for reprocessing or resale. The last sentence confirms that the paragraph is about the difference between final and intermediate goods. The main idea is found in the first two sentences.

3. A

Choice D is tempting, but it conveys only half the main idea of the paragraph. Choices B and C are broad generalizations that do not necessarily have to do with the details provided in the paragraph itself.

4. H

Choice F is a generalization that is not well supported by the information in the passage. Choice G is misleading because a better, more expensive lawyer may be the reason people with higher incomes saw fewer convictions. However, this is not stated in the passage. Choice J may be true, but it is a detail extrapolated from the paragraph, not the idea that ties it together. H is the only logical choice that express-es the main idea of the paragraph.

5. D

Choice A grows out of a single detail in the passage; furthermore, the passage itself does not indicate whether the author believes people should try skydiv-ing. Choice B incorrectly uses information presented in the paragraph—it is meant to trick you. Choice C is too extreme, carrying a single example in the passage to a broad, unfounded generalization. Only choice D is well supported by the details in the passage.

Chapter 9
Items and Answer Choices

▬ Items

On the actual ACT Reading Test you will read the items (questions) after you read the passage. You read each item and the answer choices and then go back to the passage to identify the correct answer.

Every question can be answered from the information in the passage, but the items are written so they can be hard to answer. Some refer directly to the information in a passage. Others ask you to draw a conclusion or to make an inference based on the passage. In this chapter you will learn how to crack the different types of items and answer choices on the ACT Reading Test.

Item Statements and Questions

Each item begins with a statement to complete or a question to answer. Carefully read each statement or question. It will tell you which topic to look for in the passage.

Look at the following example of how the ACT could get at information through a sentence-completion item and a question item.

EXAMPLES

The **sentence-completion** item below begins with a statement ending with the word *because*. The colon signals that this is a completion item. The word *because* signals that the correct completion choice will explain why some cities in the United States have established teen curfew laws.

1. Some cities in the United States have established teen curfew laws because:

   A. they believe parents need help caring for their children responsibly.
   B. statistics show that most juvenile crimes are committed late at night.
   C. city governments want to keep streets quiet for older residents.
   D. teenagers are less capable than other adults of driving at night.

The correct choice is B. The statement, together with the correct answer, form a sentence that is true.

The following item begins with a **question**. The word *How* at the beginning of the question signals that the correct answer will explain how TV stations make a profit.

2. How do television networks use viewer ratings to make a profit?

    F. Each viewer pays a fee depending on which network he or she watches.
    G. Networks make merchandise and sell it to their viewers.
    H. A portion of television sales go to the most popular networks.
    J. Networks sell advertising time that is priced based on popularity.

The correct choice is J, the only appropriate answer to the question.

Answer Choices

Each multiple-choice item has four answer choices. The correct choice correctly completes the item statement or answers the item question. The correct choice usually restates the writer's words, purpose, or tone. Occasionally you may come across a correct choice taken word-for-word from the passage, but this is very rare.

Incorrect choices are written to make you think they are correct. These are called *distracters*. Distracters introduce doubt and turn your thinking from the correct answer. Spotting and eliminating these distracters is an important key to scoring well on the ACT Reading Test. The more choices you can eliminate, the easier it is to choose the correct answer. Eliminate answer choices you know are false.

Following are the most common categories of distracters on the ACT. Not every answer choice fits exactly into one of these categories, and there is certainly no reason for remembering their names, but these categories will help you think about and pick out incorrect choices. Watch out for these distracters. They are meant to trick you!

The Weasel

The **weasel** is a distracter that misrepresents the passage. Some weasels are sly and just change the author's wording or meaning. Other weasels are sneaky and turn the author's words or ideas around. Yet other weasels are tricky and take words from the passage out of context. Weasels pop up more often than any other type of distracter, so keep a sharp eye out for them. Look at the following example of weaseling.

EXAMPLE

Read this short passage.

> Advertisers use color and line to manipulate the visual impression of print ads and billboards. They also carefully select words and images for high emotional impact so that viewers' initial response will make them more likely to buy a product.

1. How do advertisers persuade viewers to buy their products?

    A. Advertisers use color and line to anticipate viewers' initial responses.
    B. Viewers' emotional responses manipulate the words and images in advertisements.
    C. Words and images cause all viewers to respond to advertisements in the same emotional way.
    D. They carefully select words and images so that viewers' initial response will make them buy a product.

Look at these examples of weasels to see how test writers might try to trick you.

A. Advertisers use color and line to anticipate viewers' initial responses.

This statement does not accurately reflect the passage. The words are taken out of context. Color and line are not the tools advertisers use to predict emotional responses. Advertisers more likely use a knowledge of psychology to determine which emotional response will incline viewers to buy a product. Then they use color and line to produce that effect.

B. Viewers' emotional responses manipulate the words and images in advertisements.

This statement turns the author's ideas around. The author does not say that viewers' responses manipulate advertising. The author does say that advertisers use words and images in advertisements to influence viewers.

C. Words and images cause all viewers to respond to advertisements in the same emotional way.

Just see how this statement weasels around to try to convince you that it is correct. Almost all the words are from the passage. But the statement misrepresents the meaning of the passage.

D. They carefully select words and images so that viewers' initial response will make them buy a product.

This statement is incorrect because the words *high emotional impact* and *more likely to* are omitted. Without understanding that the words and images are influencing viewers' emotions, it's difficult to determine why they are buying a product. In addition, they are only *more likely* to buy the product; not every person who sees the ad will definitely buy the product.

The Shift

The **shift** is an incorrect choice that could be the correct answer to another item.

EXAMPLE

Read this short passage.

> Earthquakes occur when the surface of Earth's crust (the ground) moves. Earthquakes can be triggered by a variety of causes, some natural and some the result of human enterprise. Tectonic movement, or the shifting of continental plates, is the most frequent natural cause of earthquakes. Other natural causes of earthquakes include massive landslides and volcanic activity. Human beings can also cause earthquakes through mine blasts or nuclear experimentation.

Read the item below. Cross off the incorrect responses. The choice remaining is correct.

1. According to the passage, which tectonic factor can result in an earthquake?

    A. The movement of ground on Earth's surface
    B. Mine blasts and nuclear experiments
    C. The movement of continental plates
    D. Landslides and volcanoes

All the incorrect answer choices are examples of the shift. Look at the explanations below.

A. The movement of ground on Earth's surface

This choice is incorrect, but it is the correct answer to a question about what the definition of an earthquake is.

B. Mine blasts and nuclear experiments

This choice is incorrect, but it is the correct answer to a question about what are some human causes of earthquakes.

C. The movement of continental plates

You could have arrived at this correct choice by eliminating the incorrect choices. Also, the only factor identified as tectonic in the passage is the shifting of continental plates, and the question asks about tectonic factors specifically.

D. Landslides and volcanoes

This choice is incorrect, but it is the correct answer to a question about the natural causes of earthquakes other than tectonic activity.

The Enticer and the Extreme

The **enticer** is an incorrect answer choice that entices (tempts) with incorrect but very appealing wording. The **extreme** is an incorrect answer choice that might be true if it did not include extreme words such as *always*, *completely*, *perfectly*, etc. If an answer choice sounds too idealistic or too extreme or absolute, it is probably not correct.

EXAMPLES

Read this passage.

> The revival of *Hair* on Broadway has far surpassed the expectations of many audience members and critics. Some see this newest edition of the production as particularly relevant to current politics. Certainly, there are strong parallels between the events depicted in the musical and this country's present situation. A number of the songs and most of the opinions, however, are so confined to the particular troubles of the 1960s that any outside application of the ideas is a stretch that is better left unattempted. Most who see the show are simply awed by the spectacle of the production. Grandiose set pieces and outlandish costumes make for an appealing visual experience. The large number of cast members, also, makes chorus segments an intense display of daring choreography and dazzling physical feats. However, some supporting roles have been placed in less-than-capable hands. The missed notes and torpid movements of these actors distract from an otherwise fantastic evening of musical theater.

Read the items below. Cross off the incorrect responses. The choice remaining is correct.

1. According to the passage, the current revival of *Hair* on Broadway is:

   A. a spectacularly entertaining evening of musical theater.
   B. a perfect representation of the country's current political troubles.
   C. mostly enjoyable but with a few distractions.
   D. a reminder of the old values to which the country should return.

2. The critic finds fault with some of the weaker performances because:

   F. Broadway actors always deliver exceptional performances.
   G. the performers miss notes and execute choreography poorly.
   H. the actors' dancing makes the audience dizzy.
   J. they miss the essential political lesson in the script.

1. According to the passage, the current revival of *Hair* on Broadway is:

   A. a spectacularly entertaining evening of musical theater.

This choice is incorrect and is an example of an extreme. The words *spectacularly entertaining* are exaggerated, and they actually contradict the overall tempered opinion the reviewer gives of the show.

   B. a perfect representation of the country's current political troubles.

This is another example of an extreme. The word *perfect* is like the simplistic words *always* and *never*, which can tip you off that a broad (and probably inaccurate) generalization is being made.

   C. mostly enjoyable but with a few distractions.

You could have arrived at this answer through the process of elimination, but it is also the only choice that matches the actual opinion in the passage.

   D. a reminder of the old values to which the country should return.

This sounds so nice and so enticing. The image may be appealing, but there is no basis for the statement in the passage. Resist the temptation to choose this type of answer on the actual ACT.

2. The critic finds fault with some of the weaker performances because:

   F. Broadway actors always deliver exceptional performances.

There's that word: *always*. That almost guarantees that the choice is an extreme. Additionally, while Broadway actors are probably very talented, this does not necessarily mean they give performances deserving of the description *exceptional*.

   G. the performers miss notes and execute choreography poorly.

This is the only choice that is accurately supported by the information in the passage.

H. the actors' dancing makes the audience dizzy.

Incorrect. The conclusion drawn here is hasty and extreme. A look back at the passage shows you that the word *dizzying* is actually used positively, to describe the actors' physical feats.

J. they miss the essential political lesson in the script.

This enticing statement is appealing, almost irresistible, and incorrect. There is nothing in the passage to confirm this statement. While an "essential political lesson" would be admirable, the author clearly states that it is probably not to be found in this musical set 50 years in the past.

Practice

There are four paragraphs in the following exercise: one prose fiction, one social science, one humanities, and one natural science. There are two ACT-Type items for each paragraph. These items will help you practice eliminating the different types of incorrect answer choices.

Read each paragraph in turn and read the items for each paragraph. Then find the correct answers by crossing off the incorrect answer choices for each item. Write Weasel, Shift, Enticer, Extreme, or Correct beside each answer choice.

(*Answers on pages 225–226*)

PROSE FICTION

Cole Matthews knelt defiantly in the bow of the aluminum skiff as he faced forward into a cold September wind. Worn steel handcuffs bit at his wrists each time the small craft slapped into another wave. Overhead, a gray-matted sky hung like a bad omen. Cole strained at the cuffs even though he had agreed to wear them until he was freed on the island to begin his banishment. Agreeing to spend a whole year alone in Southeast Alaska had been his only way of avoiding a jail cell in Minneapolis.

1. What can you infer about Cole Matthews from this paragraph?

   A. He's a bad kid.
   B. He's a sailor.
   C. He will be reformed.
   D. He has committed a crime.

2. Why might the author have chosen to emphasize the color gray in this paragraph?

   F. It fits nicely with the weather.
   G. It is reminiscent of jail bars.
   H. It is the most depressing color he could use.
   J. It foreshadows Cole's coming freedom.

SOCIAL SCIENCE

The presence of Japanese and Chinese immigrants in America was an important factor in the ultimate development of martial arts in the United States. Two disciplines of fighting predominated: judo and karate (including kung fu). The first known exposure of an American to judo came in 1879, when former U.S. President Ulysses S. Grant was in Japan for a visit and was invited to witness a demonstration of judo by Jigoro Kano, who would eventually become an influential fighting teacher of the fighting art. Almost 25 years later, Yoshiaki Yamashita arrived from Japan to teach judo in America. In 1902, Yamashita traveled between New York and Chicago performing demonstrations, and was eventually invited to the White House to illustrate the strong points of judo. Yamashita was pitted in a contest against a Naval Academy wrestling coach; Yamashita won handily. Roosevelt not only decided to take judo lessons from Yamashita, but he arranged for Yamashita to teach judo at the Naval Academy.

1. According to the passage, which contributed MOST to the development of martial arts in the United States?

A. President Roosevelt
B. Japanese and Chinese immigrants
C. the Naval Academy
D. Yoshiaki Yamashita

2. According to the passage, when were Americans introduced to judo?

F. When Jigoro Kano came to the U.S.
G. In 1902
H. It was always a part of U.S. history.
J. In the nineteenth century

HUMANITIES

Like popcorn and Milk Duds, the biopic has long been a Hollywood staple, and often a big money-maker. You took a celebrity (Georg C. Scott, Peter O'Toole, Sissy Spacek) playing an even bigger celebrity (Patton, T. E. Lawrence, Loretta Lynn), the story wrote itself, and the Oscars swallowed the bait. But in the last five years, the biopic has begun to feel as dusty and outdated as the set of *Encyclopedia Britannicas* in your parents' attic. There has been a handful of hits, usually involving musicians—*Ray, Walk the Line*—but that's probably because the music can rescue a mediocre script, and audiences will pay to see a nonsinging actor warble. For the most part, though, Hollywood has had trouble keeping the genre relevant in our YouTube-obsessed, attention-pressed times: even a best-picture nominee such as *Frost/Nixon* sank at the box office.

1. Based on the information in the article, a biopic is:

A. a movie about somebody's life.
B. a boring movie nobody wants to watch.
C. a surefire way for Hollywood to make money.
D. a movie about a musician.

2. What reason does the author give for the failure of biopics?

F. Nonsinging actors cannot carry a tune.
G. YouTube is more interesting to watch.
H. People may not see their relevance.
J. Only best-picture nominees do well.

NATURAL SCIENCE

Glass bends in response to any force that is exerted on any one of its surfaces; when the limit of its elasticity is reached, the glass fractures. Frequently, fractured window glass reveals information about the force and direction of an impact; such knowledge may be useful for reconstructing events at a crime-scene investigation. The penetration of ordinary window glass by a projectile, whether a bullet or a stone, produces a familiar fracture pattern in which cracks both radiate outward and encircle the hole. The radiating lines are appropriately known as radial fractures, and the circular lines are termed concentric fractures.

1. According to the passage, what causes glass to fracture?

A. Force bends a surface in glass.
B. The limit of glass's elasticity is reached.
C. A pattern radiates outward from a hole.
D. A specific projectile causes a specific pattern.

2. Fractured glass can provide details about:

F. radial and circular lines.
G. the cause, or motive, behind a crime.
H. the penetration of a projectile.
J. the force and direction of an impact.

Steps for Taking the ACT Reading Test

The first step when you're confronted with the Reading ACT is to decide in what order you will read the passages. The order of passages on the ACT Reading Test is always the same:

Passage I—Prose Fiction

Passage II—Social Science

Passage III—Humanities

Passage IV—Natural Science

However, you don't have to work on the passages in that order. Flip through the test booklet and just glance at each passage. This is also a good way to preview the material.

The general wisdom is to *read the easier passages first.* You may decide the order in advance, or you may base your decision on the apparent difficulty of the passages, but *decide the order quickly.*

Write 1, 2, 3, and 4 next to the passage numbers on the test to show the order of difficulty. Write the numbers big and circle them. Complete the passages in that order. Just remember to match the passage with the correct section on the answer sheet.

Four Steps for Choosing the Correct Answer Choice

Read the passages and write the main idea for each paragraph. Then follow these steps to respond to the items. You have already reviewed these steps. Now you'll practice using all of them.

Step 1. Read the item statement or question.

Each item begins with an item statement or a question. Read it carefully to be sure you know exactly what the question is asking.

Step 2. Go to the part of the passage most likely to contain the answer.

The item specifically mentions the part of the passage about 25 percent of the time. The item may identify a particular paragraph by number, or the item may refer to particular lines in the passage. In these cases, you know exactly where to look for the answer.

Step 3. Read the answer choices, eliminating incorrect choices.

You know how to do this. Cross off the answer choices you're sure are incorrect. This is an important step for finding the correct choice. It's usually easier to spot incorrect choices than to spot correct choices. Your chances of choosing the correct answer increase significantly with each incorrect choice you eliminate.

Step 4. Choose the correct answer from the remaining choices and check the passage to make sure it's correct.

Look at the answer choices that are not crossed off. Choose the correct answer from among the remaining choices. If you are not sure which of the remaining answers is correct, guess. Do not leave any questions on the answer sheet blank.

Practice ACT Passage

Passages on the ACT look something like the one on the following page. Each passage begins with its number. The circled 1 at the top of our passage indicates that we have "decided" to read this passage first.

Next comes the type of passage. The social science passage is the second passage on the ACT Reading Test. Then comes the source of the passage and, on some forms of the test, one sentence telling what the passage is about. This introductory information can help prepare you for the material you're about to read.

The passage and items on the actual ACT are set in two columns. Lines in the passage are numbered by fives. Immediately after the passage are 10 questions. The items for the passage on the next page are numbered 21 to 30 since it is the second passage on the test and not the first. This passage shows you most of the item types you will find on the actual reading test.

Read each paragraph and write the main idea next to it. This has been done for you in the example passage. Then use the four-step approach to respond to each item. The entire process for reading the passage and answering the questions is discussed immediately following the questions.

PASSAGE II

SOCIAL SCIENCE: This passage is adapted from *Psychology* by Carl R. Green and William R. Sanford.

Id vs. superego

Sometimes the competing demands of the id and superego trap the hardworking ego into a no-win position. Imagine you've just backed Dad's car into a neighbor's expensive new car. The id tells you to just leave, while the superego tells you it would be wrong to run away.

Defense mechanisms

5   Both drives are too strong to be ignored. Caught in such a bind, the ego often chooses a response that disguises or compromises the id's socially unacceptable desires. In this case, the ego might choose to stay with the damaged car, thus obeying the law. To reduce the anxiety level, the ego may also choose to distort reality by rationalizing the accident by "saying" that it was a choice between hitting the car or hitting a small child
10   who ran out behind the car. Freud made one of his most enduring contributions to psychology when he identified a number of these ego-protecting behaviors. Known as *defense mechanisms*, their use is thought to be largely unconscious. Even though you may in time become expert at spotting their use by others, you're unlikely to be aware of the degree to which you depend on one or more of the following defense mecha-
15   nisms.

Repression

Repression protects you from disturbing memories, forbidden desires, or painful feelings by burying such material in the unconscious. Repressed feelings can remain "alive," however, capable of influencing behavior without the person's awareness. For example, say that a girl named Rachel was attacked by a large watchdog when she was
20   seven, but she escaped serious injury. Part of Rachel wants to like dogs, but whenever she gets close to one, the old repressed fear takes over.

Repression and illness

Similarly, repressed material can affect normal physical drives such as hunger or sex. Doctors also know that repression can lead to physical ailments. Anna O., one of Freud's earliest patients, was an extreme example of someone who experienced a *psy-*
25   *chosomatic illness.* Even today, some medical experts estimate that up to 40 percent of the patients a physician sees each day may be suffering from illnesses with origins that are psychological, not physical.

Repression and Recovery

Since you can't "remember" what you have repressed, it sometimes takes a lengthy period of therapy before the hidden material can be uncovered, and when it is
30   unearthed, you must still accept and deal with what you've repressed. In Rachel's case, that would not be too difficult; her fear of dogs gives an obvious clue where to look. But repression also acts to conceal drives and feelings that people cannot admit

having—even to themselves. In such cases, the patient often vigorously resists any attempt to open up the repressed material.

Displacement

35 When you can't focus your feelings on the person or thing that caused them, you often strike out at a less threatening person or object. Freud called this *displacement*. Usually we displace anger, often on weaker people, animals, or inanimate objects. But people sometimes displace nervousness or fear by chewing gum or picking at their finger-nails. Some psychologists have described prejudice as displaced aggression, as when
40 an unemployed worker blames all of his problems on a minority group.

Sublimation

Sublimation is a defense mechanism that turns powerful, frustrated drives into socially useful behavior. Freud believed that civilization could not exist without sublimation, for it allows people to contribute to society while also achieving their own inner peace. In this way, a rock-throwing youngster in trouble with the law might find
45 release from his inner tension on the baseball field. Or a woman who has just ended a love affair might feel better if she puts all her energies into creating beautiful ceramic figures. Sublimation does not always absorb all the energy created by frustration, however. The aggressive rock thrower might find success in baseball—but still often lose his temper when an umpire's decision goes against him.

21. Psychological defense mechanisms can be thought of as:

   A. reflecting reality.
   B. mostly unconscious.
   C. psychosomatic illness.
   D. protecting the id.

22. Which phrase BEST describes the defense mechanism of repression?

   F. Affects a person's awareness
   G. Responsible for up to 40 percent of visits to physicians
   H. Makes it impossible to remember something
   J. Might lead to overeating

23. According to the passage, repressed feelings result from:

   A. attacks by animals.
   B. a need for protection.
   C. psychosomatic illnesses.
   D. inability to open up.

24. The passage notes an inconsistency about a defense mechanism in that, while the defense mechanism may lead to suffering and illness,

   F. it may enable a person to achieve personal satisfaction.
   G. it may lead to the development of psychosomatic illnesses.

   H. its cause often can't be remembered.
   J. it may have the effect of distorting reality.

25. Which BEST expresses the main idea of paragraph 5 (lines 28–34)?

   A. The fear of dogs is a common form of repressed memory.
   B. Repression protects a person from feelings and drives that he or she cannot accept.
   C. Repression is a particularly difficult defense mechanism to deal with.
   D. A person is unlikely to be aware of how much he or she depends on a defense mechanism.

26. By focusing on the defense mechanism of displacement, this passage best illustrates how:

   F. outcomes of defense mechanisms are reflected in society.
   G. defense mechanisms usually single out weaker individuals.
   H. those employing a defense mechanism are nervous or fearful.
   J. defense mechanisms can be a force for good.

27. Based on the passage, all of the following could be examples of the outcome of a defense mechanism EXCEPT:

   A. a player arguing during a baseball game with a referee's decision that went against him.

B. a child with much displaced anger who finds an outlet for that anger by playing on a soccer team.

C. a person developing an illness from repressed thoughts and feelings.

D. a child being unexpectedly attacked by a watchdog or some other animal when he or she is very young.

28. Repressed thoughts or feelings might result in which of the following symptoms?

     I. Illness without a physical cause
    II. Nervous tics
   III. Fear

F. II only
G. I and III only
H. II and III only
J. I, II, and III

29. As used in the second paragraph in line 12, the word *unconscious* means:

A. knocked out or asleep.
B. in a hypnotic trance.

C. without thought.
D. without awareness.

30. You can infer from the passage that Freud's investigations of psychology led him to believe which of the following?

F. Repression can be the most deadly defense mechanism because it is the hardest to uncover and accept.

G. Everything about a person can be explained by which defense mechanisms he or she uses and the behaviors resulting from the use of these mechanisms.

H. His work with defense mechanisms has rid many people of suffering and has enabled them to live happier, more creative lives.

J. Being able to describe defense mechanisms in concrete terms makes it possible for people to better understand these mechanisms.

Practice Item Responses Explained

Follow this review of the steps for responding to the items. The first step (to read the passage and write the topic next to each paragraph) is already done. The topic for each paragraph is given below, along with a brief explanation of how the topic was arrived at.

Paragraph	Topic	Explanation
1	*Id. vs. superego*	The first sentence contains the words *competing demands of the id and superego.*
2	*Defense mechanisms*	The italicized words and the last sentence are the best clues to this topic.
3	*Repression*	The first word in the paragraph gives the topic.
4	*Repression and illness*	The last sentence gives the best clue to this topic.
5	*Repression and recovery*	The first and last sentences talk about what is required to recover from repression. You may have a better topic.
6	*Displacement*	The italicized word clearly identifies this.
7	*Sublimation*	The italicized word clearly identifies this.

Use the Four Steps to Find the Correct Answer Choice

The following analysis shows how to use the four steps to find the correct answer choice for each item. Refer to the passage on pages 216–217 as you read along.

Item 21

This is a statement to complete. The answer is going to be an acceptable definition or description of defense mechanisms.

Step 1. Read the item statement or question.

21. Psychological defense mechanisms can be thought of as:

Step 2. Go to the part of the passage most likely to contain the answer.

The item is about psychological defense mechanisms. That's the topic of paragraph 2. Go there.

Not correct. The paragraph implies these mechanisms are a defense against reality.

Maybe

Step 3. Read the answer choices, eliminating incorrect choices.

A. reflecting reality.
B. mostly unconscious.
C. psychosomatic illness.
D. protecting the id.

Not correct. The passage says that defense mechanisms can cause psychosomatic illnesses—not that they are psychosomatic illnesses. This choice is a weasel.

Maybe

Step 4. Choose the correct answer from the remaining choices and check the passage to make sure it's correct.

Choices B and D remain. Go back to the second paragraph to find the answer. The paragraph says that defense mechanisms are "largely unconscious." Choice B restates this with the words *mostly unconscious*. The paragraph states that the ego "chooses a response that disguises or compromises the id's socially unacceptable desires," which is not the same as protecting the id.

B is the correct choice.

Item 22

The correct answer will describe repression.

Step 1. Read the item statement or question.

22. Which phrase BEST describes the defense mechanism of repression?

Step 2. Go to the part of the passage most likely to contain the answer.

The third paragraph is about repression and the fourth and fifth paragraphs are related to repression. Go there.

Maybe

Step 3. Read the answer choices, eliminating incorrect choices.

F. Affects a person's awareness

G. Responsible for up to 40 percent of visits to physicians

H. Makes it impossible to remember something

J. Might lead to overeating

Not correct. This is the correct answer to a different question—a shift. The fourth paragraph says that up to 40 percent of patient visits are caused by psychological problems in general, not by repression.

Not correct. The word *impossible* makes this answer incorrect. The passage says that repressed material can be remembered, but that it can be difficult.

Step 4. Choose the correct answer from the remaining choices and check the passage to make sure it's correct.

Choices F and J remain. Go back to the third paragraph. The paragraph says repression can influence behavior without a person being aware. Choice J, that repression might lead to overeating, may be true, but there is no specific support for it in the passage.

F is the correct choice.

Maybe

Item 23

1 **23.** According to the passage, repressed feelings result from:

2 The answer will be in paragraph 3, 4, or 5.

3 **A.** attacks by animals.

B. a need for protection.

C. psychosomatic illnesses.

D. inability to open up.

4 The only choice remaining is B, and this choice is confirmed in paragraph 3, when it says that "Repression protects you from . . ."

B is the correct choice.

The correct choice will give the cause of repressed feelings.

Not correct. The passage cites one example where an animal attack was repressed. However, it does not cite this as a cause of repressed feelings.

Maybe

Not correct. The passage indicates that repression may cause psychosomatic illness, not the other way around.

Not correct. Inability to open up is given as a reason why repressed thoughts are difficult to deal with, not as a cause of the thoughts.

Item 24

24. The passage notes an inconsistency about a defense mechanism in that, while the defense mechanism may lead to suffering and illness,

2 Paragraphs 4 and 5 are about repression and illness and recovery. This item asks about defense mechanisms, so we are probably going to look elsewhere in the passage as well.

3
F. it may enable a person to achieve personal satisfaction.
G. it may lead to the development of psychosomatic illnesses.
H. its cause often can't be remembered.
J. it may have the effect of distorting reality.

4 Three choices were eliminated without knowing if they were correct or incorrect, because they did not fit the "good" category. A look back at the passage confirms that sublimation, the defense mechanism identified in the last paragraph, can turn "powerful, frustrated drives into socially useful behavior."

F is the correct choice.

The correct choice will name something about defense mechanisms that is inconsistent with suffering and illness. In other words, it will name something "positive" or "good."

Maybe. This choice fits into the "good" category.

Not correct. This definitely is not "good."

Not correct. Not remembering a cause may be "good" or it may be "bad."

Not correct. This definitely is not "good."

Item 25

25. Which BEST expresses the main idea of paragraph 5 (lines 28–34)?

2 The item tells you to look at paragraph 5, lines 28–34.

3
A. The fear of dogs is a common form of repressed memory.
B. Repression protects a person from feelings and drives that he or she cannot accept.
C. Repression is a particularly difficult defense mechanism to deal with.
D. A person is unlikely to be aware of how much he or she depends on a defense mechanism.

4 Three answer choices remain. The correct choice will be related to the topic of this paragraph, *Repression and recovery*. Choice B is true but incorrect. It is not related to the topic of recovery. Perhaps we could have eliminated this choice earlier, but it had a ring of truth to it, and we needed to go back to the paragraph to be sure. Choice C is true, and it is related to the topic and seems to convey the main thought in the paragraph. Choice D is true, and it explains one reason why recovery from repression is so difficult. However, it does not convey the full meaning of the paragraph.

C is the correct choice.

This question asks directly for the main idea. The answer will best convey the meaning of the passage.

Not correct. The words *common form* make this choice incorrect. The question is not about common forms of repression; it is about the paragraph's main idea.

Maybe

Maybe

Maybe

Item 26

The passage gives several illustrations or examples of displacement. The correct answer will describe the theme found in one of its examples of displacement.

|1| **26.** By focusing on the defense mechanism of displacement, this passage best illustrates how:

|2| Displacement is the topic of the next-to-last paragraph. Go there.

|3| **F.** outcomes of defense mechanisms are reflected in society.

   G. defense mechanisms usually single out weaker individuals.

   H. those employing a defense mechanism are nervous or fearful.

   J. defense mechanisms can be a force for good.

Maybe

Maybe

Maybe

|4| You couldn't just eliminate choices F, G, and H, because they reflect words and phrases found in the next-to-last paragraph. They have to be examined more carefully. Choice F seems correct. The example of prejudice in the passage is an example of how outcomes of defense mechanisms are reflected in society. Choice G incorrectly states the wording in the paragraph. Defense mechanisms don't single out weaker people. Rather, people tend to displace their anger on weaker individuals. Choice H also incorrectly states information from the passage, which says that people sometimes displace nervousness or fear.

Not correct. Overall, the information in this passage is not about defense mechanisms being a force for good.

F is the correct choice.

Item 27

The correct answer will NOT be an example of the outcome of a defense mechanism.

|1| **27.** Based on the passage, all of the following could be examples of the outcome of a defense mechanism EXCEPT:

|2| Just about the entire passage is involved. Focus on the examples of outcomes of the different defense mechanisms.

Not correct. This outcome of a defense mechanism is described in the last sentence of the paragraph on sublimation.

|3| **A.** a player arguing during a baseball game with a referee's decision that went against him.

   B. a child with much displaced anger who finds an outlet for that anger by playing on a soccer team.

Not correct. This outcome of a defense mechanism is described in the sublimation paragraph.

   C. a person developing an illness from repressed thoughts and feelings.

Not correct. This outcome is described in the paragraph on repression and illness.

   D. a child being unexpectedly attacked by a watchdog or some other animal when he or she is very young.

|4| D is the only choice remaining. This choice is a cause of repression, not an outcome.

Probably.

D is the correct choice.

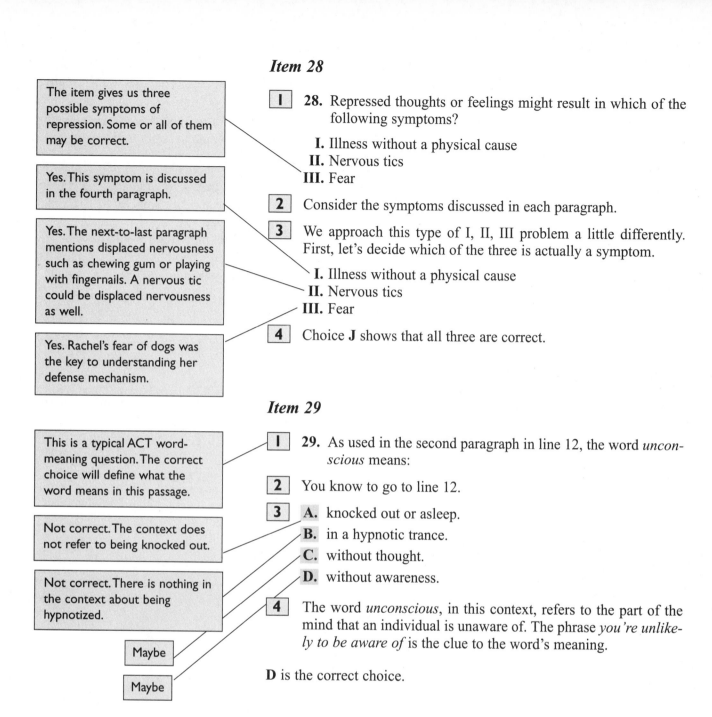

Item 28

The item gives us three possible symptoms of repression. Some or all of them may be correct.

1 28. Repressed thoughts or feelings might result in which of the following symptoms?

  I. Illness without a physical cause
 II. Nervous tics
III. Fear

Yes. This symptom is discussed in the fourth paragraph.

2 Consider the symptoms discussed in each paragraph.

3 We approach this type of I, II, III problem a little differently. First, let's decide which of the three is actually a symptom.

Yes. The next-to-last paragraph mentions displaced nervousness such as chewing gum or playing with fingernails. A nervous tic could be displaced nervousness as well.

  I. Illness without a physical cause
 II. Nervous tics
III. Fear

Yes. Rachel's fear of dogs was the key to understanding her defense mechanism.

4 Choice **J** shows that all three are correct.

Item 29

This is a typical ACT word-meaning question. The correct choice will define what the word means in this passage.

1 29. As used in the second paragraph in line 12, the word *unconscious* means:

2 You know to go to line 12.

3 **A.** knocked out or asleep.

Not correct. The context does not refer to being knocked out.

 B. in a hypnotic trance.

 C. without thought.

Not correct. There is nothing in the context about being hypnotized.

 D. without awareness.

Maybe

Maybe

4 The word *unconscious*, in this context, refers to the part of the mind that an individual is unaware of. The phrase *you're unlikely to be aware of* is the clue to the word's meaning.

D is the correct choice.

Item 30

The correct answer will be the most reasonable of the four inferences about what Freud believed. The inference must be based on the passage.

1 30. You can infer from the passage that Freud's investigations of psychology led him to believe which of the following?

2 The choices could be from anywhere in the passage.

3 **F.** Repression can be the most deadly defense mechanism because it is the hardest to uncover and accept.

Maybe

 G. Everything about a person can be explained by which defense mechanisms he or she uses and the behaviors resulting from the use of these mechanisms.

Not true. The word *everything* is a clue that this answer choice is too inclusive.

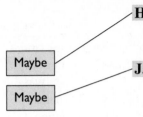

H. His work with defense mechanisms has rid many people of suffering and has enabled them to live happier, more creative lives.

J. Being able to describe defense mechanisms in concrete terms makes it possible for people to better understand these mechanisms.

4 Choice F is certainly true. More time is spent discussing repression than any of the other defense mechanisms. So this is a reasonable inference from the passage. Choice H is certainly true, but it is an enticer. It is not a belief that Freud would have developed from his investigations of psychology. Choice J may be true, but there is nothing is the passage to support this choice.

F is the correct choice.

ANSWERS

PROSE FICTION (page 213)

1. A. Extreme. We don't know anything about Cole Matthews, and just because he is on his way to a *banishment* means only that he's done something wrong, not that he's bad through and through. This choice oversimplifies Cole's character.

B. Weasel. This choice uses details in the passage—that Cole is on a boat—to try to trick you into picking it.

C. Enticer. It's nice to think that every time somebody does something wrong and then the person is punished, that the punishment will bring about a change of character. However, we don't know if that will happen for Cole.

D. This is the only reasonable choice.

2. F. Enticer. This choice sounds good, as if the passage would be consistent and coherent with a gray theme. However, the reason is not powerful enough—an author doesn't choose imagery just because it "fits nicely." He or she chooses imagery to convey a sense or mood.

G. You could arrive at this correct choice by eliminating the other choices. There are also clues in the passage, like *steel handcuffs* and *jail cell*, that support this choice.

H. Extreme. First, some might disagree that gray is the most depressing and say black is more morbid. Second, this choice is a hasty generalization, which quickly disqualifies it as the right answer.

J. Weasel. Cole is not actually going to be free where he is going. The passage clearly states that even though he'll get to take off the handcuffs at his destination, that destination is to serve as a punishment, a substitute for a prison term.

SOCIAL SCIENCE (pages 213–214)

1. A. Enticer. This choice pulls on Americans' sense of patriotism, and it makes the idea of training the Naval Academy in judo seem like something Roosevelt initiated, instead of something Roosevelt realized he should do after seeing a particularly powerful demonstration.

B. The first sentence of the passage directly supports this as the correct choice.

C. Enticer. Like choice A, this appeals to a sense of American patriotism.

D. Weasel. This choice twists the ideas in the passage; Yamashita was a leader and a teacher, but that does not necessarily mean that he was the primary influence that led to the growth of martial arts in the U.S.

2. F. Weasel. President Grant was introduced to judo when he saw Jigoro Kano in Japan. The passage does not say Kano came to the United States.

G. Correct. You could arrive at this answer just by eliminating the incorrect choices.

H. Extreme. The word *always* is a hint that this choice is incorrect. Nothing in the passage supports this.

J. Weasel. One American (President Grant) was exposed to judo in 1879, but Americans as a group had to wait until 1902, when Yoshiaki Yamashita traveled around the United States.

HUMANITIES (page 214)

1. A. The clue to this correct answer is the prefix *bio-*, which means "life." A biopic is a movie (*pic*) about someone's life.

B. Extreme. Some people might find some biopics boring, but this statement generalizes that feeling to everyone. The absolute word *nobody* is your clue that this is a wrong choice.

C. Enticer. It would be nice to think that there were a foolproof way to make money on a movie, but that isn't realistic.

D. Weasel. The passage does state that some biopics, mostly the ones about musicians, are still popular. However, this choice does not address what a biopic really is.

2. F. Weasel. This choice uses the author's words about nonsinging actors performing in some biopics, but the passage does not say that these actors cannot sing well.

G. Shift. This might be an answer to a question about why people today have a hard time paying attention to long movies, but it does not answer why biopics are faltering.

H. The passage states this directly: "Hollywood has had trouble keeping the genre relevant."

J. Extreme. Not only does this choice oversimplify the argument for which biopics will succeed, it also directly contradicts information about *Frost/Nixon* in the passage.

NATURAL SCIENCE (page 214)

1. **A.** Extreme. Force can bend a glass surface, but it does not cause it to break until the force bends the surface too far. This choice overstates the consequences of simply bending a glass surface.
   B. You could reach this correct choice by a process of elimination, or you could refer to the first sentence in the passage.
   C. Weasel. In this choice, words from the passage are directly used, but they have to do with fracture patterns, not with why glass fractures.
   D. Shift. This would be an answer about projectiles.

2. **F.** Weasel. The choice turns around the language about radial and circular lines, which then tell about a projectile.
   G. Extreme. This choice overstates the scope of the passage. The passage does not get to the motive behind the crime but talks only about what might be immediately apparent at a crime scene.
   H. Weasel. Here it sounds like the projectile is being penetrated, when in fact it is the projectile that penetrates the glass.
   J. This is the only choice that is supported by the information in the passage.

Diagnostic Reading ACT

Take this Diagnostic ACT after you have completed the Reading review. This Diagnostic ACT is just like a real ACT, and it is the first of four Reading ACTs in this book. This Diagnostic ACT is different from the Reading ACT Practice Tests because it is specially designed to help you decide which parts of the Reading section to review in more detail.

Take the Diagnostic Reading ACT under simulated test conditions. Allow 35 minutes to answer the 40 test questions. Use the Answer Sheet on the following page to mark your answers. Use a pencil to mark the answer sheet, and answer the questions in the Test 3 (Reading) section.

Review the answer explanations on pages 239–241. After you have marked the test, complete the Diagnostic Checklist on page 238. The checklist directs you to the reading skills you should review in more detail.

The test scoring chart on page 7 shows you how to convert the number of correct answers to an ACT scale score. The checklist on page 238 shows you how to find the Social Studies/Sciences and Arts/Literature subscores.

DO NOT leave any answers blank. There is no penalty for guessing on the ACT. Remember that the test is yours. You may mark up, write on, or draw on the test.

When you are ready, note the time and turn to the Diagnostic Reading ACT. Stop in exactly 35 minutes.

ANSWER SHEET

The ACT answer sheet looks something like this. Use a No. 2 pencil to completely fill the circle corresponding to the correct answer. If you erase, erase completely; incomplete erasures may be read as answers.

TEST 1—English

1 Ⓐ Ⓑ Ⓒ Ⓓ	11 Ⓐ Ⓑ Ⓒ Ⓓ	21 Ⓐ Ⓑ Ⓒ Ⓓ	31 Ⓐ Ⓑ Ⓒ Ⓓ	41 Ⓐ Ⓑ Ⓒ Ⓓ	51 Ⓐ Ⓑ Ⓒ Ⓓ	61 Ⓐ Ⓑ Ⓒ Ⓓ	71 Ⓐ Ⓑ Ⓒ Ⓓ
2 Ⓕ Ⓖ Ⓗ Ⓙ	12 Ⓕ Ⓖ Ⓗ Ⓙ	22 Ⓕ Ⓖ Ⓗ Ⓙ	32 Ⓕ Ⓖ Ⓗ Ⓙ	42 Ⓕ Ⓖ Ⓗ Ⓙ	52 Ⓕ Ⓖ Ⓗ Ⓙ	62 Ⓕ Ⓖ Ⓗ Ⓙ	72 Ⓕ Ⓖ Ⓗ Ⓙ
3 Ⓐ Ⓑ Ⓒ Ⓓ	13 Ⓐ Ⓑ Ⓒ Ⓓ	23 Ⓐ Ⓑ Ⓒ Ⓓ	33 Ⓐ Ⓑ Ⓒ Ⓓ	43 Ⓐ Ⓑ Ⓒ Ⓓ	53 Ⓐ Ⓑ Ⓒ Ⓓ	63 Ⓐ Ⓑ Ⓒ Ⓓ	73 Ⓐ Ⓑ Ⓒ Ⓓ
4 Ⓕ Ⓖ Ⓗ Ⓙ	14 Ⓕ Ⓖ Ⓗ Ⓙ	24 Ⓕ Ⓖ Ⓗ Ⓙ	34 Ⓕ Ⓖ Ⓗ Ⓙ	44 Ⓕ Ⓖ Ⓗ Ⓙ	54 Ⓕ Ⓖ Ⓗ Ⓙ	64 Ⓕ Ⓖ Ⓗ Ⓙ	74 Ⓕ Ⓖ Ⓗ Ⓙ
5 Ⓐ Ⓑ Ⓒ Ⓓ	15 Ⓐ Ⓑ Ⓒ Ⓓ	25 Ⓐ Ⓑ Ⓒ Ⓓ	35 Ⓐ Ⓑ Ⓒ Ⓓ	45 Ⓐ Ⓑ Ⓒ Ⓓ	55 Ⓐ Ⓑ Ⓒ Ⓓ	65 Ⓐ Ⓑ Ⓒ Ⓓ	75 Ⓐ Ⓑ Ⓒ Ⓓ
6 Ⓕ Ⓖ Ⓗ Ⓙ	16 Ⓕ Ⓖ Ⓗ Ⓙ	26 Ⓕ Ⓖ Ⓗ Ⓙ	36 Ⓕ Ⓖ Ⓗ Ⓙ	46 Ⓕ Ⓖ Ⓗ Ⓙ	56 Ⓕ Ⓖ Ⓗ Ⓙ	66 Ⓕ Ⓖ Ⓗ Ⓙ	
7 Ⓐ Ⓑ Ⓒ Ⓓ	17 Ⓐ Ⓑ Ⓒ Ⓓ	27 Ⓐ Ⓑ Ⓒ Ⓓ	37 Ⓐ Ⓑ Ⓒ Ⓓ	47 Ⓐ Ⓑ Ⓒ Ⓓ	57 Ⓐ Ⓑ Ⓒ Ⓓ	67 Ⓐ Ⓑ Ⓒ Ⓓ	
8 Ⓕ Ⓖ Ⓗ Ⓙ	18 Ⓕ Ⓖ Ⓗ Ⓙ	28 Ⓕ Ⓖ Ⓗ Ⓙ	38 Ⓕ Ⓖ Ⓗ Ⓙ	48 Ⓕ Ⓖ Ⓗ Ⓙ	58 Ⓕ Ⓖ Ⓗ Ⓙ	68 Ⓕ Ⓖ Ⓗ Ⓙ	
9 Ⓐ Ⓑ Ⓒ Ⓓ	19 Ⓐ Ⓑ Ⓒ Ⓓ	29 Ⓐ Ⓑ Ⓒ Ⓓ	39 Ⓐ Ⓑ Ⓒ Ⓓ	49 Ⓐ Ⓑ Ⓒ Ⓓ	59 Ⓐ Ⓑ Ⓒ Ⓓ	69 Ⓐ Ⓑ Ⓒ Ⓓ	
10 Ⓕ Ⓖ Ⓗ Ⓙ	20 Ⓕ Ⓖ Ⓗ Ⓙ	30 Ⓕ Ⓖ Ⓗ Ⓙ	40 Ⓕ Ⓖ Ⓗ Ⓙ	50 Ⓕ Ⓖ Ⓗ Ⓙ	60 Ⓕ Ⓖ Ⓗ Ⓙ	70 Ⓕ Ⓖ Ⓗ Ⓙ	

TEST 2—Mathematics

1 Ⓐ Ⓑ Ⓒ Ⓓ Ⓔ	9 Ⓐ Ⓑ Ⓒ Ⓓ Ⓔ	17 Ⓐ Ⓑ Ⓒ Ⓓ Ⓔ	25 Ⓐ Ⓑ Ⓒ Ⓓ Ⓔ	33 Ⓐ Ⓑ Ⓒ Ⓓ Ⓔ	41 Ⓐ Ⓑ Ⓒ Ⓓ Ⓔ	49 Ⓐ Ⓑ Ⓒ Ⓓ Ⓔ	57 Ⓐ Ⓑ Ⓒ Ⓓ Ⓔ
2 Ⓕ Ⓖ Ⓗ Ⓙ Ⓚ	10 Ⓕ Ⓖ Ⓗ Ⓙ Ⓚ	18 Ⓕ Ⓖ Ⓗ Ⓙ Ⓚ	26 Ⓕ Ⓖ Ⓗ Ⓙ Ⓚ	34 Ⓕ Ⓖ Ⓗ Ⓙ Ⓚ	42 Ⓕ Ⓖ Ⓗ Ⓙ Ⓚ	50 Ⓕ Ⓖ Ⓗ Ⓙ Ⓚ	58 Ⓕ Ⓖ Ⓗ Ⓙ Ⓚ
3 Ⓐ Ⓑ Ⓒ Ⓓ Ⓔ	11 Ⓐ Ⓑ Ⓒ Ⓓ Ⓔ	19 Ⓐ Ⓑ Ⓒ Ⓓ Ⓔ	27 Ⓐ Ⓑ Ⓒ Ⓓ Ⓔ	35 Ⓐ Ⓑ Ⓒ Ⓓ Ⓔ	43 Ⓐ Ⓑ Ⓒ Ⓓ Ⓔ	51 Ⓐ Ⓑ Ⓒ Ⓓ Ⓔ	59 Ⓐ Ⓑ Ⓒ Ⓓ Ⓔ
4 Ⓕ Ⓖ Ⓗ Ⓙ Ⓚ	12 Ⓕ Ⓖ Ⓗ Ⓙ Ⓚ	20 Ⓕ Ⓖ Ⓗ Ⓙ Ⓚ	28 Ⓕ Ⓖ Ⓗ Ⓙ Ⓚ	36 Ⓕ Ⓖ Ⓗ Ⓙ Ⓚ	44 Ⓕ Ⓖ Ⓗ Ⓙ Ⓚ	52 Ⓕ Ⓖ Ⓗ Ⓙ Ⓚ	60 Ⓕ Ⓖ Ⓗ Ⓙ Ⓚ
5 Ⓐ Ⓑ Ⓒ Ⓓ Ⓔ	13 Ⓐ Ⓑ Ⓒ Ⓓ Ⓔ	21 Ⓐ Ⓑ Ⓒ Ⓓ Ⓔ	29 Ⓐ Ⓑ Ⓒ Ⓓ Ⓔ	37 Ⓐ Ⓑ Ⓒ Ⓓ Ⓔ	45 Ⓐ Ⓑ Ⓒ Ⓓ Ⓔ	53 Ⓐ Ⓑ Ⓒ Ⓓ Ⓔ	
6 Ⓕ Ⓖ Ⓗ Ⓙ Ⓚ	14 Ⓕ Ⓖ Ⓗ Ⓙ Ⓚ	22 Ⓕ Ⓖ Ⓗ Ⓙ Ⓚ	30 Ⓕ Ⓖ Ⓗ Ⓙ Ⓚ	38 Ⓕ Ⓖ Ⓗ Ⓙ Ⓚ	46 Ⓕ Ⓖ Ⓗ Ⓙ Ⓚ	54 Ⓕ Ⓖ Ⓗ Ⓙ Ⓚ	
7 Ⓐ Ⓑ Ⓒ Ⓓ Ⓔ	15 Ⓐ Ⓑ Ⓒ Ⓓ Ⓔ	23 Ⓐ Ⓑ Ⓒ Ⓓ Ⓔ	31 Ⓐ Ⓑ Ⓒ Ⓓ Ⓔ	39 Ⓐ Ⓑ Ⓒ Ⓓ Ⓔ	47 Ⓐ Ⓑ Ⓒ Ⓓ Ⓔ	55 Ⓐ Ⓑ Ⓒ Ⓓ Ⓔ	
8 Ⓕ Ⓖ Ⓗ Ⓙ Ⓚ	16 Ⓕ Ⓖ Ⓗ Ⓙ Ⓚ	24 Ⓕ Ⓖ Ⓗ Ⓙ Ⓚ	32 Ⓕ Ⓖ Ⓗ Ⓙ Ⓚ	40 Ⓕ Ⓖ Ⓗ Ⓙ Ⓚ	48 Ⓕ Ⓖ Ⓗ Ⓙ Ⓚ	56 Ⓕ Ⓖ Ⓗ Ⓙ Ⓚ	

TEST 3—Reading

1 Ⓐ Ⓑ Ⓒ Ⓓ	6 Ⓕ Ⓖ Ⓗ Ⓙ	11 Ⓐ Ⓑ Ⓒ Ⓓ	16 Ⓕ Ⓖ Ⓗ Ⓙ	21 Ⓐ Ⓑ Ⓒ Ⓓ	26 Ⓕ Ⓖ Ⓗ Ⓙ	31 Ⓐ Ⓑ Ⓒ Ⓓ	36 Ⓕ Ⓖ Ⓗ Ⓙ
2 Ⓕ Ⓖ Ⓗ Ⓙ	7 Ⓐ Ⓑ Ⓒ Ⓓ	12 Ⓕ Ⓖ Ⓗ Ⓙ	17 Ⓐ Ⓑ Ⓒ Ⓓ	22 Ⓕ Ⓖ Ⓗ Ⓙ	27 Ⓐ Ⓑ Ⓒ Ⓓ	32 Ⓕ Ⓖ Ⓗ Ⓙ	37 Ⓐ Ⓑ Ⓒ Ⓓ
3 Ⓐ Ⓑ Ⓒ Ⓓ	8 Ⓕ Ⓖ Ⓗ Ⓙ	13 Ⓐ Ⓑ Ⓒ Ⓓ	18 Ⓕ Ⓖ Ⓗ Ⓙ	23 Ⓐ Ⓑ Ⓒ Ⓓ	28 Ⓕ Ⓖ Ⓗ Ⓙ	33 Ⓐ Ⓑ Ⓒ Ⓓ	38 Ⓕ Ⓖ Ⓗ Ⓙ
4 Ⓕ Ⓖ Ⓗ Ⓙ	9 Ⓐ Ⓑ Ⓒ Ⓓ	14 Ⓕ Ⓖ Ⓗ Ⓙ	19 Ⓐ Ⓑ Ⓒ Ⓓ	24 Ⓕ Ⓖ Ⓗ Ⓙ	29 Ⓐ Ⓑ Ⓒ Ⓓ	34 Ⓕ Ⓖ Ⓗ Ⓙ	39 Ⓐ Ⓑ Ⓒ Ⓓ
5 Ⓐ Ⓑ Ⓒ Ⓓ	10 Ⓕ Ⓖ Ⓗ Ⓙ	15 Ⓐ Ⓑ Ⓒ Ⓓ	20 Ⓕ Ⓖ Ⓗ Ⓙ	25 Ⓐ Ⓑ Ⓒ Ⓓ	30 Ⓕ Ⓖ Ⓗ Ⓙ	35 Ⓐ Ⓑ Ⓒ Ⓓ	40 Ⓕ Ⓖ Ⓗ Ⓙ

TEST 4—Science Reasoning

1 Ⓐ Ⓑ Ⓒ Ⓓ	6 Ⓕ Ⓖ Ⓗ Ⓙ	11 Ⓐ Ⓑ Ⓒ Ⓓ	16 Ⓕ Ⓖ Ⓗ Ⓙ	21 Ⓐ Ⓑ Ⓒ Ⓓ	26 Ⓕ Ⓖ Ⓗ Ⓙ	31 Ⓐ Ⓑ Ⓒ Ⓓ	36 Ⓕ Ⓖ Ⓗ Ⓙ
2 Ⓕ Ⓖ Ⓗ Ⓙ	7 Ⓐ Ⓑ Ⓒ Ⓓ	12 Ⓕ Ⓖ Ⓗ Ⓙ	17 Ⓐ Ⓑ Ⓒ Ⓓ	22 Ⓕ Ⓖ Ⓗ Ⓙ	27 Ⓐ Ⓑ Ⓒ Ⓓ	32 Ⓕ Ⓖ Ⓗ Ⓙ	37 Ⓐ Ⓑ Ⓒ Ⓓ
3 Ⓐ Ⓑ Ⓒ Ⓓ	8 Ⓕ Ⓖ Ⓗ Ⓙ	13 Ⓐ Ⓑ Ⓒ Ⓓ	18 Ⓕ Ⓖ Ⓗ Ⓙ	23 Ⓐ Ⓑ Ⓒ Ⓓ	28 Ⓕ Ⓖ Ⓗ Ⓙ	33 Ⓐ Ⓑ Ⓒ Ⓓ	38 Ⓕ Ⓖ Ⓗ Ⓙ
4 Ⓕ Ⓖ Ⓗ Ⓙ	9 Ⓐ Ⓑ Ⓒ Ⓓ	14 Ⓕ Ⓖ Ⓗ Ⓙ	19 Ⓐ Ⓑ Ⓒ Ⓓ	24 Ⓕ Ⓖ Ⓗ Ⓙ	29 Ⓐ Ⓑ Ⓒ Ⓓ	34 Ⓕ Ⓖ Ⓗ Ⓙ	39 Ⓐ Ⓑ Ⓒ Ⓓ
5 Ⓐ Ⓑ Ⓒ Ⓓ	10 Ⓕ Ⓖ Ⓗ Ⓙ	15 Ⓐ Ⓑ Ⓒ Ⓓ	20 Ⓕ Ⓖ Ⓗ Ⓙ	25 Ⓐ Ⓑ Ⓒ Ⓓ	30 Ⓕ Ⓖ Ⓗ Ⓙ	35 Ⓐ Ⓑ Ⓒ Ⓓ	40 Ⓕ Ⓖ Ⓗ Ⓙ

Diagnostic Reading ACT

40 Questions—35 minutes

INSTRUCTIONS: There are four passages on this test with 10 items about each passage. Choose the best answer for each item based on the passage. Then fill in the appropriate circle on the answer sheet (page 238). Check pages 239–241 for answers and explanations.

PASSAGE I

PROSE FICTION: This passage is from Jack London's *The Call of the Wild.*

Buck did not read the newspapers, or he would have known that trouble was brewing, not alone for himself, but for every tidewater dog, strong of muscle and with warm, long
5 hair, from Puget Sound to San Diego. Because men, groping in the Arctic darkness, had found a yellow metal, and because steamship and transportation companies were booming the find, thousands of men
10 were rushing into the Northland. These men wanted dogs, and the dogs they wanted were heavy dogs, with strong muscles by which to toil, and furry coats to protect them from the frost.

15 Buck lived at a big house in the sun-kissed Santa Clara Valley. Judge Miller's place, it was called. It stood back from the road, half hidden among the trees, through which glimpses could be caught of the wide
20 cool veranda that ran around its four sides. The house was approached by graveled driveways which wound about through wide-spreading lawns and under the interlacing boughs of tall poplars. At the rear things were
25 on even a more spacious scale than at the front. There were great stables, where a dozen grooms and boys held forth, rows of vine-clad servants' cottages, an endless and orderly array of outhouses, long grape arbors, green
30 pastures, orchards, and berry patches. Then there was the pumping plant for the artesian well, and the big cement tank where Judge Miller's boys took their morning plunge and kept cool in the hot afternoon.

35 And over this great demesne Buck ruled. Here he was born, and here he had lived the four years of his life. It was true, there were other dogs. There could not but be other dogs on so vast a place, but they did not count.
40 They came and went, resided in the populous kennels, or lived obscurely in the recesses of the house after the fashion of Toots, the Japanese pug, or Ysabel, the Mexican hairless—strange creatures that rarely put nose
45 out of doors or set foot to ground. On the other hand, there were the fox terriers, a score of them at least, who yelped fearful promises at Toots and Ysabel looking out of the windows at them and protected by a legion of
50 housemaids armed with brooms and mops.

But Buck was neither housedog nor kennel dog. The whole realm was his. He plunged into the swimming tank or went hunting with the Judge's sons; he escorted
55 Mollie and Alice, the Judge's daughters, on long twilight or early morning rambles; on wintry nights he lay at the Judge's feet before the roaring library fire; he carried the Judge's grandsons on his back, or rolled them in the
60 grass, and guarded their footsteps through wild adventures down to the fountain in the stable yard, and even beyond, where the paddocks were, and the berry patches. Among the terriers he stalked imperiously, and Toots
65 and Ysabel he utterly ignored, for he was king—king over all creeping, crawling, flying things of Judge Miller's place, humans included.

His father, Elmo, a huge St. Bernard, had
70 been the Judge's inseparable companion and Buck did fair to follow in the way of his father. He was not so large—he weighed only

one hundred and forty pounds—for his mother, Shep, had been a Scotch shepherd dog. Nevertheless, one hundred and forty pounds, to which was added the dignity that comes of good living and universal respect, enabled him to carry himself in right royal fashion. During the four years since his puppyhood he had lived the life of a sated aristocrat; he had a fine pride in himself, was ever a trifle egotistical, as country gentlemen sometimes become because of their insular situation. But he had saved himself by not becoming a mere pampered housedog. Hunting and kindred outdoor delights had kept down the fat and hardened his muscles; and to him, as to the cold-tubbing races, the love of water had been a tonic and a health preserver.

And this was the manner of dog Buck was in the fall of 1897, when the Klondike strike dragged men from all the world into the frozen North. But Buck did not read the newspapers, and he did not know that Manuel, one of the gardener's helpers, was an undesirable acquaintance. Manuel had one besetting sin. He loved to play Chinese lottery. Also, in his gambling, he had one besetting weakness—faith in a system; and this made his damnation certain. For to play a system requires money, while the wages of a gardener's helper do not lap over the needs of a wife and numerous progeny.

The Judge was at a meeting of the Raisin Growers' Association, and the boys were busy organizing an athletic club, on the memorable night of Manuel's treachery. No one saw him and Buck go off through the orchard on what Buck imagined was merely a stroll. And with the exception of a solitary man, no one saw them arrive at the little flag station known as College Park. This man talked with Manuel, and money chinked between them.

1. What is the setting of the passage?

  A. Puget Sound
  B. the Arctic
  C. Northland
  D. Santa Clara Valley

2. According to the passage, men need dogs:

  F. for company on lonely evenings in the Arctic.
  G. for physical warmth and comfort.
  H. to assist them in their search for gold.
  J. to serve as watchdogs.

3. What is Judge Miller's relationship to Buck?

  A. Buck is the favorite dog on Judge Miller's estate.
  B. Buck is a sled dog for Judge Miller.
  C. Judge Miller prefers Toots and Ysabel.
  D. Judge Miller wants to sell Buck.

4. Which choice does NOT generally describe Judge Miller's place?

  F. Sunny and warm
  G. Luxurious and comfortable
  H. Woody and expansive
  J. Dangerous and threatening

5. What does it mean that Buck was "king over all" on Judge Miller's place?

  A. Buck had trained the other dogs to obey his rules.
  B. Buck had a regal demeanor and seemed to have control over life at Judge Miller's place.
  C. King was his real name; Buck was only a nickname.
  D. Buck was the father of the other dogs.

6. Toots and Ysabel are:

  F. Buck's sisters.
  G. other dogs at Judge Miller's place.
  H. Judge Miller's daughters.
  J. Buck's best friends.

7. Which word BEST describes Buck?

  A. Pampered
  B. Energetic
  C. Lonely
  D. Lazy

8. The author describes Buck's strength and size (lines 69–90) to:

  F. show that Buck deserved to be king.
  G. indicate that he is the type of dog for whom trouble was brewing.
  H. give the reader a mental picture of Buck.
  J. show that Buck is bigger than Ysabel and Toots.

9. The author discusses the Arctic in the first paragraph, then discusses Buck's life, then returns to the Arctic in lines 91–94 to:

A. show that Buck is happy and lucky.

B. contrast Buck's happy life with the difficult life he will have in the future.

C. demonstrate that Buck and Judge Miller have a special relationship.

D. point out that Manuel is a gambler.

10. The author states that "money chinked between" Manuel and the man at the park:

F. to indicate that Manuel is gambling there.

G. to show that Manuel is paying for services.

H. because the man is buying Buck from Manuel.

J. because the men are going to buy supplies.

PASSAGE II

SOCIAL SCIENCE: This passage is from *Current Issues in American Democracy* by Gerson Antell and Walter Harris.

Freedom of the Press

The founders of the United States did not invent the idea of freedom of the press. It is a right that earlier generations of Americans had fought for. In 1735, for example, a news-
5 paper printer named John Peter Zenger was arrested and put on trial for printing articles that criticized New York's royal governor. After Zenger had been in jail for nine months, he was acquitted. Zenger became a free man.
10 The jury decided that because the articles Zenger had printed about the governor were true, he could not be punished for printing them. The Zenger case became a landmark in the history of the press in the United States.

15 Freedom of the press was one of the major provisions of the First Amendment to the U.S. Constitution. This provision would soon be clarified by actual events, such as the passage of the Alien and Sedition Acts in
20 1798 and the protests that followed. The United States was involved in an undeclared war with France on the high seas in 1798. At the same time, a wave of French immigrants was arriving on America's shores. Worried
25 about their loyalty, Congress obliged President John Adams with the passage of three Alien Acts. They attempted to restrict further immigration. In attempting to restrict the pro-French press, the Sedition Act made
30 any speech or writing against the president or

Congress a crime punishable by fine or imprisonment. Twenty-five people (most of them newspaper editors) were arrested; most were convicted. Thomas Jefferson and other
35 Americans protested against the Alien and Sedition Acts. Jefferson made the acts one of the key issues in the election of 1800. When he became president in 1801, he pardoned all the editors and printers convicted under the
40 act. The First Amendment was reaffirmed.

Events in modern history have both furthered and hindered the principle of freedom-of-the-press. Wars place excessive stress on upholding it. During the Civil War, for exam-
45 ple, President Abraham Lincoln ordered the federal government to shut down newspapers that Union officials considered disloyal.

In World War I, the U.S. government censored some publications, citing violations of
50 the federal Espionage Act of 1917. Socialist party leader Charles Schenck had published pamphlets urging American men to resist the draft. The government convicted him of obstructing the war effort. Schenck appealed
55 his case all the way to the Supreme Court. While Schenck claimed that the Espionage Act violated freedom of the press, the Court ruled otherwise in 1919. It said that Schenck's actions created a "clear and present danger"
60 to the U.S. government and people.

During World War II, the press was censored by most participating countries. Each wanted to control information that might divide a country and give information to its
65 enemies. The U.S. Congress passed laws ban-

ning publications that might interfere with the war effort or harm national security. Reporters who roamed the battle zones found, however, that their dispatches were rarely
70 censored by the U.S. government. In most instances, the reporters sensibly refrained from including sensitive information about troop movements—information that would have helped the enemy. The principle of a free
75 press's behaving responsibly was clearly demonstrated before the eyes of the men and women who were fighting for freedom.

In a more recent U.S. military engagement, the press was prevented from accompa-
80 nying the troops. In 1983, when U.S. forces invaded the island of Grenada, reporters were not allowed to go along with the invading troops. Military leaders felt that the presence of reporters would endanger the secrecy of the
85 mission. During the Allied war against Iraq in 1991, some reporters were allowed to accompany the troops to Saudi Arabia. But the U.S. military censored the reporters' stories before they could be sent back to the United States.
90 The amount of freedom that the U.S. government allows is not constant. Freedom of the press is continually defined and redefined.

Even in peacetime, the courts have ruled that freedom of the press does not mean that
95 the press can publish anything, no matter how irresponsible. There are limits to what the press can publish without risking legal penalties. For instance, the press is forbidden to publish anything that is obscene or libelous. Something is
100 obscene when it is designed only to inflame sexual desires. It is libelous when it publicly and untruthfully harms a person's reputation.

What is more, there are many times when the press's freedom comes into conflict with
105 another right. In such cases, the courts have to decide which right is more important in the particular circumstances.

11. The author's purpose in this passage is to:

A. demonstrate that freedom of the press is the most important right of Americans.
B. show that America's founders did not invent freedom of the press.

C. indicate that though freedom of the press is an important right, its boundaries are always changing.
D. describe the effect of the press on U.S. wars.

12. John Peter Zenger was found not guilty for printing articles that criticized the royal governor of New York because:

F. he didn't write the articles.
G. he was protected under the U.S. Constitution.
H. the governor forgave him.
J. his criticisms of the governor were true.

13. Based on the information in this passage, who did NOT act as an advocate for freedom of the press?

A. Thomas Jefferson
B. John Peter Zenger
C. John Adams
D. Charles Schenck

14. The John Peter Zenger trial is significant to American history because:

F. it defined when the press could be censored.
G. Zenger was the nation's leading journalist.
H. the trial recognized freedom of the press as a critical right.
J. his criticisms of the royal governor demonstrated that America should seek freedom from England.

15. Why does the U.S. government often block the freedom of the press during wartime?

A. Reading about what really happens during wartime might frighten people.
B. The enemy might learn American troop plans, putting soldiers in even more danger.
C. Americans have the right to know only what the government wants them to know.
D. Reporters are not soldiers, so they do not fully understand what is happening.

16. According to this passage, Congress passed the Sedition Act in 1798:

F. to prevent advocates of the French from persuading Americans to turn against their government.

G. to stop French people from immigrating to the United States.

H. to show that Congress and the U.S. government were above criticism.

J. to end the war against the French.

17. Which is protected by the freedom of the press?

A. Obscenity

B. Purposely harming another person's reputation

C. Speaking out against government

D. Publication of military secrets

18. Based on the information in this passage, which is NOT a restriction on the press?

F. Blocking or deleting information that may be considered harmful

G. Setting guidelines for what reporters can and cannot write about during wartime

H. Refusing to allow reporters to accompany troops

J. Printing libelous informatiom criticizing the government

19. According to this article, freedom of the press is:

A. a right that can never be denied.

B. constantly being redefined.

C. dangerous to the safety of Americans.

D. designed to protect newspaper publishers, not writers.

20. A free press behaves responsibly:

F. because someone who criticizes the government can be aquitted by a jury.

G. when reporters refrain from reporting information that can endanger Americans.

H. if reporters never write anything obscene.

J. if reporters never include libelous statements in their articles.

PASSAGE III

HUMANITIES: This passage is from *Western Civilization* by Gerson Antell and Walter Harris.

The artists of the Italian Renaissance may be said to have captured the spirit of humanism in paint, marble, and bronze. In doing so, they studied anatomy and returned to an ideal-
5 ization of the human body like that which appears in Greek sculpture.

Giotto, who lived from 1276 to 1336, is considered the first Renaissance painter. Though his frescoes retained some of the
10 stiffness of medieval works, his figures are full of human feeling. His compositions are dramatic in their groupings of figures. And, by varying the intensity of his colors from bright to dark, Giotto gives both people and
15 settings a lifelike quality.

Another early realist, Masaccio, was influenced by Giotto. The monumental figures in his wall paintings—done early in the fifteenth century—seem to have been carved
20 from stone. Unlike those of Giotto, however, they are creatures of flesh and blood. Masaccio was one of the first painters to master perspective—the representation of three dimensions on a two-dimensional surface so
25 that distance and distant objects appear as they would to the eye.

The late fifteenth and early sixteenth centuries witnessed such a flowering of art that this period is called the High Renaissance.
30 The four greatest Italian artists of this period were Leonardo da Vinci, Michelangelo, Raphael, and Titian.

Leonardo da Vinci came closer to being an all-round genius than any other person in his-
35 tory. Born in 1452, he designed a flying machine, lathes, pumps, and weapons. His notebooks contain accurate drawings of a human embryo and of human muscles and organs. Leonardo's most famous painting,
40 *Mona Lisa*, shows a lovely woman with a mysterious smile. Everything in the painting

seems to be seen through a slight haze. The wall painting *The Last Supper* is often called Leonardo's greatest work. The figure of Christ is isolated at the center. He has just told the disciples, "One of you shall betray me," and all of the emotions that this statement evoked can be seen in their faces and gestures.

Michelangelo Buonarotti, like Leonardo, was a man of wide-ranging talents. His masterpiece is the huge painting on the ceiling of the Sistine Chapel in the Vatican. For more than four years, from 1508 to 1512, Michelangelo lay on his back and worked night and day. The result was the biblical story of Genesis, from the Creation to the Flood. Twenty-two years later, he painted the *The Last Judgment*, which covers the great wall behind the altar of the Sistine Chapel.

Michelangelo was also a great sculptor, possibly the greatest of the Renaissance. He made marble come to life in his youthful *David*, in the sorrowful *Pietà*, and in his mighty statue of Moses, the majestic law-giver.

Raphael Santi, while not an innovator, had the ability to select and adapt what he had learned from others and to impart to his paintings a fresh and lasting beauty. His figures are as powerful as those on the Sistine ceiling. And his paintings of the Madonna exhibit a dignified yet appealing womanly beauty.

Titian, or Tiziano Vecelli, was probably the greatest Venetian painter of the Renaissance. His use of color was unsurpassed. He painted landscapes, portraits, and historical and mythological scenes. The viewer always sees real men and women, vital and alive. Titian, unlike Leonardo and Michelangelo, painted in oils on canvas. This technique gave artists greater freedom to correct, refine, and add dimension and depth to their paintings.

21. According to the passage, the admiration and idealization of the human form reflected the same trends in:

 A. Egyptian mummies.
 B. American art.
 C. Byzantine paintings.
 D. Greek sculpture.

22. Which was NOT a Renaissance artist?

 F. Mona Lisa
 G. Raphael
 H. Titian
 J. Giotto

23. According to this passage, Leonardo da Vinci was:

 A. an artist.
 B. a scientist.
 C. an inventor.
 D. all of the above.

24. When the authors of this passage note that Masaccio mastered "perspective" in his art, they mean that Masaccio:

 F. had an objective viewpoint of his subjects.
 G. viewed things differently from his peers.
 H. created paintings that looked as though they were three-dimensional.
 J. created only three-dimensional art.

25. According to the information presented in the passage, an important subject for most artists of the Renaissance was:

 A. self-portraits.
 B. buildings.
 C. science.
 D. biblical stories.

26. Raphael was best known for:

 F. his brilliant colors.
 G. his innovative painting style.
 H. his use of clay.
 J. his adaptation of skills he learned to impart new beauty in his art.

27. The technique NOT mentioned in this discussion of Renaissance art is:

 A. pastels.
 B. sculpture.
 C. frescoes.
 D. oil painting.

28. Because Giotto had not mastered perspective, the people in his paintings are:

    F. realistic.
    G. flat.
    H. unpleasant.
    J. dark.

29. Based on the information in this passage, the period called the High Renaissance took place during:

    A. the late 1400s and early 1500s.
    B. the late 1300s and early 1400s.

    C. the late 1500s and early 1600s.
    D. the late 1200s and early 1300s.

30. The main point in this passage is that:

    F. the Renaissance began with Giotto's art.
    G. many beautiful works of art as well as artistic advances were made in the Renaissance.
    H. Leonardo da Vinci designed the first airplane.
    J. Titian should be known as the greatest Renaissance painter.

PASSAGE IV

NATURAL SCIENCE: This passage is from *Chemistry: A Contemporary Approach* by Paul S. Cohen.

The Modern Periodic Table

The work set in motion by the Mendeleev–Meyer system of classification led to further developments during the latter half of the 19th century. By 1900 the noble
5 gas elements—helium, neon, argon, xenon, and krypton—had been discovered and added to the table. One problem, however, was as yet unresolved. Why did a few elements, when grouped by atomic mass, fail to appear
10 in their proper places?

This problem was finally resolved in 1913, when a 26-year-old English physicist, Henry Moseley, was able to determine the atomic number of each of the elements. When
15 the elements were grouped by atomic number, instead of by atomic mass, every element fell into its proper group, with elements of similar properties. Thus the periodic law was revised, and the development of the modern periodic
20 table was possible.

The *revised periodic law* states: The properties of the elements are periodic functions of their atomic numbers. Recall that the atomic number indicates the number of pro-
25 tons, and also of electrons, in an atom. In other words, when the elements are arranged in order of increasing atomic number, the properties of the elements repeat regularly. For example, in this arrangement, argon
30 (atomic number 18) precedes potassium (atomic number 19), which has a lower atomic mass than argon. The same reversal of order occurs with cobalt and nickel and with tellurium and iodine. The properties of these
35 pairs of elements now fall into place.

Organization of the Periodic Table

The modern periodic table arranges the elements in order of increasing atomic number. The elements fall into horizontal rows and vertical columns. Horizontal rows, called
40 periods, are labeled 1, 2, 3 and . . . Vertical columns, called groups or families, are labeled with Roman numerals and letters, such as IIA and IIB. The subgroups became the Group B elements, while the main groups
45 became the Group A elements.

A final change in the periodic table was made by the International Union of Pure and Applied Chemistry. The A and B designations were discarded entirely, and the groups were
50 simply numbered consecutively, from 1 to 18. The A group elements are now often called the "representative elements," while the elements in the B groups are called "transition elements."

55 Since both forms of the periodic table are commonly used by chemists, the table we use gives both the old designations and the new designations for the groups on the table.

60 Atomic masses are shown below atomic numbers in the table. Atomic masses are based on the carbon-12 standard—that is, the masses are determined on a scale in which the most common isotope of carbon is assigned a mass of exactly 12.00. The mass numbers 65 reflect the weighted average of the naturally occurring isotopes.

On some periodic tables, the electron configuration of an atom is also given for each element. In addition, the covalent atomic 70 radius and the relative size of an atom may be provided. This information applies to some of the periodic properties of the elements.

In our table, as in most periodic tables now in use, the row of elements 58–71 (lan-75 thanides) and the row of elements 90–103 (actinides) appear separately at the bottom. This placement makes it easier to follow the regularities of all the other elements.

The Periodic Table

Key
6 — Atomic number
C — Symbol
12.01 — Atomic mass

1 IA																	18 O
1 H 1.008	2 IIA											13 IIIA	14 IVA	15 VA	16 VIA	17 VIIA	2 He 4.003
3 Li 6.941	4 Be 9.012				TRANSITION ELEMENTS							5 B 10.81	6 C 12.01	7 N 14.01	8 O 16.00	9 F 19.00	10 Ne 20.18
11 Na 22.99	12 Mg 24.31	3 IIIB	4 IVB	5 VB	6 VIB	7 VIIB	8	9 VIIIB	10	11 IB	12 IIB	13 Al 26.98	14 Si 28.09	15 P 30.97	16 S 32.07	17 Cl 35.45	18 Ar 39.95
19 K 39.10	20 Ca 40.08	21 Sc 44.96	22 Ti 47.88	23 V 50.94	24 Cr 52.00	25 Mn 54.94	26 Fe 55.85	27 Co 58.93	28 Ni 58.69	29 Cu 63.55	30 Zn 65.39	31 Ga 69.72	32 Ge 72.61	33 As 74.92	34 Se 78.96	35 Br 79.90	36 Kr 83.80
37 Rb 85.47	38 Sr 87.62	39 Y 88.91	40 Zr 91.22	41 Nb 92.91	42 Mo 95.94	43 Tc (98)	44 Ru 101.1	45 Rh 102.9	46 Pd 106.4	47 Ag 107.9	48 Cd 112.4	49 In 114.8	50 Sn 118.7	51 Sb 121.8	52 Te 127.6	53 I 126.9	54 Xe 131.3
55 Cs 132.9	56 Ba 137.3	57 La 138.9	72 Hf 178.5	73 Ta 181.0	74 W 183.8	75 Re 186.2	76 Os 190.2	77 Ir 192.2	78 Pt 195.1	79 Au 197.0	80 Hg 200.6	81 Tl 204.4	82 Pb 207.2	83 Bi 209.0	84 Po (209)	85 At (210)	86 Rn (222)
87 Fr (223)	88 Ra 226.0	89 Ac 227.0	104 Rf (261)	105 Db (262)	106 Sg (263)	107 Bh (262)	108 Hs (265)	109 Mt (268)	110 Ds (281)	111 Rg (272)	112 Cn (285)	113 Uut (284)	114 Uuq (289)	115 Uup (288)	116 Uuh (292)	117 Uus	118 Uuo (294)

PERIOD

58 Ce 140.1	59 Pr 140.9	60 Nd 144.2	61 Pm (145)	62 Sm 150.4	63 Eu 152.0	64 Gd 157.3	65 Tb 158.9	66 Dy 162.5	67 Ho 164.9	68 Er 167.3	69 Tm 168.9	70 Yb 173.0	71 Lu 175.0	LANTHANIDE SERIES
90 Th 232.0	91 Pa 231.0	92 U 238.0	93 Np 237.0	94 Pu (244)	95 Am (243)	96 Cm (247)	97 Bk (247)	98 Cf (251)	99 Es (252)	100 Fm (257)	101 Md (258)	102 No (259)	103 Lr (260)	ACTINIDE SERIES

31. The periodic table was revised in the early 20th-century because:

A. the Mendeleev-Meyer system covered all the important information.
B. scientists felt that all the periodic elements needed to be updated.
C. Henry Moseley discovered that the original table was incorrect.
D. not all of the elements adhered to the properties that they were categorized by in the previous periodic table.

32. According to this passage, which element is NOT a noble gas?

F. Oxygen
G. Helium
H. Krypton
J. Neon

33. The atomic number of an element is determined by:

A. weighing the element.
B. counting the number of atoms in an element.
C. examining the number of protons and electrons in an element.
D. squaring the atomic mass.

34. The main idea of lines 14–18 is:

F. atomic mass is the best way to group the periodic elements.
G. English scientists were far advanced in the field of physics.
H. determining the atomic number of an element allows scientists to group together elements with similar properties.
J. The Mendeleev–Meyer system was completely wrong.

35. What is the suggested connection between the revised periodic law and the revised periodic table?

A. The revised table clearly describes this revised law.
B. Following the revised periodic law, the revised table groups the elements by their atomic number.
C. They both use Roman numerals.
D. The law does not apply to the lanthanide and actinide series.

36. According to this passage, what is the connection between atomic number and atomic mass?

F. They are always the same.
G. Elements arranged in order of their atomic number are also arranged in order of their atomic mass.
H. An element's atomic mass can change, but the atomic number remains the same.
J. The passage draws no clear connection between these two properties.

37. The name that describes the horizontal rows on the revised periodic table is:

A. groups.
B. families.
C. periods.
D. series.

38. This passage suggests that the A and B designations for elements are still reflected on the table, even though these designations have been replaced by the terms "representative elements" and "transition elements," because:

F. some scientists prefer the older designations.
G. the old designations are more descriptive than the new designations.
H. you can't understand one designation without the other.
J. the Mendeleev-Meyer-Moseley system uses both designations.

39. The row of elements 58–71 (lanthanides) and the row of elements 90–103 (actinides) are set apart from the rest of the table because:

A. they are radioactive.
B. they do not conform well to the properties of the other elements.
C. these are the most important elements.
D. they were discovered later than the other elements.

40. No information is given in this passage or periodic table about:

F. noble gases.
G. the carbon-12 standard.
H. relative size.
J. half-life.

Diagnostic Reading Checklist

Answer	Check if Missed	Social Studies/ Sciences	Arts/ Literature	Answer	Check if Missed	Social Studies/ Sciences	Arts/ Literature
1. D	❑		❑	21. D	❑		❑
2. H	❑		❑	22. F	❑		❑
3. A	❑		❑	23. D	❑		❑
4. J	❑		❑	24. H	❑		❑
5. B	❑		❑	25. D	❑		❑
6. G	❑		❑	26. J	❑		❑
7. B	❑		❑	27. A	❑		❑
8. G	❑		❑	28. G	❑		❑
9. B	❑		❑	29. A	❑		❑
10. H	❑		❑	30. G	❑		❑
11. C	❑	❑		31. D	❑	❑	
12. J	❑	❑		32. F	❑	❑	
13. C	❑	❑		33. C	❑	❑	
14. H	❑	❑		34. H	❑	❑	
15. B	❑	❑		35. B	❑	❑	
16. F	❑	❑		36. J	❑	❑	
17. C	❑	❑		37. C	❑	❑	
18. J	❑	❑		38. F	❑	❑	
19. B	❑	❑		39. B	❑	❑	
20. G	❑	❑		40. J	❑	❑	

Number Correct:

Social Studies/Sciences _____

Arts/Literature _____

Total _____

Review the answer explanations on the following pages. Then go back to the items you missed. Apply the four steps on page 215 to find out how the steps lead you to the correct answers.

Diagnostic Reading ACT Answers Explained

PASSAGE I

1. D

The passage mentions all four locations, but the first sentence of paragraph 2 says that the setting is Santa Clara Valley.

2. H

The author says (line 7) that men "had found a yellow metal." The men searching for the gold needed strong work dogs to assist them, as the passage states: "the dogs they wanted were heavy dogs, with strong muscles by which to toil" (lines 11–13).

3. A

According to the passage, Buck is the favored dog on Judge Miller's estate. He is "king" over everyone on the estate; "The whole realm [was] his."

4. J

No threatening, frightening, or otherwise negative words are used to describe Judge Miller's place. Judge Miller's place has a warm climate. The area is "sun-kissed," and the children use a pool to keep cool. There is a lot of land, a "great demesne" covered with orchards and trees. There are stables and servants' quarters.

5. B

The passage implies that because of his favored status and his physical strength, Buck appeared to have control over everyone. As far as Buck is concerned, the other dogs "don't count." Buck is his real name. He has not fathered any puppies.

6. G

The passage describes them as a Japanese pug and a Mexican hairless, two different breeds of dogs. Since they are of different breeds, Buck and these two dogs cannot be related. Since Buck "utterly ignored" (line 65) these two dogs, they are not his best friends. Judge Miller's daughters are Mollie and Alice.

7. B

Buck goes hunting and swimming, and he plays with and protects the Judge's daughters and grandsons. He is not lazy or lonely. Paragraph 5 says that Buck was not pampered.

8. G

The first paragraph indicates that "trouble was brewing . . . for every tidewater dog, strong of muscle and with warm, long hair. . . ." The later description of Buck indicates that he is strong and furry, which gives the reader a sense of foreboding about Buck's situation.

9. B

The opening paragraph indicates that there will be trouble for Buck; the last two paragraphs confirm this, describing how Buck is removed from his happy and comfortable life.

10. H

The implication is that Manuel commits an act of treachery by selling Buck to get money to pay off his gambling debt. Manuel is not paying for services or buying supplies. On the contrary, he is receiving money for Buck.

PASSAGE II

11. C

This passage discusses how the freedom of the press has fluctuated in America. It does not state that this is Americans' most important right, but it does state that the founding fathers did not invent the right. Most often, these fluctuations stem from wartime decisions; however, these wars are not the focus of the passage.

12. J

Because Zenger told the truth in his articles, the jury decided that he should be acquitted. Since there was not yet a U.S. Constitution, he was being protected under British (not American) rule. It was not the governor who forgave him, but President Jefferson.

13. C

The passage lists each person in the answer except John Adams as exerting the rights of freedom of the press. Of those listed, only John Adams is noted for acting against freedom of the press, by signing into law the Alien and Sedition Acts.

14. H

This was the first case in America that supported freedom of the press. There is no information in the passage to indicate that F, G, or J is true.

15. B

According to this passage, there was concern that information could endanger the secrecy of missions, reveal information about troop movements, and otherwise endanger the war effort.

16. F

Because of the wartime situation, John Adams and Congress wanted to stifle any anti-American, pro-French writing. The Alien Acts prevented the immigration of more French to the United States. The Sedition Act simply prevented anyone from speaking out against the government. The passage does not contain any statement to support either H or J.

17. C

Choices A, B, and D are all things that should not be published; therefore, they are not protected (or allowed) by freedom of the press. Since the Sedition Act was revoked in 1801, citizens of the United States have had the right to speak out against the American—or any other—government.

18. J

The first three choices are all examples of cases where the freedom of the press was not violated. However, printing libelous information is not considered freedom of the press.

19. B

The authors state (lines 91–92) that freedom of the press is constantly being redefined. The remainder of the passage gives examples that support this statement.

20. G

In describing U.S. censorship, the authors note that many reporters were not censored during World War II because they made sure not to give out information that would endanger the troops (lines 70–74). Choice F is more like an excuse for a press that behaves irresponsibly. While it may be true that a responsible press would not print obscenities or libel, neither of these is broad enough to define that responsibility as a whole.

PASSAGE III

21. D

The authors note (lines 3–6) that Renaissance art is reflective of Greek sculpture.

22. F

Mona Lisa is the subject of one of Leonardo da Vinci's most famous paintings, not an artist herself.

23. D

Leonardo da Vinci was a true "Renaissance man." In other words, he was skilled in many areas. The authors note many of Leonardo's achievements in fields other than art.

24. H

The authors discuss perspective as distinguishing the spatial relationship of objects. Masaccio's paintings were advanced because he could make a two-dimensional surface appear to be three-dimensional.

25. D

In this passage, much of the art discussed reflects religious themes, like Leonardo's *The Last Supper*, Michelangelo's work at the Sistine Chapel, and Raphael's *Madonna*.

26. J

According to the authors, Raphael was not an innovator. Instead, he adapted the skills he learned from others to paint powerful and beautiful pictures. The passage states that other painters used bold colors but does not say this of Raphael. It also does not mention Raphael using clay.

27. A

Giotto is known for fresco, Michelangelo for sculpture, and Titian for oil painting. Pastel may have been used, but it is not mentioned in this article.

28. G

Because his paintings were not "three-dimensional," Giotto's figures are described as "stiff" as opposed to Masaccio, whose figures are "creatures of flesh and blood."

29. A

The late fifteenth and early sixteenth centuries witnessed the High Renaissance. These centuries correspond with the late 1400s and early 1500s.

30. G

The authors describe the best artists, their works, and their artistic advances. While the other statements may or may not be true, they are supporting details, not the main point of the passage.

PASSAGE IV

31. D

The author indicates (lines 9–10) that, under the rules of the old table, some elements failed to "appear in their proper places." In lines 14–18, the author indicates that in Henry Moseley's table, "every element fell into its proper group."

32. F

Oxygen is a gas, but only helium, krypton, argon, xenon, and neon are noble gases.

33. C

The author notes (lines 23–25) that the atomic number indicates the number of protons and electrons in an atom.

34. H

Elements ordered by atomic number, *not by atomic mass*, fall into groups with other elements with similar properties. The Mendeleev-Meyer system was not wrong; it just did not answer all questions.

35. B

In the third paragraph, the author defines the revised periodic law: "The properties of the elements are periodic functions of their atomic numbers." Two sentences later, he notes that when "the elements are arranged in order of increasing atomic number, the properties of the elements repeat regularly." You can infer that the table, which reflects the revised periodic law, arranges the elements in order of increasing atomic number. Lines 36–78 also describe the arrangement of the periodic table.

36. J

Whether or not there is a concrete connection between these two concepts is not strongly indicated in this passage. Clearly, atomic mass and atomic number are not always the same; if they were, the old periodic table would have worked as well as the revised table. The author notes that, occasionally, elements with higher atomic masses are placed before elements with lower atomic masses.

37. C

The author notes (lines 39–40) that horizontal rows are called periods, while vertical columns are called groups, or families. This is reinforced by the notation on the periodic table, which labels the horizontal rows as periods.

38. F

Lines 55–58 indicate that both the A and B designations as well as the "representative" and "transition" designations are commonly used by modern scientists. Therefore, both designations are preserved. There is no such thing as the Mendeleev-Meyer-Moseley system.

39. B

The author notes (lines 73–78) that these rows appear separately to make it "easier to follow the regularities of all the other elements." This statement implies that the rows set aside do not show the regularities of other elements in the table. There is no indication that these elements are any more important or more recently discovered than the other elements in the table, and there is no mention of radioactivity in the passage.

40. J

Noble gases, the carbon-12 standard, and relative size are all mentioned in the article. There is no mention of half-life.

Section IV

Model English and Reading Tests

Model English and Reading ACT I

With Answers Explained

This Model English and Reading ACT I is just like a real ACT. Take this test after you take the Diagnostic English ACT and the Diagnostic Reading ACT. If you plan to take the optional ACT Writing Test, you should also complete the Developmental ACT Writing Test on pages 362–370.

Take this model test under simulated test conditions. Allow 45 minutes to answer the 75 English items and 35 minutes to answer the 40 Reading items. Use the Answer Sheet on the following page to mark your answers. Use a pencil to mark the answer sheet, and color in the circles for the correct choices in the Test 1 (English) and Test 3 (Reading) sections.

Use the Scoring Keys on pages 269–271 to score the answer sheet. Review the answer explanations on pages 272–280.

The test scoring charts on pages 6 and 7 show you how to convert the number of correct answers to ACT scale scores. The Scoring Keys on pages 269–271 show you how to find the Usage/Mechanics and Rhetorical Skills subscores and the Social Studies/ Sciences and Arts/Literature subscores.

DO NOT leave any answers blank. There is no penalty for guessing on the ACT. Remember that the test is yours. You may mark up, write on, or draw on the test.

When you are ready, note the time and begin.

ANSWER SHEET

The ACT answer sheet looks something like this. Use a No. 2 pencil to completely fill the circle corresponding to the correct answer. If you erase, erase completely; incomplete erasures may be read as answers.

TEST 1—English

1 Ⓐ Ⓑ Ⓒ Ⓓ	11 Ⓐ Ⓑ Ⓒ Ⓓ	21 Ⓐ Ⓑ Ⓒ Ⓓ	31 Ⓐ Ⓑ Ⓒ Ⓓ	41 Ⓐ Ⓑ Ⓒ Ⓓ	51 Ⓐ Ⓑ Ⓒ Ⓓ	61 Ⓐ Ⓑ Ⓒ Ⓓ	71 Ⓐ Ⓑ Ⓒ Ⓓ
2 Ⓕ Ⓖ Ⓗ Ⓙ	12 Ⓕ Ⓖ Ⓗ Ⓙ	22 Ⓕ Ⓖ Ⓗ Ⓙ	32 Ⓕ Ⓖ Ⓗ Ⓙ	42 Ⓕ Ⓖ Ⓗ Ⓙ	52 Ⓕ Ⓖ Ⓗ Ⓙ	62 Ⓕ Ⓖ Ⓗ Ⓙ	72 Ⓕ Ⓖ Ⓗ Ⓙ
3 Ⓐ Ⓑ Ⓒ Ⓓ	13 Ⓐ Ⓑ Ⓒ Ⓓ	23 Ⓐ Ⓑ Ⓒ Ⓓ	33 Ⓐ Ⓑ Ⓒ Ⓓ	43 Ⓐ Ⓑ Ⓒ Ⓓ	53 Ⓐ Ⓑ Ⓒ Ⓓ	63 Ⓐ Ⓑ Ⓒ Ⓓ	73 Ⓐ Ⓑ Ⓒ Ⓓ
4 Ⓕ Ⓖ Ⓗ Ⓙ	14 Ⓕ Ⓖ Ⓗ Ⓙ	24 Ⓕ Ⓖ Ⓗ Ⓙ	34 Ⓕ Ⓖ Ⓗ Ⓙ	44 Ⓕ Ⓖ Ⓗ Ⓙ	54 Ⓕ Ⓖ Ⓗ Ⓙ	64 Ⓕ Ⓖ Ⓗ Ⓙ	74 Ⓕ Ⓖ Ⓗ Ⓙ
5 Ⓐ Ⓑ Ⓒ Ⓓ	15 Ⓐ Ⓑ Ⓒ Ⓓ	25 Ⓐ Ⓑ Ⓒ Ⓓ	35 Ⓐ Ⓑ Ⓒ Ⓓ	45 Ⓐ Ⓑ Ⓒ Ⓓ	55 Ⓐ Ⓑ Ⓒ Ⓓ	65 Ⓐ Ⓑ Ⓒ Ⓓ	75 Ⓐ Ⓑ Ⓒ Ⓓ
6 Ⓕ Ⓖ Ⓗ Ⓙ	16 Ⓕ Ⓖ Ⓗ Ⓙ	26 Ⓕ Ⓖ Ⓗ Ⓙ	36 Ⓕ Ⓖ Ⓗ Ⓙ	46 Ⓕ Ⓖ Ⓗ Ⓙ	56 Ⓕ Ⓖ Ⓗ Ⓙ	66 Ⓕ Ⓖ Ⓗ Ⓙ	
7 Ⓐ Ⓑ Ⓒ Ⓓ	17 Ⓐ Ⓑ Ⓒ Ⓓ	27 Ⓐ Ⓑ Ⓒ Ⓓ	37 Ⓐ Ⓑ Ⓒ Ⓓ	47 Ⓐ Ⓑ Ⓒ Ⓓ	57 Ⓐ Ⓑ Ⓒ Ⓓ	67 Ⓐ Ⓑ Ⓒ Ⓓ	
8 Ⓕ Ⓖ Ⓗ Ⓙ	18 Ⓕ Ⓖ Ⓗ Ⓙ	28 Ⓕ Ⓖ Ⓗ Ⓙ	38 Ⓕ Ⓖ Ⓗ Ⓙ	48 Ⓕ Ⓖ Ⓗ Ⓙ	58 Ⓕ Ⓖ Ⓗ Ⓙ	68 Ⓕ Ⓖ Ⓗ Ⓙ	
9 Ⓐ Ⓑ Ⓒ Ⓓ	19 Ⓐ Ⓑ Ⓒ Ⓓ	29 Ⓐ Ⓑ Ⓒ Ⓓ	39 Ⓐ Ⓑ Ⓒ Ⓓ	49 Ⓐ Ⓑ Ⓒ Ⓓ	59 Ⓐ Ⓑ Ⓒ Ⓓ	69 Ⓐ Ⓑ Ⓒ Ⓓ	
10 Ⓕ Ⓖ Ⓗ Ⓙ	20 Ⓕ Ⓖ Ⓗ Ⓙ	30 Ⓕ Ⓖ Ⓗ Ⓙ	40 Ⓕ Ⓖ Ⓗ Ⓙ	50 Ⓕ Ⓖ Ⓗ Ⓙ	60 Ⓕ Ⓖ Ⓗ Ⓙ	70 Ⓕ Ⓖ Ⓗ Ⓙ	

TEST 2—Mathematics

1 Ⓐ Ⓑ Ⓒ Ⓓ Ⓔ	9 Ⓐ Ⓑ Ⓒ Ⓓ Ⓔ	17 Ⓐ Ⓑ Ⓒ Ⓓ Ⓔ	25 Ⓐ Ⓑ Ⓒ Ⓓ Ⓔ	33 Ⓐ Ⓑ Ⓒ Ⓓ Ⓔ	41 Ⓐ Ⓑ Ⓒ Ⓓ Ⓔ	49 Ⓐ Ⓑ Ⓒ Ⓓ Ⓔ	57 Ⓐ Ⓑ Ⓒ Ⓓ Ⓔ
2 Ⓕ Ⓖ Ⓗ Ⓙ Ⓚ	10 Ⓕ Ⓖ Ⓗ Ⓙ Ⓚ	18 Ⓕ Ⓖ Ⓗ Ⓙ Ⓚ	26 Ⓕ Ⓖ Ⓗ Ⓙ Ⓚ	34 Ⓕ Ⓖ Ⓗ Ⓙ Ⓚ	42 Ⓕ Ⓖ Ⓗ Ⓙ Ⓚ	50 Ⓕ Ⓖ Ⓗ Ⓙ Ⓚ	58 Ⓕ Ⓖ Ⓗ Ⓙ Ⓚ
3 Ⓐ Ⓑ Ⓒ Ⓓ Ⓔ	11 Ⓐ Ⓑ Ⓒ Ⓓ Ⓔ	19 Ⓐ Ⓑ Ⓒ Ⓓ Ⓔ	27 Ⓐ Ⓑ Ⓒ Ⓓ Ⓔ	35 Ⓐ Ⓑ Ⓒ Ⓓ Ⓔ	43 Ⓐ Ⓑ Ⓒ Ⓓ Ⓔ	51 Ⓐ Ⓑ Ⓒ Ⓓ Ⓔ	59 Ⓐ Ⓑ Ⓒ Ⓓ Ⓔ
4 Ⓕ Ⓖ Ⓗ Ⓙ Ⓚ	12 Ⓕ Ⓖ Ⓗ Ⓙ Ⓚ	20 Ⓕ Ⓖ Ⓗ Ⓙ Ⓚ	28 Ⓕ Ⓖ Ⓗ Ⓙ Ⓚ	36 Ⓕ Ⓖ Ⓗ Ⓙ Ⓚ	44 Ⓕ Ⓖ Ⓗ Ⓙ Ⓚ	52 Ⓕ Ⓖ Ⓗ Ⓙ Ⓚ	60 Ⓕ Ⓖ Ⓗ Ⓙ Ⓚ
5 Ⓐ Ⓑ Ⓒ Ⓓ Ⓔ	13 Ⓐ Ⓑ Ⓒ Ⓓ Ⓔ	21 Ⓐ Ⓑ Ⓒ Ⓓ Ⓔ	29 Ⓐ Ⓑ Ⓒ Ⓓ Ⓔ	37 Ⓐ Ⓑ Ⓒ Ⓓ Ⓔ	45 Ⓐ Ⓑ Ⓒ Ⓓ Ⓔ	53 Ⓐ Ⓑ Ⓒ Ⓓ Ⓔ	
6 Ⓕ Ⓖ Ⓗ Ⓙ Ⓚ	14 Ⓕ Ⓖ Ⓗ Ⓙ Ⓚ	22 Ⓕ Ⓖ Ⓗ Ⓙ Ⓚ	30 Ⓕ Ⓖ Ⓗ Ⓙ Ⓚ	38 Ⓕ Ⓖ Ⓗ Ⓙ Ⓚ	46 Ⓕ Ⓖ Ⓗ Ⓙ Ⓚ	54 Ⓕ Ⓖ Ⓗ Ⓙ Ⓚ	
7 Ⓐ Ⓑ Ⓒ Ⓓ Ⓔ	15 Ⓐ Ⓑ Ⓒ Ⓓ Ⓔ	23 Ⓐ Ⓑ Ⓒ Ⓓ Ⓔ	31 Ⓐ Ⓑ Ⓒ Ⓓ Ⓔ	39 Ⓐ Ⓑ Ⓒ Ⓓ Ⓔ	47 Ⓐ Ⓑ Ⓒ Ⓓ Ⓔ	55 Ⓐ Ⓑ Ⓒ Ⓓ Ⓔ	
8 Ⓕ Ⓖ Ⓗ Ⓙ Ⓚ	16 Ⓕ Ⓖ Ⓗ Ⓙ Ⓚ	24 Ⓕ Ⓖ Ⓗ Ⓙ Ⓚ	32 Ⓕ Ⓖ Ⓗ Ⓙ Ⓚ	40 Ⓕ Ⓖ Ⓗ Ⓙ Ⓚ	48 Ⓕ Ⓖ Ⓗ Ⓙ Ⓚ	56 Ⓕ Ⓖ Ⓗ Ⓙ Ⓚ	

TEST 3—Reading

1 Ⓐ Ⓑ Ⓒ Ⓓ	6 Ⓕ Ⓖ Ⓗ Ⓙ	11 Ⓐ Ⓑ Ⓒ Ⓓ	16 Ⓕ Ⓖ Ⓗ Ⓙ	21 Ⓐ Ⓑ Ⓒ Ⓓ	26 Ⓕ Ⓖ Ⓗ Ⓙ	31 Ⓐ Ⓑ Ⓒ Ⓓ	36 Ⓕ Ⓖ Ⓗ Ⓙ
2 Ⓕ Ⓖ Ⓗ Ⓙ	7 Ⓐ Ⓑ Ⓒ Ⓓ	12 Ⓕ Ⓖ Ⓗ Ⓙ	17 Ⓐ Ⓑ Ⓒ Ⓓ	22 Ⓕ Ⓖ Ⓗ Ⓙ	27 Ⓐ Ⓑ Ⓒ Ⓓ	32 Ⓕ Ⓖ Ⓗ Ⓙ	37 Ⓐ Ⓑ Ⓒ Ⓓ
3 Ⓐ Ⓑ Ⓒ Ⓓ	8 Ⓕ Ⓖ Ⓗ Ⓙ	13 Ⓐ Ⓑ Ⓒ Ⓓ	18 Ⓕ Ⓖ Ⓗ Ⓙ	23 Ⓐ Ⓑ Ⓒ Ⓓ	28 Ⓕ Ⓖ Ⓗ Ⓙ	33 Ⓐ Ⓑ Ⓒ Ⓓ	38 Ⓕ Ⓖ Ⓗ Ⓙ
4 Ⓕ Ⓖ Ⓗ Ⓙ	9 Ⓐ Ⓑ Ⓒ Ⓓ	14 Ⓕ Ⓖ Ⓗ Ⓙ	19 Ⓐ Ⓑ Ⓒ Ⓓ	24 Ⓕ Ⓖ Ⓗ Ⓙ	29 Ⓐ Ⓑ Ⓒ Ⓓ	34 Ⓕ Ⓖ Ⓗ Ⓙ	39 Ⓐ Ⓑ Ⓒ Ⓓ
5 Ⓐ Ⓑ Ⓒ Ⓓ	10 Ⓕ Ⓖ Ⓗ Ⓙ	15 Ⓐ Ⓑ Ⓒ Ⓓ	20 Ⓕ Ⓖ Ⓗ Ⓙ	25 Ⓐ Ⓑ Ⓒ Ⓓ	30 Ⓕ Ⓖ Ⓗ Ⓙ	35 Ⓐ Ⓑ Ⓒ Ⓓ	40 Ⓕ Ⓖ Ⓗ Ⓙ

TEST 4—Science Reasoning

1 Ⓐ Ⓑ Ⓒ Ⓓ	6 Ⓕ Ⓖ Ⓗ Ⓙ	11 Ⓐ Ⓑ Ⓒ Ⓓ	16 Ⓕ Ⓖ Ⓗ Ⓙ	21 Ⓐ Ⓑ Ⓒ Ⓓ	26 Ⓕ Ⓖ Ⓗ Ⓙ	31 Ⓐ Ⓑ Ⓒ Ⓓ	36 Ⓕ Ⓖ Ⓗ Ⓙ
2 Ⓕ Ⓖ Ⓗ Ⓙ	7 Ⓐ Ⓑ Ⓒ Ⓓ	12 Ⓕ Ⓖ Ⓗ Ⓙ	17 Ⓐ Ⓑ Ⓒ Ⓓ	22 Ⓕ Ⓖ Ⓗ Ⓙ	27 Ⓐ Ⓑ Ⓒ Ⓓ	32 Ⓕ Ⓖ Ⓗ Ⓙ	37 Ⓐ Ⓑ Ⓒ Ⓓ
3 Ⓐ Ⓑ Ⓒ Ⓓ	8 Ⓕ Ⓖ Ⓗ Ⓙ	13 Ⓐ Ⓑ Ⓒ Ⓓ	18 Ⓕ Ⓖ Ⓗ Ⓙ	23 Ⓐ Ⓑ Ⓒ Ⓓ	28 Ⓕ Ⓖ Ⓗ Ⓙ	33 Ⓐ Ⓑ Ⓒ Ⓓ	38 Ⓕ Ⓖ Ⓗ Ⓙ
4 Ⓕ Ⓖ Ⓗ Ⓙ	9 Ⓐ Ⓑ Ⓒ Ⓓ	14 Ⓕ Ⓖ Ⓗ Ⓙ	19 Ⓐ Ⓑ Ⓒ Ⓓ	24 Ⓕ Ⓖ Ⓗ Ⓙ	29 Ⓐ Ⓑ Ⓒ Ⓓ	34 Ⓕ Ⓖ Ⓗ Ⓙ	39 Ⓐ Ⓑ Ⓒ Ⓓ
5 Ⓐ Ⓑ Ⓒ Ⓓ	10 Ⓕ Ⓖ Ⓗ Ⓙ	15 Ⓐ Ⓑ Ⓒ Ⓓ	20 Ⓕ Ⓖ Ⓗ Ⓙ	25 Ⓐ Ⓑ Ⓒ Ⓓ	30 Ⓕ Ⓖ Ⓗ Ⓙ	35 Ⓐ Ⓑ Ⓒ Ⓓ	40 Ⓕ Ⓖ Ⓗ Ⓙ

Model English ACT 1

75 Questions—45 Minutes

INSTRUCTIONS: Certain words or phrases in the following five passages are underlined and numbered. There is a corresponding item for each underlined portion. Each item offers three suggestions for changing the underlined portion to conform to standard written English or to make it more understandable or consistent with the rest of the passage. If the underlined portion is not improved by one of the three suggested changes, mark NO CHANGE. Some items are about the entire passage, and the numbers for these items come at the end of the passage.

Choose the best answer for each question based on the passage. Then fill in the appropriate circle on the answer sheet.

Check pages 269–270 and 272–277 for answers and explanations.

PASSAGE 1

It seems that each year we invent new ways to keep human beings from meeting each other. ☐1☐

Home entertainment is fast becoming the leisure of choice, as more and more people take advantage of the wide assortment
 2
of electronic entertainment available. Video stores sprout everywhere; videotapes and DVDs siphon customers from theaters and museums: and now video games' attract those
 3   4
who once would have participated in traditional out-of-home sports such as bowling.

We now have all kinds of food establishments racing to *deliver*
 5
food. Is this the beginning of the end-of-the-restaurant renaissance? Going to a restaurant involves parking, walking, and sometimes waiting in line. Compare this to the no-walking, no-parking, no-waiting, no-hassle way of life we
 6
have in our own homes when we have our meals delivered.

1. Which option might BEST explain why the author has opened this article with this one-sentence paragraph?

   A. To emphasize the passage of time, as more sentences will follow this one
   B. Because she could not figure out how to elaborate on this idea in greater detail
   C. In order to highlight and emphasize the thesis of the essay that follows
   D. To demonstrate her great skill as a writer

2. F. NO CHANGE
   G. have taken
   H. had taken
   J. took

3. A. NO CHANGE
   B. museums;
   C. museums,
   D. museums

4. F. NO CHANGE
   G. video game
   H. video games
   J. video game's

Even preparing our own food is less of a hassle. With
prepackaged meals getting better and better and microwave
ovens making nuking food quick and efficient.

Futurist's call this social phenomenon "cocooning," where
families stay close to the homestead and interact very little
with their outside surroundings. Home-shopping networks,
faxed mail, home computers and offices—such things threaten
to rip the social fabric by keeping people from interacting with
each other. In the long run, this cannot be healthy for our
culture. 12

Mingling with other people and exploring our surroundings
should not be abandoned because of advanced home-
entertainment technologies. What we do in our spare time
should not be decided in a combat between cocooning
technology and the lure of their public places. There should
be equally time for both.

5. Which choice BEST explains why the
   author chose to italicize the word
   deliver?
   A. To emphasize that people are
      having food brought to them so
      that they won't have to leave their
      homes
   B. To differentiate between delivery
      and take-out options
   C. To indicate that food arrives very
      quickly
   D. To show that food is being mailed
      to people

6. Which choice represents the MOST
   logical order for the underlined
   phrases?
   F. NO CHANGE
   G. no-parking, no-walking, no-
      waiting
   H. no-waiting, no-parking, no-
      walking
   J. no-parking, no-waiting, no-
      walking

7. A. NO CHANGE
   B. hassle, with
   C. hassle! With
   D. hassle? With

8. F. NO CHANGE
   G. frying
   H. zapping
   J. cooking

9. A. NO CHANGE
   B. Futurists'
   C. Futurist
   D. Futurists

10. F. NO CHANGE
    G. interacting
    H. interacts
    J. interacted

11. A. NO CHANGE
    B. offices. Such
    C. offices! such
    D. offices; such

12. Based on the language in this paragraph, which choice BEST reflects the author's attitudes toward cocooning?

    F. Indifference
    G. Elation
    H. Concern
    J. Shame

13. **A.** NO CHANGE
    B. there
    C. they're
    D. our

14. **F.** NO CHANGE
    G. equal
    H. equated
    J. equalest

Question 15 asks about the entire passage.

---

15. Which information would strengthen this article?

    A. An explanation of the cocooning process in caterpillars
    B. An explication of the movie *Cocoon*
    C. Examples proving how society is becoming less interactive
    D. Descriptions of how to use modern technology, such as fax machines and computers

PASSAGE II

In the forests of southeastern Canada and the eastern United

States. Indians lived as hunters and farmers. For both
    16

activities, they use tools and weapons made of chipped stone,
    17

bone, and they were also made of wood. Not until the arrival
    18

of Europeans in the 1500s did the Indians obtain metal axes

and knives.

16. **F.** NO CHANGE
    G. States, Indians
    H. States; Indians
    J. States Indians

17. **A.** NO CHANGE
    B. using
    C. uses
    D. used

[1] One of the largest groups of Indians in the Eastern Woodlands area <u>was</u> the Iroquois. [2] Five tribes
19
formed the Iroquois League of Five <u>Nations Seneca,</u>
20
Cayuga, Mohawk, Onondaga, and Oneida. [3] (The Tuscaroras later joined the group, making it the League of Six Nations.) [4] The purpose of the League was to keep peace among the five tribes <u>who belonged to the Iroquois League.</u> [5] The unity and
21
fighting ability of the <u>Iroquois</u> made them very powerful. [23]
22

In their tribal councils, the Iroquois practiced a type of democracy. <u>Acting as servants of the people, the tribe elected
24
public officials.</u> The government of the League was in the
24
hands of 50 men called sachems. The leading women of the tribe chose the sachems. [25]

Anyone could attend meetings of the <u>Council, at</u> these
26
meetings, proposals were either accepted or <u>trashed.</u> After a
27
great deal of discussion and speechmaking, the sachems would reach a decision about each proposal. Some historians believe that the men who planned the government of the United States may have gotten some of their ideas from the way the League of Five Nations <u>operated. Women</u> had a great deal of authority
28
among the Iroquois. A woman headed each clan, or group of related families. The women owned all of the family goods. No one could inherit anything except from his or her mother. Young men and women could not choose whom they would marry. Mothers arranged all marriages.

18. **F.** NO CHANGE
    G. the tools were also made of wood
    H. wood
    J. wooden tools

19. **A.** NO CHANGE
    B. were
    C. was,
    D. were,

20. **F.** NO CHANGE
    G. Nations: Seneca
    H. Nations; Seneca
    J. Nations. Seneca

21. **A.** NO CHANGE
    B. who were League of Five Nations members
    C. for the League of Five Nations
    D. OMIT the underlined portion.

22. **F.** NO CHANGE
    G. Iroquoises
    H. Iroquois'
    J. Iroquoises'

23. For the greatest coherence in this paragraph, where should sentence 5 be placed?
    A. NO CHANGE
    B. After Sentence 1
    C. After Sentence 2
    D. At the beginning of the paragraph

24. **F.** NO CHANGE
    G. Acting as servants of the tribe, the people elected public officials.
    H. Acting as servants of the people, the public officials represented the tribe members.
    J. Acting as servants of the people, the tribe had public officials.

25. What information is necessary to clarify the meaning of this paragraph?
    A. An explanation of the duties of the sachem
    B. A definition of democracy
    C. A list of all the men chosen to be sachem
    D. A detailed explanation of how the women chose the sachem

26. **F.** NO CHANGE
    G. Council at
    H. Council . . . at
    J. Council. At

27. **A.** NO CHANGE
    B. they were trashed
    C. rejected
    D. blown off

28. **F.** NO CHANGE
    G. operated! Women
    H. operated. (begin new paragraph)
    Women
    J. operated! (begin new paragraph)
    Women

Questions 29 and 30 ask about the entire passage.

---

29. Assume that the author's assignment was to write an essay focused on the strength of Iroquois women. Does he complete this assignment?

    A. Yes, because he spends a paragraph discussing women's roles.
    B. No, because most of the essay focuses on the Iroquois tribe as a whole, not just the function of women.
    C. No, because women cannot be sachems.
    D. Yes, because women were the heads of clans.

30. Based on the language of this essay, which choice BEST describes the author's intended audience?

    F. Professors of history
    G. Native-American women
    H. Senior citizens
    J. People who are unfamiliar with the Iroquois and their traditions

PASSAGE III

The paragraphs in this passage may or may not be in the most appropriate order. The number of each paragraph is in brackets above the paragraph. The last item for this passage asks for the correct order of paragraphs that will make this passage most sensible.

[1]

Late in 1799, the Department of Aveyron in central France buzzes with gossip touched off by
₃₁
an unusual event. Hunters and farmers told of seeing a boy about 14 years old, who lived alone all by himself in the woods of the region.
₃₂
The reports described the boy as wild and uncivilized. They said that he dug for roots and bulbs, drank from streams, and runs on all fours.
₃₃

[2]

When he was finally captured, the Wild Boy came under the care of Jean-Marc Itard. A physician at the
₃₄
National Institute of Deaf-Mutes. Itard believed that he could civilize the child, but many people disagreed. The debate created by Itard's efforts centered on the question, "Was Victor (as the boy came to be called) abandoned because he was an idiot, or was he an idiot because he was abandoned."
₃₅

[3]

Jean-Marc Itard, however, had opened new doors for the education of children. His work with Victor. Rather,
₃₆

31. **A.** NO CHANGE
    B. buzzed
    C. has buzzed
    D. buzzing

32. **F.** NO CHANGE
    G. alone by himself
    H. alone with himself
    J. alone

33. **A.** NO CHANGE
    B. is running
    C. ran
    D. had run

34. **F.** NO CHANGE
    G. Jean-Marc Itard, a physician
    H. Jean-Marc Itard; a physician
    J. Jean Marc Itard a physician

35. **A.** NO CHANGE
    B. abandoned.
    C. abandoned?"
    D. abandoned!"

36. **F.** NO CHANGE
    G. Victor, rather,
    H. Victor, for example,
    J. Victor for example

37. **A.** NO CHANGE
    B. famous, Italian, educator
    C. famous Italian, educator
    D. famous Italian educator

38. **F.** NO CHANGE
    G. physically and intellectual
    H. physical and intellectual
    J. physical and intellectually

inspired Maria Montessori, the famous, Italian educator. Her
37
approach to teaching children, revolutionary when she opened

her first school in the early years of the 20th century,

emphasizes that children should be free to develop their own

capacities for physically and intellectually development.
38
Thanks to the Wild Boy of Aveyron, Montessori children learn

carpentry, household tasks, and other how-to jobs in addition

to art, music, and the traditional subjects.

[4]

Itard stubbornly maintained that Victor could be helped

and refused to be convinced otherwise. After all, he pointed
39
out, the boy had managed to exist in the woods, living by his

wits, for an unknown length of time! Victor, he believed,
40
possessed a normal intelligence stunted by a lack of contact

with loving parents and the social interaction of everyday

family life. [41]

[5]

Despite Itard's five year training program, Victor did not
42
learn to speak more than a few words. He was never

fully comfortable in clothing or sleeping in a bed, although he

would do this to please the people who cared for him. Victor
43
died in 1828, still "fearful, half-wild, and unable to learn to
44
speak, despite all the efforts that were made."
44

39. **A.** NO CHANGE
    B. and refuses to be convinced
       otherwise.
    C. and refused to be convinced.
    D. OMIT the phrase; end with a
       period.

40. **F.** NO CHANGE
    G. time?
    H. time.
    J. time,

41. What, if any, information is needed
    to clarify the information in this
    sentence?

    A. Definition of normal intelligence
    B. Description of Victor's parents
    C. Explanation of the social
       interaction of everyday family
       life
    D. No information is necessary.

42. **F.** NO CHANGE
    G. five-year
    H. five years
    J. five-years

43. **A.** NO CHANGE
    B. that
    C. both
    D. OMIT this word.

44. The writer puts this part of the
    sentence in quotation marks to:

    F. show that this description is
       directly quoted from a source,
       such as a book.
    G. put emphasis on these phrases.
    H. show that this description is
       ironic.
    J. highlight his or her own opinion.

Question 45 asks about the entire passage.

45. Which sequence of paragraphs
    makes the essay MOST logical?

    A. NO CHANGE
    B. 1, 5, 2, 4, 3
    C. 2, 1, 3, 4, 5
    D. 1, 2, 4, 5, 3

PASSAGE IV

> The paragraphs in this passage may or may not be in the most appropriate order. The number of each paragraph is in brackets above the paragraph. The last item for this passage asks for the correct order of paragraphs that will make this passage the most sensible.

[1]

How is it possible for people today to know about the distant past, especially in those <u>long</u> centuries before the
₄₆
invention of <u>writing the</u> answer has to do with the science of
₄₇
archeology, which uses a variety of <u>different</u> techniques.
₄₈

[2]

[1] As for very ancient remains of humans and their artifacts, scientists <u>are on the ball about</u> the surroundings in
₄₉
which they are found. [2] In general, the lower something is in an archeological "dig," the older it is. [3] <u>Therefore</u>, the
₅₀
more crudely something is made, the older it is. [4] If human remains are found together with the bones of an animal that became extinct 50,000 years ago, we know that the remains are at least 50,000 years old. [5] <u>Any once-living thing, plant</u>
₅₁
<u>or animal, gives off certain rays at a known rate for thousands</u>
₅₁
<u>of years after its death.</u> [6] Still another archeological
₅₁
technique is radiocarbon dating. [7] By measuring its rays in a special machine, archeologists can estimate an
<u>objects</u> age.
₅₂

46. **F.** NO CHANGE
    G. hundred-year-long
    H. longest
    J. OMIT the word.

47. **A.** NO CHANGE
    B. writing. The
    C. writing? The
    D. writing, the

48. **F.** NO CHANGE
    G. different,
    H. various
    J. OMIT the word.

49. **A.** NO CHANGE
    B. are hip to
    C. pay special attention to
    D. OMIT the underlined portion.

50. **F.** NO CHANGE
    G. However
    H. For example
    J. Also

51. To maintain a logical and orderly flow in this paragraph, where should sentence 5 be located?

    A. NO CHANGE
    B. After Sentence 1
    C. After Sentence 6
    D. At the beginning of the paragraph

52. **F.** NO CHANGE
    G. thing's
    H. object
    J. object's

53. **A.** NO CHANGE
    B. grain, it
    C. grain. It
    D. grain . . . it

[3]

Archeologists, like detectives, make informed guesses from the clues they find. If a "dig" contains a mortar for grinding grain; it is a safe guess that the people probably knew

[53]

how to farm. If an ancient site yields a bit of amber that could only have come from hundreds of miles away, the inhabitants were probably traders. Burials with many artifacts give a great

[54]

deal of information. This is especially true with the Egyptians, for Egypt's dry climate has preserved even cloth and wood for thousands of years.

[4]

Of course, with Egypt and most later civilizations, archeologists have written symbols to guide them, for a long

[55]

time, however, no one knew how to read ancient writings. The Greek word for Egyptian writing, hieroglyphics, means "sacred carving"; the Greeks believed that these symbols were magical and could be understood only by Egyptian priests. [56]

[5]

Thus through a combination of science, scholarship, and chance discovery, we are constantly learning more and more about the creatures—both human and nonhuman, who came

[57]

before us on this planet. And new and exciting insights into the

[58]

history of life on earth.

[58]

---

54. F. NO CHANGE
G. was
H. weren't
J. are

55. A. NO CHANGE
B. them for
C. them! For
D. them. For

56. What information, if any, would BEST support the information provided in this paragraph?

F. No information is necessary.
G. An explanation of how archeologists learned to read ancient writings
H. A detailed description of the complex relationship between the Greek and Egyptian cultures
J. Pictures of hieroglyphic writing

57. A. NO CHANGE
B. nonhuman—
C. nonhuman
D. nonhuman.

58. F. NO CHANGE
G. New and exciting insights into the history of life on earth.
H. However, this gives new and exciting insights into the history of life on earth.
J. This gives new and exciting insights into the history of life on earth.

Questions 59 and 60 ask about the entire passage.

59. Does this essay answer the question posed by the author in the opening paragraph?

    A. No, because the author does not discuss "people today."

    B. No, because the author discusses only Greek and Egyptian civilizations.

    C. Yes, because the author introduces the subject of archeology and describes how it helps us decipher the past.

    D. Yes, because the author is an archeologist.

60. Which sequence of paragraphs will make the essay MOST logical?

    F. NO CHANGE
    G. 2, 3, 4, 5, 1
    H. 5, 4, 3, 2, 1
    J. 2, 1, 3, 4, 5

PASSAGE V

The paragraphs in this passage may or may not be in the most appropriate order. The number of each paragraph is in brackets above the paragraph. The last item for this passage asks for the correct order of paragraphs that will make this passage most sensible.

[1]

After the tornado passed I roamed around and <u>find</u> a
                             61
broken power line. It banged violently by the Penn Avenue
curb; it was shooting sparks into the street. I <u>couldnt</u> bring
                                          62
myself to leave the spot.

61. **A.** NO CHANGE
    B. finds
    C. found
    D. founded

62. **F.** NO CHANGE
    G. can't
    H. could'nt
    J. couldn't

63. **A.** NO CHANGE
    B. morning the
    C. morning. The
    D. morning? The

[2]

A tornado hit our neighborhood one morning, the tornado
                                              63
broke all the windows in the envelope factory on Penn Avenue

and ripped down mature oaks and maples on Richland Lane

and its side streets trees about which everyone would make,
                64
in my view, an unconscionable fuss, not least perhaps because
    65
they would lie across the streets for a week.

[3]

The power line was loosing a fireball of sparks that melted

the asphalt from a solid to a liquidy substance. It was a thick,
              66
twisted steel cable usually strung overhead along Penn Avenue;
                    67
it carried power—4,500 kilovolts of it, from Wilkinsburg to

major sections of Pittsburgh, to Homewood and Brushton,

Shadyside, and Squirrel Hill.

[4]

1 The live wire's hundred twisted ends spat a thick sheaf

of useless yellow sparks that hissed. 2 The sparks were

cooking the asphalt gummy; burning a hole. 3 I watched the
                                 68
cable relax and sink into its own pit; I watched the yellow
                   69
sparks pool and crackle around the cable's torn end and splash

out of the pit and over the asphalt in a stream toward the curb

and my shoes. 4 It was melting a pit for itself in the street.
                                                   70
5 My bare shins could feel the heat. 6 I smelled tarry

melted asphalt and steel so hot it smoked.

[5]

"If you touch that," my father said, needlessly "your
                                    71   72
a goner."

64. F. NO CHANGE
    G. streets. Trees
    H. streets—trees
    J. streets; trees

65. A. NO CHANGE
    B. (place after "perhaps")
    C. (place after "week")
    D. OMIT underlined portion.

66. F. NO CHANGE
    G. from a solid to a liquid
    H. from a liquid to a solid
    J. OMIT the underlined portion.

67. A. NO CHANGE
    B. (place after "thick")
    C. (place after "It")
    D. (place after "twisted")

68. F. NO CHANGE
    G. were burning a hole
    H. holes burning through the ground
    J. they were burning a hole

69. A. NO CHANGE
    B. (place after "relax")
    C. (place after "cable")
    D. (place after "watched")

70. Where does sentence 4 logically
    belong in this paragraph?

    F. NO CHANGE
    G. After Sentence 6
    H. After Sentence 1
    J. After Sentence 5

71. A. NO CHANGE
    B. needlessly,
    C. needlessly.
    D. needlessly:

72. F. NO CHANGE
    G. youre
    H. you're
    J. you

73. Suppose the author of this passage was assigned to write an essay on the effects of tornadoes. Does she fulfill this assignment?

    A. Yes, because she tells about the effects of a tornado on her town.
    B. Yes, because she presents her own personal experience with tornado damage.
    C. No, because the article focuses more on the author's fascination with the live power line than on the tornado.
    D. No, because the author doesn't talk about the effects of a tornado.

74. Is it appropriate that the author uses "I" in this passage?

    F. Yes, because she is relating an autobiographical experience from her childhood.
    G. No, because it is never appropriate to use the first-person "I" in an essay.
    H. No, because the essay focuses on the tornado, not her life.
    J. Yes, because the first-person I should be used in all essays.

75. Which sequence of paragraphs makes the essay MOST logical?

    A. NO CHANGE
    B. 2, 1, 3, 4, 5
    C. 1, 3, 4, 5, 2
    D. 5, 4, 3, 2, 1

END OF ENGLISH TEST I

Model Reading ACT 1

40 Questions—35 Minutes

INSTRUCTIONS: There are four passages on this test with 10 items about each passage. Choose the best answer for each item based on the passage. Then fill in the appropriate circle on the answer sheet (page 246).
Check pages 271 and 277–280 for answers and explanations.

PASSAGE 1

PROSE FICTION: This passage is from "Her First Ball" by Katherine Mansfield.

Exactly when the ball began Leila would have found it hard to say. Perhaps her first real partner was the cab. It did not matter that she shared the cab with the Sheridan girls and
5 their brother. She sat back in her own little corner of it, and the bolster on which her hand rested felt like the sleeve of an unknown young man's dress suit; and away they bowled, past waltzing lamp-posts and houses
10 and fences and trees.

"Have you really never been to a ball before, Leila? But, my child, how too weird—" cried the Sheridan girls.

"Our nearest neighbor was fifteen miles,"
15 said Leila softly, gently opening and shutting her fan.

Oh, dear, how hard it was to be indifferent like the others! She tried not to smile too much; she tried not to care. But every single thing was
20 so new and exciting . . . Meg's tuberoses, Jose's long loop of amber, Laura's little dark head, pushing above her white fur like a flower through snow. She would remember forever. It even gave her a pang to see her cousin Laurie
25 throw away the wisps of tissue paper he pulled from the fastenings of his new gloves. She would like to have kept those wisps as a keepsake, as a remembrance. Laurie leaned forward and put his hand on Laura's knee.

30 "Look here, darling," he said. "The third and the ninth as usual. Twig?"

Oh, how marvelous to have a brother! In her excitement Leila felt that if there had been time, if it hadn't been impossible, she couldn't
35 have helped crying because she was an only child, and no brother had ever said "Twig?" to her; no sister would ever say, as Meg said to Jose that moment, "I've never known your hair go up more successfully than it has
40 tonight!"

But, of course, there was no time. They were at the drill hall already; there were cabs in front of them and cabs behind. The road was bright on either side with moving fan-
45 like lights, and on the pavement happy couples seemed to float through the air; little satin shoes chased each other like birds.

"Hold on to me, Leila; you'll get lost," said Laura.

50 "Come on, girls, let's make a dash for it," said Laurie.

Leila put two fingers on Laura's pink velvet cloak, and they were somehow lifted past the big golden lantern, carried along the pas-
55 sage, and pushed into the little room marked "Ladies." Here the crowd was so great there was hardly space to take off their things; the noise was deafening. Two benches on either side were stacked high with wraps. Two old
60 women in white aprons ran up and down tossing fresh armfuls. And everybody was pressing forward trying to get at the little dressing-table and mirror at the far end.

A great quivering jet of gas lighted the
65 ladies' room. It couldn't wait; it was dancing

already. When the door opened again and there came a burst of tuning from the drill hall, it leaped almost to the ceiling.

Dark girls, fair girls were patting their
70 hair, tying ribbons again, tucking handkerchiefs down the fronts of their bodices, smoothing marble-white gloves. And because they were all laughing it seemed to Leila that they were all lovely.

75 "Aren't there any invisible hair-pins?" cried a voice. "How most extraordinary! I can't see a single invisible hair-pin."

"Powder my back, there's a darling," cried someone else.

80 "But I must have a needle and cotton. I've torn simply miles and miles of the frill," wailed a third.

Then, "Pass them along, pass them along!" The straw basket of programs was tossed from
85 arm to arm. Darling little pink-and-silver programs, with pink pencils and fluffy tassels. Leila's fingers shook as she took one out of the basket. She wanted to ask someone, "Am I meant to have one too?" but she had just time
90 to read: "Waltz 3. *Two, Two in a Canoe.* Polka 4. *Making the Feathers Fly,*" when Meg cried, "Ready, Leila?" and they pressed their way through the crush in the passage towards the big double doors of the drill hall.

1. The statement "Have you really never been to a ball before, Leila? But, my child, how too weird—" indicates that:

   A. Leila must be some sort of social outcast.
   B. all of the Sheridan girls and their friends have been to balls before.
   C. the Sheridan girls do not like Leila and wish that she were not coming with them to the ball.
   D. the ball is an uninteresting event.

2. Leila's relation to the other young people in the cab is that:

   F. they are friends from school.
   G. they are her siblings.
   H. they are her cousins.
   J. they are her dates for the ball.

3. The phrase "waltzing lamp-posts" is significant because it:

   A. shows that the world Leila and the Sheridan children are in is magical.
   B. conveys Leila's sense of excitement and anticipation of dancing at the ball.
   C. indicates that the cab was moving very quickly.
   D. reminds Leila of dance lessons.

4. Leila's general mood is:

   F. happy excitement and anticipation.
   G. melancholy sadness.
   H. oscillating between excitement and fear.
   J. great loneliness.

5. The statement "And because they were all laughing it seemed to Leila that they were all lovely" means that:

   A. Leila believes that people who do not laugh are ugly.
   B. Leila is upset because she believes the laughing women around her are more attractive than she is.
   C. Leila believes that all the women around her are laughing at her naiveté.
   D. Leila believes the women's laughter makes them lovely because they are part of the happy excitement of the ball.

6. According to Leila, she has never been to a ball because:

   F. as an only child, she could not go unchaperoned.
   G. her parents disapproved of balls.
   H. she is an orphan and could not get a new dress.
   J. she lives in a rural area where they do not have balls.

7. It gives Leila a "pang to see her cousin Laurie throw away the wisps of tissue paper he pulled from the fastenings of his new gloves" because:

   A. she believes that paper should be recycled.
   B. she cannot afford such nice, new gloves.
   C. she believes that every little thing associated with the ball is special and should be preserved.
   D. she knows that Laurie will need the tissue paper to repack the gloves later.

8. Based on the information in this passage, the Sheridan family is probably:

    F. middleclass.
    G. poor but happy.
    H. miserly and unhappy.
    J. upperclass and fashionable.

9. Leila wonders, "Am I meant to have one too?" when the dance programs are passed out because:

    A. she is at the ball only as a spectator, not to dance.
    B. the programs are expensive, and she cannot afford one.

C. she finds it hard to believe that she is actually a part of the excitement going on around her.
D. she doesn't know how to read.

10. Leila's fingers shake as she removes a program from the basket because:

    F. she is excited to be at the ball.
    G. she's afraid she'll be caught stealing.
    H. she wants to make sure she gets a program.
    J. she is terrified of being at the ball.

PASSAGE II

SOCIAL SCIENCE

G.I. Jane Breaks the Combat Barrier

As the convoy rumbled up the road in Iraq, Specialist Veronica Alfaro was struck by the beauty of fireflies dancing in the night. Then she heard the unmistakable
5 pinging of tracer rounds and, in a Baghdad moment, realized the insects were illuminated bullets.

She jumped from behind the wheel of her gun truck, grabbed her medical bag and
10 sprinted 50 yards to a stalled civilian truck. On the way, bullets kicked up dust near her feet. She pulled the badly wounded driver to the ground and got to work.

Her heroism that January night last year
15 earned Specialist Alfaro a Bronze Star for valor. She had already received a combat action badge for fending off insurgents as a machine gunner.

"I did everything there," Spc. Alfaro, 25,
20 said of her time in Iraq. "I gunned. I drove. I served as a truck commander. And underneath it all, I was a medic."

Before 2001, America's military women had rarely seen ground combat. Their jobs
25 kept them mostly away from enemy lines, as military policy dictates.

But the Afghanistan and Iraq wars, often fought in marketplaces and alleyways, have changed that. In both countries, women have
30 repeatedly proved their mettle in combat. The number of high-ranking women and women who command all-male units has climbed considerably along with their status in the military.

35 "Iraq has advanced the cause of full integration for women in the Army by leaps and bounds," said Peter R. Mansoor, a retired Army colonel who served as executive officer to Gen. David H. Petraeus while he was the
40 top American commander in Iraq. "They have earned the confidence and respect of male colleagues."

Their success, widely known in the military, remains largely hidden from public view.
45 In part, this is because their most challenging work is often the result of a quiet circumvention of military policy. Women are barred from joining combat branches like the infantry, armor, Special Forces and most field
50 artillery units and from doing support jobs while living with those smaller units. Women can lead some male troops into combat as officers, but they cannot serve with them in battle.

55 Yet, over and over, in Iraq and Afghanistan, Army commanders have resorted to bureaucratic trickery when they needed more

soldiers for crucial jobs, like bomb disposal and intelligence. On paper, for instance,
60 women have been "attached" to a combat unit rather than "assigned."

Nonetheless, as soldiers in the Iraq and Afghanistan wars, women have done nearly as much in battle as their male counterparts:
65 patrolled streets with machine guns, served as gunners on vehicles, disposed of explosives, and driven trucks down bomb-ridden roads. They have proved indispensable in their ability to interact with and search Iraqi and
70 Afghan women for weapons, a job men cannot do for cultural reasons. The Marine Corps has created revolving units—"lionesses"—dedicated to just this task.

A small number of women have even
75 conducted raids, engaging the enemy directly in total disregard of existing policies. Many experts, including David W. Barno, a retired lieutenant general who commanded forces in Afghanistan, Dr. Mansoor, who now teaches
80 military history at Ohio State University, and John A. Nagl, a retired lieutenant colonel who helped write the Army's new counterinsurgency field manual, say it is only a matter of time before regulations that have restricted
85 women's participation in war will be adjusted to meet the reality forged over the last eight years.

The Marine Corps, which is overwhelmingly male and designed for combat, recently
90 opened two more categories of intelligence jobs to women, recognizing the value of their work in Iraq and Afghanistan. In gradually admitting women to combat, the United States will be catching up to the rest of the
95 world. More than a dozen countries allow women in some or all ground combat occupations. Among those pushing boundaries most aggressively is Canada, which has recruited women for the infantry and sent them to
100 Afghanistan.

Poll numbers show that a majority of the public supports allowing women to do more on the battlefield. Fifty-three percent of the respondents in a *New York Times*/CBS News
105 poll said they would favor permitting women to "join combat units, where they would be directly involved in the ground fighting."

11. It can reasonably be inferred from this passage that the author believes:

   A. women may be better suited than are their male counterparts for certain jobs in the military.
   B. women are better prepared for the rigors of close combat than most of the males in the military.
   C. women will eventually have more combat responsibilities.
   D. women should not be exempted from the military draft, as they currently are.

12. Which is BEST supported by lines 43–54?

   F. Women may serve only in support roles.
   G. Women have gained importance in intelligence work.
   H. Women are regularly placed in combat units.
   J. Women may not serve as helicopter pilots.

13. Reviewing the details in the passage shows which of the following is FALSE?

   A. Women cannot lead male troops into combat as officers.
   B. Women cannot serve with male troops in battle.
   C. Women are barred from joining the Special Forces.
   D. Women serve in battle by circumventing rules.

14. The main purpose of the fourth paragraph in relation to the entire passage is to:

   F. establish that women in the American armed forces are engaged in combat just like women from other countries.
   G. establish that women in the American armed forces are already engaged in combat, even though the rules do not specifically permit it.
   H. describe a unique exception in which this one American armed forces member was engaged in armed combat.
   J. show how the American forces use propaganda about women in combat, even though these women are not really involved because the rules forbid it.

15. When the author writes "forged over the last eight years" in lines 86–87, she most likely means that:

A. weapons have been fabricated in special iron forges during the last eight years.

B. battle reports have been forged to misrepresent what actually happened in military operations.

C. actual practices were developed during the last eight years.

D. fraudulent activities have been reported during the last eight years.

16. According to the first paragraph of the passage:

F. a new type of ammunition was being used in which bullets were disguised as fireflies.

G. Specialist Veronica Alfaro was wounded by a bullet that looked like a firefly.

H. Specialist Veronica Alfaro was affected by the appearance of the illuminated bullets.

J. fireflies look beautiful at night near Baghdad in Iraq.

17. Which statement BEST summarizes the author's view about the impact of the wars in Iraq and Afghanistan?

A. These wars have caused a high number of civilian casualties in marketplaces.

B. These wars have seen women officers lead some male troops into combat.

C. The wars in Iraq and Afghanistan have cost the lives of women soldiers.

D. The wars in Iraq and Afghanistan have established women as combat soldiers.

18. The author's reference to the words "attached" and "assigned" in lines 60–61:

F. emphasizes the use of synonyms in a military context.

G. shows how commanders use subtle differences in meanings to circumvent official language.

H. demonstrates how, in the military, different words can have the same official meaning.

J. points out how women in the military flagrantly break the rules.

19. The author MOST likely provides the poll numbers in the final paragraph to:

A. show that almost half of the people responding to the poll do not support a combat role for women.

B. show that there is support for allowing women to take on a greater role in the military.

C. introduce statistics into the historical account.

D. reveal that polls by more liberal news organizations can produce unreliable results.

20. The author's opinion of the American "regulations that have restricted women's participation in war" is that the regulations:

F. represent a disconnect from reality.

G. are the official policy of the United States armed services.

H. are not shared by many other countries.

J. are used to circumvent what actually happens in the field.

PASSAGE III

HUMANITIES

Film Food, Ready for Its "Bon Appétit"

When the director Nora Ephron began shooting a pivotal scene in her movie *Julie and Julia*, it quickly became clear that the sole meunière might become the food stylist's Waterloo.
5 Susan Spungen, the movie's food stylist, had spent a dozen years as Martha Stewart's food editor. She had been a caterer before that. She understood pressure. But she knew she was in the weeds the moment she arrived at a
10 Manhattan restaurant to shoot the scene.

For starters, the chef that Ms. Ephron had recruited to cook on the show was instead pressed into service as the scene's waiter.

That left Ms. Spungen uncharacteristically unprepared. The restaurant didn't have a non-stick pan, and the chef forgot to tell her that the secret to the dish was a light coat of Wondra flour.

Worse, she had only about 10 of the expensive fillets to work with. That wouldn't allow for many mistakes. And even if she cooked one perfectly, how was she going to make sure the big fillet sizzled enough so the camera would pick it up?

"I have no idea how, but we finally just got one that didn't stick," she said. That scene became Ms. Ephron's favorite food moment in the film. For Ms. Spungen, it is just one of several food miracles in a film where what the actors eat is as important as the actors themselves. Although movies have long relied on half-cooked turkeys colored with motor oil, fruit made of plastic, and ice cream carved from Crisco, food in film is increasingly edible and even delicious.

"Everybody thinks it's all shellacked," said Colin Flynn, a New York-based chef and stylist who worked with Ms. Spungen on the film. "In the '70s and '80s it was more like that. Food looked more like Plasticine. Nowadays it's almost always real food."

For food stylists, most of whom began as cooks, it's a welcome change. It's also good for audiences, who have become more sophisticated about food and expect more realistic images. And directors believe that well-prepared food can improve the actors' performances and the look of the final scene.

"The challenge always is making it seem delicious and hyper-real," said John Lyons, president of production for Focus Features. "If it doesn't look hyper-real, it doesn't work in the movie." That means a dish needs to be fresh-looking and well-prepared to begin with, and then enhanced with a bit of oil here and a little fake steam there. On films without the money for a stylist, the props department might rely on a local restaurant or even a crew member's boyfriend who happens to be a good cook.

Mr. Lyons produced *Pieces of April*, about a dysfunctional family Thanksgiving.

They had precious few turkeys in the budget. In cases like that, the camera doesn't linger too long and the actors put as little food in their mouths as possible. But on films with a budget for food stylists, "food becomes very much the fabric of the movie," he said.

A good stylist always has enough replacement food. Often, no one knows what part of a dish an actor will eat until the scene is shot or how many takes the director will want. Johanna Weinstein, a food stylist based in Toronto, said, "It's guerrilla kind of stuff, because you are all about making quantity so the actors have enough of the one thing they have to eat 100 times and then correcting things on the fly."

And things change fast. For the 2000 movie *American Psycho*, Ms. Weinstein had prepared several vegetarian dishes for the actor Willem Dafoe, who, she was told, didn't eat meat. But at the last minute, he decided his character was a carnivore. In deference to his Method Acting technique, she had to send out for steaks and figure out how to cook them on the set.

Even when a little Hollywood magic has to be used, food stylists still try to keep it at least looking real. Two actresses in the cop thriller *Pride and Glory* were vegan. So, the assistant property master for the film called in a vegan chef to help style a dinner scene that had a ham as the centerpiece. The chef ended up piling slices of sham ham made from soybeans near the real stuff, careful to make sure the two versions never touched.

Of course, there are plenty of times a food stylist has to employ tricks. Cherry pies are filled with mashed potatoes, poultry is partly roasted and painted with Kitchen Bouquet, glycerin and water make beads of sweat on glasses, and ice cream is wrapped around dry-ice nuggets so it won't melt.

When Amy Adams, an actress in the movie, drops a fruit Bavarian on the sidewalk, she is actually dropping a special breakaway mold filled with whipped cream and raspberry puree. The stuffing in a chicken that she drops on her kitchen floor had to be doused in heavy cream so it splatted properly.

21. According to the passage, the food shown in movies was mostly real starting in the:

A. 1960s.
B. 1970s.
C. 1980s.
D. 1990s.

22. The main point of this passage is best summarized by which of the following?

F. It is best to use real food in film scenes and not try to deceive the audience.
G. In film, it's what food looks like, not what food really is that matters.
H. Film food is often inedible because of all the preservatives that must be added to it.
J. Film actors need the real food in films so they can effectively portray their roles.

23. In the first sentence, when the author writes "the sole meunière might become the stylist's Waterloo," she MOST likely means that:

A. there was one, sole, dish featured in the program that was likely to cause problems.
B. sole meunière could be impossible to prepare properly.
C. the actors might refuse to eat the sole because many people do not like fish.
D. a famous restaurant named Waterloo was forced to close after some of its customers became sick.

24. According to the passage, food stylists who design food for movies usually:

F. work for famous personalities or actors.
G. started out as cooks.
H. began their careers as artists.
J. usually have someone else to do the cooking.

25. We can infer from the passage that the film was based on two women who:

A. were food stylists.
B. owned a restaurant.
C. were chefs.
D. were vegans.

26. In lines 67–68, when Mr. Lyons says "food becomes very much the fabric of the movie," he MOST likely means:

F. the food itself is an important part of the movie.
G. the fabric in the movie was colored with vegetable dye.
H. much of the fabric for the costumes contained designs that looked like food.
J. the food was a fabrication, not real.

27. The author's development of the passage mainly relies on:

A. persuasion.
B. narration.
C. reflection.
D. technical details.

28. Based on the passage, one major success of the film *Julie and Julia* is that:

F. the food was as important as the acting.
G. the film had a pivotal scene.
H. the film had food stylists.
J. there were only 10 expensive fillets to work with.

29. Based on the passage, the greatest challenge for a food stylist is to:

A. use real food unless it is impossible.
B. keep the food looking as real as possible.
C. be prepared for the unexpected.
D. have a lot of food available in case there is an emergency.

30. The "Method Acting" mentioned on line 85 means that:

F. the actor had a particular method of using a knife and a fork.
G. the actor ate food that his character would eat but that he normally would not eat.
H. an actor must always obey the director's method, even if he disagrees.
J. the actor had a mental method to make himself believe the steak was really made of soybeans.

PASSAGE IV

NATURAL SCIENCE: This passage is from "Is Time Travel Possible?" by Mark Davidson.

Contrary to the old warning that time waits for no one, time slows down when you are on the move. It also slows down more as you move faster, which means astronauts
5 someday may survive so long in space that they would return to an Earth of the distant future. If you could move at the speed of light, 186,282 miles a second, your time would stand still. If you could move faster
10 than light, outpacing your shadow, your time would move backward.

Although no form of matter yet discovered moves as fast as or faster than light, scientific experiments have confirmed that
15 accelerated motion causes a voyager's time to be stretched. Einstein predicted this in 1905, when he introduced the concept of relative time as part of his Special Theory of Relativity. A search is now underway to con-
20 firm the suspected existence of particles of matter that move faster than light and therefore possibly might serve as our passports to the past.

Einstein employed a definition of time,
25 for experimental purposes, as that which is measured by a clock. He regarded a clock as anything that measured a uniformly repeating physical process. In accordance with his definition, time and time's relativity are
30 measurable by any sundial, hourglass, metronome, alarm clock, or an atomic clock that can measure a billionth of a second because its "tick" is based on the uniformly repeating wobble of the spinning-top motion
35 of electrons.

With atomic-clock application of Einstein's definition of time, scientists have demonstrated that an ordinary airplane flight is like a brief visit to the Fountain of Youth. In
40 1972, for example, scientists who took four atomic clocks on an airplane trip around the world discovered that the moving clocks moved slightly slower than atomic clocks which had remained on the ground. If you fly
45 around the world, preferably going eastward

to gain the advantage of the added motion of the Earth's rotation, the atomic clocks show that you'll return younger than you would have been if you had stayed home. Frankly,
50 you'll be younger by only 40 billionths of a second. Such an infinitesimal saving of time hardly makes up for all the hours you age while waiting at airports, but any saving of time proves that time can be stretched.
55 Moreover, atomic clocks have demonstrated that the stretching of time, or "time dilation," increases with speed.

Here is an example of what you can expect if tomorrow's space-flight technology—
60 employing the energy of thermonuclear fusion, matter-antimatter annihilation, or whatever—enables you to move at ultra-high speeds. Imagine you're an astronaut with a twin who stays home. If you travel back and
65 forth to the nearest star at about half the speed of light, you'll be gone for eighteen Earth years. When you return, your twin will be eighteen years older, but you'll have aged only sixteen years. Your body will be two
70 years younger than your twin's because time aboard the flying spaceship will have moved slower than time on Earth. You will have aged normally, but you will have been in a slower time zone. If your spaceship moves at about
75 90 percent of light-speed, you'll age only 50 percent as much as your twin. If you whiz along at 99.86 percent of light-speed, you'll age only 5 percent as much. These examples of time-stretching, of course, cannot be tested
80 with any existing spacecraft. Yet, they are based on mathematical projections of relativity science, as confirmed by the atomic-clock experiments.

Speed is not the only factor that slows
85 time; so does gravity. Einstein determined in his General Theory of Relativity (the 1915 sequel to his 1905 Special Theory of Relativity) that the force of an object's gravity "curves" the space in the object's gravitation-
90 al field. When gravity curves space, Einstein reasoned, gravity also must curve time, because space and time are linked in a space-time continuum. The concept of the space-

time continuum, developed by one of
Einstein's former professors, simply means
that time and space must be considered
together because time is a fourth dimension
of space.

Numerous atomic-clock experiments
have confirmed Einstein's calculation that the
closer you are to the Earth's center of gravity,
which is the Earth's core, the slower you will
age. In one of these experiments, an atomic
clock was taken from the National Bureau of
Standards in Washington, D.C., near sea
level, and moved to mile-high Denver. The
results demonstrated that people in Denver
age more rapidly by a tiny amount than people in Washington.

If you would like gravity's space-time
warp to extend your life, get a home at the
beach and a job as a deep-sea diver. Avoid
living in the mountains or working in a sky-
scraper. If you're taking airplane trips to slow
your aging, make sure you fly fast enough to
cancel out the gravity-reduction effect of
being high above the Earth's surface. That
advice, like the advice about flying around
the world, will enable you to slow your aging
by only a few billionths of a second.

Nevertheless, those tiny fractions of a second add up to more proof that time-stretching
is a reality. The proof involving gravity suggests that you could have an unforgettable ren-
dezvous with a black hole, where gravity is
believed to be so powerful that it imprisons
light. In a black hole—a huge, burned-out star
that has collapsed into infinite density and,
therefore, infinite gravity—the object's
extreme warp of space-time would make your
time stand still. Granted, a black hole would
be an awfully dark and dreary place to spend
eternity, but think of all the time you'd have to
redecorate.

31. According to the theories in this article, in
order for time to move backward, an object
must move:

A. fast enough to break the time barrier.
B. at 186,282 miles a second.
C. at the speed of light.
D. faster than the speed of light.

32. The results of the atomic-clock experiment
related in the fourth paragraph show that time:

F. cannot be measured in outer space.
G. continues at a normal pace.
H. slows down.
J. speeds up.

33. Which theory was NOT developed by
Einstein?

A. Space-time continuum
B. General Theory of Relativity
C. Special Theory of Relativity
D. None of the above theories were
developed by Einstein.

34. People in Denver age more rapidly than
people in Washington, D.C., because:

F. the average age of the population in
Denver is older than that in
Washington, D. C.
G. the climate is healthier for people on the
East Coast.
H. Washington, D.C., is closer than Denver
to sea level.
J. the air in Denver contains ash from Mount
St. Helens.

35. Time for humans is NOT affected by:

A. gravity.
B. life expectancy.
C. speed of travel.
D. closeness to Earth's center.

36. Which statement BEST reflects the author's
main point in this passage?

F. Black holes are very dangerous.
G. Atomic clocks are unreliable indicators of
time.
H. Einstein was the greatest scientist in
history.
J. Time can be affected by factors such as
speed and gravity.

37. In its context in line 81, the word *projections*
means:

A. visual images on a television screen.
B. predicted outcomes.
C. objects that stick out of the ground.
D. proofs.

38. In a place of infinite gravity, time:

   F. speeds up dramatically.
   G. slows down slightly.
   H. reverses completely.
   J. stops completely.

39. In the last sentence the author mentions redecorating while living in a black hole:

   A. because when the sun dies, all humans will live in a black hole.
   B. to demonstrate that the concept of black holes is ridiculous.

   C. to prove that life is in fact dark and dreary.
   D. to add a playful note to an otherwise serious scientific discussion.

40. If one 20-year-old woman travels in space at half the speed of light for 18 years and her twin stays on Earth, the space traveler's age when she returns will be:

   F. 30.
   G. 35.
   H. 36.
   J. 20.

END OF READING TEST I

Model ACT I English Scoring Key

Item and Answer	Usage/ Mechanics	Rhetorical Skills	Review These Pages	Item and Answer	Usage/ Mechanics	Rhetorical Skills	Review These Pages
1. C		❏	133–141	28. H		❏	145–150
2. F	❏		67–75	29. B		❏	133–141
3. B	❏		108–111	30. J		❏	133–141
4. H	❏		56–58, 118–120	31. B	❏		67–75
5. A		❏	133–141	32. J		❏	156–160
6. G		❏	145–150	33. C	❏		79–83
7. B	❏		38–42	34. G	❏		103–108
8. J		❏	133–141	35. C	❏		121–125
9. D	❏		118–120	36. H	❏		103–108, 133–141
10. F	❏		68–70	37. D	❏		103–108
11. A	❏		108–115	38. H	❏		84–90
12. H		❏	133–141	39. D		❏	156–160
13. D	❏		59–63	40. H	❏		120–122
14. G	❏		84–90	41. D		❏	133–141
15. C		❏	133–141	42. G	❏		111–115
16. G	❏		103–108	43. C		❏	59–63
17. D	❏		65–67	44. F	❏		133–141
18. H	❏		79–83	45. D		❏	145–150
19. A	❏		76–79, 103–108	46. J		❏	156–160
20. G	❏		108–111	47. C	❏		120–122
21. D		❏	156–160	48. J		❏	156–160
22. F	❏		56–58	49. C		❏	133–141
23. A		❏	145–150	50. J		❏	133–141
24. H	❏		43–47	51. C		❏	145–150
25. A		❏	133–141	52. J	❏		118–120
26. J	❏		34–38	53. B	❏		103–108
27. C		❏	133–141	54. F	❏		61–70

Item and Answer	Usage/ Mechanics	Rhetorical Skills	Review These Pages	Item and Answer	Usage/ Mechanics	Rhetorical Skills	Review These Pages
55. D	❑		34–38	66. J		❑	156–160
56. G		❑	133–141	67. A		❑	133–141
57. B	❑		111–115	68. J	❑		108–111
58. J		❑	133–141	69. A		❑	43–47
59. C		❑	133–141	70. H		❑	145–150
60. F		❑	145–150	71. B	❑		123–125
61. C	❑		67–75	72. H	❑		118–120
62. J	❑		118–120	73. C		❑	133–141
63. C	❑		34–38	74. F		❑	133–141
64. H	❑		111–115	75. B		❑	145–150
65. A		❑	156–160				

Number Correct:

Usage/Mechanics _____

Rhetorical Skills _____

Total _____

Model ACT I Reading Scoring Key

Item and Answer	Social Studies/ Sciences	Arts/ Literature	Item and Answer	Social Studies/ Sciences	Arts/ Literature	Item and Answer	Social Studies/ Sciences	Arts/ Literature
1. B		❏	15. C	❏		28. F		❏
2. H		❏	16. H	❏		29. B		❏
3. B		❏	17. D	❏		30. G		❏
4. F		❏	18. G	❏		31. D	❏	
5. D		❏	19. B	❏		32. H	❏	
6. J		❏	20. F	❏		33. A	❏	
7. C		❏	21. D		❏	34. H	❏	
8. J		❏	22. G		❏	35. B	❏	
9. C		❏	23. B		❏	36. J	❏	
10. F		❏	24. G		❏	37. B	❏	
11. C	❏		25. C		❏	38. J	❏	
12. G	❏		26. F		❏	39. D	❏	
13. A	❏		27. B		❏	40. H	❏	
14. G	❏							

Number Correct:

Social Studies/Sciences _____

Arts/Literature _____

Total _____

Model ACT I English Answers Explained

PASSAGE I

1. C
This sentence presents the thesis of the essay that follows. Clearly, the author is quite capable of elaborating on this idea, for she does so for the remainder of the passage. However, there is nothing special about this sentence that indicates the author to be a great writer. And finally, the author of this passage gives no indication that the passage of time needs to be emphasized here.

2. F
In order for this sentence to maintain proper construction, the verbs in the sentence must be in the same tense. Therefore, the verb *take* must be in the same tense as the earlier present tense verb *is*.

3. B
A semicolon should be used to separate items in a list when those items are long and complex and when they are independent clauses.

4. H
The author is referring to more than one video game, so the correct answer must be plural. A verb follows the noun *video games*, so the word cannot be a possessive.

5. A
In context with the language in the passage, the word *deliver* is emphasized to show that people have the option of remaining at home while someone else brings food directly to their door. There is no discussion of mail, how quickly food is brought to the home, or the take-out option in this paragraph.

6. G
Because this sentence repeats ideas mentioned in the previous sentence, the phrases should logically fall in the same order. Since the previous sentence refers first to parking, then to walking, and then to waiting, the items in this sentence should match this order.

7. B
The second "sentence" here is not a sentence. It is a parenthetical adverbial clause describing why preparing our own food is getting easier, making it a fragment. Therefore, it needs to be joined to the preceding independent clause and then set apart from the remainder of the sentence by a comma.

8. J
Since microwave use has become common, the slang verb *to nuke* was created to describe this type of cooking. However, this is not formal English; therefore, it is inappropriate for a formal essay. Choices G and H are also slang terms for cooking food in the microwave.

9. D
The subject of this sentence is followed directly by a verb. If *futurists* were a possessive, it would be an adjective describing the actual subject of the sentence. Since no noun follows, *futurists* stands alone as the subject. Also important, note that the verb that follows (*call*) is plural; therefore, the subject must be plural as well.

10. F
Since this verb refers to the subject *families* and it should be parallel with the verb *stay, interact* must be a plural verb in the present tense.

11. A
A period, exclamation point, or semicolon would separate a dependent clause from an independent clause, making the first part of this sentence a fragment. A dash functions here to separate the explanation of the elements already mentioned.

12. H
The author doesn't take any personal responsibility for the occurrence of cocooning, so it doesn't make her ashamed. Choosing to write about this subject shows that the author is not indifferent about it. Her choice of words indicates that she thinks cocooning is not "healthy" and it will "rip the social fabric"; this clearly indicates that she is very concerned about the future of society.

13. D
Throughout this essay, the author has been speaking in the first person plural, using *us, we,* and *our.* A switch in pronouns here would not only be uncharacteristic of this essay, it also would show that the author is not a part of the society she's describing. Since she has already described herself as part of this society, the choice of *our* here is the best, most consistent answer.

14. G
The word *equal* should be an adjective describing the word *time. Equally* is an adverb, which cannot describe a noun. *Equated* is a verb, which is also an inappropriate choice. There is no such word as *equalest*, because *equal* is an absolute adjective that

cannot be made into a superlative. Something cannot be more or less equal, otherwise it would not be equal.

15. C

Choices A, B, and D provide irrelevant information that would distract rather than inform the reader. Choice C offers information that would clarify the author's argument.

PASSAGE II

16. G

The first "sentence" as it is written is a fragment. This fragment is an adverb phrase used to describe where the Indians lived. A long adverb phrase that begins a sentence is separated from the main, independent clause of the sentence by a comma.

17. D

In the first sentence, the author discusses the Indians in the past tense. To remain consistent, this verb should also be in the past tense.

18. H

To maintain parallel construction, the third item in the list should be presented in the same manner as the first two—a single noun.

19. A

The subject of this sentence is *one.* Therefore, the verb must be singular. No comma should separate the verb from the remainder of the sentence.

20. G

A colon is the appropriate punctuation to set off a list of items from the sentence. A period or semicolon would make the list of tribes a sentence fragment.

21. D

In this paragraph, the author has already discussed the Iroquois League (League of Five Nations) and the five tribes that united to form this group. Adding any of the phrases given here would be redundant.

22. F

The word *Iroquois* is both a singular and a plural, like *English* or *French.* Just as you wouldn't say *the Frenches,* you wouldn't say *the Iroquoises.* This is also shown in sentence 1 of this paragraph. The word is not possessive here because *of the Iroquois* is used instead to indicate possession.

23. A

This sentence makes the most sense at the end of the paragraph, where it is already located. The entire paragraph builds ideas that are summed up in this final statement.

24. H

The individuals acting as *servants of the people* are the elected officials, not the tribe. In the other choices, the opening adverbial clause appears to describe the tribe rather than the officials.

25. A

The author assumes that the reader of this essay is familiar with the term *democracy.* However, the reader is probably not familiar with the term *sachem* and the way the sachem functioned in the Iroquois governing body. Though an explanation of how the sachem were chosen might be interesting, it is not as helpful as the description of the duties of the sachem. A list of all the men chosen to be sachem would take up a great deal of space and provide no useful information to the reader.

26. J

Choice F presents the reader with a comma splice, a run-on sentence in which the two independent clauses are joined only by a comma. Choice G is a run-on sentence where no punctuation is used to join the two independent clauses. An ellipsis can be used to bridge two sentences, but it would replace missing words—and there do not seem to be any missing words here. Choice J breaks the run-on into two complete sentences.

27. C

The other options present common slang expressions that have similar meanings to *rejected.* In the formal context of this passage, especially following the formal word *accepted,* the word *rejected* is most appropriate.

28. H

The discussion of women here introduces a new idea; therefore, the author should begin a new paragraph. Because no special emphasis is needed for the sentence ending with *operated,* a period is the appropriate punctuation.

29. B

Though the author does mention the powerful roles of women in the Iroquois League, the majority of the article focuses on the League itself and its government. Only one paragraph focuses on the role of women.

30. J

This essay is most likely too basic for professors of history. While G and H are possible audiences for this essay, the essay is designed to present general information to anyone unfamiliar with this group of people.

PASSAGE III

31. B
Choice B is the past tense, which is consistent with the discussion of an event in 1799 and the tense of the other verbs in the paragraph.

32. J
The phrases *by himself, all by himself,* and *with himself* all repeat the meaning of the word *alone,* making the phrases redundant. Since these phrases simply repeat the word, rather than modifying it, they are unnecessary.

33. C
In order to maintain parallel construction in this sentence, all of the verbs must be in the same tense. *Dug* and *drank* are both past tense, so *ran* is correct.

34. G
The comma is necessary to set off Jean-Marc Itard's name from the modifying clause that follows it and provides additional information about him. A period or a semicolon would create a sentence fragment.

35. C
Because the quotation is in the form of a question, it should end with a question mark, followed by closing quotation marks.

36. H
His work with Victor is a sentence fragment because it has no verb. Furthermore, the word *rather* makes little sense, whereas *for example,* set off by commas, connects the first and second sentences of the paragraph.

37. D
Both B and C are incorrect because a comma should not separate the adjective and the word it is describing. Because the adjective *famous* modifies the noun phrase *Italian educator,* the same rule applies. Therefore, no commas are necessary here.

38. H
In choice F, adverb forms are given for both words, but the words describe a noun and not a verb. In choice G, the adverb *physically* is being used in place of the adjective *physical* to describe the noun *development.* In choice J, the opposite is true.

39. D
The clauses *refused to be convinced* or *refused [or refuses] to be convinced otherwise* are unnecessary because *stubbornly maintained* in the opening clause implies that Itard would not allow others to influence his opinions.

40. H
This is not a question or a statement that requires enough emphasis to need an exclamation point. It is, however, the end of a sentence, so a period rather than a comma is appropriate.

41. D
Most readers will not need a definition as in choices A and C. Choice B is impossible to discover, since Itard and his peers did not know who Victor's parents were or what they were like. Though it rests on the general assumptions of normal intelligence and everyday family life, the sentence needs no further information.

42. G
The words *five-year* form a compound adjective that modifies *training program.* When a compound adjective precedes the word or phrase it describes, it is hyphenated.

43. C
The writer lists two things that Victor was uncomfortable doing. The adjectives *this* and *that* both indicate a single action. *Both* indicates two actions, so C is the best option.

44. F
Quotation marks should be used for only a few specific purposes: to set off direct quotations, to set off titles of short works, and to set off words that are being used in an unusual manner. This quotation is not a title. Earlier in the paragraph the writer indicates that these words accurately describe Victor's condition. These words must be a direct quotation from a book or another source.

45. D
Paragraph 3 sums up how Jean-Marc Itard's work affected future researchers. When paragraph 3 is moved to the end of the passage, the other four paragraphs tell an orderly story about the progression of Itard's experiment. (1, 2, 4, 5).

PASSAGE IV

46. J
No century is any longer than the others, so *long* is unnecessary. There is no need to explain that is a century is 100 years.

47. C

This sentence begins with the word *How*, which indicates that a question likely will be asked. Since this first independent clause is asking a question, the proper end punctuation here is a question mark, not a period. As this sentence stands, it is a run-on. Choice D is a comma splice, a run-on where the two independent clauses are connected by a comma.

48. J

Both the words *different* and *various* are redundant. No other word is necessary to convey the idea that there are different ways archeologists examine the past. A comma should not separate an adjective from a noun.

49. C

The scientists must learn about the surroundings where they find objects; in other words, they must *pay special attention to* the area. Choices A and B reflect similar concepts, but both are slang phrases that are out of place in a formal essay. If this phrase were completely omitted, the sentence would be missing a verb and therefore would be an incomplete thought.

50. J

In this paragraph, the author lists the different ways an archeologist can determine the age of an item. This is the second item mentioned, so *also* provides an appropriate transition. *Therefore* implies that there is a connection between this and the preceding sentence, but there is no logical connection between these statements. *However* implies that the second sentence contradicts the first; this also is not logical. Finally, *for example* indicates that the second sentence provides an example of what was described in the first sentence, when actually, it provides another topic of discussion.

51. C

This sentence describes the emitting of radiocarbons and should therefore follow the introduction of the term, which occurs in sentence 6. Any other location in the paragraph would be confusing because it separates two sentences about the same idea.

52. J

Because the article *an* precedes this word, we know two things: the word must begin with a vowel (so *thing's* cannot be correct), and it must be singular (so *objects* is incorrect). Additionally, the word must be a possessive because it describes the age of the object.

53. B

Because a long adverbial clause opens this sentence, it must be set apart from the remainder of the sentence by a comma. A period makes the adverbial clause a sentence fragment. Ellipses generally indicate that words have been removed from a sentence, though that does not seem to be the case here.

54. F

This sentence discusses the habits of people who lived thousands of years ago, so the verb must be in the past tense. Preceded by the noun *inhabitants*, the verb must also be plural to match the plural subject. Though *weren't* is grammatically correct in this sentence, it is logically incorrect, for the archeologists are making hypotheses about how these ancient people lived. In the previous sentence, a similar structure is created, noting that if the people did a certain action, then they probably had certain knowledge. Logically, this sentence, which has the same structure, would follow the same pattern.

55. D

This sentence contains two independent clauses that must be separated into two complete, independent sentences. It is currently a comma splice. Choice B is a run-on sentence. Though choice C is grammatically correct, it adds unnecessary emphasis.

56. G

The writer states that "no one knew how to read ancient writings." However, he has already stated that archeologists can decipher this ancient writing. Since readers of this article most likely do not know how archeologists broke this ancient written code, an explanation is helpful for the logical flow of this article. Though pictures of hieroglyphics would be interesting, they would not provide any significant information. A description of the relationship between the Greeks and the Egyptians would steer readers away from the central discussion of archeology.

57. B

Nonessential information should be set off from the remainder of the sentence by a pair of dashes, commas, or parentheses.

58. J

Choice J offers the only logical and complete sentence to fill this space. Choices F and G are both sentence fragments that are missing subjects and verbs. Although choice H is a complete sentence, the word *However* implies that the information that follows will contradict the information given in previous sentences. Since this sentence agrees with rather than contradicts the previous sentence, choice J is correct.

59. C

The author poses a question in the first sentence of this essay. In the following sentence, the author points out that the answer to this question can be found through the many techniques of archeology. The remainder of this essay fills in the details of these techniques in response to the opening question. Choice D also answers the question affirmatively, but the reader has no way of knowing whether the author of this passage is an archeologist. Furthermore, whether he is an archeologist has no relevance to whether he answered the question. Therefore, this is not the best possible answer. Choice A is incorrect because the entire essay is focused on "people today," even if the author does not use these words. It is "people today" who are doing the archeological digs and making hypotheses. Choice B is inappropriate because the author offers a general discussion of archeology, using the Greek and Egyptian cultures as examples. The author does not claim to mention every ancient culture that archeologists have explored.

60. F

In an essay that discusses the different techniques of archeology, it's logical to begin by introducing the subject of archeology and its function. All of the other options introduce the techniques of archeology before introducing the subject itself.

PASSAGE V

61. C

In order to maintain parallel construction in this sentence, both verbs that refer to the sentence's one subject must be in the same tense. Since the initial verb (*roamed*) is in the past tense, we must also have the past-tense form of *find*, which is *found*. *Founded* is an actual past-tense verb, but it means "to start up" (usually an organization or a business).

62. J

The contraction of *could not* requires an apostrophe to show that the *o* has been removed: *couldn't*.

63. C

As this sentence is currently written, it is a comma splice. These independent clauses must be separated by a period.

64. H

The part of the sentence beginning with *trees* is an appositive, or extra information. Therefore, it should be set off with a comma or a dash, as in choice H.

Inserting a period or a semicolon before *trees* makes the second part of the sentence a fragment.

65. A

This phrase indicates that it is the author's personal opinion that the fuss about the trees was *unconscionable*. If the phrase were placed after *perhaps* or *week*, it would seemingly indicate that the *in my view* refers to the trees remaining in the street, which is not a matter of opinion, rather than the nature of the fuss that is being made about them. By removing this phrase, it would appear that the author's opinion is a fact, which it cannot be.

66. J

This adverbial clause is redundant because it simply repeats the idea that is indicated by the word *melted*. Choice G is a diversion to throw the reader off because something cannot melt from a liquid to a solid.

67. A

This power line, which normally ran along Penn Avenue, had fallen to the ground. The word *usually* refers to the normal location of this line. The other conditions, what it looked like and what it was made of, are still true; therefore, they cannot be modified by *usually*.

68. J

A semicolon is used between independent clauses to join complete, connected thoughts. Choice J offers the only independent clause.

69. A

This phrase follows the word *sink* because a wire can *sink into* something. If the phrase *sink into* is placed in any location other than directly after *sink*, the meaning of the sentence is altered or becomes illogical.

70. H

Sentence 4 provides the first mention that the wire was melting a pit into the street. Sentences 2, 3, and 6 all refer to the effects of this melting. Therefore, the information that this pit was being melted must come prior to sentence 2, which must build upon the information in sentence 4. Choice H is the only option that allows sentence 4 to be placed before sentence 2.

71. B

When you introduce a quotation with an introductory tag (such as "my father said" or "Jenny claimed"), the introductory tag must be followed by a comma. If the introductory tag were an independent clause or the following quotation were formal, a colon would be acceptable, but neither is the case here. Since the two halves of the quotation (indicated by the first quotation's final comma) are part of the same statement, they cannot be separated by a period.

72. H
This quotation is directed toward the author as *you.* That means the word *your* is supposed to be a contraction for *you are,* choice H.

73. C
The author focuses on a live wire that falls on the ground as the result of a tornado, not on the tornado and its general effects on the town. Though she does mention these effects briefly, they are not the focus of this essay. She also focuses only on her personal experience with one tornado rather than the general information about the effects of tornadoes that this assignment should contain.

74. F
The author is directly relating an experience she remembers from her youth. Because this experience is autobiographical, the use of *I* is logical and appropriate. Choices G and J use the words *never* and *all,* which probably make these choices extremes.

75. B
In paragraph 2, the author introduces us to the tornado. The other paragraphs describe the aftermath of this event. Therefore, the paragraph that tells about the tornado hitting should logically come before the paragraphs that describe how the tornado knocked down a high-voltage power line. Choice B is the only option that places paragraph 2 first.

Model ACT I Reading Answers Explained

PASSAGE I

1. B
In the social circle of the Sheridan girls, all young women are able to attend balls, and they do. This means the Sheridan girls have certainly been to balls. Nothing in the passage supports the other choices, and choice D seems to directly contradict the narration.

2. H
When Leila discusses her companions in the cab, she refers to her cousin Laurie. She then notes that Laurie is the brother of Laura, and that Meg and Jose are sisters. They are the Sheridan children and Leila's cousins.

3. B
The personification of the lamp-posts is significant, especially as they are waltzing. Since Leila is excited and happy about the possibility of waltzing later in the evening, she imagines that the world is waltzing with her.

4. F
The passage notes that Leila had to "try not to smile too much." Leila could not hide her excitement. Though she contemplates how under other circumstances she might be sad at the lack of a sibling, she does not allow herself to be sad or lonely. There is also nothing in the passage to indicate that she is fearful.

5. D
Whether or not these women are actually lovely, Leila sees their happiness and laughter as part of the beauty of the ball. These women are not laughing at her, nor does Leila necessarily believe that these women are more attractive than she is.

6. J
When her cousins question her about not having gone to a ball, Leila claims that it is because she lives in an area where the neighbors live far away from each other. She implies that this distance prevents people from having balls.

7. C
Leila wishes she could keep the tissue paper as a remembrance or a keepsake. She believes that this paper, as much as everything else, is an important part of this momentous occasion in her life. Because the event is so important to her, she wishes she could preserve everything.

8. J
The Sheridan girls seem to be dressed in new, fancy clothes, as is their brother. The indication is that they and all the other ball attendees are of wealthy families with social standing.

9. C
Leila questions her participation in the ball because she cannot believe that something this wonderful

can be happening to her. Clearly, she is meant to be a part of the dancing and other activities. There is no indication that these programs cost any money. Since Leila reads the dance program, she must be literate.

10. F

Everything in the passage leading up to this sentence demonstrates Leila's excitement at being at the ball. As a natural reaction, her hands begin to shake as her fantasy begins to become reality. F is the only choice that reflects this happy excitement.

PASSAGE II

11. C

The theme that women will eventually have more combat responsibility than they do now runs through the article. Choices A and B are incorrect because the author never makes these claims. The author never comments on the military draft.

12. G

The paragraph specifically mentions the Marines' use of women in intelligence. Choice F is incorrect because the paragraph mentions that the Marines are gradually admitting women to combat. The paragraph never claims that women are in combat units or that women cannot serve as helicopter pilots.

13. A

Lines 51–54 specifically mention that women can lead male troops into combat as officers. Choice A is best because it is false. All the other choices are true and are supported by information in the passage.

14. G

Women are involved in combat, although regulations do not yet permit it. Choice F is incorrect because women from other countries are more involved than American women in combat. Choice H is also incorrect because the story about this one woman soldier is meant to be an example of the role of all American women soldiers. Choice J is incorrect because the involvement of American women in combat is a fact, not propaganda.

15. C

In this context the word *forged* means "developed." In this context *forged* does not mean "created" or "faked."

16. H

In this context, the word *struck* means "to be affected (moved or touched)" by the fireflies, which turned out to be illuminated bullets; it does not mean "to be hit."

Choice J is incorrect because Specialist Alfaro never actually saw fireflies.

17. D

The recurring theme throughout the passage is that women have been fully integrated into combat operations, which established them as combat soldiers. Choices A and C are incorrect because the article never mentions either civilian or military casualties. Choice B does not describe the author's view about the wars, even though the statement is factually true.

18. G

Lines 60–61 describe the practice in choice G. Choices F and H are incorrect because *assigned* and *attached* are not synonyms, and they do not have the same official meaning. Nothing in the passage says that women in the military flagrantly break the rules.

19. B

The poll numbers show that there is support for the author's point of view about a combat role for women. The article emphasizes the increased role of women in the military, but choice A supports the opposite point of view. Choice C is incorrect because it's what the statistics say and not the statistics themselves that matter. Choice D is incorrect because the author would not want poll results that supported her position to be revealed as unreliable.

20. F

The article establishes that women are already involved in combat, contrary to the regulations. Choice G is incorrect because the author believes these are the published policies, but not the real policies. Choice H is true, but it is not the author's opinion of the American military regulations. It's what happened in the field that was used to circumvent the regulations, and not the other way around, as stated in choice J.

PASSAGE III

21. D

In the fifth paragraph we're told that in the '70s and '80s food looked more like Plasticine. That eliminates A, B, and C as possible choices, because these dates were during or before the '70s and '80s.

22. G

The appearance of the food is emphasized throughout the article. An audience can't taste the food; they can only see it. Choice F is incorrect because the article contains many examples of audience deception.

Choice H is true, but it is not the main theme of this passage. J is incorrect because there are many examples in the passage of actors who portrayed their characters without real food.

23. B

In the Battle of Waterloo, Napoleon's army suffered a disastrous defeat. The food stylist might not be able to "conquer" the recipe for sole meunière. Choice A is incorrect because in this context *sole* refers to a fish; it is not a synonym for *only*. Nothing in the passage supports choices C and D.

24. G

Lines 42–43 state that most food stylists began as cooks.

25. C

It makes the most sense to make a cooking movie if Julie and Julia were chefs. It makes less sense to make a movie about two food stylists or restaurant owners. There is nothing in the passage to suggest that Julie and Julia were vegans.

26. F

In the context, the word *fabric* means that food is an important aspect of the movie. Choices G and H are incorrect because the passage doesn't mention cloth. The word *fabric* does not mean a *fabrication*, something misleading.

27. B

The author is narrating (telling) a story about food in film. The article was not written to persuade the audience of a particular point of view. The author did not write the passage to reflect on the meaning of an outcome or event, nor does she share technical details—although the passage naturally includes some of these details, it is driven mainly by the narration and not by the details.

28. F

The writer emphasizes that the food in the movie is as important as the acting. Neither a pivotal scene nor the food stylists were a major success of the film. Choice J is incorrect because the number of fillets was a limitation, not a major success of the film.

29. B

Lines 49–53 state that the challenge is always making the food seem delicious and hyper-real. Choices A, C and D are challenges, but they are not the greatest challenge to a food stylist.

30. G

In Method Acting, actors try to create in themselves the attributes of the person they are portraying. Choice G offers the best example of Method Acting, and in the passage, that example explains Method Acting because the actor responds in the way his character would, not in the way he personally would respond. Choices F, H, and J do not describe a situation in which the actor tries to incorporate the characteristics of the person being portrayed.

PASSAGE IV

31. D

In paragraph 1, the author notes that if an object can move faster than the speed of light (more than 186,282 miles per second), time for that object will move backward.

32. H

The author reports in paragraph 4 that the scientists discovered that "the moving clocks moved slightly slower than atomic clocks which had remained on the ground."

33. A

According to paragraph 6, the space-time continuum was developed by one of Einstein's professors. In paragraphs 2 and 6, the author indicates that Einstein introduced the Special Theory of Relativity and the General Theory of Relativity.

34. H

Because Washington, D.C., is near to sea level and Denver is a mile above sea level, Washington is closer to Earth's core and therefore has a stronger gravity pull.

35. B

Life expectancy is determined by time; it does not control time. All the other choices are cited in the article as factors that affect time for humans.

36. J

This passage focuses on how time can be speeded up, slowed down, or even stopped by the forces of speed and gravity. All the choices except J are details in the article, but none encompasses the main idea of the article as a whole.

37. B

When the author describes *mathematical projections,* he is discussing the results when certain scientific and mathematical theories are applied to specific occurrences. In this instance, scientists predict a certain occurrence using a mathematical formula.

38. J
In the last paragraph, the author claims that in a black hole, a place of infinite gravity, time stands still.

39. D
Choice A is an extreme because it uses the word *all* too broadly. Choice C also generalizes, and does so in a way irrelevant to the article. The author clearly believes in the existence of black holes, so the concept could not be ridiculous to him. The author provides humor to keep the reader interested and to lighten up an essay filled with abstract theories.

40. H
According to the information in paragraph 5, someone traveling at half the speed of light for 18 years will age only 16 years: $20 + 16 = 36$.

Model English and Reading ACT II

With Answers Explained

This Model English and Reading ACT II is just like a real ACT. Take this test after you take the Model English and Reading ACT I. If you plan to take the optional ACT Writing Test, you should also complete the ACT Writing Test I on pages 378–384.

Take this model test under simulated test conditions. Allow 45 minutes to answer the 75 English items and 35 minutes to answer the 40 Reading items. Use the Answer Sheet on the following page to mark your answers. Use a pencil to mark the answer sheet, and color in the circles from the correct choices in the Test 1 (English) and Test 3 (Reading) sections.

Use the Scoring Keys on pages 305–307 to score the answer sheet. Review the answer explanations on pages 308–315.

The test scoring charts on pages 6 and 7 show you how to convert the number of correct answers to ACT scale scores. The Scoring Keys on pages 305–307 show you how to find the Usage/Mechanics and Rhetorical Skills subscores and the Social Studies/ Sciences and Arts/Literature subscores.

DO NOT leave any answers blank. There is no penalty for guessing on the ACT. Remember that the test is yours. You may mark up, write on, or draw on the test.

When you are ready, note the time and begin.

ANSWER SHEET

The ACT answer sheet looks something like this. Use a No. 2 pencil to completely fill the circle corresponding to the correct answer. If you erase, erase completely; incomplete erasures may be read as answers.

TEST 1—English

1 Ⓐ Ⓑ Ⓒ Ⓓ	11 Ⓐ Ⓑ Ⓒ Ⓓ	21 Ⓐ Ⓑ Ⓒ Ⓓ	31 Ⓐ Ⓑ Ⓒ Ⓓ	41 Ⓐ Ⓑ Ⓒ Ⓓ	51 Ⓐ Ⓑ Ⓒ Ⓓ	61 Ⓐ Ⓑ Ⓒ Ⓓ	71 Ⓐ Ⓑ Ⓒ Ⓓ
2 Ⓕ Ⓖ Ⓗ Ⓙ	12 Ⓕ Ⓖ Ⓗ Ⓙ	22 Ⓕ Ⓖ Ⓗ Ⓙ	32 Ⓕ Ⓖ Ⓗ Ⓙ	42 Ⓕ Ⓖ Ⓗ Ⓙ	52 Ⓕ Ⓖ Ⓗ Ⓙ	62 Ⓕ Ⓖ Ⓗ Ⓙ	72 Ⓕ Ⓖ Ⓗ Ⓙ
3 Ⓐ Ⓑ Ⓒ Ⓓ	13 Ⓐ Ⓑ Ⓒ Ⓓ	23 Ⓐ Ⓑ Ⓒ Ⓓ	33 Ⓐ Ⓑ Ⓒ Ⓓ	43 Ⓐ Ⓑ Ⓒ Ⓓ	53 Ⓐ Ⓑ Ⓒ Ⓓ	63 Ⓐ Ⓑ Ⓒ Ⓓ	73 Ⓐ Ⓑ Ⓒ Ⓓ
4 Ⓕ Ⓖ Ⓗ Ⓙ	14 Ⓕ Ⓖ Ⓗ Ⓙ	24 Ⓕ Ⓖ Ⓗ Ⓙ	34 Ⓕ Ⓖ Ⓗ Ⓙ	44 Ⓕ Ⓖ Ⓗ Ⓙ	54 Ⓕ Ⓖ Ⓗ Ⓙ	64 Ⓕ Ⓖ Ⓗ Ⓙ	74 Ⓕ Ⓖ Ⓗ Ⓙ
5 Ⓐ Ⓑ Ⓒ Ⓓ	15 Ⓐ Ⓑ Ⓒ Ⓓ	25 Ⓐ Ⓑ Ⓒ Ⓓ	35 Ⓐ Ⓑ Ⓒ Ⓓ	45 Ⓐ Ⓑ Ⓒ Ⓓ	55 Ⓐ Ⓑ Ⓒ Ⓓ	65 Ⓐ Ⓑ Ⓒ Ⓓ	75 Ⓐ Ⓑ Ⓒ Ⓓ
6 Ⓕ Ⓖ Ⓗ Ⓙ	16 Ⓕ Ⓖ Ⓗ Ⓙ	26 Ⓕ Ⓖ Ⓗ Ⓙ	36 Ⓕ Ⓖ Ⓗ Ⓙ	46 Ⓕ Ⓖ Ⓗ Ⓙ	56 Ⓕ Ⓖ Ⓗ Ⓙ	66 Ⓕ Ⓖ Ⓗ Ⓙ	
7 Ⓐ Ⓑ Ⓒ Ⓓ	17 Ⓐ Ⓑ Ⓒ Ⓓ	27 Ⓐ Ⓑ Ⓒ Ⓓ	37 Ⓐ Ⓑ Ⓒ Ⓓ	47 Ⓐ Ⓑ Ⓒ Ⓓ	57 Ⓐ Ⓑ Ⓒ Ⓓ	67 Ⓐ Ⓑ Ⓒ Ⓓ	
8 Ⓕ Ⓖ Ⓗ Ⓙ	18 Ⓕ Ⓖ Ⓗ Ⓙ	28 Ⓕ Ⓖ Ⓗ Ⓙ	38 Ⓕ Ⓖ Ⓗ Ⓙ	48 Ⓕ Ⓖ Ⓗ Ⓙ	58 Ⓕ Ⓖ Ⓗ Ⓙ	68 Ⓕ Ⓖ Ⓗ Ⓙ	
9 Ⓐ Ⓑ Ⓒ Ⓓ	19 Ⓐ Ⓑ Ⓒ Ⓓ	29 Ⓐ Ⓑ Ⓒ Ⓓ	39 Ⓐ Ⓑ Ⓒ Ⓓ	49 Ⓐ Ⓑ Ⓒ Ⓓ	59 Ⓐ Ⓑ Ⓒ Ⓓ	69 Ⓐ Ⓑ Ⓒ Ⓓ	
10 Ⓕ Ⓖ Ⓗ Ⓙ	20 Ⓕ Ⓖ Ⓗ Ⓙ	30 Ⓕ Ⓖ Ⓗ Ⓙ	40 Ⓕ Ⓖ Ⓗ Ⓙ	50 Ⓕ Ⓖ Ⓗ Ⓙ	60 Ⓕ Ⓖ Ⓗ Ⓙ	70 Ⓕ Ⓖ Ⓗ Ⓙ	

TEST 2—Mathematics

1 Ⓐ Ⓑ Ⓒ Ⓓ Ⓔ	9 Ⓐ Ⓑ Ⓒ Ⓓ Ⓔ	17 Ⓐ Ⓑ Ⓒ Ⓓ Ⓔ	25 Ⓐ Ⓑ Ⓒ Ⓓ Ⓔ	33 Ⓐ Ⓑ Ⓒ Ⓓ Ⓔ	41 Ⓐ Ⓑ Ⓒ Ⓓ Ⓔ	49 Ⓐ Ⓑ Ⓒ Ⓓ Ⓔ	57 Ⓐ Ⓑ Ⓒ Ⓓ Ⓔ
2 Ⓕ Ⓖ Ⓗ Ⓙ Ⓚ	10 Ⓕ Ⓖ Ⓗ Ⓙ Ⓚ	18 Ⓕ Ⓖ Ⓗ Ⓙ Ⓚ	26 Ⓕ Ⓖ Ⓗ Ⓙ Ⓚ	34 Ⓕ Ⓖ Ⓗ Ⓙ Ⓚ	42 Ⓕ Ⓖ Ⓗ Ⓙ Ⓚ	50 Ⓕ Ⓖ Ⓗ Ⓙ Ⓚ	58 Ⓕ Ⓖ Ⓗ Ⓙ Ⓚ
3 Ⓐ Ⓑ Ⓒ Ⓓ Ⓔ	11 Ⓐ Ⓑ Ⓒ Ⓓ Ⓔ	19 Ⓐ Ⓑ Ⓒ Ⓓ Ⓔ	27 Ⓐ Ⓑ Ⓒ Ⓓ Ⓔ	35 Ⓐ Ⓑ Ⓒ Ⓓ Ⓔ	43 Ⓐ Ⓑ Ⓒ Ⓓ Ⓔ	51 Ⓐ Ⓑ Ⓒ Ⓓ Ⓔ	59 Ⓐ Ⓑ Ⓒ Ⓓ Ⓔ
4 Ⓕ Ⓖ Ⓗ Ⓙ Ⓚ	12 Ⓕ Ⓖ Ⓗ Ⓙ Ⓚ	20 Ⓕ Ⓖ Ⓗ Ⓙ Ⓚ	28 Ⓕ Ⓖ Ⓗ Ⓙ Ⓚ	36 Ⓕ Ⓖ Ⓗ Ⓙ Ⓚ	44 Ⓕ Ⓖ Ⓗ Ⓙ Ⓚ	52 Ⓕ Ⓖ Ⓗ Ⓙ Ⓚ	60 Ⓕ Ⓖ Ⓗ Ⓙ Ⓚ
5 Ⓐ Ⓑ Ⓒ Ⓓ Ⓔ	13 Ⓐ Ⓑ Ⓒ Ⓓ Ⓔ	21 Ⓐ Ⓑ Ⓒ Ⓓ Ⓔ	29 Ⓐ Ⓑ Ⓒ Ⓓ Ⓔ	37 Ⓐ Ⓑ Ⓒ Ⓓ Ⓔ	45 Ⓐ Ⓑ Ⓒ Ⓓ Ⓔ	53 Ⓐ Ⓑ Ⓒ Ⓓ Ⓔ	
6 Ⓕ Ⓖ Ⓗ Ⓙ Ⓚ	14 Ⓕ Ⓖ Ⓗ Ⓙ Ⓚ	22 Ⓕ Ⓖ Ⓗ Ⓙ Ⓚ	30 Ⓕ Ⓖ Ⓗ Ⓙ Ⓚ	38 Ⓕ Ⓖ Ⓗ Ⓙ Ⓚ	46 Ⓕ Ⓖ Ⓗ Ⓙ Ⓚ	54 Ⓕ Ⓖ Ⓗ Ⓙ Ⓚ	
7 Ⓐ Ⓑ Ⓒ Ⓓ Ⓔ	15 Ⓐ Ⓑ Ⓒ Ⓓ Ⓔ	23 Ⓐ Ⓑ Ⓒ Ⓓ Ⓔ	31 Ⓐ Ⓑ Ⓒ Ⓓ Ⓔ	39 Ⓐ Ⓑ Ⓒ Ⓓ Ⓔ	47 Ⓐ Ⓑ Ⓒ Ⓓ Ⓔ	55 Ⓐ Ⓑ Ⓒ Ⓓ Ⓔ	
8 Ⓕ Ⓖ Ⓗ Ⓙ Ⓚ	16 Ⓕ Ⓖ Ⓗ Ⓙ Ⓚ	24 Ⓕ Ⓖ Ⓗ Ⓙ Ⓚ	32 Ⓕ Ⓖ Ⓗ Ⓙ Ⓚ	40 Ⓕ Ⓖ Ⓗ Ⓙ Ⓚ	48 Ⓕ Ⓖ Ⓗ Ⓙ Ⓚ	56 Ⓕ Ⓖ Ⓗ Ⓙ Ⓚ	

TEST 3—Reading

1 Ⓐ Ⓑ Ⓒ Ⓓ	6 Ⓕ Ⓖ Ⓗ Ⓙ	11 Ⓐ Ⓑ Ⓒ Ⓓ	16 Ⓕ Ⓖ Ⓗ Ⓙ	21 Ⓐ Ⓑ Ⓒ Ⓓ	26 Ⓕ Ⓖ Ⓗ Ⓙ	31 Ⓐ Ⓑ Ⓒ Ⓓ	36 Ⓕ Ⓖ Ⓗ Ⓙ
2 Ⓕ Ⓖ Ⓗ Ⓙ	7 Ⓐ Ⓑ Ⓒ Ⓓ	12 Ⓕ Ⓖ Ⓗ Ⓙ	17 Ⓐ Ⓑ Ⓒ Ⓓ	22 Ⓕ Ⓖ Ⓗ Ⓙ	27 Ⓐ Ⓑ Ⓒ Ⓓ	32 Ⓕ Ⓖ Ⓗ Ⓙ	37 Ⓐ Ⓑ Ⓒ Ⓓ
3 Ⓐ Ⓑ Ⓒ Ⓓ	8 Ⓕ Ⓖ Ⓗ Ⓙ	13 Ⓐ Ⓑ Ⓒ Ⓓ	18 Ⓕ Ⓖ Ⓗ Ⓙ	23 Ⓐ Ⓑ Ⓒ Ⓓ	28 Ⓕ Ⓖ Ⓗ Ⓙ	33 Ⓐ Ⓑ Ⓒ Ⓓ	38 Ⓕ Ⓖ Ⓗ Ⓙ
4 Ⓕ Ⓖ Ⓗ Ⓙ	9 Ⓐ Ⓑ Ⓒ Ⓓ	14 Ⓕ Ⓖ Ⓗ Ⓙ	19 Ⓐ Ⓑ Ⓒ Ⓓ	24 Ⓕ Ⓖ Ⓗ Ⓙ	29 Ⓐ Ⓑ Ⓒ Ⓓ	34 Ⓕ Ⓖ Ⓗ Ⓙ	39 Ⓐ Ⓑ Ⓒ Ⓓ
5 Ⓐ Ⓑ Ⓒ Ⓓ	10 Ⓕ Ⓖ Ⓗ Ⓙ	15 Ⓐ Ⓑ Ⓒ Ⓓ	20 Ⓕ Ⓖ Ⓗ Ⓙ	25 Ⓐ Ⓑ Ⓒ Ⓓ	30 Ⓕ Ⓖ Ⓗ Ⓙ	35 Ⓐ Ⓑ Ⓒ Ⓓ	40 Ⓕ Ⓖ Ⓗ Ⓙ

TEST 4—Science Reasoning

1 Ⓐ Ⓑ Ⓒ Ⓓ	6 Ⓕ Ⓖ Ⓗ Ⓙ	11 Ⓐ Ⓑ Ⓒ Ⓓ	16 Ⓕ Ⓖ Ⓗ Ⓙ	21 Ⓐ Ⓑ Ⓒ Ⓓ	26 Ⓕ Ⓖ Ⓗ Ⓙ	31 Ⓐ Ⓑ Ⓒ Ⓓ	36 Ⓕ Ⓖ Ⓗ Ⓙ
2 Ⓕ Ⓖ Ⓗ Ⓙ	7 Ⓐ Ⓑ Ⓒ Ⓓ	12 Ⓕ Ⓖ Ⓗ Ⓙ	17 Ⓐ Ⓑ Ⓒ Ⓓ	22 Ⓕ Ⓖ Ⓗ Ⓙ	27 Ⓐ Ⓑ Ⓒ Ⓓ	32 Ⓕ Ⓖ Ⓗ Ⓙ	37 Ⓐ Ⓑ Ⓒ Ⓓ
3 Ⓐ Ⓑ Ⓒ Ⓓ	8 Ⓕ Ⓖ Ⓗ Ⓙ	13 Ⓐ Ⓑ Ⓒ Ⓓ	18 Ⓕ Ⓖ Ⓗ Ⓙ	23 Ⓐ Ⓑ Ⓒ Ⓓ	28 Ⓕ Ⓖ Ⓗ Ⓙ	33 Ⓐ Ⓑ Ⓒ Ⓓ	38 Ⓕ Ⓖ Ⓗ Ⓙ
4 Ⓕ Ⓖ Ⓗ Ⓙ	9 Ⓐ Ⓑ Ⓒ Ⓓ	14 Ⓕ Ⓖ Ⓗ Ⓙ	19 Ⓐ Ⓑ Ⓒ Ⓓ	24 Ⓕ Ⓖ Ⓗ Ⓙ	29 Ⓐ Ⓑ Ⓒ Ⓓ	34 Ⓕ Ⓖ Ⓗ Ⓙ	39 Ⓐ Ⓑ Ⓒ Ⓓ
5 Ⓐ Ⓑ Ⓒ Ⓓ	10 Ⓕ Ⓖ Ⓗ Ⓙ	15 Ⓐ Ⓑ Ⓒ Ⓓ	20 Ⓕ Ⓖ Ⓗ Ⓙ	25 Ⓐ Ⓑ Ⓒ Ⓓ	30 Ⓕ Ⓖ Ⓗ Ⓙ	35 Ⓐ Ⓑ Ⓒ Ⓓ	40 Ⓕ Ⓖ Ⓗ Ⓙ

Model English ACT II

75 Questions—45 Minutes

INSTRUCTIONS: Certain words or phrases in the following five passages are underlined and numbered. There is a corresponding item for each underlined portion. Each item offers three suggestions for changing the underlined portion to conform to standard written English or to make it more understandable or consistent with the rest of the passage. If the underlined portion is not improved by one of the three suggested changes, mark NO CHANGE. Some items are about the entire passage, and the numbers of these items come at the end of the passage.

Choose the best answer for each question based on the passage. Then fill in the appropriate circle on the answer sheet.

Check pages 305–306 and 308–312 for answers and explanations.

PASSAGE I

> The paragraphs in this passage may or may not be in the most appropriate order. The number of each paragraph is in brackets above the paragraph. The last item for this passage asks for the correct order of paragraphs that will make this passage most sensible.

> Read the whole passage before answering questions 1 and 2.

[1]

<u>It</u> began on October 29, 1929, in the United States. For
1
months, Americans had been on a stock-buying spree. Returns were high, and millions of people dreamed of striking it rich. Suddenly, stock prices fell and continued to fall rapidly. Panic swept the nation. People rushed to sell their stocks, often at a fraction of what they had paid. Millions lost all or most of the money they had invested. ☐2☐

[2]

This was the Crash, and it was followed by something much <u>worse! The</u> Great Depression. The Crash affected mainly
3
Americans who had invested in the stock market, but the Depression affected almost everyone. <u>With less income,</u>
4

1. The author begins this passage with a pronoun rather than the specific name for the event to which she is referring:
   A. because the name of the event is unimportant.
   B. for dramatic effect.
   C. because the title of the article states the event.
   D. to build suspense.

2. Choose the BEST reason why the author used the word *millions* twice in the opening paragraph.
   F. To emphasize how many people were affected by this disaster
   G. To show that one million people each lost $1 million
   H. To emphasize the risks of investing in the stock market
   J. One refers to how many people, and the other refers to how much money.

employees were laid off by businesses that were cutting
production. One out of every four workers were unemployed.
Many banks had invested in stocks, and their losses caused
them to lose their shirts. Thus people often lost most of their
life's savings in bank failures.

[3]

The Crash did not cause the Depression, but was instead a
symptom of deep and widespread problems. Prosperity had
returned to most of the Western world in the 1920s, but it
had a shaky foundation. [7] Much of the wealth was
merely paper wealth. After 1929 the United States could
no longer lend money to Europe, and its economy also fell
apart? Millions of workers in the industrialized nations of
Europe lost their jobs, while European farmers suffered from
the steep decline in prices for they're goods.

[4]

Measures taken to combat the Great Depression varied
in many ways from country to country, but in general they
involved government intervention of some sort. Recovery was
well under way by the late 1930s. In many country's, however,
recovery was due in large part to increased military spending.
As preparations for war mounted, Europe and America's
unemployed found jobs in factories, farms, and the armed
forces. However, for millions the relief was only temporary
for a short time as the miseries of an economic crisis were
replaced by the horrors of total war.

---

3. **A.** NO CHANGE
   B. worse. The
   C. worse: the
   D. worse; the

4. **F.** NO CHANGE
   G. With less income, employees cut business production and were laid off.
   H. Businesses began cutting production and laying off employees with less income.
   J. With less income, businesses began cutting production and laying off employees.

5. **A.** NO CHANGE
   B. was
   C. are
   D. were to have been

6. Which expression BEST fits in with the tone of the article?

   F. NO CHANGE
   G. lost their minds.
   H. go flat broke.
   J. go out of business.

7. What information, if any, would be MOST useful to support this sentence in the paragraph?

   A. An example of "paper wealth"
   B. A definition of wealth
   C. A discussion of different types of wealth
   D. No other information is necessary.

8. **F.** NO CHANGE
   G. apart, millions
   H. apart. Millions
   J. apart! Millions

9. **A.** NO CHANGE
   B. their
   C. its
   D. there

10. **F.** NO CHANGE
    G. differently
    H. changes
    J. OMIT the underlined portion.

11. **A.** NO CHANGE
    B. countrys,
    C. countries'
    D. countries,

12. **F.** NO CHANGE
    G. jobs, in
    H. jobs. In
    J. jobs; in

13. **A.** NO CHANGE
    B. for a little while
    C. for a brief period
    D. OMIT the underlined portion.

Questions 14 and 15 ask about the entire passage.

14. The author uses shorter, action-oriented sentences in the opening paragraph of this essay:

    F. so she can quickly move on to the more important information about the Great Depression.
    G. because shorter sentences are easier to read.
    H. to demonstrate the excitement of the time and the quickness with which the rise and fall of the stock market took place.
    J. to indicate that stockbuying is a dangerous and risky proposition.

15. Which is the MOST logical order for the paragraphs in the article?

    A. NO CHANGE
    B. 2, 3, 1, 4
    C. 4, 3, 2, 1
    D. 1, 3, 2, 4

PASSAGE II

The paragraphs in this passage may or may not be in the most appropriate order. The number of each paragraph is in brackets above the paragraph. The last item for this passage asks for the correct order of paragraphs that will make this passage the most sensible.

[1]

Because of their steadily increasing rate of change, <u>many thoughtful individuals recognized that the coming years would hold even more change.</u> The Industrial Revolution
16
was <u>beginning, those</u> affected by it could detect change
17
<u>in the course of their own lifetimes.</u>
18

[2]

Until modern <u>times. The</u> rate of change in the way humans
19
live was so slow as to make the process unnoticeable in the course of any one <u>person's</u> lifetime. It was therefore the
20
illusion of mankind that change did not take place. <u>In the</u>
21
<u>face of that illusion,</u> when a change had clearly taken <u>place the</u>
21   22
response was to view it as something that should not have taken place, as something that represented a degeneration from the <u>"good old days."</u>
23

16. **F.** NO CHANGE
   G. many individuals thoughtfully recognized that the coming years would hold even more change.
   H. recognizing thoughtful individuals, the coming years would hold even more change.
   J. the coming years were recognized by thoughtful individuals as holding even more changes.

17. **A.** NO CHANGE
   B. beginning, and those
   C. beginning those
   D. beginning, yet those

18. **F.** NO CHANGE
   G. (place after "it")
   H. (place after "detect")
   J. OMIT the underlined portion.

19. **A.** NO CHANGE
   B. times, the
   C. times; the
   D. times—the

20. **F.** NO CHANGE
   G. persons
   H. person
   J. persons'

21. **A.** NO CHANGE
   B. (place after "change" and capitalize the *w* in *when*)
   C. (place after "place" and capitalize the *w* in *when*)
   D. (place after "view," but separate clause from "view" with a comma and capitalize the *w* in *when*)

[3]

Some people grew to understand that not only was change taking place, but that it would continue to take place after their deaths, for the first time. It meant there would come to be

24

changes still greater than a person had lived to see. Changes

25

that he would never see. This gave rise to a new curiosity—perhaps the first really new curiosity developed in historic

times; that of wondering what life on Earth would be like after

26

one was no longer alive. The literary response to that new

27

curiosity was what we now call "science fiction."

22. F. NO CHANGE
    G. place, the
    H. place. The
    J. place? The

23. Which option BEST explains why the author puts "good old days" in quotation marks?

    A. To show these words are directly quoted from someone else
    B. To show that the "good old days" are better than the present time
    C. To indicate that he is attributing a commonly used, though possibly inaccurate, cliché to many people
    D. To emphasize these words

24. F. NO CHANGE
    G. (place after "people")
    H. (place after "only")
    J. (place after the first "place")

25. A. NO CHANGE
    B. see, changes
    C. see; changes
    D. see! Changes

26. F. NO CHANGE
    G. times—that
    H. times that
    J. times . . . that

27. A. NO CHANGE
    B. alive, the
    C. alive? The
    D. alive! The

Questions 28–30 ask about the entire passage.

28. What information would BEST supplement this passage?

    F. A definition of science-fiction writing
    G. Examples of how "curiosity killed the cat"
    H. A list of changes that have occurred over the past century
    J. A list of science-fiction authors

29. The writer of this passage was assigned to write an article to explain why and how science-fiction writing was created. Does the writer succeed?

  A. No, because the writer doesn't mention science fiction until the last sentence of the passage.
  B. No, because most of the essay is on change, not on science fiction.
  C. No, because the writer gives no examples of science fiction.
  D. Yes, because the article describes the conditions that brought about the curiosity that led to science fiction writing.

30. Which sequence of paragraph will make the essay MOST logical?

  F. NO CHANGE
  G. 3, 2, 1
  H. 2, 1, 3
  J. 2, 3, 1

PASSAGE III

The people of ancient Israel the Hebrews, never built a
                  ———————————
                        31
large empire. But their religious and moral ideas changed the

world. The Hebrews were the first people to believe in one

God. This belief is called *monotheism*. It gradually replaced
                                         ——————————————
                                              32
polytheism. Hebrew teachings about justice and the principles
——————
   32
of right and wrong, combined with their belief in monotheism,

gave rise to Judaism it became one of the major religions of
             —————————
                 33
the world. Eventually, Jewish teachings influenced the
           ——————————
                34
development of two other major religions, Christianity and

Islam.

31. A. NO CHANGE
  B. Israel. The Hebrews,
  C. Israel, the Hebrews,
  D. Israel: the Hebrews,

32. What, if any, information would BEST support this statement?

  F. Definition of polytheism
  G. A list of polytheistic cultures
  H. A list of monotheistic cultures
  J. Nothing should be added.

33. A. NO CHANGE
  B. Judaism! It
  C. Judaism, it
  D. Judaism. It

34. F. NO CHANGE
  G. Yet
  H. Therefore
  J. However

Much of the history of the Hebrews is written in the Old Testament of the Bible. The Hebrews' were originally at first tribes of wandering herders from Mesopotamia. They were brought to Israel, also called Canaan, by Abraham. During a time of famine, some Hebrews moved to Egypt, where they were made slaves. After a long period of captivity, the Hebrews were freed and led back to Israel by Moses. Needing a code of moral standards, God came to Moses on Mount Sinai and gave him the Ten Commandments to give to the Hebrews.

From about 1200 to 600 B.C., the Hebrews develop an advanced civilization. Around 1025 B.C., the tribes united under Saul, their first king. Saul led the fight against the Philistines, a neighboring people, who wanted control of Israel. He was followed on the throne by David. The great king built the city of Jerusalem and made it his capital.

The Hebrew Kingdom reached its peak of strength and wealth under David's son, Solomon. During his rule, from about 975 B.C. to 935 B.C., Solomon made alliances with other kings, sent ships to trade in distant lands, and Jerusalem was made beautiful. He built a great temple in Jerusalem. It's size and beauty amazed those who saw it. The Temple of Solomon became the center of Jewish religious life. [43]

[1] After Solomon's death, his kingdom split into two parts, and civil wars weakened the Hebrew kingdoms. [2] Israel did not become an independent nation again until A.D. 1948. [3] Many different people conquered the Jews.

35. **A.** NO CHANGE
    B. Hebrew's
    C. Hebrews
    D. Hebrew

36. **F.** NO CHANGE
    G. at one time
    H. the first
    J. OMIT the underlined portion.

37. **A.** NO CHANGE
    B. slaves after
    C. slaves? After
    D. slaves, after

38. **F.** NO CHANGE
    G. Needing a code of moral standards, Moses was given the Ten Commandments to give to the Hebrews from God.
    H. Needing a code of moral standards, Moses took the Ten Commandments from God to give to the Hebrews.
    J. Needing a code of moral standards, the Hebrews followed the Ten Commandments, which God had given them through Moses.

39. **A.** NO CHANGE
    B. will develop
    C. develops
    D. developed

40. **F.** NO CHANGE
    G. people, that wanted
    H. people who wanted
    J. people, which wanted

41. **A.** NO CHANGE
    B. and Jerusalem became beautiful
    C. and beautified Jerusalem
    D. and beautifulled Jerusalem

42. **F.** NO CHANGE
    G. Their
    H. They're
    J. Its

[4] In time (63 B.C.), Israel became part of the Roman Empire. [5] To punish the Jews for their constant rebellions, the Romans destroyed Jerusalem and scattered many of the Jews around the world (about A.D. 135). [45]

43. Based on the language in the paragraph, which sentence BEST explains what the author means by "The Temple of Solomon became the center of Jewish religious life"?

A. The Temple was located at the center of the city of Jerusalem.
B. The Temple of Solomon was in the middle of the religious community.
C. The Temple was the focus of the Jewish religion.
D. The religious activity of Jews revolved around the events and services that took place at the Temple of Solomon.

44. F. NO CHANGE
G. two various parts
H. two separate parts
J. two different parts

45. What is the MOST logical order for the sentences in the paragraph?

A. 1, 4, 3, 2, 5
B. 1, 5, 2, 3, 4
C. 1, 3, 4, 5, 2
D. 4, 5, 1, 2, 3

PASSAGE IV

> The paragraphs in this passage may or may not be in the most appropriate order. The number of each paragraph is in brackets above the paragraph. The last item for this passage asks for the correct order of paragraphs that will make this passage the most sensible.

[1]

Sample a typical days headlines: "War Breaks Out in the
                    46
Middle East." "Child Killed in Gang Shooting." "Bribery

Scandal Rocks City Hall." "Stock Market Falls."

46. F. NO CHANGE
G. days'
H. day's
J. day

47. A. NO CHANGE
B. while. A
C. while: a
D. while . . . a

[2]

Once in a <u>while, a</u> note of hope creeps in: "Doctors
₄₇

Conquer Fatal Illness." "Neighbors Aid Homeless Family."

"Hero Risks Life to Rescue Fire Victim."

[3]

The word *psychology* comes from the Greek *psyche*, which

means "soul," and *logos*, which has come to mean "logic" or

<u>"science" in practice</u>, however, this "science of the soul" is
₄₈

defined as <u>a modern definition,</u> *the study of human behavior.*
₄₉

[4]

People, apparently, are capable of great cruelty. <u>And great</u>
₅₀

<u>compassion.</u> If so, you might wonder why humanity so often
₅₀

chooses violence over <u>caring.</u> After all, poets and artists have
₅₁

created great art <u>and we are reminded</u> of the heights to which
₅₂

our species can aspire. A play by Shakespeare or a painting by

Rembrandt speaks to the human potential within everyone.

<u>Shakespeare and Rembrandt, however, don't tell us *how* to</u>
₅₃

<u>achieve inner peace. That's the task the psychologist has</u>
₅₃

<u>taken on.</u>
₅₃

[5]

Psychologists use the scientific method to collect data

about <u>behavior. Using</u> the insights gained through <u>checking</u>
₅₄ ₅₅

<u>stuff out</u> and experimentation, they answer some of life's most
₅₅

important questions: Why do people act as they do? Can

behavior be predicted or changed? Can people's lives be made

48. F. NO CHANGE
  G. "science," in practice
  H. "science". In practice
  J. "science." In practice

49. A. NO CHANGE
  B. the definition,
  C. a definition
  D. OMIT the underlined portion.

50. F. NO CHANGE
  G. And also of great compassion.
  H. They are also capable of great compassion.
  J. And their great compassion.

51. A. NO CHANGE
  B. caring?
  C. caring!
  D. caring:

52. F. NO CHANGE
  G. that reminds us
  H. who reminds us
  J. we were reminded

53. Which choice BEST explains why the author chose to italicize the word *how*?

  A. To show his anger that the art will not give us the answers that humans seek
  B. To reveal that artists like Shakespeare and Rembrandt are unable to reach inner peace themselves, so they don't know how to show others
  C. To emphasize that artists like Shakespeare and Rembrandt can demonstrate inner peace, but they cannot tell someone how to achieve it as a psychologist tries to do
  D. To imply that art is insignificant

54. F. NO CHANGE
  G. behavior using
  H. behavior, using
  J. behavior, but using

happier and more productive? What can be done to help people who have lost touch with reality?

[6]

[1] If people were simple creatures like dogs or horses, the answers to these questions would be relatively easy. [2] Human beings are <u>very uniquely</u> gifted with the power of reason and language and the ability to create a complex culture. [3] Psychologists, therefore, have their work cut out for them. [4] The study of behavior yields few easy answers. [5] But our lives are not controlled by the same instincts and drives that dominate other forms of animal life. [57]

55. **A.** NO CHANGE
  B. checking information out
  C. observing stuff
  D. observation

56. **F.** NO CHANGE
  G. strongly uniquely
  H. most uniquely
  J. uniquely

57. What is the BEST, most logical order for the sentences in this paragraph?

  A. 1, 3, 2, 4, 5
  B. 5, 4, 3, 2, 1
  C. 1, 5, 4, 3, 2
  D. 1, 5, 2, 3, 4

Questions 58–60 ask about the entire passage.

58. Which choice BEST describes the author's intended audience for this passage?

  F. Medical doctors
  G. People who are unfamiliar with the field of psychology
  H. People who are currently undergoing psychiatric treatment
  J. Young women

59. The reason that BEST explains why the author begins this passage by quoting negative and positive headlines is:

  A. to show he is abreast of current events.
  B. to demonstrate the wide range of human behavior.
  C. to engage the reader's emotions.
  D. to paint a picture of modern society.

60. What is the MOST logical order for the paragraphs in this passage?

  F. 1, 2, 3, 4, 6, 5
  G. 6, 5, 4, 3, 2, 1
  H. 1, 3, 4, 2, 5, 6
  J. 1, 2, 4, 3, 5, 6

PASSAGE V

> The paragraphs in this passage may or may not be in the most appropriate order. The number of each paragraph is in brackets above the paragraph. The last item for this passage asks for the correct order of paragraphs that will make this passage most sensible.

[1]

Ever since I was a small <u>young</u> girl in school, I've been
₆₁
aware of what the school textbooks say about Indians. I am <u>a</u>
₆₂
Indian and, naturally, am interested in what the school teaches

about natives of this land.

[2]

One day in the grammar school I attended, I read that a

delicacy of American Indian people was dried <u>fish. Which,</u>
₆₃
according to the textbook, tasted <u>"like an old shoe, or was like</u>
₆₄
<u>chewing on dried leather."</u> To this day I can remember my
₆₄
utter dismay at reading these words. We called this wind-dried

fish <u>"sleetschus,"</u> and to us, it was our favorite delicacy and,
₆₅
indeed, it did not taste like shoe leather. It took many hours of

long and hard work to cure the fish in just this particular

fashion. Early fur traders and other non-Indians must have

agreed, for they often used this food for subsistence as they

traveled around isolated areas.

[3]

[1] My father was the youngest son of one of the last

chiefs of the Nooksack Indian Tribe of Whatcom County in the

state of Washington. [2] I brought the textbook home to show

it to my father, leader of my tribe at that time. [3] On this

61. **A.** NO CHANGE
    B. little
    C. child
    D. OMIT the word.

62. **F.** NO CHANGE
    G. an
    H. the
    J. A

63. **A.** NO CHANGE
    B. fish! Which,
    C. Fish. Which,
    D. fish, which,

64. Which option BEST explains why the author put these words in quotation marks?

    F. To show that this quotation is taken directly from the textbook
    G. To emphasize the importance of these words
    H. To show that these words are false
    J. To indicate that she has spoken these words out loud

65. **A.** NO CHANGE
    B. "sleetchus"
    C. sleetschus,
    D. sleetschus

66. **F.** NO CHANGE
    G. Indians
    H. Indians'
    J. Indian

67. **A.** NO CHANGE
    B. well,
    C. good
    D. goodest

particular day, he told me in his wise and humble manner that the outside world did not always understand Indian's people, and that I should not let it hinder me from learning the well parts of education. 68 69

[4]

Since those early years I have learned we were much better off with our own delicacies, which did not rot our teeth and bring about the various dietary problems that plague Indian people in modern times, I was about eight years old when this incident happened, and it does much to sharpen my desire to pinpoint terminology in books used to describe American Indian people, books which are, most often, not very complimentary?

---

68. Which is the MOST logical arrangement of the sentences in this paragraph?

   F. NO CHANGE
   G. 2, 3, 1
   H. 2, 1, 3
   J. 3, 2, 1

69. Based on the information in this paragraph, the author's feelings about her father are:

   A. hostile and angry.
   B. respectful and proud.
   C. embarrassed.
   D. indifferent.

70. **F.** NO CHANGE
   G. times I
   H. times . . . I
   J. times. I

71. **A.** NO CHANGE
   B. had done
   C. done
   D. did

72. **F.** NO CHANGE
   G. complimentary.
   H. complimentary,
   J. complimentary!

Questions 73–75 ask about the entire passage.

---

73. The audience the writer of this essay seems to be targeting is:

   A. people living in mainstream American culture.
   B. members of her own tribe.
   C. historians who are examining the behavior of Native Americans.
   D. researchers who are studying the dietary habits of Native Americans.

74. Based on the language in this passage, which choice seems to BEST describe the author's reason for recounting this episode from her childhood?

    F. To describe the tastiness of sleetschus to those people who have never tried it

    G. To criticize the modern dietary habits of Indians

    H. To comment on the negative way many people in mainstream America describe Native Americans and their culture

    J. To pay tribute to her tribe

75. What is the MOST appropriate order for the paragraphs in this essay?

    A. NO CHANGE

    B. 1, 4, 3, 2

    C. 4, 3, 2, 1

    D. 1, 2, 4, 3

END OF ENGLISH TEST II

Model Reading ACT II

40 Questions—35 Minutes

INSTRUCTIONS: There are four passages on this test with 10 items about each passage. Choose the best answer for each item based on the passage. Then fill in the appropriate circle on the answer sheet (page 282).
Check pages 307 and 313–315 for answers and explanations.

PASSAGE I

PROSE FICTION: This passage is adapted from "One Throw" by W. C. Heinz.

I checked into a hotel called the Olympia, which is right on the main street and the only hotel in the town. After lunch I was hanging around the lobby, and I got to talking
5 to the guy at the desk. I asked him if this wasn't the town where that kid named Maneri played ball.

"That's right," the guy said. "He's a pretty good ballplayer."

10 He was leaning on the desk, talking to me and looking across the hotel lobby. He nodded his head. "This is a funny thing," he said. "Here he comes now."

The kid had come through the door from
15 the street.

"Hello, Nick," he said to the guy at the desk.

"I'm sorry, Pete," the guy at the desk said, "but no mail today."

20 "That's all right, Nick," the kid said.

"Excuse me," I said, "but you're Pete Maneri?"

"That's right," the kid said, turning and looking at me.

25 "Excuse me," the guy at the desk said, introducing us. "Pete, this is Mr. Franklin. Pete's a good ballplayer," the guy said.

"Not very," the kid said. "Don't take his word for it, Mr. Franklin."

30 That's the way I got talking with the kid.

"What do you do, Mr. Franklin?" he said.

"I sell hardware," I said. "I can think of some things I'd like better. I played some ball once myself, and I was going to ask you how
35 you like playing in this league."

"Well," the kid said, "I suppose it's all right. I guess I've got no kick coming."

"Oh, I don't know," I said. "I understand you're too good for this league. What are
40 they trying to do to you? Who manages this ball club?"

"Al Dall," the kid said. "Maybe he's all right, but I don't get along with him. He's on my neck all the time. If I get the big hit or
45 make the play, he never says anything. The other night I tried to take second on a loose ball and I got caught in the rundown. He bawled me out in front of everybody. There's nothing I can do."

50 "Oh, I don't know," I said. "This is probably a guy who knows he's got a good thing in you, and he's looking to keep you around."

"That's what I mean," the kid said. "When the Yankees sent me down here they
55 said, 'Don't worry. We'll keep an eye on you.' So Dall never sends back a good report on me. Nobody ever comes down to look me over. What chance is there for a guy like Eddie Brown or somebody like that coming
60 down to see me here?"

"You have to remember that Eddie Brown's the big shot," I said, "the great Yankee scout."

"Sure," the kid said, "and I'll never see
65 him in this place. I have an idea that if they

ever ask Dall about me, he'll knock me down."

"Why don't you go after Dall?" I said. "I had trouble like that once myself, but I fig-
70 ured out a way to get attention."

"You did?" the kid said.

"I threw a couple of balls over the first baseman's head," I said. "I threw a couple of games away, and that really got the manager
75 sore. I was lousing up his ball club and his record. So what does he do? He blows the whistle on me, and what happens? That gets the brass curious, and they come to see what's wrong."

80 "Is that so?" the kid said. "What hap-pened?"

"Two weeks later, I was up with Columbus. I'd try it," I said.

"I might," the kid said. "Are you coming
85 out to the park tonight?"

"I wouldn't miss it," I said.

The first game wasn't much, with the home club winning something like 8 to 1. The second game was different, though.

90 I was trying to wish the ball down to the kid, just to see what he'd do with it, when the batter drives one on one big bounce to the kid's right.

The kid was off for it when the ball started.
95 He made a backhand stab and grabbed it. He was deep now, and he turned in the air and fired. If it goes over the first baseman's head, it's two runs in and a panic—but it's the pret-tiest throw you'd want to see. It's right on a
100 line, and the runner is out by a step, and it's the ball game.

I walked back to the hotel, thinking about the kid. I sat around the lobby until I saw him come in.

105 "Why didn't you throw that ball away?" I said.

"I don't know," the kid said. "I had it in my mind before he hit it, but I couldn't."

"You're going to be a major-league
110 ballplayer," I said, "because you couldn't

throw that ball away, and because I'm not a hardware salesman and my name's not Harry Franklin."

"What do you mean?" the kid said.

115 "I mean," I explained to him, "that I tried to needle you into throwing that ball away because I'm Eddie Brown."

1. The narrator checks into the Olympia hotel:

    A. to spend the night in town so he can sell hardware.
    B. because he is visiting relatives.
    C. because he has been stranded in town.
    D. because he is scouting Pete Maneri for the Yankees.

2. The narrator tries to convince Pete to make a bad throw:

    F. because he is working with Al Dall to keep Pete in the minor leagues.
    G. to psych out the players on the opposing team.
    H. because he wants to see if Pete is worthy of playing in the major leagues.
    J. because he thinks it would make the game more entertaining.

3. Pete is so frustrated with Al Dall because:

    A. Al is trying to throw him off the team.
    B. Al criticizes him and seems to be holding him back from the major leagues.
    C. Al Dall keeps substituting other players for Pete.
    D. Al Dall used to play for the Yankees, and Pete does not play for them.

4. Based on the information given in the story, to "throw the ball away" means:

    F. to take the baseball and put it in the trash can.
    G. to throw the ball at the batter.
    H. to purposely throw the ball poorly.
    J. to throw the ball into the stands.

5. What is significant about the desk clerk's statement to Pete that there is "no mail today"?

    A. Pete has not received any word from the major leagues.

B. Pete's family, embarrassed by his failure, will no longer write to him.

C. It's a national holiday, so no mail was delivered.

D. No one knows where Pete lives, so he never gets mail at the hotel.

6. Which does NOT describe Pete Maneri?

F. He is not fond of his manager.

G. He will never play major league baseball.

H. He is a good baseball player.

J. He is frustrated because he isn't playing for the Yankees.

7. Eddie Brown is:

A. Mr. Franklin's cousin.

B. the desk clerk.

C. a famous scout.

D. the team coach.

8. Pete says that he is not a very good ballplayer because:

F. he is having a terrible season.

G. he takes Al Dall's criticisms to heart.

H. he got caught trying to steal second base.

J. he is a modest and frustrated young man.

9. In the doubleheader played by Pete's team:

A. they won both games.

B. they won one game and lost one.

C. they lost both games.

D. the second game was called on account of rain.

10. Why does Eddie Brown sit around the lobby at the end of the story?

F. He is tired from the game.

G. He is enjoying his time off work.

H. He is waiting to meet with a client.

J. He wants to talk to Maneri.

PASSAGE II

SOCIAL SCIENCE: This passage is from *Psychology: A Way to Grow* by Carl R. Green and William R. Sanford.

Humanist psychology is based on the research and influence of Abraham Maslow (1908–1970). An American psychologist, Maslow told his fellow psychologists to stop the practice of defining personality in terms of their disturbed patients. Instead, he said, psychology should study healthy people.

Along with Carl Rogers, the other guiding spirit of the humanist movement, Maslow believed that all members of society should be given the chance to realize their full potential as human beings. This goal is achievable, he thought, because people are basically good. His beliefs contrast with those of Freud, who seemed to define human beings as victims of their biological and psychological past. Not so, Maslow claimed. If their basic needs are met, most men and women build happy, productive lives for themselves.

Maslow criticized the older schools of psychology for what he saw as their negative attitudes toward human nature. He attempted to paint a brighter, more optimistic picture of emotional life. In doing so, Maslow defined five basic concepts that relate to the human personality.

1. Humanity's essential nature is made up of needs, capacities, and tendencies that are good (or natural) rather than harmful.

2. Full, healthy personality development comes when people develop their basic natures and fulfill their potential. People must grow from within rather than be shaped from without. Unless they do, they can never reach true maturity.

3. Mental illness results when people's basic needs are not satisfied, thereby frustrating or twisting their inner nature. The role of the therapist is to restore the patient to the path of growth and self-knowledge along the lines dictated by the patient's own inner nature.

4. Each person's inner nature is weak, delicate, and subtle, unlike the overpowering

instincts of animals. Although a person's
45 inner nature can grow tall and strong, it
begins as a tiny seed. As it grows, it can easily be stunted by cultural pressures, the failure
to satisfy basic needs, or unhealthy habits. No
one's basic goodness ever disappears, even
50 though it may be submerged for a while under
self-defeating behaviors.

5. As people mature, their potential goodness shows itself even more clearly. The *self-
actualizing* person, as humanist psychologists
55 describe the fully mature personality, stands out
in any environment. Perhaps only a few people
reach full self-actualization. But even those who
are making progress toward that level of maturity are recognized and sought after by others.

11. Maslow's theory differs from that of many
other psychologists because:

A. he bases his theories on animal behavior.
B. he bases all of his theories on Freud's
theories.
C. he believes psychologists should base
their studies on the lives of well-adjusted
humans.
D. his theories show that no one is truly
mentally healthy.

12. If a child is deprived of basic needs such as
food and love:

F. he or she will have more difficulty
coming to terms with his or her inner
nature.
G. his or her inner nature will not be affected.
H. his or her inner nature will bloom.
J. he or she will mature and fully develop.

13. According to the information in this passage:

A. Maslow and Rogers agree with Freud's
theory that a person's past dictates his or
her psychological future.
B. Maslow, unlike Rogers, believes that
people can lead successful, happy lives
despite their troubled pasts.
C. Maslow believes that a person can achieve
full potential despite his or her past
experiences.
D. Neither Maslow nor Rogers believes that
self-fulfillment is possible.

14. According to the information in the final
paragraph, a *self-actualizing* person:

F. can create herself.
G. is fully developed.
H. can find himself in others.
J. is selfish.

15. It is NOT true that:

A. a person's inner nature is fragile in its
early stages.
B. a person's inner nature never varies in
strength.
C. a person's inner nature can be harmed by
outside influences.
D. a person's inner nature is always basically
good.

16. Carl Rogers is:

F. the author of this article.
G. the partner of Abraham Maslow.
H. a pupil of Sigmund Freud.
J. a humanist psychologist.

17. According to Maslow:

A. people are always riddled with self-doubt.
B. people are basically angry and violent.
C. no matter what happens, people are
always happy.
D. people are innately good.

18. According to Maslow, mental illness will
affect a person who:

F. is deprived of basic needs.
G. must always live alone.
H. is innately evil.
J. is always depressed.

19. Maslow's outlook on human nature would be
described as:

A. pessimistic.
B. fatalistic.
C. positive.
D. superficial.

20. Maslow would MOST likely say that a good
therapist should:

F. help patients discover their own true path
to self-actualization.
G. tell patients exactly how to live their lives.
H. encourage people to suppress their
harmful emotions.
J. encourage everyone to seek therapy.

Latin American Art

Latin American art in the first half of the twentieth century was shaped by three dominant trends. In the first two decades, innovative artists in all countries sought to distance them-
5 selves from the academic style of art predominant among trained artists in the late nineteenth century. Having consciously shed involvement with this aesthetic mode, many artists traveled to Europe where they sought to assimilate
10 *avant-garde* styles that were quickly gaining acceptance there, particularly *cubism* and its various offshoots and, to a lesser extent, *expressionism*. Upon returning to their native countries, the vast majority of painters and sculptors
15 turned their attention to exploring subject matter that was concerned with national identity and local social and cultural issues. Many combined their desire to experiment artistically with involvement in social and political struggles
20 that championed the disadvantaged.

Modernist Styles

The creative arts in Europe (visual arts, writing, music) experienced an explosion of new approaches and styles in the early part of the twentieth century. Artists rebuffed previous
25 academic styles that they considered stale, restrictive and inadequate to respond to changing social realities. *Avant-garde* refers to artists and their works that are seen at the time to be innovative, experimental, or unconventional.
30 Latin American artists embraced the avant-garde in order to create a new artistic language that could reflect the essence of Latin American cultural identity. Although this was dominated by a desire to break with the dominance of the
35 older European tradition, Latin American artists were also a part of the international avant-garde dialogue that sought to generate revolutionary changes in society, politics, and the arts.

Cubism

Cubism was developed between 1907 and
40 1912 by the artist Pablo Picasso (1882–1973)
and the French artist Georges Braque (1882–1963). They were influenced by African tribal art and the work of the French post-impressionist painter Paul Cézanne, who advo-
45 cated a geometric approach to art. Cézanne stated that artists should treat nature "in terms of the cylinder, the sphere, and the cone."

The key concept of cubism is that the essence of objects can only be captured if
50 they are shown from multiple points of view simultaneously. In cubist paintings, the subject matter is broken up, analyzed, and then reassembled. Compositions show an abstracted world in which the subject is broken into
55 planes with open edges that slide into each other. In a portrait a face may be shown frontally and in profile at the same time.

Although cubism had run its course by the early 1920s, it exerted an influence on
60 other modernist movements

Expressionism

Expressionism was an artistic and literary movement centered in Germany during the early years of the twentieth century. Its roots can actually be traced to certain trends in
65 Nordic and German art during the European Middle Ages that emerged especially during times of social change and spiritual crisis. Expressionism emphasizes the artist's subjective emotional responses to objects and
70 events, rather than an objective or realistic rendering of a subject. The artist strives to express his or her own inner experience through a variety of means, including exaggeration, fantasy, distortion, and the vivid,
75 even jarring, application of formal elements. Colors are usually bright and intense.

Artist Close Ups

Diego Rivera (1896–1957)

Mexican Artist Diego Rivera showed such a passion for drawing that his father covered a room in their house with paper so that
80 young Diego could paint all over the walls. Rivera received a classical art education in

Mexico and departed for Spain in 1907 on a travel grant. He settled in Paris, where he lived and painted for the next 14 years. Influenced by the work of Cézanne and Picasso, Rivera created more than 200 paintings in the cubist style from 1913 to 1917.

Rivera returned to Mexico in 1921. He joined the Communist Party in 1923, committed to a modernist vision that would fuse art with politics and social concerns. The Mexican government charged him with creating large-scale public murals that celebrated national identity. Rivera used techniques that he had learned by studying the Italian fresco painters.

Frida Kahlo (1907–1954)

Frida Kahlo is possibly Mexico's most widely recognized and appreciated painter. Mainly self-taught, she belonged to a circle of innovative and influential artists in Mexico and internationally. Kahlo was married to the artist Diego Rivera. She was also an active participant in the cultural and political movements of her time. Her work combines folk-art elements with highly personal symbolism that can be mysterious and disquieting. Her self-portraits painted between 1925 and 1954 offer both a compelling and complex autobiography, exploring both physical and psychological pain. Kahlo contracted polio as a child and as a teenager was involved in a serious bus accident that required many surgeries throughout her life. Her stormy relationship with Rivera was a source of conflicting emotions as well.

21. When the author writes that the "Mexican government charged him [Diego Rivera] with creating large scale public murals," he MOST likely means that the government:
   A. brought Rivera up on charges for creating the murals.
   B. actually imprisoned Rivera for popularizing the Communist cause.
   C. gave Rivera the responsibility for creating the murals.
   D. ordered Rivera to pay a fine for creating the murals.

22. A MAIN point the author makes is that:
   F. European art was almost entirely cubist or impressionist.
   G. European art was influenced by Latin American art.
   H. all Latin American art has a cubist influence.
   J. Latin American art was influenced by European art.

23. What is one way to identify a cubist painting?
   A. It seems to show the subject from many perspectives simultaneously.
   B It reveals political and social struggles.
   C. It reveals the artist's inner struggles.
   D. It shows only cylinders, cubes, and cones.

24. According to the author, the term *avant-garde* most nearly means:
   F. a particular art movement founded internationally in the early 1900s.
   G. a form of painting and sculpture associated primarily with France.
   H. art that is not the standard of the time.
   J. art that has modernist roots.

25. Which statement is BEST supported by the passage?
   A. The focus of Latin American art was not a break from the European tradition.
   B. The roots of expressionism can be traced to Latin American art.
   C. Cubist art was not developed by Paul Cézanne.
   D. European art relied mainly on old approaches in the early part of the 20th century.

26. The author of the passage implies that the relationship between the featured artists (Diego Rivera and Frida Kahlo):
   F. created conflicting personal emotions.
   G. created conflicting nationalistic beliefs.
   H. contrasted cubism and folk art.
   J. was based on both artists' Mexican nationality.

27. The passage states on lines 8–10 that "many Artists traveled to Europe where they sought to assimilate *avant-garde* styles." This MOST nearly means that the artists:

A. tried to find alternatives to the avant-garde styles.
B. favored the more traditional artistic styles found in Europe.
C. sought to incorporate avant-garde styles in their own works.
D. sought to start their own approach to avant-garde art.

28. We can infer from the paragraph on expressionism that:

F. it was a central characteristic of Latin American art.
G. German artists traveled to Latin America to spread expressionist ideals.
H. it was not limited to art.
J. it was primarily focused on objects and events.

29. When the author refers to Paul Cézanne as a post-impressionist painter, we can infer that:

A. impressionism and expressionism are related artistic styles.
B. the impressionist style preceded cubism.
C. African tribal art influenced impressionism.
D. cubism influenced impressionism.

30. In the last paragraph, the author writes that Kahlo's work offers a "compelling and complex autobiography," MOST likely meaning:

F. a summary of the struggles of the downtrodden in Latin America.
G. an overstated and difficult to understand summary of life in Mexico.
H. a forceful and intricate summary of Kahlo's life.
J. a direct and complete summary of the lives of her fellow artists.

PASSAGE IV

NATURAL SCIENCE: This passage is from "Smart Skin" by Shawna Vogel.

If we're ever to have the future promised us by *The Jetsons*, we're at the very least going to need personal robots that can serve us breakfast. But to do that those robots will
5 have to be able to sense the difference between a glass of orange juice and a soft-boiled egg, and to hold each with just enough pressure to keep it from either breaking or dropping to the floor. At the moment such a
10 fine-tuned grip is beyond the capacity of any robot in existence.

Robots have no innate "feel" for the objects they are handling primarily because they lack one of our most useful sense organs:
15 skin. That isn't to say they can't get a grip on things. Industrial robots can repeatedly pick up objects like carburetors by exerting a pre-programmed pressure on them. But robots capable of functioning autonomously will
20 need a "smart skin" to sense whether they should, say, grasp a wrench more firmly or ease up their death grip on a tomato.

One of the most sophisticated approaches to this goal is being developed at the
25 University of Pisa by Italian engineer Danilo De Rossi, who has closely modeled an artificial skin on the inner and outer layers of human skin: the dermis and epidermis. His flexible, multilayered sheathing even has the
30 same thickness as human skin—roughly that of a dime.

De Rossi's artificial dermis is made of a water-swollen conducting gel sandwiched between two layers of electrodes that monitor
35 the flow of electricity through the squishy middle. Like the all-natural human version, this dermis senses the overall pressure being exerted on an object. As pressure deforms the gel, the voltage between the electrodes
40 changes; the harder the object being pressed, the greater the deformation. By keeping tabs on how the voltage is changing, a skin-clad robot could thus distinguish between a rubber ball and a rock.

45 For resolving the finer details of surface texture, De Rossi has created an epidermal layer of sensor-studded sheets of plastic placed between thin sheets of rubber. The

sensors are pinhead-size disks made of piezo-
50   electric substances, which emit an electric
charge when subjected to pressure. These
disks can sense texture as fine as the bumps
on a braille manuscript.

Other researchers have developed texture-
55   sensitive skin, but De Rossi's has a unique
advantage. Because his disks respond to pressure from any direction—including forces
pulling sideways across the surface of the
skin—they can also sense friction. "No other
60   sensor today can do that," says De Rossi. Most
smart skins detect only pressure perpendicular
to the surface and cannot feel lateral deformation. But a robot wearing De Rossi's skin could
easily feel the tug from a sticky piece of tape
65   or, conversely, sense an alarming lack of friction when a greased motor bearing is slipping
from its grasp.

Either of De Rossi's layers could be used
separately to meet the specialized needs of
70   industrial robots, but he envisions them as
parts of an integrated skin for multipurpose
mechanical hands. At the moment, however,
De Rossi faces a small dilemma: his two layers
are incompatible. The water essential to the
75   working of the dermis invariably short-circuits
the sensitive epidermis. De Rossi will need to
separate the two layers, but no matter what
material he chooses he will probably have to
compromise among several ideals, such as
80   extreme thinness, strength, and flexibility.

Even if he does manage to unite his layers,
there will still be a number of hurdles to get
over before a robot with artificial skin can
become as adept as a human. Foremost among
85   them is the basic question of how to coordinate all the tactile information transmitted.
Robotics engineers still puzzle over how people use all the tactile messages conveyed by
their hands to accomplish a feat as simple as
90   threading a nut onto the end of a bolt.

31. The scientific name for the outer layer of
skin is:

A. dermis.
B. extradermis.
C. intradermis.
D. epidermis.

32. Danilo De Rossi is:

F. a Renaissance painter.
G. the author of this article.
H. an Italian engineer.
J. the name of a special robot.

33. The unique property of De Rossi's artificial
skin is that:

A. it can feel hard and soft objects.
B. it can sense friction by responding to
pressure from all angles.
C. it can decide whether or not something is
fragile.
D. it can fit on robots of any size.

34. According to the author, a robot has trouble
gripping different types of objects because:

F. it cannot be programmed to hold different
objects.
G. it can hold only special magnetic items.
H. it has no inborn way to determine the
difference between one item and another.
J. robots crush every object that they hold
because they are too powerful for man-
made items.

35. The BEST description of the situation of
"smart-skinned" robots is:

A. they will be on the market in the very near
future.
B. they will never exist.
C. scientists must do more research if this
experiment is to succeed.
D. they have existed for years.

36. Based on De Rossi's present experiment,
what will allow a robot to determine the
difference between a fragile object and a
durable one?

F. Special computer chips that allow
computers to think about each object
individually
G. The changing voltage of the electrodes in
the skin
H. The amount of gel used when the robot
picks up a new object
J. The water that short-circuits the system
when an object is fragile

37. The MAIN purpose of this article is:

   A. to demonstrate that someday robots with skin will be able to grip objects of varying strengths, sizes, and frictions.
   B. to show that De Rossi's is certain to fail.
   C. to relate modern life with the science-fiction cartoon *The Jetsons*.
   D. to prove that robots will never be able to do the jobs that most humans now do.

38. The materials used to make "smart skin" need to be assessed for all of these, EXCEPT:

   F. flexibility.
   G. strength.
   H. thinness.
   J. color.

39. According to the author, once "smart skin" is perfected, the next hurdle faced by scientists will be to:

   A. enable robots to boil an egg.
   B. find a way to process all the information received by the sensitive skin.
   C. find a way for robots to use the four other senses.
   D. find a way to keep the smart skin on the robot without it falling off whenever the robot moves.

40. The word *tactile* is used twice in the final paragraph. Based on its context, its meaning is related to:

   F. pressure.
   G. touch.
   H. military tactics.
   J. electricity.

END OF READING TEST II

Model ACT II English Scoring Key

Item and Answer	Usage/ Mechanics	Rhetorical Skills	Review These Pages	Item and Answer	Usage/ Mechanics	Rhetorical Skills	Review These Pages
1. B		❑	133–144	27. A	❑		120–122
2. F		❑	133–144	28. F		❑	133–144
3. C	❑		108–111	29. D		❑	133–144
4. J	❑		43–47	30. H		❑	145–152
5. B	❑		76–79	31. C	❑		103–108
6. J		❑	133–144	32. J		❑	133–144
7. A		❑	133–144	33. D	❑		34–38
8. H	❑		120–122	34. F		❑	133–144
9. B	❑		56–63	35. C	❑		56–58
10. J		❑	156–160	36. J		❑	156–160
11. D	❑		56–58	37. A	❑		120–122
12. F	❑		103–111, 120–122	38. J	❑		43–47
13. D		❑	156–160	39. D	❑		67–75
14. H		❑	133–144	40. H	❑		103–108
15. A		❑	145–152	41. C	❑		79–83
16. J	❑		43–47	42. J	❑		56–63
17. B	❑		34–38	43. D		❑	133–144
18. F		❑	156–160	44. F		❑	156–160
19. B	❑		103–108	45. C		❑	145–152
20. F	❑		118–120	46. H	❑		118–120
21. A		❑	133–144	47. A	❑		103–108
22. G	❑		103–108	48. J	❑		34–38, 123–125
23. C		❑	156–160	49. D		❑	156–160
24. G		❑	156–160	50. H	❑		38–43
25. B	❑		103–108	51. A	❑		120–122
26. G	❑		113–115	52. G	❑		79–83

Item and Answer	Usage/ Mechanics	Rhetorical Skills	Review These Pages	Item and Answer	Usage/ Mechanics	Rhetorical Skills	Review These Pages
53. C		❏	133–144	65. A	❏		123–125
54. F	❏		34–38	66. J	❏		84–90
55. D		❏	133–144	67. C	❏		84–90
56. J		❏	156–160	68. H		❏	145–152
57. D		❏	145–152	69. B		❏	133–144
58. G		❏	133–144	70. J	❏		34–38
59. C		❏	133–144	71. D	❏		67–75
60. J		❏	145–152	72. G	❏		120–122
61. D		❏	156–160	73. A		❏	133–144
62. G	❏		56–58	74. H		❏	133–144
63. D	❏		38–43	75. A		❏	145–152
64. F	❏		123–125				

Number Correct:

Usage/Mechanics _____

Rhetorical Skills _____

Total _____

Model ACT II Reading Scoring Key

Item and Answer	Social Studies/ Sciences	Arts/ Literature	Item and Answer	Social Studies/ Sciences	Arts/ Literature	Item and Answer	Social Studies/ Sciences	Arts/ Literature
1. D		❑	15. B	❑		28. H		❑
2. H		❑	16. J	❑		29. B		❑
3. B		❑	17. D	❑		30. H		❑
4. H		❑	18. F	❑		31. D	❑	
5. A		❑	19. C	❑		32. H	❑	
6. G		❑	20. F	❑		33. B	❑	
7. C		❑	21. C		❑	34. H	❑	
8. J		❑	22. J		❑	35. C	❑	
9. A		❑	23. A		❑	36. G	❑	
10. J		❑	24. H		❑	37. A	❑	
11. C	❑		25. C		❑	38. J	❑	
12. F	❑		26. F		❑	39. B	❑	
13. C	❑		27. C		❑	40. G	❑	
14. G	❑							

Number Correct:

Social Studies/Sciences _____

Arts/Literature _____

Total _____

Model ACT II English Answers Explained

PASSAGE I

1. B
Clearly, the name of the event is important. She leaves the event unnamed at first to give the article dramatic effect.

2. F
Both times the author uses the word *millions*, she is referring to a number of people, not an amount of money. She specifically chose to use this number twice for emphasis. Nothing in the passage supports the other choices.

3. C
Since *the Great Depression* explains what was *much worse*, a colon is needed to separate the original statement from the explanation that follows. Using a period, semicolon, or exclamation point creates a sentence fragment.

4. J
Since the businesses were bringing in less money, they were responsible for cutting production and laying off employees. Therefore, the phrase *with less income* needs to be followed by a statement about the businesses, not one about the employees.

5. B
The subject of this sentence is the singular *One*. Therefore, the verb must be singular.

6. J
The other expressions are too casual. The author's tone is serious and so is the subject.

7. A
Because the term *paper wealth* is unusual, an explanation might be useful. However, *paper wealth* could also be explained by example. A definition of *wealth* would not be helpful because it has a very different meaning from *paper wealth*. A full discussion of different types of wealth would give the reader too much information, because the discussion here focuses on only one type of wealth.

8. H
The first sentence is neither a question nor a point of special emphasis. It is, however, an independent clause, as is the second sentence. Therefore, the two sentences must be separated by a period. A comma would create a comma splice.

9. B
This word should be a pronoun that refers to the European farmers.

10. J
All of the choices simply repeat the meaning of *varied*. Therefore, the phrase is redundant and should be omitted.

11. D
The word should be the correct plural form of *country*: *countries*.

12. F
This sentence is fine as it is. If you put in a period or a semicolon, you separate a dependent clause from an independent clause and thus create a fragment. No comma is necessary to separate *jobs* from the list that follows.

13. D
These phrases all repeat the meaning of *temporary*; therefore, the phrase is not needed.

14. H
The tone of this entire passage (not just the introduction) is short, choppy, and exciting. The passage emphasizes how quickly and forcefully the stock market crash affected the lives of millions of people.

15. A
The article describes a progression of events starting with the stock market crash, then the Great Depression and the events that followed. Any other order would be confusing.

PASSAGE II

16. J
The "coming years," rather than "thoughtful individuals," have a "steadily increasing rate of change." Because this opening adverbial clause contains the pronoun *their*, the pronoun should refer to the subject of the sentence. In choices F and G, *thoughtful individuals* seems to be the subject of the sentence. The ordering of the phrases in choice H does not make sense.

17. B
As this sentence stands, it is a comma splice (two independent clauses joined together by only a comma). Choice C, with no punctuation, is also a run-on sentence. While choice D is grammatically

correct, it implies that despite the Industrial Revolution, change occurred, but that is not the intended meaning of the sentence. Choice B correctly indicates that change occurred as a result of the Industrial Revolution.

18. F

This clause makes the most sense in its current position in the sentence. This clause adds relevant information to the paragraph, so it should not be deleted. By moving the clause before the word *it*, it appears that the clause refers to the Industrial Revolution rather than change. Moving the clause after the word *detect* makes the sentence awkward because it breaks up the verb and the object of the sentence.

19. B

In a sentence with an opening adverbial clause (which in this case explains when an action takes place), the adverbial clause is generally separated from the remainder of the sentence by a comma. Placing a period after *times* creates a sentence fragment. Neither a semicolon nor a dash can be used to separate a dependent clause from an independent clause.

20. F

This should be a singular possessive because it describes whose lifetime the author is referring to. The singular *person* should end in *'s*.

21. A

"In the face of that illusion" indicates that an illusion has already been mentioned. Therefore, this clause must come after the mention of the illusion. Furthermore, this clause should come before and lead into the information that contradicts the illusion mentioned. Thus the clause fits best where it is already located.

22. G

When a change had clearly taken place is an adverbial clause, and so it should be separated from the rest of the sentence by a comma. The sentence as it is written is confusing. Inserting a period would create a fragment. A question mark is inappropriate because the first part of the sentence is a statement, not a question.

23. C

By putting quotation marks around *the good old days*, the author attributes this cliché to generations of people, not to one person in particular. The language of this paragraph does not indicate that the author genuinely believes that these old days were better than the present time, nor does he place any

special emphasis on these words, which are not the focus of the paragraph. There is also no reason to believe the words are directly quoted.

24. G

This adverbial clause refers to how some people had just begun to realize that change would continue. By placing this clause after *only* or *place*, the clause seems to indicate that change was actually taking place for the first time, which is clearly false. By placing the clause after *deaths*, it seems as though change would really begin to take place only after some people's deaths.

25. B

A comma is needed to separate this clause from the remainder of the sentence. All of the other options listed make the final dependent clause a sentence fragment.

26. G

This nonessential clause needs to be set off from the rest of the sentences by a dash.

27. A

The period breaks up two independent clauses. Choice B is a comma splice. While choices C and D are grammatically correct, this sentence is not a question, nor does it need any special emphasis.

28. F

This paragraph ends by referring to the broad category of science fiction. To someone very familiar with the genre, the meaning of this term would be obvious. However, this term could be clarified for most people by the addition of a definition. Changes that have occurred and lists of science fiction authors would not help the readers grasp the concept of the genre of science fiction. Choice G is designed to throw the reader off with a cliché that has nothing to do with the information conveyed by the writer.

29. D

Although the article doesn't mention science fiction until the end, the author describes the conditions that led up to the creation of science fiction. The essay builds the historical precedent before it introduces the main subject.

30. H

The second paragraph introduces the concept of change in modern society, and therefore it should come first. While paragraphs 1 and 3 both expand upon this notion of change, paragraph 1 directly builds upon the information presented in paragraph 2, explaining how the rate of change was increasing.

Paragraph 3 builds upon the ideas in the previous two paragraphs, demonstrating how this increasing change brought about science fiction writing.

PASSAGE III

31. C

The phrase *the Hebrews* is nonessential and does not significantly affect the meaning of the sentence; it adds extra information. Nonessential clauses should be set off from the sentence by commas.

32. J

It is clear from the context that polytheism is the opposite of the belief in one god; it is the belief in more than one god. The other choices are not relevant to the topic.

33. D

This sentence is a run-on. Adding a comma, as in choice C, makes the sentence into a comma splice. To break the run-on into two sentences, end punctuation is necessary. Since there is no special emphasis on the first part of this sentence, an exclamation point is inappropriate. A period is the best solution.

34. F

Choices G and J imply that a contradiction to what has already been stated will follow. However, the sentence does not contradict the prior sentence. Choice H implies a cause-and-effect relationship, though in this case the effect is stated before the cause. *Eventually* indicates that Judaism *became* a major religion over time, as is stated in the prior sentence.

35. C

Since the passage refers to the people of Israel as *the Hebrews*, this reference should also be plural.

36. J

This phrase is not necessary because it repeats the idea that is conveyed by the word *originally*.

37. A

These are two perfectly logical sentences. When the period is removed, the sentence becomes a run-on. When a comma is substituted, the sentence becomes a comma splice. Since the first sentence is not a question, a question mark is not appropriate.

38. J

The phrase *needing a code of moral standards* modifies *the Hebrews*, not *God* (who creates the moral standards) or *Moses*. Therefore, *the Hebrews* should directly follow the modifier.

39. D

Because the sentence describes events that took place in the past, the past-tense *developed* is correct.

40. H

The phrase *a neighboring people* is not an appositive here. It is a definition of *Philistines*. So the comma after *people* is incorrect. This may be clearer if you reread the sentence and imagine a colon in place of the comma.

41. C

Choice C is the only one that achieves parallel structure. There is no such word as *beautifulled*.

42. J

It's is a contraction of *it is*. The pronoun *its* to describe the Temple is correct.

43. D

The word *center* in this sentence does not refer to the physical positioning of the Temple of Solomon; therefore, choices A and B are incorrect. Choice D indicates that the Temple of Solomon is a symbol that represents the activities that take place within the physical structure of the temple, which is more accurate than saying the temple itself was the focus in the Jewish religion, as in choice C.

44. F

The insertion of any of the given words between *two* and *parts* is redundant. These parts must be separate and different, otherwise they would not be parts.

45. C

With the sentences in this order, the paragraph shows the logical progression of how Israel and the Hebrews were defeated by outside forces. The final sentence explains that in 1948, Israel once again became an independent country. You could also have used the progression of dates in the paragraph—chronological order—to figure out the answer.

PASSAGE IV

46. H

The headlines belong to a particular day. Therefore, a possessive must be used. Since the sentence refers to one typical day, the possessive must be singular.

47. A

Once in a while is an adverbial clause that describes when a particular action takes place, so it is set apart from the main clause of the sentence by a comma. A period or a colon would make the adverbial clause a sentence fragment. Ellipses are generally used to indicate missing words, which does not seem to be the case here.

48. J

This sentence is a run-on because it contains two independent clauses not connected by a conjunction such as *and* or *but.* By adding a comma, the sentence becomes a comma splice. A period is the best choice for punctuation (and note that it is placed inside the quotation mark).

49. D

Obviously, a word is defined by a definition. Using the word twice is redundant. The sentence is more direct when the phrase is left out.

50. H

Choices F, G, and J are all sentence fragments that do not contain a subject or a verb. Only choice H is an independent clause and a complete sentence. It is also parallel in structure to the preceding sentence.

51. A

This sentence contains an indirect question, which tells what has been asked but does not directly quote the speaker's words. Because it is not a direct question, it does not take a question mark. The exclamation point would indicate an unneeded emphasis on this sentence. Since no definition or list follows the punctuation here, a colon is also inappropriate.

52. G

Choices F and J show a shift in sentence construction from the active voice to the passive voice. In order to remain in the active voice, *we* must be the object of the art's reminding. Choice H is illogical because *who* cannot refer to art, which is an inanimate object rather than a person.

53. C

The author emphasizes *how* to demonstrate that psychologists have a special function. Unlike artists, psychologists can actually tell you ways that you might be able to achieve inner peace. The *how* in the first sentence stresses that artists cannot do this, while psychologists can.

54. F

Choice G turns these two independent clauses into one long run-on sentence. Choice H turns them into a comma splice. Choice J connects the two ideas with a conjunction, but the conjunction *but* implies that a contradiction will follow. Since the remainder of the sentence does not contradict the first part of the sentence, choice J is also incorrect.

55. D

All of these answers convey the same meaning, but choices A, B, and C are too casual for a formal essay on a scientific procedure. The word *observation* is formal and names part of the scientific process, and it is parallel to *experimentation.*

56. J

The adjective *unique* means "one of a kind." Because this word has an absolute meaning, it cannot be modified by other adjectives, or in the case of the adverb *uniquely*, by other adverbs.

57. D

In the opening sentence of this paragraph, the author compares humans to horses and dogs. Sentence 5 follows up on this idea, noting that humans have different instincts from animals. Sentence 2 then focuses more specifically on what makes humans unique. Therefore, sentence 5 should be inserted between sentences 1 and 2.

58. G

Both medical doctors and psychiatric patients would most likely have a more in-depth knowledge of the field of psychology and its methods. Though this passage may be intended for young women as well as young men, there is nothing in the language that indicates the passage was directed at young women specifically. Since the explanations here are very basic, the passage is written for someone with little or no knowledge of psychology.

59. C

This author attempts to capture the reader's attention by giving headlines that might engage the reader's emotions.

60. J

Paragraphs 1 and 2 belong at the beginning of the passage. That narrows the answer choices to F and J. The current paragraph 4 follows logically from the current paragraph 2. So the first three paragraphs should be 1, 2, 4. J is the only choice that correctly orders these first three paragraphs.

PASSAGE V

61. D

The words *little, young,* and *child* are redundant, repeating the meanings of *small* and *girl.* This word can be omitted.

62. G

Because the word *Indian* begins with a vowel, the proper article is *an.*

63. D

In choices A, B, and C, the sentence beginning with *which* is a sentence fragment. The sentence has a verb (*tasted*), but no subject. *Which* is a pronoun that refers to the subject but does not replace it.

64. F

The words just prior to this statement indicate that they are "according to the textbook." Direct quotations are always put in quotation marks.

65. A

You would use single quotation marks only for something inside double quotation marks. Choice D does not contain the comma necessary to lead into the coordinating conjunction and second independent clause in this compound sentence. Choice C removes the quotation marks, which is incorrect because the author is telling what the Nooksack called this food. Other tribes might have another name for it.

66. J

Indian is an adjective describing the word *people*, not a possessive showing ownership of the people. Choice G is incorrect because when the name of a culture is used as an adjective, it should not be plural.

67. C

The word *well* means "in a good manner" or refers to a state of feeling (an adverb), therefore it cannot describe parts of *education* (a noun). *Goodest* is an incorrect superlative. Only *good* is the correct adjective here.

68. H

In order for there to be a smooth transition among ideas, this paragraph should begin by referring to the story in the textbook mentioned in the previous paragraph. Additionally, the description of the father's lineage makes more sense following his connection to the textbook story and the author's reference to him as the leader of her tribe. Therefore, the first and second sentences should be in reverse order.

69. B

The author describes her father's prestigious lineage and position within the tribe. She also describes him with the adjectives *wise* and *humble*, which are both good and noble characteristics. Obviously, she has great respect for her father. There are no indications that she is hostile toward or embarrassed by him,

and, based on the tone of this paragraph, she is not indifferent to him.

70. J

As it stands, this long sentence is a comma splice. Choice G is a run-on sentence. The use of ellipses in choice H would indicate that words have been left out of this sentence, which does not seem to be the case. Therefore, it is correct to use a period to break up the two sentences.

71. D

In order for the construction of this sentence to remain parallel, the verb tenses must agree. The second verb must be in past tense to remain parallel to the verb *was* in the previous clause.

72. G

This sentence is a statement, not a question or a point for unusual emphasis. A period is the correct end punctuation.

73. A

The author describes the deep-seated prejudices of mainstream American culture—prejudices that most people in her own tribe would have experienced themselves. Both historians and researchers would most likely not need this very general information about Native Americans. However, many Americans would not recognize these prejudices in themselves. This essay awakens Americans to the negative picture of Native Americans that is portrayed in schools, textbooks, and elsewhere.

74. H

Although this essay focuses on criticism of a particular type of food considered a delicacy by Native Americans, the subject of the essay really isn't about food. The subject of food is just one example of the "not very complimentary" way the mainstream portrays Native Americans.

75. A

The essay begins with the author looking back on an experience that occurred when she was eight years old, tells the story in chronological order, then returns to the present to explain why she has told this story. The paragraphs are in the correct order.

Model ACT II Reading Answers Explained

PASSAGE I

1. D
At the end of the story, the narrator reveals that he is actually a major-league baseball scout. Because he asks about Maneri when he arrives in town, it can be inferred that he has come to watch Maneri play.

2. H
When Pete cannot explain why he didn't make a bad throw, the narrator responds, "You're going to be a major-league ballplayer because you couldn't throw that ball away." The narrator implies that a truly great player would never throw the ball away; Pete's decision shows that he has what it takes to be a professional.

3. B
Pete says of Al Dall, "He bawled me out in front of everybody," which supports choice B.

4. H
The narrator tells Pete that he once threw a ball over the first baseman's head. In other words, he purposely forced the first baseman to miss the catch to cause problems for his coach.

5. A
Pete is waiting desperately to hear from the Yankee management, most likely through the mail. The desk clerk says there is no mail *today*, which implies that this is something Pete asks for every day.

6. G
The story implies that Pete will play major-league baseball because he is a talented young man. As a scout, Eddie Brown will most likely now recommend that the Yankees bring him up to the major league.

7. C
The narrator uses the name Mr. Franklin, an alias that allows him to test Pete without being recognized. However, at the end of the story, the narrator admits that he is actually Eddie Brown, the famous Yankee scout.

8. J
Through the details given about Pete in the story, we can infer that he is an excellent ballplayer who is being held back from the major leagues. He is frustrated by this. Moreover, his dialogue shows him to be a likable and modest young man.

9. A
The narrator tells us that the home team (which we know to be Pete's, since the scout comes to this town where "that kid Maneri played ball") won the first game. Because of Pete's skill and integrity, he gets the final player on the opposing team out in the second game, winning the game for his team.

10. J
The fact that Eddie Brown gives Pete the news that he's in the major leagues while they're in the lobby shows that Eddie Brown was waiting for him. The other choices might be tempting, but they are not supported by the events in the story.

PASSAGE II

11. C
The author notes (lines 3–7) that Maslow's humanist psychology is based on information discovered from healthy patients rather than disturbed patients.

12. F
Item 3 from the list in the passage states that when people's (including children's) needs are not satisfied, their inner nature becomes frustrated or twisted.

13. C
The author notes (lines 14–19) that Maslow disagrees with the basic tenets of Freud's theories, which indicate that a person is ruled by his or her psychological experiences. Rogers agreed with Maslow. All the other choices contradict this.

14. G
The author defines a self-actualizing person as a fully mature personality—in other words, one who has fully developed.

15. B
A person's inner nature can grow stronger or weaker depending on outside influences and other factors, according to the information in lines 42–48. Therefore, a person's inner nature is not constant. Also, according to lines 12–15, that nature is always good.

16. J
Carl Rogers is described as the "other guiding spirit of the humanist movement" (lines 8–9). Though he and Maslow held similar ideas about human nature, there is nothing in the article to indicate that they were partners.

17. D

In lines 12–14 and 27–29, the author reiterates Maslow's concept that people are basically good at heart.

18. F

Maslow believed that every disturbed person has unmet needs. According to Maslow, depression would indicate that the person was deprived of some basic needs.

19. C

The author describes Maslow's outlook as optimistic, or positive (line 23).

20. F

The author notes that a good therapist will help to restore a patient to the path of self-knowledge (lines 38–41), leading to eventual self-actualization.

PASSAGE III

21. C

The word *charged* has several meanings. In this passage, it means being given the responsibility for doing something, in this case creating large-scale public murals. There is no evidence in the article that choices A, B, or D occurred.

22. J

The first paragraph mentions that Latin American artists traveled to Europe and then returned. The paragraph cites that travel is one of the three dominant trends in Latin American art. Choice F is incorrect because the second paragraph refers to European art as avant-garde. Choice G is incorrect because the article does not mention that European art was influenced by Latin American art, and if that influence did occur, it is not a main point of this article. The word *all* in choice H is an indication that the answer is not the best choice. A single counterexample will make the choice incorrect. Frida Kahlo's folk art provides that counterexample.

23. A

Choice A restates the first sentence in the fourth paragraph (lines 48–50), which says that in cubist art objects are shown from multiple points of view simultaneously.

24. H

The explanation for choice H is found in the second paragraph, where the author writes that *avant-garde* means things that are "seen at that time" to be "experimental." The other choices are incorrect because, while an art movement referred to as avant-garde was founded in the early 1900s and was associated with modernist styles, the art movement itself is not the meaning of *avant-garde*.

25. C

The beginning of the third paragraph specifically states that cubism was developed by Picasso and Braque. These artists were influenced by Cézanne, but Cézanne did not develop cubist art. All the other choices contradict information in the passage.

26. F

Rivera and Kahlo were married, while the last line in the passage indicates that their relationship was "stormy." Choice G is incorrect because the passage indicates that it was their personal relationship, not their nationalistic beliefs, that created conflicting emotions. Choice H is incorrect because, although Rivera was a cubist and Kahlo was a folk artist, this difference is not discussed as a feature of their relationship. The passage does not mention that their relationship was based on their nationality.

27. C

The key to the correct answer is the word *assimilate*, which means "to incorporate." Choice A is incorrect because the artists actually wanted to incorporate avant-garde styles, not find alternatives to them. Choice B is incorrect because avant-garde represented a break with traditional styles. Choice D is incorrect because the artists were not seeking a different approach to the avant-garde style, but rather to assimilate (incorporate) that style.

28. H

The paragraph mentions that expressionism was both a literary and an artistic movement. This paragraph does not mention Latin American art, nor is there mention of German artists traveling to Latin America, although German art is noted as being at the roots of expressionism. Choice J is incorrect because expressionism primarily focused on emotional responses, not on objects and events themselves.

29. B

Post-impressionism means "after" impressionism. Cézanne's work developed before cubism, so impressionism must have developed before cubism. The passage does not identify impressionism and expressionism as related. The passage states that African tribal art influenced the cubists Picasso and Braque.

30. H

The words *forceful* and *intricate* are similar to the words *compelling* and *complex*, and *summary of her life* means the same as *autobiography*. Choice F is incorrect because the paragraph does not mention struggles of the downtrodden. Choice G is not the best because *overstated and difficult* do not have the same meaning as *compelling and complex*. J is incorrect because it mentions a summary of the lives of others, which is not an autobiography.

PASSAGE IV

31. D.

The author writes about the "inner and outer layers of human skin: the dermis and epidermis." The outer layer is the epidermis.

32. H.

According to the article, De Rossi is an Italian engineer who has created a type of "smart skin."

33. B

The author notes that the advantage of De Rossi's artificial skin is that it can sense friction (lines 54–59).

34. H

Robots can hold on to a variety of different objects, but they cannot sense the differences among objects that need to be held with firm grips, soft grips, or other grips. The author indicates this in the first two paragraphs. Choice F contradicts information in the article, and choices G and J are not supported by anything in the passage.

35. C

The article indicates that De Rossi has many problems with his current model of "smart skin." However, the article implies that these problems will most likely be worked out through continued experimentation. The article does not imply the robots will be available soon or that they will never exist.

36. G

According to lines 32–44, pressure deforms the gel that is encapsulated between two layers of electrodes. As the pressure changes, so will the voltage between these electrodes. This will send a message to the robot that the object requires a specific type of grip.

37. A

The purpose of this article is to discuss how the development of "smart skin" can affect and improve the grips of robots.

38. J

The author lists certain important factors that affect De Rossi's attempts to fix the problems with his "soft skin," but color is never mentioned.

39. B

According to the final paragraph of the article, once the scientists are able to collect data, they must figure out how to coordinate—or process—all of the information they have received. This exactly matches choice B.

40. G

The author refers to "tactile information" and "tactile messages" that are conveyed by the hands of robots with "smart skin" and by humans. All this is related to the sense of touch.

Model English and Reading ACT III

With Answers Explained

This Model English and Reading ACT III is just like a real ACT. Take this test after you take the Model English and Reading ACT II. If you plan to take the optional ACT Writing Test, you should also complete the ACT Writing Test II on pages 385–392.

Take this model test under simulated test conditions. Allow 45 minutes to answer the 75 English items and 35 minutes to answer the 40 Reading items. Use the Answer Sheet on the following page to mark your answers. Use a pencil to mark the answer sheet, and color in the circles for the correct choices in the Test 1 (English) and Test 3 (Reading) sections.

Use the Scoring Keys on pages 340–342 to score the answer sheet. Review the answer explanations on pages 343–351.

The test scoring charts on pages 6 and 7 show you how to convert the number of correct answers to ACT scale scores. The Scoring Keys on pages 340–342 show you how to find the Usage/Mechanics and Rhetorical Skills subscores and the Social Studies/ Sciences and Arts/Literature subscores.

DO NOT leave any answers blank. There is no penalty for guessing on the ACT. Remember that the test is yours. You may mark up, write on, or draw on the test.

When you are ready, note the time and begin.

ANSWER SHEET

The ACT answer sheet looks something like this. Use a No. 2 pencil to completely fill the circle corresponding to the correct answer. If you erase, erase completely; incomplete erasures may be read as answers.

TEST 1—English

1 Ⓐ Ⓑ Ⓒ Ⓓ	11 Ⓐ Ⓑ Ⓒ Ⓓ	21 Ⓐ Ⓑ Ⓒ Ⓓ	31 Ⓐ Ⓑ Ⓒ Ⓓ	41 Ⓐ Ⓑ Ⓒ Ⓓ	51 Ⓐ Ⓑ Ⓒ Ⓓ	61 Ⓐ Ⓑ Ⓒ Ⓓ	71 Ⓐ Ⓑ Ⓒ Ⓓ
2 Ⓕ Ⓖ Ⓗ Ⓙ	12 Ⓕ Ⓖ Ⓗ Ⓙ	22 Ⓕ Ⓖ Ⓗ Ⓙ	32 Ⓕ Ⓖ Ⓗ Ⓙ	42 Ⓕ Ⓖ Ⓗ Ⓙ	52 Ⓕ Ⓖ Ⓗ Ⓙ	62 Ⓕ Ⓖ Ⓗ Ⓙ	72 Ⓕ Ⓖ Ⓗ Ⓙ
3 Ⓐ Ⓑ Ⓒ Ⓓ	13 Ⓐ Ⓑ Ⓒ Ⓓ	23 Ⓐ Ⓑ Ⓒ Ⓓ	33 Ⓐ Ⓑ Ⓒ Ⓓ	43 Ⓐ Ⓑ Ⓒ Ⓓ	53 Ⓐ Ⓑ Ⓒ Ⓓ	63 Ⓐ Ⓑ Ⓒ Ⓓ	73 Ⓐ Ⓑ Ⓒ Ⓓ
4 Ⓕ Ⓖ Ⓗ Ⓙ	14 Ⓕ Ⓖ Ⓗ Ⓙ	24 Ⓕ Ⓖ Ⓗ Ⓙ	34 Ⓕ Ⓖ Ⓗ Ⓙ	44 Ⓕ Ⓖ Ⓗ Ⓙ	54 Ⓕ Ⓖ Ⓗ Ⓙ	64 Ⓕ Ⓖ Ⓗ Ⓙ	74 Ⓕ Ⓖ Ⓗ Ⓙ
5 Ⓐ Ⓑ Ⓒ Ⓓ	15 Ⓐ Ⓑ Ⓒ Ⓓ	25 Ⓐ Ⓑ Ⓒ Ⓓ	35 Ⓐ Ⓑ Ⓒ Ⓓ	45 Ⓐ Ⓑ Ⓒ Ⓓ	55 Ⓐ Ⓑ Ⓒ Ⓓ	65 Ⓐ Ⓑ Ⓒ Ⓓ	75 Ⓐ Ⓑ Ⓒ Ⓓ
6 Ⓕ Ⓖ Ⓗ Ⓙ	16 Ⓕ Ⓖ Ⓗ Ⓙ	26 Ⓕ Ⓖ Ⓗ Ⓙ	36 Ⓕ Ⓖ Ⓗ Ⓙ	46 Ⓕ Ⓖ Ⓗ Ⓙ	56 Ⓕ Ⓖ Ⓗ Ⓙ	66 Ⓕ Ⓖ Ⓗ Ⓙ	
7 Ⓐ Ⓑ Ⓒ Ⓓ	17 Ⓐ Ⓑ Ⓒ Ⓓ	27 Ⓐ Ⓑ Ⓒ Ⓓ	37 Ⓐ Ⓑ Ⓒ Ⓓ	47 Ⓐ Ⓑ Ⓒ Ⓓ	57 Ⓐ Ⓑ Ⓒ Ⓓ	67 Ⓐ Ⓑ Ⓒ Ⓓ	
8 Ⓕ Ⓖ Ⓗ Ⓙ	18 Ⓕ Ⓖ Ⓗ Ⓙ	28 Ⓕ Ⓖ Ⓗ Ⓙ	38 Ⓕ Ⓖ Ⓗ Ⓙ	48 Ⓕ Ⓖ Ⓗ Ⓙ	58 Ⓕ Ⓖ Ⓗ Ⓙ	68 Ⓕ Ⓖ Ⓗ Ⓙ	
9 Ⓐ Ⓑ Ⓒ Ⓓ	19 Ⓐ Ⓑ Ⓒ Ⓓ	29 Ⓐ Ⓑ Ⓒ Ⓓ	39 Ⓐ Ⓑ Ⓒ Ⓓ	49 Ⓐ Ⓑ Ⓒ Ⓓ	59 Ⓐ Ⓑ Ⓒ Ⓓ	69 Ⓐ Ⓑ Ⓒ Ⓓ	
10 Ⓕ Ⓖ Ⓗ Ⓙ	20 Ⓕ Ⓖ Ⓗ Ⓙ	30 Ⓕ Ⓖ Ⓗ Ⓙ	40 Ⓕ Ⓖ Ⓗ Ⓙ	50 Ⓕ Ⓖ Ⓗ Ⓙ	60 Ⓕ Ⓖ Ⓗ Ⓙ	70 Ⓕ Ⓖ Ⓗ Ⓙ	

TEST 2—Mathematics

1 Ⓐ Ⓑ Ⓒ Ⓓ Ⓔ	9 Ⓐ Ⓑ Ⓒ Ⓓ Ⓔ	17 Ⓐ Ⓑ Ⓒ Ⓓ Ⓔ	25 Ⓐ Ⓑ Ⓒ Ⓓ Ⓔ	33 Ⓐ Ⓑ Ⓒ Ⓓ Ⓔ	41 Ⓐ Ⓑ Ⓒ Ⓓ Ⓔ	49 Ⓐ Ⓑ Ⓒ Ⓓ Ⓔ	57 Ⓐ Ⓑ Ⓒ Ⓓ Ⓔ
2 Ⓕ Ⓖ Ⓗ Ⓙ Ⓚ	10 Ⓕ Ⓖ Ⓗ Ⓙ Ⓚ	18 Ⓕ Ⓖ Ⓗ Ⓙ Ⓚ	26 Ⓕ Ⓖ Ⓗ Ⓙ Ⓚ	34 Ⓕ Ⓖ Ⓗ Ⓙ Ⓚ	42 Ⓕ Ⓖ Ⓗ Ⓙ Ⓚ	50 Ⓕ Ⓖ Ⓗ Ⓙ Ⓚ	58 Ⓕ Ⓖ Ⓗ Ⓙ Ⓚ
3 Ⓐ Ⓑ Ⓒ Ⓓ Ⓔ	11 Ⓐ Ⓑ Ⓒ Ⓓ Ⓔ	19 Ⓐ Ⓑ Ⓒ Ⓓ Ⓔ	27 Ⓐ Ⓑ Ⓒ Ⓓ Ⓔ	35 Ⓐ Ⓑ Ⓒ Ⓓ Ⓔ	43 Ⓐ Ⓑ Ⓒ Ⓓ Ⓔ	51 Ⓐ Ⓑ Ⓒ Ⓓ Ⓔ	59 Ⓐ Ⓑ Ⓒ Ⓓ Ⓔ
4 Ⓕ Ⓖ Ⓗ Ⓙ Ⓚ	12 Ⓕ Ⓖ Ⓗ Ⓙ Ⓚ	20 Ⓕ Ⓖ Ⓗ Ⓙ Ⓚ	28 Ⓕ Ⓖ Ⓗ Ⓙ Ⓚ	36 Ⓕ Ⓖ Ⓗ Ⓙ Ⓚ	44 Ⓕ Ⓖ Ⓗ Ⓙ Ⓚ	52 Ⓕ Ⓖ Ⓗ Ⓙ Ⓚ	60 Ⓕ Ⓖ Ⓗ Ⓙ Ⓚ
5 Ⓐ Ⓑ Ⓒ Ⓓ Ⓔ	13 Ⓐ Ⓑ Ⓒ Ⓓ Ⓔ	21 Ⓐ Ⓑ Ⓒ Ⓓ Ⓔ	29 Ⓐ Ⓑ Ⓒ Ⓓ Ⓔ	37 Ⓐ Ⓑ Ⓒ Ⓓ Ⓔ	45 Ⓐ Ⓑ Ⓒ Ⓓ Ⓔ	53 Ⓐ Ⓑ Ⓒ Ⓓ Ⓔ	
6 Ⓕ Ⓖ Ⓗ Ⓙ Ⓚ	14 Ⓕ Ⓖ Ⓗ Ⓙ Ⓚ	22 Ⓕ Ⓖ Ⓗ Ⓙ Ⓚ	30 Ⓕ Ⓖ Ⓗ Ⓙ Ⓚ	38 Ⓕ Ⓖ Ⓗ Ⓙ Ⓚ	46 Ⓕ Ⓖ Ⓗ Ⓙ Ⓚ	54 Ⓕ Ⓖ Ⓗ Ⓙ Ⓚ	
7 Ⓐ Ⓑ Ⓒ Ⓓ Ⓔ	15 Ⓐ Ⓑ Ⓒ Ⓓ Ⓔ	23 Ⓐ Ⓑ Ⓒ Ⓓ Ⓔ	31 Ⓐ Ⓑ Ⓒ Ⓓ Ⓔ	39 Ⓐ Ⓑ Ⓒ Ⓓ Ⓔ	47 Ⓐ Ⓑ Ⓒ Ⓓ Ⓔ	55 Ⓐ Ⓑ Ⓒ Ⓓ Ⓔ	
8 Ⓕ Ⓖ Ⓗ Ⓙ Ⓚ	16 Ⓕ Ⓖ Ⓗ Ⓙ Ⓚ	24 Ⓕ Ⓖ Ⓗ Ⓙ Ⓚ	32 Ⓕ Ⓖ Ⓗ Ⓙ Ⓚ	40 Ⓕ Ⓖ Ⓗ Ⓙ Ⓚ	48 Ⓕ Ⓖ Ⓗ Ⓙ Ⓚ	56 Ⓕ Ⓖ Ⓗ Ⓙ Ⓚ	

TEST 3—Reading

1 Ⓐ Ⓑ Ⓒ Ⓓ	6 Ⓕ Ⓖ Ⓗ Ⓙ	11 Ⓐ Ⓑ Ⓒ Ⓓ	16 Ⓕ Ⓖ Ⓗ Ⓙ	21 Ⓐ Ⓑ Ⓒ Ⓓ	26 Ⓕ Ⓖ Ⓗ Ⓙ	31 Ⓐ Ⓑ Ⓒ Ⓓ	36 Ⓕ Ⓖ Ⓗ Ⓙ
2 Ⓕ Ⓖ Ⓗ Ⓙ	7 Ⓐ Ⓑ Ⓒ Ⓓ	12 Ⓕ Ⓖ Ⓗ Ⓙ	17 Ⓐ Ⓑ Ⓒ Ⓓ	22 Ⓕ Ⓖ Ⓗ Ⓙ	27 Ⓐ Ⓑ Ⓒ Ⓓ	32 Ⓕ Ⓖ Ⓗ Ⓙ	37 Ⓐ Ⓑ Ⓒ Ⓓ
3 Ⓐ Ⓑ Ⓒ Ⓓ	8 Ⓕ Ⓖ Ⓗ Ⓙ	13 Ⓐ Ⓑ Ⓒ Ⓓ	18 Ⓕ Ⓖ Ⓗ Ⓙ	23 Ⓐ Ⓑ Ⓒ Ⓓ	28 Ⓕ Ⓖ Ⓗ Ⓙ	33 Ⓐ Ⓑ Ⓒ Ⓓ	38 Ⓕ Ⓖ Ⓗ Ⓙ
4 Ⓕ Ⓖ Ⓗ Ⓙ	9 Ⓐ Ⓑ Ⓒ Ⓓ	14 Ⓕ Ⓖ Ⓗ Ⓙ	19 Ⓐ Ⓑ Ⓒ Ⓓ	24 Ⓕ Ⓖ Ⓗ Ⓙ	29 Ⓐ Ⓑ Ⓒ Ⓓ	34 Ⓕ Ⓖ Ⓗ Ⓙ	39 Ⓐ Ⓑ Ⓒ Ⓓ
5 Ⓐ Ⓑ Ⓒ Ⓓ	10 Ⓕ Ⓖ Ⓗ Ⓙ	15 Ⓐ Ⓑ Ⓒ Ⓓ	20 Ⓕ Ⓖ Ⓗ Ⓙ	25 Ⓐ Ⓑ Ⓒ Ⓓ	30 Ⓕ Ⓖ Ⓗ Ⓙ	35 Ⓐ Ⓑ Ⓒ Ⓓ	40 Ⓕ Ⓖ Ⓗ Ⓙ

TEST 4—Science Reasoning

1 Ⓐ Ⓑ Ⓒ Ⓓ	6 Ⓕ Ⓖ Ⓗ Ⓙ	11 Ⓐ Ⓑ Ⓒ Ⓓ	16 Ⓕ Ⓖ Ⓗ Ⓙ	21 Ⓐ Ⓑ Ⓒ Ⓓ	26 Ⓕ Ⓖ Ⓗ Ⓙ	31 Ⓐ Ⓑ Ⓒ Ⓓ	36 Ⓕ Ⓖ Ⓗ Ⓙ
2 Ⓕ Ⓖ Ⓗ Ⓙ	7 Ⓐ Ⓑ Ⓒ Ⓓ	12 Ⓕ Ⓖ Ⓗ Ⓙ	17 Ⓐ Ⓑ Ⓒ Ⓓ	22 Ⓕ Ⓖ Ⓗ Ⓙ	27 Ⓐ Ⓑ Ⓒ Ⓓ	32 Ⓕ Ⓖ Ⓗ Ⓙ	37 Ⓐ Ⓑ Ⓒ Ⓓ
3 Ⓐ Ⓑ Ⓒ Ⓓ	8 Ⓕ Ⓖ Ⓗ Ⓙ	13 Ⓐ Ⓑ Ⓒ Ⓓ	18 Ⓕ Ⓖ Ⓗ Ⓙ	23 Ⓐ Ⓑ Ⓒ Ⓓ	28 Ⓕ Ⓖ Ⓗ Ⓙ	33 Ⓐ Ⓑ Ⓒ Ⓓ	38 Ⓕ Ⓖ Ⓗ Ⓙ
4 Ⓕ Ⓖ Ⓗ Ⓙ	9 Ⓐ Ⓑ Ⓒ Ⓓ	14 Ⓕ Ⓖ Ⓗ Ⓙ	19 Ⓐ Ⓑ Ⓒ Ⓓ	24 Ⓕ Ⓖ Ⓗ Ⓙ	29 Ⓐ Ⓑ Ⓒ Ⓓ	34 Ⓕ Ⓖ Ⓗ Ⓙ	39 Ⓐ Ⓑ Ⓒ Ⓓ
5 Ⓐ Ⓑ Ⓒ Ⓓ	10 Ⓕ Ⓖ Ⓗ Ⓙ	15 Ⓐ Ⓑ Ⓒ Ⓓ	20 Ⓕ Ⓖ Ⓗ Ⓙ	25 Ⓐ Ⓑ Ⓒ Ⓓ	30 Ⓕ Ⓖ Ⓗ Ⓙ	35 Ⓐ Ⓑ Ⓒ Ⓓ	40 Ⓕ Ⓖ Ⓗ Ⓙ

Model English ACT III

75 Questions–45 Minutes

INSTRUCTIONS: Certain words or phrases in the following five passages are underlined and numbered. There is a corresponding item for each underlined portion. Each item offers three suggestions for changing the underlined portion to conform to standard written English or to make it more understandable or consistent with the rest of the passage. If the underlined portion is not improved by one of the three suggested changes, mark NO CHANGE. Some items are about the entire passage, and the numbers for these items come at the end of the passage.

Choose the best answer for each question based on the passage. Then fill in the appropriate circle on the answer sheet.

Check pages 340–341 and 343–347 for answers and explanations.

PASSAGE I

Computer Freeze Up!

My computer and I have some serious problems. It just does not get along with me, and I'm always asking my friends for help. Sometimes I feel like using my computer is more <u>frustrating, than</u> anything
1
else I do. Suddenly, and for no apparent reason,

<u>the screen freezes up.</u>
2

The screen freezing up must mean, <u>literally</u>, the
3
computer has died. But let me <u>be specific when</u> the
4
computer freezes, I am always concerned that I have lost all my data, and that my life as a student is over.

The first thing I <u>try is pressing the Enter Key</u>.
5
Then I press the space bar. But the pressed keys

<u>don't respond; are ill suited</u> to solving the problem. I
6
pick up the phone and start calling my list of friends.

1. **A.** NO CHANGE
   B. frustrating than
   C. frustrating than,
   D. frustrating, then

2. **F.** NO CHANGE
   G. the characters on the screen freeze up.
   H. the words on the screen freeze up.
   J. the computer suddenly seems very cold.

3. **A.** NO CHANGE
   B. conclusively
   C. effectively
   D. in a sense

4. **F.** NO CHANGE
   G. be specific! When
   H. be specific: when
   J. be specific, when

5. What is the BEST placement of the underlined phrase?

   A. NO CHANGE
   B. Place after *space bar* in the next sentence.
   C. Place after *then*.
   D. Place after *data* in the previous paragraph.

Included in that list are people who know about
computers. I explain that no matter what I do, the
computer program had never continue.

⬛ Why does the screen freeze up so frequently?

⬛ I guess it's because there are some real issues
with my computer and it is trying to let me know that.

⬛ If that is really the case I'll just have to listen
to my friend who said, "Reboot the computer
to continue." ⬜ ⬜

6. **F.** NO CHANGE
   G. don't respond. Are ill suited
   H. don't respond and are ill suited
   J. don't respond, are ill suited

7. **A.** NO CHANGE
   B. is
   C. was
   D. OMIT the word.

8. **F.** NO CHANGE
   G. program will never
   H. program is never
   J. program are never

9. **A.** NO CHANGE
   B. its'
   C. its
   D. it'is

10. **F.** NO CHANGE
    G. case, I'll
    H. case. I'll
    J. case; I'll

11. **A.** NO CHANGE
    B. to continue!
    C. to continue"?
    D. to continue?"

12. For the sake of coherence, what is
    the BEST placement of sentence 2?

    F. NO CHANGE
    G. Before sentence 1
    H. After sentence 3
    J. OMIT the sentence.

13. Given the tone of the piece, a
    closing sentence could read:

    A. Computer errors like the one I
    describe here are often the result
    of the way others have used the
    computer.
    B. The school should give classes
    on how to avoid these kinds of
    computer problems.
    C. I guess I should ask before I get
    so upset about computer errors.
    D. It's okay to hate your computer.

14. The author has been asked to submit an article on computer use to a business magazine. Will this passage be suitable?

   F. Yes, because it describes computers and how they function.
   G. Yes, because the article is very easy to understand.
   H. No, because the article is too informal for a business magazine.
   J. No, because the article does not talk enough about computer use.

15. A good title for this piece would be:

   A. "Computers Are Death Traps"
   B. "Staying Cool With Your Computer"
   C. "Computer Errors Can Ruin Your Day"
   D. "Computers Are Unresponsive"

PASSAGE II

The Play

[1]

Auditions for the school play were rapidly approaching.

I had never been an actor, but my father thought

their little son Tyler should try for a part. I'm
    16
Tyler, but I'm not little. "Tyler" my parents told me,
                                  17
"go to those auditions." They thought I was good

enough, since the casting director for the play did not
          18
know that. Parents are funny that way, like the time

they said I should invite the Homecoming Queen to

the prom. Luckily, I never did.

16. F. NO CHANGE
    G. my
    H. our
    J. his

17. A. NO CHANGE
    B. "Tyler," my parents told me
    C. "Tyler," my parents told me,
    D. "Tyler" my parents told me

18. F. NO CHANGE
    G. but
    H. unless
    J. and

[2]

With the old drama teacher, the choice for being in the school play had been based on acting ability.
19
[20] That was the quality that mattered, on which all decisions were made. That applied regardless of
21
whether the person was the most handsome boy or
21
most beautiful girl in the school, or worse, a friend of the drama teacher. The actual talent of the potential
22
actor was the determining factor. Things have changed. For example, an actor is now chosen based on "looks," and created by an equivalent number of
23
attractiveness points to measure the actor's value. Of
23
course, it is not an objective measure as well; that is,
24
it is subject to ever-changing standards. (I'm just wondering if you can tell that I am not considered to be good-looking.) [25]

[3]

[26] [1] It was about England in the 1800s, and I had lines about English money like "pence ha'pence
27
and farthings were copper." [2] I never knew what
27
the lines meant. [3] Believe it or not I got a part.

[4] The money described in the play was so confusing that I had to dress up like an old English banker who came out at the very beginning of the play to explain the money back then. [5] I had to speak these exact lines: "The coins were issued by the Royal Mint, but the banknotes got its name because
28
they were issued by the Bank of England." [6] It's

19. **A.** NO CHANGE
    B. will be
    C. would be
    D. was being

20. The writer considers adding the following sentence after the first sentence in paragraph 2.

    Today the choices are made quite differently.

    The most logical reason for NOT including the sentence is that:

    F. it does not flow logically from the sentence before it.
    G. it changes the focus from the past to the present, and the next sentence refers again to the past.
    H. it seems to say that the way choices are made is better now.
    J. it suggests that Tyler knows that now the choices are made differently.

21. Which BEST represents the idea that it does not matter how the person was chosen?

    A. NO CHANGE
    B. even if
    C. depending on whether
    D. except for when

22. **F.** NO CHANGE
    G. condition
    H. values
    J. possibility

23. **A.** NO CHANGE
    B. "looks," which are used to measure an actor's value created by specific attractiveness points.
    C. "looks," which are used to measure an actor's value.
    D. "looks," which are created by specific attractiveness points used to measure an actor's value.

24. **F.** NO CHANGE
    G. as well that is
    H. as well, that is
    J. OMIT the underlined portion.

weird how things happened. [7] I thought I would never get a part because I wasn't good-looking. [8] My parents are happy. [9] However, I think I'll put an end to my acting ambitions. [10] Now my parents think that with this experience, I might become a banker. [11] You figure that one out. [29]

25. This sentence is in parentheses because it:

   A. is unrelated to the other information in the paragraph.
   B. provides additional information through an explanation.
   C. is the last sentence in the paragraph.
   D. includes a definition of looks.

26. A good introductory sentence for this paragraph would be:

   F. NO CHANGE
   G. So I tried out for the play.
   H. England has a unique monetary system.
   J. England is the setting for many plays.

27. A. NO CHANGE
   B. pence, ha'pence, and farthings
   C. pence ha'pence, and farthings
   D. pence, ha'pence and farthings,

28. F. NO CHANGE
   G. it's name
   H. their name
   J. their names

29. The author wants to add this sentence to paragraph 3.

   I probably got the part because I was just good-looking enough to be a banker.

   Where should it go?

   A. After sentence 5
   B. After sentence 6
   C. After sentence 7
   D. As a parenthetical sentence after sentence 8

30. A good title for this essay might be:

   F. "To Be or Not to Be, That is the Question"
   G. "Parents Are People Too"
   H. "Good Looks Aren't Everything"
   J. "My Adventures with English Money"

Just Desserts

[1]

New York restaurateur Warner LeRoy once said, "A restaurant is a fantasy—a kind of living fantasy in which diners are the most important members of the cast." He might have added, "and dessert is the more
<u>31</u>   <u>32</u>
important prop on the stage," unless nothing is closer
<u>32</u>   <u>33</u>
to fantasy than dessert.

[2]

You can try to make a case for chocolate as a major food group (I've tried for years), or for getting
<u>34</u>
your Recommended Dietary Allowance of calcium by eating gobs of whipped cream, but it's a no-go. The only reason for dessert is pleasure; pure and simple.
<u>35</u>
And that pleasure doubles when dessert is beautiful
<u>36</u>
presented in a restaurant.

[3]

1 The evening depends upon this last impression.
2 All the chefs who handle the savory portion of a restaurant meal will surely protest,
<u>37</u>
but anyone with a serious sweet tooth believes that appetizers and main courses are merely the stage directions for dessert.   3 We save room for it
<u>38</u>
and expect it to deliver.   39

31. **A.** NO CHANGE
    B. cast".
    C. cast?"
    D. cast"!

32. **F.** NO CHANGE
    G. the better important
    H. the most important
    J. the best important

33. **A.** NO CHANGE
    B. however
    C. since
    D. as a result

34. **F.** NO CHANGE
    G. group I've tried for years,
    H. group, I've tried for years
    J. group; I've tried for years,

35. **A.** NO CHANGE
    B. pleasure. Pure and simple.
    C. pleasure, pure and simple.
    D. pleasure, pure, and simple.

36. **F.** NO CHANGE
    G. more beautiful
    H. beauty
    J. beautifully

37. **A.** NO CHANGE
    B. sure
    C. surly
    D. sureful

38. **F.** NO CHANGE
    G. entrance
    H. props
    J. setup

39. Which is the BEST order of sentences in paragraph 3?

    A. 2, 1, 3
    B. 1, 3, 2
    C. 2, 3, 1
    D. 3, 1, 2

[4]

Pastry chefs impress us first by serving up drama—spun-sugar cages, gravity-defying pastry towers, and cocoa-speckled plates make all of us smile like little kids at the circus. But while the look is often architectural, the foundation is always <u>the same; rich flavor.</u>

40

[5]

[1] If there's a trend today, it's toward even more taste. [2] America's top pastry chefs are working to extract as much flavor as they can from every ingredient. [3] Chocolate is bitter as well as sweet; nuts are toasted for intensity; cream is infused with <u>not-so-subtle flavors, often</u> with herbs and

41

unusual spices; and fruit purees, sauces, and syrups are so concentrated that they often taste fruitier than the fruit itself. [4] Sure, chefs fuss over presentation—everyone knows we eat with our eyes first—but it's taste that captures their imaginations and <u>galvanizes</u> their creativity. [43]

42

40. F. NO CHANGE
   G. the same: rich flavor.
   H. the same rich flavor.
   J. the same, rich, flavor.

41. A. NO CHANGE
   B. not-so-subtle flavors; often
   C. not-so-subtle flavors: often
   D. not so subtle, flavors, often

42. F. NO CHANGE
   G. destroys
   H. manifests
   J. liquidates

43. The author wants to insert the following parenthetical comment in paragraph 5:

(Of course, the chefs make sure the flavors enhance one another, rather than overpowering other ingredients or the entire dish.)

It should be placed:

   A. after sentence 1.
   B. after sentence 2.
   C. after sentence 3.
   D. before sentence 1.

> Questions 44 and 45 ask about the entire passage.

44. Suppose the author had been asked to write an article that focused on the effect of the health craze in diners. Would this essay have fulfilled that assignment?

   F. Yes, because the essay focuses on the fact that diners are still eating desserts even today.
   G. Yes, because the essay focuses on the varied ingredients included in the desserts the chefs are creating.
   H. No, because the essay does not make a connection between the health craze and eating dessert.
   J. No, because the essay focuses on the failure of diners to stop eating desserts.

45. The writer wants to add the following sentence to the essay.

No matter how simple the main courses, dessert is always elegant and well presented.

The sentence MOST logically fits in:

A. paragraph 1.
B. paragraph 2.
C. paragraph 4.
D. paragraph 5.

PASSAGE IV

Best Friends

[1]

1 Finding and working is one of the primary initiations of the shaman <u>with an animal helper.</u> **2** In a
46
worldwide folk-story the younger son or daughter who <u>are</u>
47
sent out into the wide world without goods or friends invariably meets with an animal or series of <u>animals</u> which
48
help and <u>enable</u> them. **3** Many Celtic saints are associated
49
with animals: St. Gobhnat of Ballyvourny in County Cork is led to her monastic foundation by nine white deer, and her enclosure is guarded by bees, while St. Kevin of County Wicklow offers <u>it's</u> hand for a blackbird <u>as a nest</u> and learns
50   51
patience while the eggs hatch. **4** These stories have little to do with "kindness to animals." 52 53

[2]

The notion that animals can teach humans is <u>profoundly</u>
54
present in shamanic work. The animal helpers whom we meet in the inner-worlds are wiser in the ways of the otherworld

46. F. NO CHANGE
G. (place before *finding* with capitalization corrected)
H. (place after *working*)
J. (place after *initiations*)

47. A. NO CHANGE
B. were
C. is
D. aren't

48. F. NO CHANGE
G. animals's
H. animals'
J. animal's

49. Which word BEST portrays the idea that the animals lend the people strength?

A. NO CHANGE
B. entrap
C. empower
D. entreat

50. F. NO CHANGE
G. their
H. its
J. his

than we, and we discover they can be trusted to help <u>her</u> in
₅₅
ways unknown to us. The animals we meet in the world about
us teach us the simple and manifest truths about life and
relationship to <u>life-forms, which</u> are extraordinarily
₅₆
therapeutic for human beings who have forgotten their place
in the universe. The memory of the animals helps them
remember their <u>paradisal interconnection.</u>
₅₇

[3]

The destiny of human beings is often regulated by or
connected with helping animals, which may be seen as
properly totemic to a person or tribe. [58]

51. **A.** NO CHANGE
   B. (place after *for*)
   C. (place after *hatch*)
   D. (place after *hand*)

52. The author wishes to add the following sentence to paragraph 1:

   Rather, they concern a total understanding of and attunement to the animal teachers of the natural world.

   Where would it BEST fit?

   F. Before sentence 1
   G. As part of sentence 2, added on at the end, with a comma separating *them* from *rather*, and with a lowercase *r* in *rather*
   H. At the end of the last sentence, with a semicolon after *animals* and before *rather*, and with a lowercase *r* in *rather*
   J. Between sentences 2 and 3

53. The main idea of paragraph 1 is BEST stated as:

   A. animals can talk and help people.
   B. in folklore, being kind to animals eventually helps people.
   C. in shamanic lore, being kind to animals helps people but does not give them understanding of those animals.
   D. in shamanic folklore, people often gain an understanding of the animal world through animal teachers, rather than just learning the lesson to be kind to animals.

54. The word *profoundly* is used here to mean:

   F. eerily.
   G. uneasily.
   H. shallowly.
   J. intensely.

55. **A.** NO CHANGE
   B. his
   C. our
   D. us

56. F. NO CHANGE
G. life-forms; which
H. life-forms: which
J. life-forms. Which

57. Which phrase BEST expresses the idea that we are part of heaven?

A. NO CHANGE
B. heretical connection
C. edenic separation
D. earthly spirit

58. This sentence should:

F. be part of paragraph 1 because it talks about helping animals.
G. be part of paragraph 2 because it discusses connections.
H. remain as the start of paragraph 3 because it begins a new idea: the regulation of our destiny.
J. be placed as the opening paragraph before paragraph 1 because it talks about destiny.

Questions 59 and 60 ask about the entire passage.

59. The author wants to add the following sentences:

In one story, a boy gains his name (The Hound of Culainn) after fighting the smith's hound. As compensation for killing the dog, he then becomes the smith's watchdog. It is then his duty never to eat meat. Similarly, it is another man's duty never to hunt wild boar. In the end, both men die because they violate their duties—eating meat and hunting boar.

These sentences would BEST fit:

A. in paragraph 1, which gives examples of men meeting with animals.
B. in paragraph 3, which gives examples of how human destinies are regulated by animals.

C. in paragraph 2 because the animals teach the men their duties.
D. as an introductory paragraph because they provide initial examples of animals in stories about men.

60. The overall theme of this essay seems to suggest that:

F. many people learn through stories that the animal kingdom can help them understand the world better.
G. many people learn to be kind to animals through shaman stories.
H. many people learn not to hunt boar through shaman stories.
J. if you fail at your duty, you will die.

PASSAGE V

[1]

Standing in a circle of adult students in a <u>bright</u> lit
                                              61
classroom, Christine Youngblood signals a classmate with a

wink and a smile. What might appear to be <u>sultry</u> body
                                            62
language is an American Sign Language continuing-

education class.

[2]

As students perfect the <u>wink. One</u> of many facial
                          63
expressions that accompany signing, instructor Myrna

Orleck-Aiello <u>offers</u> gestures of encouragement. The
               64
classroom <u>are</u> silent except for some laughter while the
           65
students struggle through <u>one's</u> beginning phrases. Orleck-
                            66
Aiello, like all sign-language instructors at the university, is

deaf, and there is no oral communication even on the first

day of <u>class?</u>
         67

61. A. NO CHANGE
    B. brighter
    C. brightly
    D. brightest

62. What word BEST conveys the idea of flirtatious and inviting?

    F. NO CHANGE
    G. surly
    H. elated
    J. melodic

63. A. NO CHANGE
    B. wink; one
    C. wink, one
    D. wink one

64. F. NO CHANGE
    G. offer
    H. offered
    J. were offering

[3]

In any language, experts have concluded, the faster and
                                                    68
best way to learn is through total immersion. Though
68
beginning sign-language students find it tough at first not to

vocalize their questions, they grow used to gesturing and

raising their eyebrows at one another as pleas for help. 69

[4]

The dozen pupil here range from a new high school
            70
graduate to a grandmother. There reasons for learning sign
                                71
language also are diverse. One woman is preparing for law

school and has chosen this intensive two-week class to
          72
broaden her potential client base. Another woman and her

husband speak singular languages in public to keep people
              73
nearby from understanding their conversations. "But a lot of
                                                   74
people already know French and Spanish," she laments. "I'm

trying to get him to learn sign language with me, so we can

keep our secrets to ourselves."

65. **A.** NO CHANGE
    B. were
    C. were being
    D. is

66. **F.** NO CHANGE
    G. their
    H. her
    J. its

67. **A.** NO CHANGE
    B. of class!
    C. of class,
    D. of class.

68. **F.** NO CHANGE
    G. faster and better
    H. fastest and better
    J. fastest and best

69. Which sentence would BEST fit in paragraph 3?

    A. However, they find speaking and asking questions much easier.
    B. Since they must either communicate or be shut out from the conversation, they find it easier to learn than to protest.
    C. They need help because they find it very difficult to learn this way.
    D. Sign language is not like any other language.

70. **F.** NO CHANGE
    G. pupiles
    H. pupils
    J. pupil's

71. **A.** NO CHANGE
    B. They're
    C. Their
    D. Her

72. **F.** NO CHANGE
    G. had chosen
    H. has choose
    J. will choose

73. Which word BEST conveys the idea of many languages?

   A. NO CHANGE
   B. various
   C. generous
   D. melded

74. F. NO CHANGE
   G. As a result,
   H. Therefore,
   J. So

> Question 75 asks about the entire passage.

75. The author has been asked to add a sentence stating that learning sign language is similar to learning French or Spanish. In which paragraph should it go?

   A. Paragraph 4
   B. Paragraph 2
   C. Paragraph 3
   D. Paragraph 1

END OF ENGLISH TEST III

Model Reading ACT III

40 Questions–35 Minutes

INSTRUCTIONS: There are four passages on this test with 10 items about each passage. Choose the best answer for each item based on the passage. Then fill in the appropriate circle on the answer sheet (page 317).
Check pages 342 and 348–351 for answers and explanations.

PASSAGE I

PROSE FICTION

This passage is adapted from *Nineteen Minutes* by Jodi Picoult.

In nineteen minutes, you can order a pizza and get it delivered. You can read a story to a child or have your oil changed. You can walk a mile. You can sew a hem.

5 In nineteen minutes, you can stop the world, or you can just jump off of it.

In nineteen minutes, you can get revenge.

As usual, Alex Cormier was running late. It took thirty-two minutes to drive from her
10 house in Sterling to the superior court in Grafton County, New Hampshire, and that was only if she speeded through Oxford. She hurried downstairs, carrying the files she'd brought home with her over the weekend. She
15 twisted her thick copper hair into a knot and anchored it at the base of her neck with bobby pins, transforming herself into the person she needed to be before she left her house.

Alex had been a superior court judge now
20 for thirty-four days. She'd believed that, having proved her mettle as a district court judge for the past five years, this time around the appointment might be easier. But at forty, she was still the youngest judge in the state. Her
25 history as a public defender preceded her into the courtroom, and prosecutors assumed she'd side with the defense. When Alex had submitted her name years ago for the bench, it had been with the sincere desire to make
30 sure that people in this legal system were innocent until proven guilty. She just never

anticipated that as a judge, she might not be given the same benefit of the doubt.

The smell of freshly brewed coffee drew
35 Alex into the kitchen. Her daughter was hunched over a steaming mug at the kitchen table, poring over a textbook. Josie looked exhausted—her blue eyes were bloodshot; her chestnut hair was a knotty ponytail. "Tell
40 me you haven't been up all night." Alex said.

Josie didn't even glance up. "I haven't been up all night," she parroted.

Alex poured herself a cup of coffee and slid into the chair opposite her. "Honestly?"

45 "You asked me to tell you something," Josie said. "You didn't ask for the truth."

Alex frowned. "You shouldn't be drinking coffee."

"And you shouldn't be smoking ciga-
50 rettes."

Alex felt her face heat up. "I don't–"

"Mom," Josie sighed, "even when you open up the bathroom windows, I can still smell it on the towels." She glanced up, dar-
55 ing Alex to challenge her other vices.

Josie had once been so proud to have a mother as a judge. She'd asked Alex about her cases and her decisions. That had all changed three years ago, when Josie entered
60 high school, and the tunnel of communication between them slowly bricked shut. Alex didn't necessarily think that Josie was hiding anything more than any other teenager, but it was different: a normal parent might meta-

65 phorically judge her child's friends, whereas
Alex could do it legally.

"What's on the docket today?" Alex said.

"Unit test. What about you?"

"Arraignments," Alex replied. She squinted
70 across the table, trying to read Josie's textbook
upside down, "Chemistry?"

"Catalysts." Josie rubbed her temples.

Alex weighed the costs of being even five
minutes later, or getting another black mark
75 against her in the cosmic good-parenting
tally. *Shouldn't a seventeen-year-old be able
to take care of herself in the morning?* Alex
started pulling items out of the refrigerator:
eggs, milk, bacon.

80 "I still don't get why I have to eat breakfast if you don't," Josie muttered.

"Because you have to be a certain age to
earn the right to ruin your own life." Alex
pointed at the scrambled eggs Josie was mix-
85 ing in the skillet. "Promise me you'll finish
that?"

Josie met her gaze. "Promise."

"Then I'm headed out."

Alex grabbed her travel mug of coffee.
90 By the time she backed her car out of the
garage, her head was already focused on the
decision she had to write that afternoon. She
was caught up in a world far from home,
where at that very moment her daughter
95 scraped the scrambled eggs from the skillet
into the trash can without ever taking a single
bite.

Josie understood how she was *supposed*
to look and *supposed* to act. She wore her
100 dark hair long and straight. She liked feeling
the eyes of other girls in the school when she
sat in the cafeteria. She liked having guys
stare at her when she walked down the hall
with Matt's arm around her.

105 But there was a part of her that wondered
what would happen if she let them all in
on the secret—that some mornings, it was
hard to get out of bed and put on someone
else's smile; that she was, standing on air,
110 a fake.

1. Which of the following would Josie MOST
likely use to describe her mother?

A. She's someone I am very proud of.
B. She's the judge and the jury.
C. Do as I say, not as I do.
D. Out of sight, out of mind.

2. When it comes to presumed innocence, Alex
has an issue with:

F. the defendants who come before her.
G. her treatment as a judge.
H. Josie's possible use of drugs.
J. the legal status of Josie's friends.

3. In the statement on lines 64–65 that a normal
parent might "metaphorically judge her child's
friends," *metaphorically* MOST nearly means:

A. a comparison based on a legal standard.
B. a comparison based on a symbolic
meaning.
C. an implied comparison of two unlike things.
D. a comparison to a specific standard.

4. In the context of this passage, Josie uses the
term *standing on air* to describe herself, most
likely implying a sense of:

F. confidence.
G. uncertainty.
H. aloofness.
J. superiority.

5. It can reasonably be inferred from this
passage that:

A. Josie's relationship with Matt is most
important because of the status it gives her.
B. Josie had been proud of her mother's role
as a judge, until her mother bricked up the
communication between them.
C. Josie and her mother had similar hairstyles.
D. Alex had been a judge at a trial for some
of Josie's friends.

6. The question on lines 76–77, *"Shouldn't a
seventeen-year-old be able to take care of
herself in the morning?"* can BEST be
characterized as:

F. a sign of concern.
G. Alex referencing herself.
H. a clue to Josie about how she should
behave.
J. a rhetorical question.

7. Which word BEST describes the mood created throughout the passage?

    A. Anxious
    B. Resigned
    C. Frustrated
    D. Desperate

8. It can reasonably be inferred from the passage that both Alex and Josie:

    F. stay up late at night.
    G. are hardworking.
    H. express themselves unconditionally.
    J. miss Josie's father.

9. Which BEST describes how the first three paragraphs function in the passage?

    A. These paragraphs bring a light tone to the passage by describing many things that can be accomplished in nineteen minutes.
    B. These paragraphs introduce a sense of foreboding by foreshadowing

something bad that will happen in nineteen minutes.
    C. These paragraphs give the author an opportunity to introduce a lot of the real-life events in the life of Alex and Josie by using the number nineteen as a literary device.
    D. These paragraphs grab the reader's attention, using the number nineteen, before the author begins to tell the rest of the story.

10. Which BEST describes the reason for the first lines of dialogue on lines 39–54?

    F. To show that Josie had been up all night studying for a test
    G. To emphasize that Alex was running late on her way to the courthouse
    H. To portray the relationship between the mother and daughter
    J. To convey a warning about the dangers associated with smoking cigarettes

---

PASSAGE II

SOCIAL SCIENCE: This passage is from "Freeze Frame: Calais Remembered" by Gordon Marsden.

Calais Falls to Edward III and His English Army

The surrender of the French Channel port of Calais to the besieging English king Edward III not only was a key element in the English successes in the early stages of the Hundred
5 Years' War but its fall and the progress of what had been an eleven-month siege illumine the complex temperament that underpinned the conduct of war by medieval chivalry.

Edward had claimed the throne of France
10 through his mother Isabella after the direct line of her Capetian brothers had died out, leaving the native claimant as Philip of Valois (who became Philip VI). His motives for the claim have been variously ascribed by historians. . . .

15 Whatever the case, the energy with which Edward conducted his campaign in France from 1340 onwards cannot be doubted. He

reaped a rich reward with his famous victory at the battle of Crécy in August 1346, where
20 the firepower of English archers wrought havoc on the heavily armored but ponderous noble cavalry of the French. His success there left him free to besiege Calais which, lying as it does at the narrowest crossing point to
25 England across the Channel, was a vital strategic objective to secure supplies and safe passage for the conduct of the invasion.

The town's defenses reflected this significance: a double wall with towers and ditches,
30 supplied by sea by Philip's forces. The town's governor, Jean de Vienne, was resourceful and ruthlessly practical in making the best of his resources, turning out of the town non-combatant men, women and children at the
35 start of the siege to save food, an occasion on which Edward showed chivalrous generosity by feeding them and allowing them to pass through the lines.

The siege tied down Edward's resources
40 of men and material—over the winter of

1346–47 his army had to be victualed by the Flemish in a wooden town he erected outside the walls to protect his troops, and via raids on the surrounding countryside. The defend-
45 ers in Calais resisted doggedly, despite dwindling supplies. The appeal of the Governor to Philip VI—"we have nothing left to subsist on, unless we eat each other"—finally moved Philip to action. He raised an army in late
50 spring 1347. . . .

Philip's attempts at relief were half-hearted: his last on July 27th, 1347, was followed by inconclusive parleying between the French forces and English heralds led by Henry
55 Grossmont, Duke of Lancaster. When these broke down, Philip declined to take the risk of battle: on August 1st, his army retreated and Calais was left to its fate.

Jean de Vienne parleyed with Edward's
60 heralds for honorable terms of surrender. He had reason to be worried: the laws of war by no means guaranteed that surrender would be followed by the defendants preserving life and limb, and persistent resistance—such as
65 Edward might well have regarded the eleven-month siege—might be met by condign punishment.

Edward initially rejected the Governor's request for his men and the remaining citizens
70 to leave unharmed, but (according to the chronicler Froissart) he softened to the extent of restricting his potential vengeance to the governor and six of Calais' leading citizens. But even they were spared when Edward's
75 pregnant wife interceded on their behalf.

Calais became an English possession. Its population was expelled, and the town, resettled with English merchants and an impressive garrison, became both a strategic strong-
80 hold and a symbol of English resolution in France. After the final debacles of English power a century later, it alone remained the sole foothold in France after 1453, remaining an English possession until it fell to the
85 French in the reign of Mary Tudor as a by-product of her husband Philip II's war with the French, the symbolic blow to national pride which allegedly led the Tudor queen to sigh, "When I am dead, they will find the
90 word 'Calais' engraved upon my heart."

11. According to the passage, Edward's motive for claiming the French throne:

   A. was to overthrow Philip of Valois.
   B. could be any one among many theories.
   C. was through his mother, Isabella.
   D. was to be able to marry a Frenchwoman.

12. According to the passage, what did Edward gain through his success at Crécy?

   F. The ability to cross the Channel at Calais
   G. Rich rewards of English firepower
   H. The freedom to attack Calais
   J. The assistance of France's noble cavalry

13. In the first paragraph, what does the author set up as the thesis for his essay?

   A. Calais' surrender was a key element in the English successes during the Hundred Years' War.
   B. King Edward III forced Calais to surrender during the Hundred Years' War.
   C. Medieval chivalry made it possible for Edward to be victorious at Calais.
   D. The fall of Calais in an almost yearlong siege shows the complexity of the conduct of war under medieval chivalry.

14. The author states that Calais was important because:

   F. Calais was a strategic crossing point from England.
   G. in this battle, Edward could finally defeat Philip and claim the throne for good.
   H. the governor of Calais was resourceful and ruthless.
   J. many of its citizens were sympathetic to the British.

15. The author implies in this passage that Philip:

   A. was a brave soldier who fought Edward for the throne.
   B. was unmotivated by the seige and not interested in fighting.
   C. worked for the surrender of Calais.
   D. rejected the governor's request not to harm his men.

16. The author includes the note about Edward feeding the townspeople and sparing the men following his wife's plea to show that:

F. Edward had power over people's lives and deaths.

G. while he was a tough commander, Edward was also benevolent and chivalrous.

H. the people of Calais should have surrendered earlier.

J. Edward was a better ruler than Jean de Vienne was.

17. According to the passage, what happened to Calais?

A. It was returned to the French after the debacles of English power a century later.

B. It was resettled with English merchants until 1453.

C. It became one of England's strongholds in France, and the only English-owned town after 1453 until Mary Tudor's time.

D. It was engraved on Mary's heart.

18. The author mentions Jean de Vienne's worry about surrender because he wants to:

F. inform the reader that the laws of surrender could not guarantee safety.

G. show that surrender guaranteed freedom from death or torture.

H. show that Edward was set on vengeance at Calais.

J. portray Jean de Vienne as a coward.

19. Are the details of the surrender of Calais and Edward's sparing of the burghers treated as fact in the passage?

A. Yes, because it states that the scene was a famous one.

B. Yes, because it portrays Edward's change of heart.

C. No, because it does not state specifically why Edward softened.

D. No, because it notes that these things happened "according to Froissart."

20. According to the author:

I. Calais was lost, in part, because Philip refused to fight.

II. Philip's forces were supplying Calais by sea.

III. Philip surrendered to Edward at Calais with Jean de Vienne.

F. I only

G. I and III only

H. II and III only

J. I and II only

PASSAGE III

HUMANITIES: This passage is from *Madwoman in the Attic* by Sandra M. Gilbert and Susan Gubar.

Frankenstein (1818) and *Wuthering Heights* (1847) are not usually seen as related works, except insofar as both are nineteenth-century literary puzzles, with Mary Shelley's
5 plaintive speculation about where she got so "hideous an idea" (for the monster in Frankenstein) finding its counterpart in the position of Heathcliff's creator as a sort of mystery woman of literature. Still, if both
10 Emily Brontë and Shelley wrote enigmatic, curiously unprecedented novels, their works are puzzling in different ways: Shelley's is an enigmatic fantasy of metaphysical horror, Brontë's an enigmatic Romantic and "mascu-
15 line" text in which the fates of subordinate female characters seem entirely dependent upon the actions of ostensibly male heroes or anti-heroes. . . .

Despite these dissimilarities, however,
20 *Frankenstein* and *Wuthering Heights* are alike in a number of crucial ways. For one thing, both works are enigmatic, puzzling, even in some sense generically problematical. Moreover, in each case the mystery of
25 the novel is associated with what seems to be its metaphysical intentions, intentions around which much critical controversy has collected. For these two "popular" novels—one a thriller, the other a romance—have con-

vinced many readers that their charismatic surfaces conceal (far more than they reveal) complex ontological depths, elaborate structures of allusion, fierce though shadowy moral ambitions. And this point in particular is demonstrated by a simpler characteristic both works have in common. Both make use of what in connection with *Frankenstein* we have called an evidentiary narrative technique, a Romantic storytelling method that emphasizes the ironic disjunctions between different perspectives on the same events as well as the ironic tensions that inhere in the relationship between surface drama and concealed authorial intention. In fact, in its use of such a technique, *Wuthering Heights* might be a deliberate copy of *Frankenstein*. Not only do the stories of both novels emerge through concentric circles of narration, both works contain significant digressions. Catherine Earnshaw's diary, Isabella's letter, Zillah's narrative, and Heathcliff's confidences to Nelly function in *Wuthering Heights* much as Alphonse Frankenstein's letter, Justine's narrative, and Safie's history do in *Frankenstein*.

Their common concern with evidence, especially with written evidence, suggests still another way in which *Wuthering Heights* and *Frankenstein* are alike: more than most novels, both are consciously literary works, at times almost obsessively concerned with books and with reading as not only a symbolic but a dramatic—plot-forwarding—activity. Can this be because, like Shelley, Brontë was something of a literary heiress? The idea is an odd one to consider because the four Brontë children, scribbling in Yorkshire's remote West Riding, seem as trapped on the periphery of nineteenth-century literary culture as Mary Shelley was embedded in its . . . center. Nevertheless, peripheral though they were, the Brontës had literary parents just as Mary Shelley did.

21. According to the passage, how are *Frankenstein* and *Wuthering Heights* different?

  A. *Frankenstein* is puzzling while *Wuthering Heights* is not.

  B. *Frankenstein* is a 19th-century work while *Wuthering Heights* was written in the 18th century.

  C. *Frankenstein* is a horror thriller while *Wuthering Heights* is a romance.

  D. *Frankenstein* is a masculine text while *Wuthering Heights* is a feminine text.

22. As used throughout this passage, the word enigmatic means:

  F. mysterious.

  G. transparent.

  H. crystalline.

  J. lucid.

23. When speaking of Brontë's work as a "masculine" text, the authors imply that:

  A. a male author actually wrote the work, despite the female name attached to it.

  B. this is positive because men are the heroes.

  C. this is negative because women are subordinated to male characters.

  D. Heathcliff's creator was a mystery woman.

24. In the first paragraph, the authors set up the idea that:

  F. Shelley and Brontë were unrelated writers.

  G. *Frankenstein* and *Wuthering Heights* are completely different books: a thriller and a romance.

  H. Shelley's work is better because it is unprecedented.

  J. although both works are puzzling, they are puzzling in different ways.

25. The authors say that despite their differences, the two works are similar because:

  I. they are both 19th-century puzzles.
  II. they are both consciously literary works.
  III. they are both evidentiary novels.

  A. None of the above

  B. I and II only

  C. I and III only

  D. All of the above

26. According to the passage, what is used as evidence in the two works?

F. The backing the authors had from literary families
G. Similar perspectives on different episodes
H. Digressions through letters and other forms of communication
J. Enigmatic fantasy and metaphysical horror

27. What reason do the authors give for the two books being highly literary?

A. Both writers were embedded in the center of literary culture.
B. Both writers had literary parents.
C. Both writers use reading as a symbolic activity.
D. Both books are obsessed with plot.

28. Overall, this passage seems to be setting up the idea that:

F. while these books and authors may appear to be dissimilar, they may in fact hide underlying similarities that should be examined.
G. most books should be studied for what they are and not be compared to other works.

H. *Frankenstein* and *Wuthering Heights* were two 19th-century books written by women.
J. most writers with literary parents will have similarities in their works.

29. According to the passage, many readers over the years have been convinced:

A. that these novels are merely "popular" reading.
B. the surfaces of these novels reveal complex depths and elaborate structures within them.
C. complex depths and structures are concealed beneath the charismatic surfaces of these novels.
D. that while these novels appear problematical, they are really simple to understand.

30. In the passage, the authors imply that:

F. *Wuthering Heights* is a copy of *Frankenstein.*
G. *Frankenstein* is a copy of *Wuthering Heights.*
H. *Frankenstein* is modeled on *Wuthering Heights.*
J. in *Wuthering Heights*, Brontë might have copied the technique Shelley used in *Frankenstein.*

PASSAGE IV

NATURAL SCIENCE

The "Mystery" of the Bermuda Triangle

Miami, Puerto Rico and Bermuda are prime holiday destinations boasting sun, beaches and coral seas. But between these idyllic settings, there is a dark side: countless
5   ships and planes have mysteriously gone missing in the one and a half million square miles of ocean separating them. About 60 years ago, the area was nicknamed the Bermuda Triangle.

Twins George and David Rothschild are
10 among the first passengers to have experienced bizarre effects in the Bermuda

Triangle. In 1952, "We had been flying for probably 20 or 30 minutes when all of a sudden the pilot yelled out that the instruments
15 were dead," says George Rothschild. After what seemed like hours, they landed safely in Norfolk, on the Florida coast.

Some speculate that it had nothing to do with the location, but rather the instruments that
20 were available at the time. Pilot Robert Grant says that back in the 1940s, navigating a plane involved a lot of guesswork since they relied completely on a magnetic compass to guide them. "Dead reckoning" was used, which
25 means that pilots would trust their compass and then estimate how the wind would influence their planned flight path to remain on track.

"No matter what your mind tells you, you must stay on that course," says Grant. "If you don't, and you start turning to wherever you think you should be going, then you're toast."

Wild Weather

The landscape of the island of Bermuda is quite unique: it is a remote coral reef precariously perched on a massive extinct volcano. Local fisherman Sloan Wakefield thinks that the weather could be responsible for some of the disappearances. "Because the island is a dot in the Atlantic Ocean, it gets weather from everywhere. One minute, you can be looking at good weather, and the next moment you've got a low front coming through," he says. He has seen 15- to 20-foot waves.

Hurricanes are common in the Bermuda Triangle area. In the Atlantic Ocean, they typically originate off the African coast and thrive off the moisture of the warm, tropical waters. Hurricane records from the past 100 years have shown that hurricanes headed west for the United States often swerve into the waters of the Bermuda Triangle at the last minute. Jim Lushine, a meteorologist at the National Hurricane Center, says that there are more hurricanes in the Bermuda Triangle than in any other area in the Atlantic basin.

But thunderstorms in the area can be just as dangerous. In 1986, a historic ship called the *Pride of Baltimore* vanished from radar screens while it was in the Bermuda Triangle, making a trip from the Caribbean to Baltimore. About four and a half days later, the wreckage and eight survivors were found, and they revealed that the ship had been hit by a microburst: 80 mile-per-hour winds emanating from a freak thunderstorm. It happened so quickly that the crew didn't have time to make a distress call. "The ship was sunk in the downburst, unfortunately with a great loss of life," says Lushine. "Similar downbursts are probably responsible for some of the sunken ships in the Bermuda Triangle."

Even more unpredictable than thunderstorms are waterspouts. These can be caused by tornadoes that move out to sea or by rotating columns of air that drop from thunderstorms, creating a vortex of spray. Jim Edds, an amateur fisherman who chases and films waterspouts for fun, says that if you are out at night and a tornado-like waterspout develops—the really big, strong ones with high velocity—it can flip your vessel over.

Bubbling Methane

Seismic activity at the bottom of the ocean can also be an explanation for disappearing ships. Scientists have discovered that huge bubbles of methane gas can violently erupt without warning from the ocean floor and at least one oil rig is thought to have sunk because of this phenomenon. Ralph Richardson, the director of the Bermuda Underwater Exploration Institute, claims that a large pocket of gas could surround a ship, causing it to lose buoyancy and disappear without warning.

At the U.S. Navy's research center in California, Bruce Denardo, an expert in fluid dynamics, has proved that bubbles from methane gas eruptions could be responsible for vanishing ships in the open ocean. Water pressure causes objects to float, and the deeper the water, the greater the pressure exerted to keep the object floating at the surface. If bubbles from methane are introduced, they lower the density of the water. They take up space, but the volume of water stays the same, causing the buoyant force to decrease. In an experiment with a ball in water, Denardo can demonstrate that the ball sinks deeper and deeper down in water as the amount of bubbles increases, until it reaches a critical point where it sinks completely. "If a ship were to take on enough water, it would sink to the bottom and stay there," says Denardo.

31. The initial section of the passage (lines 1–31) MOST strongly suggests that:

A. some events cannot reasonably be explained scientifically.

B. firsthand accounts are the best source of information about an event.

C. there are usually logical explanations for seemingly illogical events.

D. magnetic fields in the Bermuda Triangle can cause instruments to malfunction.

32. Which of the following, if true, would BEST support the idea mentioned in the passage that the instruments malfunctioned because of the location of the plane in the Bermuda Triangle?

    F. There were other, random accounts over the years that pilots had reported.
    G. The instruments from the plane mentioned in the passage were checked after the flight and found to be functioning properly.
    H. Many other planes in the same area at the same time independently reported the same instrument problems.
    J. The instruments from the plane mentioned in the passage were checked after the flight and found not to be functioning properly.

33. It is MOST reasonable to infer from the phrase that "Bermuda . . . is a remote coral reef precariously perched on a massive extinct volcano" that:

    A. Bermuda consists primarily of sand and beaches.
    B. the area around Bermuda is subject to periodic volcanic eruptions.
    C. the coral reef itself is not stable.
    D. the volcano originally formed after the appearance of the coral reef.

34. If it is true that the Bermuda Triangle itself has a bizarre effect on navigation instruments, it is MOST reasonable to assume that the cause of these effects was present:

    F. before 1952.
    G. starting in 1952.
    H. since the discovery of the magnetic north pole.
    J. since the coral reef formed near Bermuda.

35. Based on the information in the passage, which of the following, if true, would be MOST likely to weaken Denardo's argument that methane gas bubbles could be responsible for sinking large ships in the Bermuda Triangle?

    A. The huge bubbles occur infrequently.
    B. The density of water varies somewhat in the area around the Bermuda Triangle.
    C. Denardo was unable to replicate the experiment with another object.

    D. Denardo was able to replicate the experiment with only a small ship.

36. We can infer from the passage that, compared to thunderstorms, waterspouts are:

    F. more reliable.
    G. more frightening.
    H. less forseeable.
    J. less dangerous.

37. In paragraph 3, *dead reckoning* most nearly means a navigation technique that:

    A. is used when there is great danger and the possibility of an accident that might lead to death or injuries.
    B. combines instruments and guesswork.
    C. ensures an aircraft will arrive before it "dies."
    D. uses true north rather than magnetic north to determine the correct course.

38. What evidence does the passage offer to support the notion that hurricanes are more of a problem in the Bermuda Triangle than in other places in the ocean?

    F. Information about the frequency of hurricanes there
    G. Information about the origin of hurricanes
    H. The type of waters in which thunderstorms thrive
    J. Information about microbursts associated with thunderstorms

39. The author begins the passage with a description of idyllic settings because:

    A. the description provides an accurate location of the Bermuda Triangle.
    B. the sun, beaches, and coral reefs play an important role in the article.
    C. it provides a dramatic contrast to the mysterious occurrences in the same places.
    D. the author will return to this description at the end of the passage.

40. On line 103, the word *buoyant* most nearly means:

    F. having high salt content.
    G. able to float.
    H. exhibiting heaviness.
    J. exerting pressure.

END OF READING TEST III

Model ACT III English Scoring Key

Item and Answer	Usage/ Mechanics	Rhetorical Skills	Review These Pages	Item and Answer	Usage/ Mechanics	Rhetorical Skills	Review These Pages
1. B	❑		103–108	27. B	❑		103–108
2. F		❑	156–160	28. J	❑		56–63
3. D		❑	156–160	29. C		❑	145–152
4. H	❑		109–111	30. H		❑	133–141
5. A		❑	145–152	31. A	❑		123–125
6. H	❑		32–43	32. H	❑		87–90
7. A	❑		76–79	33. C		❑	133–141
8. G	❑		70–72	34. F	❑		116–118
9. A	❑		59–63	35. C	❑		103–108
10. G	❑		103–108	36. J	❑		84–87
11. A	❑		120–122	37. A	❑		84–87
12. F		❑	145–152	38. J		❑	133–141
13. C		❑	137–141	39. C		❑	145–152
14. H		❑	137–141	40. G	❑		109–111
15. B		❑	133–141	41. A	❑		103–118
16. J	❑		59–63	42. F		❑	133–141
17. C	❑		103–108	43. C		❑	145–152
18. G		❑	133–141	44. H		❑	133–141
19. A	❑		67–70	45. B		❑	145–152
20. G		❑	133–152	46. H	❑		43–47
21. A		❑	133–141	47. C	❑		76–79
22. F		❑	156–160	48. F	❑		56–58
23. C		❑	156–160	49. C		❑	133–141
24. F	❑		109–111	50. J	❑		59–63
25. B	❑		116–118	51. D	❑		43–47
26. G		❑	133–152	52. H		❑	145–152

Item and Answer	Usage/ Mechanics	Rhetorical Skills	Review These Pages	Item and Answer	Usage/ Mechanics	Rhetorical Skills	Review These Pages
53. D		❑	133–141	65. D	❑		76–79
54. J		❑	133–141	66. G	❑		59–63
55. D	❑		59–63	67. D	❑		120–122
56. F	❑		103–108	68. J	❑		87–90
57. A		❑	133–141	69. B		❑	133–141
58. H		❑	137–141, 148	70. H	❑		56–58
59. B		❑	145–152	71. C	❑		59–63
60. F		❑	133–141	72. F	❑		67–70
61. C	❑		84–87	73. B		❑	133–141
62. F		❑	133–141	74. F		❑	133–141
63. C	❑		103–108	75. C		❑	145–152
64. F	❑		67–68				

Number Correct:

Usage/Mechanics _____

Rhetorical Skills _____

Total _____

Model ACT III Reading Scoring Key

Item and Answer	Social Studies/ Sciences	Arts/ Literature	Item and Answer	Social Studies/ Sciences	Arts/ Literature	Item and Answer	Social Studies/ Sciences	Arts/ Literature
1. C		❑	15. B	❑		28. F		❑
2. G		❑	16. G	❑		29. C		❑
3. C		❑	17. C	❑		30. J		❑
4. G		❑	18. F	❑		31. C	❑	
5. A		❑	19. D	❑		32. H	❑	
6. J		❑	20. J	❑		33. C	❑	
7. B		❑	21. C		❑	34. F	❑	
8. G		❑	22. F		❑	35. C	❑	
9. B		❑	23. C		❑	36. H	❑	
10. H		❑	24. J		❑	37. B	❑	
11. B	❑		25. D		❑	38. F	❑	
12. H	❑		26. H		❑	39. C	❑	
13. D	❑		27. B		❑	40. G	❑	
14. F	❑							

Number Correct:

Social Studies/Sciences _____

Arts/Literature _____

Total _____

PASSAGE I

1. B

The sentence is one complete thought, and none of the parts should be set off by a comma. That is why choices A, C, and D are incorrect.

2. F

No change. The original wording effectively communicates the thought and fits the tone of the passage. Choices G and H do not effectively describe what is really happening on the screen. Choice J is inaccurate.

3. D

The reference to the computer dying is not meant to be taken literally. It is a figurative comment best characterized by the words in Choice D. Choices B and C are incorrect because they convey the idea that the "death" was real.

4. H

The beginning of the sentence states that the author is going to be specific. The colon separates that thought from a description of that thought. An exclamation point is not called for here. Choice J is incorrect because each part of the sentence is a complete thought and the comma creates a comma splice.

5. A

The underlined phrase belongs where it is. All the other choices create illogical sentences.

6. H

Choice H coordinates the sentence parts with the word *and.* Choices F and G are incorrect because the words following the semicolon or period create a sentence fragment. Choice J lacks a conjunction.

7. A

The subject of the sentence is *people*, so the verb should be plural. Omitting the word leaves the sentence without a main verb.

8. G

The sentence refers to what happens after the author makes the phone calls. That means the verb should be in the future tense. In all the other choices, the verbs are in the present or past tense.

9. A

The word *it's* is spelled and punctuated correctly to mean *it is.* Choice C shows the possessive form. Choices B and D are not real words.

10. G

The introductory phrase needs to be set off from the rest of the sentence with a comma. Using a period or a semicolon is incorrect because *If that really is the case* is not an independent sentence.

11. A

No change. Choice B is incorrect because the sentence is not an interjection or a command. Choices C and D are incorrect because neither the words spoken nor the sentence is a question.

12. F

No change. This sentence placement makes the most sense. Choice G puts the answer before the question. Choices H and J move the answer too far away from the question.

13. C

The writer quickly got good advice after trying and worrying about the computer problems. A is incorrect because there is no indication that someone else used the computer, and the tone in this sentence is more formal than the passage. B is incorrect because no class was needed to solve the problem, and D is incorrect because nothing in the passage suggests a reason for hating your computer, although you may occasionally feel that way.

14. H

The article is easy to understand, and it does explain computer problems. However, the tone is not formal enough for a business magazine. The clear *no* answer to the question about the article's tone explains why choices F and G are incorrect. Choice J is incorrect, although we do not know how much computer use should be discussed. It is the tone of the article that is the main reason for its inappropriateness.

15. B

The real message of the passage is to stay cool and get help. That's how the person in the passage solved the problem. Choice A is incorrect because nothing in the passage suggests that computers are death traps. Choices C and D are incorrect because nothing in the passage discusses errors or makes the generalization that computers are unresponsive. Remember that it was the screen and not the computer that was unresponsive. This does not mean that a computer problem may not occasionally ruin your day, or that computers are never unresponsive. These choices are not mentioned in the passage, and ACT questions are always about the passage.

PASSAGE II

16. J
The underlined pronoun refers to the noun *father*. That means the correct choice is *his* little son. Choice G is incorrect because the pronoun does not refer to the father. Choices F and H are incorrect because they show plural pronouns.

17. C.
Set off the phrase *my parents told me* with commas to separate this from the dialogue.

18. G.
The word *since* implies that his parents knew because the casting director did not. This cause-and-effect relationship is not present. The best choice is *but*, which emphasizes the contrast between what his parents thought and what the casting director knew. Choice J is incorrect because *and* implies the continuation of a thought, but in this sentence, the thought is turned around because the second part of the sentence contradicts the first.

19. A.
No change. The sentence is about the past, about the previous drama teacher, so the past tense is correct. Choices B and C both refer to the future. Choice D is nonsensical when it is inserted in the original sentence.

20. G
The sentence disrupts the flow of the paragraph, switching from past, to the present, and then back to the past. The information about the present already appears later in the paragraph. Choice F is incorrect because the sentence does flow logically from the sentence before it, even if it interrupts the logical flow of the paragraph as a whole. Choices H and J both contain an unreasonable argument for including the sentence in the paragraph.

21. A
The term *regardless of whether* best describes that it "does not matter how a person was chosen." Choice B shows a bias against choosing people with qualities listed in the sentence. Choices C and D indicate that it does matter how a person was chosen.

22. F
The word *talent* means the actor's actual ability. G is incorrect because *condition* is too vague. Choice H is

incorrect because a person's values would not be the determining factor for the choice of an actor. Choice J is incorrect because the word *possibility* does not refer to something actual, and the word does not make sense in this context.

23. C
This is a very wordy sentence. The best, and shortest, replacement is choice C, which clearly states, "looks are used to measure an actor's value." Choices B and D include a reference to *attractiveness points*, which is an unnecessary and wordy additions to the sentence.

24. F
The sentence consists of two independent clauses that are correctly separated by a semicolon. Choices G and H create a run-on sentence. Choice J is incorrect because omitting the underlined portion creates a comma splice.

25. B
The writer's "looks" explain about the writer and so should be set off with parentheses. Choice A is incorrect because "looks" are related to other explanations in the paragraph. Choice C is incorrect because being the last sentence in a paragraph itself is never a reason for using parentheses. Choice D does not define "looks," although a definition would be a reason for putting a sentence in parentheses.

26. G
The rest of the paragraph makes no sense unless we know the writer tried out for the play. The current first line in the paragraph needs this introductory sentence to create a coherent paragraph because the first word—*It*—needs a referent. Choices H and J are incorrect because, while true, the sentences do not provide the required lead-in for the paragraph.

27. B.
When there are three or more items in a list, always separate the items with commas. Choices A, C, and D do not include a comma between each item in the list.

28. J
The noun *banknotes* is plural, so the pronoun must be plural. This leaves choices H and J. Choice J is correct because each banknote has its own name, and so the noun following must be the plural *names*.

29. C
The sentence belongs immediately after the sentence where the writer states why he thought he would not get the part. This sentence states why he thinks he did

get the part. Choice A is incorrect because the sentence to be added has nothing to do with banknotes. Choice B puts the sentence out of order, before the sentence it should follow. Choice D does not describe anything about why his parents are happy.

30. H.

The essence of the story is that a student tried out for a play thinking that good looks would be required to get a part, and that turned out not to be true. There are some side themes about parents and England and English money, and the original, simpler title is not a bad one. However, from the choices given, this is the best title for the essay.

PASSAGE III

31. A

Punctuation must be placed inside the quotation marks, so the possible choices are A and C. However, the opening sentence is not a question, so choice C is ruled out.

32. H

Since dessert is not being compared to a singular prop or subject, *better* and *more* cannot be used. The correct superlative with *important* is *most*.

33. C

Desserts are the most fantastic items, and the word *since* shows their contribution to the concept of a restaurant as a fantasy. The words *unless* and *however* make the rest of the sentence sound as if it contradicts the first part, when it actually explains the first part. The phrase *as a result* also does not make sense because the second part of the sentence is not caused by the first.

34. F

The sentence is correct as it stands with the aside in parentheses. Choices G and H make run-on sentences. Choice J makes the second part of the sentence a fragment, which cannot be separated by a semicolon.

35. C

The sentence is incorrect because a semicolon can separate only two independent clauses, and *pure and simple* is not an independent clause. The same is true for choice B; *Pure and simple* cannot stand alone as a sentence. Choice D must be ruled out because the three items—*pleasure, pure, simple*—are not part of a list and should not be separated by commas.

36. J

The adverb *beautifully* is correct because it is modifying the verb *presented.*

37. A

The correct adverbial form of *sure* is *surely*, as used in the sentence. An adverb is necessary since the word being modified—*protest*—is a verb.

38. J

Stage directions order the movement of a play, which is not what the author is implying here. Nor are main courses and appetizers the props or the entrance. In fact, dessert has already been called the most important prop, so choice H is incorrect. Appetizers and main courses are the setup for dessert.

39. C

Sentence 1 must follow sentences 2 and 3 because otherwise the word *this* has no reference. What last impression does the evening depend upon? For the same reason, sentence 3 must follow sentence 2 because otherwise the word *it* has no referent. What do we save room for and expect to deliver? Therefore, the best order is 2, 3, 1.

40. G

Rich flavor defines *same*, so a colon is used. Using a semicolon creates a sentence fragment. Leaving all punctuation out makes the sentence confusing. While a comma might be used between the two adjectives, there should not be a comma between the second adjective and the noun.

41. A

The sentence is correct as it is. The phrase *often with herbs and unusual spices* modifies *not-so-subtle flavors.* Therefore, it should be set apart by a comma or parentheses—it cannot be separated by a semicolon. *Not-so-subtle* should remain hyphenated since the three words function together as a single adjective.

42. F

The word *galvanize* coveys the same idea as *excite* or *arouse.* The taste does not destroy creativity, or beautiful creations would have no taste. The verb *manifest* means "to make evident." Taste does not make creativity evident; instead, it inspires creativity. Finally, *liquidate* means "to convert assets into cash or determine liabilities." Therefore, this verb makes no sense in the sentence.

43. C

The parenthetical aside provides additional information about sentence 3. Therefore, it follows sentence 3.

44. H

The essay does not discuss health in any form—only taste. Choice F is incorrect because no connection is made between dessert and the health of the diners. Choice G is incorrect because the healthiness of the ingredients is not discussed. Choice J is incorrect because the essay does not say that not eating dessert is either good or bad.

45. B

Paragraph 2 discusses the beauty of a dessert being presented, so it is the only paragraph where a sentence including information about the main course fits.

PASSAGE IV

46. H

The underlined part is misplaced. The phrase *with an animal helper* is supposed to explain what a shaman is working with. The sentence doesn't make sense if the phrase is placed anywhere else.

47. C

The verb must agree with the subject. The sentence reads "son or daughter," so the verb must be singular—*is*, not *are*.

48. F

The sentence is correct as written. *Animal* is made plural by adding *s*.

49. C

The word *enable* is a synonym for *help*, so using *enable* is redundant. The animals don't entrap the shaman, or they would not be helping. The animals also don't entreat them; the word *entreat* means "to beg or plead," and the animals are aiding the humans, not begging them to do something. Therefore, the best word is *empower*, meaning "to give power to," which means the same as *lend the people strength* in the question.

50. J

The pronoun must agree with the noun. The noun is Kevin—male and singular—so the pronoun should be *his*.

51. D

The underlined portion of the sentence is misplaced. It should follow *hand*, the word it modifies. If the underlined portion is placed anywhere else, the sentence does not make sense.

52. H

For the pronoun *they* to make sense, *they* must come after what is describes: *stories*. Therefore, choice F

cannot be correct. If placed after sentence 2, the pronoun is still vague—does it refer to the humans or the animals? Therefore, placing it after sentence 4 makes the most sense.

53. D

The paragraph does not focus on animals talking, so choice A is incorrect. Choice B is in direct opposition to the final sentence, which states that the stories have little to do with being kind to animals. Choice C opposes the sentence added to the paragraph, which states that the people gain a total understanding of the animal world.

54. J

The idea in the first sentence is that animals teaching humans is common in these works. Therefore, the first three choices do not make sense. However, *intensely* conveys the right idea.

55. D

The pronoun must agree with the antecedent. In this case, the antecedent *we* needs to have the pronoun *us*.

56. F

The second part of the sentence, starting with *which*, is a dependent clause and cannot be separated from the independent clause by a period or semicolon. Choice H is incorrect because the second part is not a list relating to the first part of the sentence.

57. A

The sentence implies that humans are part of heaven. Choice C refers to humans as separated from heaven. Choice D connects humans to the Earth, rather than to heaven. Choice B connects humans to the heretical—the opposite of being connected to heaven and religion.

58. H

Each paragraph should contain one main idea. In paragraph 3, it is about how animals regulate the destiny of humans. This sentence introduces this main idea, and so it should be the first sentence in paragraph 3.

59. B

In paragraph 1, the examples are very general and refer to a person meeting with an animal. Paragraph 2 is more about the inner-worlds and outer-worlds. Neither paragraph mentions duties or destiny. Therefore, the best place for this example is in paragraph 3 as an explanation of how a person's destiny is connected with the animals.

60. F

Choices H and J refer solely to limited lessons a person might learn. Choice G refers to an incorrect lesson that may be learned from the opening paragraph. Choice F, however, refers to a general lesson provided by the entire essay.

PASSAGE V

61. C

The correct adverbial form of *bright* is *brightly*, which modifies the adjective *lit*.

62. F

The word *surly* means "arrogant or sullen, in a bad mood." The word *elated* means "extremely happy." The word *melodic* means "musical." Therefore, the best word is the one used in the sentence, *sultry*. It means "passionate or desirous," which is something a flirtatious or an inviting person would be.

63. C

The phrase *as students perfect the wink* is not an independent clause and therefore cannot be followed by a period or a semicolon. This dependent clause introduces the rest of the sentence, so it must be separated from the independent clause by a comma.

64. F

The verb must be singular and present tense because the passage is written in the present and the noun phrase *instructor Myrna Orleck-Aiello* is singular. Therefore, *offers* is correct.

65. D

The noun *classroom* is singular, so the verb must also be singular. Since the passage is in present tense, the verb should also be in present tense. The only choice that fits is D—*is*.

66. G

The pronoun must agree with the noun. *Students* is plural, so the pronoun must be the plural *their*.

67. D

The sentence states a fact—that Orleck-Aiello is deaf. The word *class* ends the sentence, so it should be followed by end punctuation, not by a comma. The sentence is not an exclamation or a question, but a direct statement. The correct punctuation is a period.

68. J

Both adjectives must be in the comparative form or in the superlative form. In this sentence, more than two things are being compared (not one form of study to another, but one form of study over all others), so both must be in superlative form.

69. B

Paragraph 3 describes why total immersion is the best way to learn. Choices A and C seem to refute this idea. Choice D states that sign language is unlike other languages, meaning that while total immersion is best for most languages, it is not best for sign language.

70. H

The adjective *dozen* takes the plural noun *pupils*. Neither *pupiles* nor *pupil's* is the correct spelling for the plural form of the noun.

71. C

The word *Their* in this sentence is a pronoun, referring to the pupils. *There* indicates a place, as in *over there*. *They're* is a contraction of "they are." *Her* is the singular form of the pronoun, but since *pupils* is plural, it takes a plural pronoun.

72. F

The correct form of the verb here is the present participle. Therefore, the verb should be *has*, not *had*. The correct post-tense form of the verb *choose* is *chosen*.

73. B

The word *singular* implies one language. The word *generous* means "abundant." The word *melded* means "two or more things joined together to form one." Therefore, *various* is the best choice, especially since the question mentions *many languages*.

74. F

The other three choices all imply that a lot of people know French or Spanish because the woman and her husband speak different languages in public. This is not the case. Instead, it is because many people speak French or Spanish that the couple is trying to learn a different language.

75. C

Paragraph 3 discusses how the best way to learn sign language is through total immersion, just as it is with any other language. This is the best place to compare sign language to other languages, like French or Spanish, in order to reinforce that idea.

Model ACT III Reading Answers Explained

PASSAGE I

1. C

Choice C is correct because in much of the dialogue Alex gives Josie advice that Alex does not follow. Choice A is incorrect because according to lines 56–61, Josie had once been proud of her mother, but that had changed in recent years. Choice B is incorrect because there is evidence in the passage of a natural give-and-take relationship between mother and daughter. Choice D is incorrect because the passage indicates that there is a continuing relationship between mother and daughter.

2. G

Choice G is correct because in the last lines of the fifth paragraph Alex indicates that she was surprised that she had not been given the same presumption of innocence that she wanted for people in the legal system. The other choices are incorrect because the passage never brings up Alex and issues in connection with the innocence of defendants, Josie, or Josie's friends, even though these issues may exist.

3. C

Choice C gives the dictionary definition of *metaphorically.* The context can help you arrive at this answer because the passage implies judgment that is not real or actual, which eliminates choice A. There is also no direct comparison in the sentence, so neither B nor D is correct. The passage does imply that compared to other parents, Alex is different, which would leave you with choice C as the correct answer.

4. G

Josie uses the phrase in the last paragraph as she wonders what would happen if people knew the truth about how she really felt. The other choices convey confidence, aloofness, and superiority, which are the opposite of what the narration tells us about Josie's feeling about herself.

5. A

The only information in the passage about Matt is how Josie felt as she was stared at when she walked down the hall with him. Choice B is incorrect because the passage indicates the communication was "bricked shut," but it does not say or imply that the blame for this fell on Alex. Choice C is incorrect because the passage identifies Alex's hair as a "knot" and Josie's hair as "straight." Choice D is incorrect because although the passage does allude to the possibility that Alex could judge Josie's friends, it never suggests that she has actually done so.

6. J

The italics indicate this was what Alex was thinking, not what she was actually saying. The statement is a rhetorical question, a question to which no answer was expected. Choice F is incorrect because Alex does not seem concerned, although she may be frustrated. Choice G is incorrect because Alex applies these words to Josie, not to herself. Choice H is incorrect because an unspoken thought can't provide a clue to someone else about how to act.

7. B

Choice A is not correct because although both characters have moments of anxiety in the passage, this is not the overall mood. The characters do seem to have resigned themselves to the roles they are expected to play and to the course their relationship has taken. Choices C and D are too strong for this passage, as both characters seem passive instead of showing the strong feelings of frustration and desperation.

8. G

There is no indication that Alex stayed up late, even though Josie clearly did. Neither character expresses herself unconditionally, as shown by Alex making Josie eat breakfast and Josie's wish to "let them all in on the secret." There is no mention of Josie's father, or of the two women missing him. Alex's achievements as a relatively young judge and Josie's staying up all night to study do show, however, that they both work hard.

9. B

These paragraphs end with a warning that something terrible is going to happen in a span of nineteen minutes. Choice A is incorrect because the light tone is quickly erased by the last sentence. Choice C is incorrect because it does not refer to the first three paragraphs, but to the following paragraphs that include the dialogue. Choice D is incorrect because the number nineteen means more than just any number; it is the number of minutes it will take for some act of revenge.

10. H

The words *BEST describes* are important here because some of the other choices might be reasonable, but this is the best one. The author uses this dialogue to establish the relationship between Josie and Alex. It reveals the nature of their relationship. Choices F and G give less important reasons for the first lines of dialogue than choice H. Choice J reflects some of the content of the dialogue, but it does not give the reason for those lines of dialogue.

PASSAGE II

11. B.
In lines 13–14, the author states that Edward's motives for claiming the throne "have been variously ascribed by historians." Choice B most closely matches this evidence from the text.

12. H
In lines 22–23, the author states that Edward's success in the battle of Crécy "left him free to besiege Calais." This statement matches choice H only.

13. D
Although choices A and B are both mentioned in the first paragraph, they are secondary to the main point—the complexity of the conduct of war under medieval chivalry. This can be seen through the organization of the sentence as *not only* did A and B occur, but the main point is the complexity of war.

14. F
The author states in lines 23–26 that Edward "was free to attack Calais which, lying as it does at the narrowest crossing point to England . . . , was a vital strategic objective."

15. B
The author states that Philip's defense was "half-hearted" (lines 51–52). Philip then retreated rather than risk battle.

16. G
The idea that Edward had the power of life and death could be made without the note about sparing the men. Even if the men had surrendered earlier, the stakes would have been the same. Also, Jean de Vienne has been shown to be a good ruler because he tried to save the lives of his citizens. However, because Edward spares the men, it shows he is not only ruthless.

17. C
The last paragraph shows that *Calais* was still settled by the English after 1453, a century later, so choices A and B are incorrect. The word *Calais* was not inscribed on Mary Tudor's heart, but she allegedly said it was to show how important the city was to her.

18. F
Jean de Vienne's worry about surrender would not have been necessary if choices G or J were correct. Also, while Edward may have wanted vengeance, he did not take it to the full extent. However, Jean de Vienne could not have known what Edward wanted, but he knew that under those laws the men were in trouble.

19. D
Since the author puts in that these details were "according to Froissart" (lines 70–71), they cannot be taken as fact.

20. J
Lines 28–30 state that Philip was supplying Calais by sea, and lines 57–58 state that once Philip retreated, Calais was left to its own fate. Therefore, I and II are both correct. However, Philip retreated and, therefore, did not surrender at Calais, so choice III is incorrect.

PASSAGE III

21. C
The first sentence states that both books are puzzling and, since both are written in the 1800s, both are 19th-century works. The last sentence of the first paragraph says that *Wuthering Heights*, Brontë's work, is a "masculine" text. It also states that Shelley's work is a thriller and Brontë's is a romance.

22. F
The word *enigmatic* means "relating to an enigma, a puzzle or mystery." You can figure this out from the words *puzzling* and *mystery* in the passage.

23. C
The authors state that Brontë's work is "masculine" because "the fates of subordinate female characters seem entirely dependent upon the actions of ostensibly male heroes or anti-heroes" (lines 15–18). In other words, in a "masculine" work, the males control the action, no matter whether they are good or bad.

24. J
The authors of the passage state that Brontë's and Shelley's works were unrelated but do not mention whether the authors were related. They also state that both are unprecedented works, not just Shelley's. Although they do say they are different types of books—a thriller and a romance—the important aspect is that the books are puzzling in different ways, since this is the focus of the rest of the essay.

25. D

From the first paragraph, we know that both are 19th-century novels that are puzzling, so item I is correct. The authors state (lines 59–60) that "more than most novels, both are consciously literary works," so item II is correct. In lines 36–39, the authors state that "Both make use of what in connection with *Frankenstein* we have called an evidentiary narrative technique," so item III is correct.

26. H

Neither the authors' families nor fantasy and horror have anything to do with evidence in the books. These stories are told through different perspectives on the same episode, rather than one narration of different episodes (as is usual in a story), but these different narratives do not constitute evidence in the two works. Lines 47–55 summarize the evidentiary technique and state that each digression is through a different type of narration (or piece of evidence)—letters, diaries, narratives, etc.

27. B

The authors wonder if both books are conscious literary novels because, "like Shelley, Brontë was something of a literary heiress" (lines 64–65)—born to literary parents.

28. F

Although H is true, it is only the starting point for the passage. Obviously the authors don't feel one should not compare books, because they are comparing these two authors. Also, while they discuss the fact that both Shelley and Brontë had literary parents, they think this may be a reason for the literary nature of the works, not for underlying similarities. The main point, set up in the first paragraph, is that while these works have been seen as unrelated, or dissimilar, they actually have similarities such as narrative digressions, puzzles, and a literary nature.

29. C

These two "popular" novels have convinced readers that the surfaces conceal the complex depths, rather than reveal them, according to lines 28–34. Although they appear simple, they are, in actuality, very complex.

30. J

G and H cannot be correct because *Frankenstein* was written before *Wuthering Heights*. In paragraph 2, the authors state that *Wuthering Heights* might be a copy of *Frankenstein* in terms of the technique of evidentiary writing, not as a whole novel.

PASSAGE IV

31. C

The third paragraph contains a logical explanation of what happened as described in the second paragraph. Choice A is incorrect because the passage presents scientific explanations of the events. Choice B is incorrect because the passage focuses more on scientific fact than on the firsthand accounts. Choice D is incorrect because there is no proof in the initial section of the passage that magnetic fields in the Bermuda Triangle cause instruments to malfunction.

32. H

A large number of simultaneous reports give the most support about the cause of the instrument malfunctions. Choice F is incorrect because sporadic reports might have many different causes. Choice G is incorrect because properly functioning instruments would not confirm or deny that there had been instrument problems, and an inspection in this case would be of only one plane, meaning the problem was unique and not experienced by many people in the area. Choice J is incorrect because improperly functioning instruments would establish that the cause had been the instruments and not the Bermuda Triangle.

33. C

The word *precarious* means "unstable," so a reef precariously perched on an extinct volcano indicates an unstable reef. Choice A is incorrect because there is nothing about a precariously perched coral reef to suggest that Bermuda consists of sand and beaches. Remember, the best answer must be based on the passage. Choice B is incorrect because the volcano is extinct, indicating that there are no volcanic eruptions. Choice D is incorrect because the passage indicates the extinct volcano would have to have formed before the coral reef.

34. F.

If the Bermuda Triangle is really responsible for bizarre navigational problems, the problems have been present before they showed up as interference with navigation instruments, and before the 1952 report in this passage. Choice G is incorrect for the same reason. Choice H is incorrect because the magnetic North Pole would have had an impact on magnetic compasses, even if the magnetic North Pole had not been discovered. Choice J is incorrect because the formation of a coral reef could not have any impact on navigation problems.

35. C

If Denardo was able to make the experiment work only with a ball, that would call into question whether the phenomenon could sink a ship and thereby weaken his argument. Choice A is incorrect because an infrequent occurrence of the bubbles would not weaken the argument that the bubbles could sink a ship. Choice B is incorrect because the bubbles could still sink ships in less dense areas. Choice D is incorrect because sinking a small ship would not weaken the argument as much as not being able to sink anything but a ball.

36. H.

The passage says that waterspouts are less predictable, which means they are less forseeable—it's harder to anticipate when a waterspout will occur than when a thunderstorm will occur. Choice F is incorrect because the passage actually indicates that waterspouts are less reliable. Choices G and J are incorrect because the passage does not indicate that waterspouts are more frightening or less dangerous than thunderstorms.

37. B

The passage says that when using dead reckoning, pilots trusted their compasses and then estimated, guessed, how wind would affect their flight path.

Choices A and C have nothing to do with dead reckoning, as described in the passage. Choice D is incorrect because the compasses pointed to magnetic north, not to true north.

38. F

Evidence means statements of fact, as described in choice F and found on lines 53–56. Choice G is incorrect because information about the origin of hurricanes does not establish that there are more hurricanes in the Bermuda Triangle. Choice H is incorrect because the types of waters that thunderstorms thrive in are not unique to the Bermuda Triangle. Choice J is incorrect because microbursts are a type of thunderstorm, not a type of hurricane.

39. C

Choice A might be factually correct, but it does not provide a strong enough reason for the vivid description the author gives. Choices B and D are inaccurate because neither is true in the passage itself. Only choice C provides a solid rationale for the author's romantic description in the opening lines.

40. G

The buoyancy of an object indicates its ability to float. Choice F means saltiness, choice H means the mass of an object, and choice J means the amount of force an object puts on something.

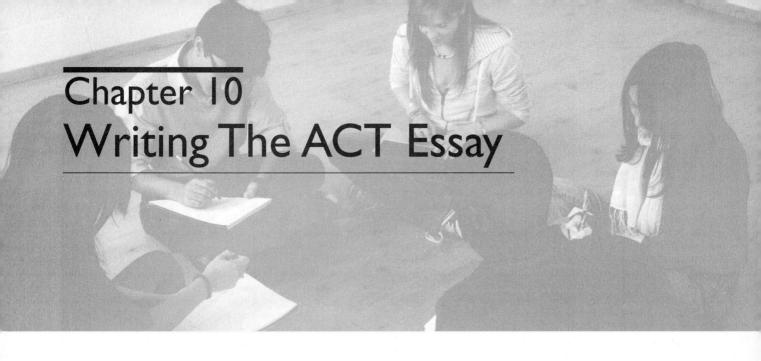

Chapter 10
Writing The ACT Essay

Overview of the Writing Test

The ACT Writing Test gives you 30 minutes to write a persuasive essay in response to a prompt. The prompt will introduce you to a particular issue and ask you to give your view on it. For example, you may write an essay about how a college should use grant funds, or whether a school should have a dress code.

ACT does not require the Writing Test; however, some colleges and scholarship programs do. Find out whether the test is recommended or required by any of the colleges or programs to which you're applying. You can use the "Search Writing Test Requirements by College" feature in the Writing Test section on the ACT Web site to see what various institutions have decided. You should contact admissions offices and scholarship agencies directly for the most up-to-date and reliable information.

Scoring the Writing Test

Two readers evaluate your essay and assign a score from 1 to 6. ACT trains its readers to score holistically by showing them many examples of essays. Holistic scoring means a reader's evaluation is based on his or her informed impression of your writing. The readers do not go into detailed analysis. If readers' scores differ by more than 1 point, a third reader also evaluates the essay.

ACT readers think about five essential questions as they rate your essay.

1. How well do you explain your position on the issue?
2. Do you maintain your focus on the issue throughout the essay?
3. Do you organize your ideas logically?
4. How thoroughly do you support your position with evidence, details, and examples?
5. Do you use language appropriately, in a way that does not distract from or interfere with a reader's understanding?

Notice that grammar is not mentioned specifically. Errors that distract a reader or interfere with a reader's understanding will lower your score. However, grammar is not the readers' primary focus.

ACT does not specify how long an essay should be, but it's worth noting in the following table that essays scored in the lower half contain fewer than 300 words, while essays scored in the upper half usually contain 400 words or more. It's not just more words but, rather, the extra detail in these higher-rated essays that makes them longer. You will probably have to write a minimum of 400 words to earn a score of 4 or higher. You will probably have to write an essay of about 500–650 words or more to earn a score of 5 or 6.

This table shows what distinguishes an essay rated in the upper half from an essay rated in the lower half. Notice that the first item on the list is your ability to clearly communicate your position on an issue.

ACT Rating Comparison

Upper Half	Lower Half
You clearly express your point of view on the issue.	You may not include a clear point of view.
You support generalizations with specific examples and details.	Your development of ideas is insufficient, too general, or repetitious.
You maintain a clear focus on the prompt throughout the essay.	Your focus strays from the issue and/or the topic of the prompt.
Your essay features a clear and logical organization with effective transitions between paragraphs.	Your essay features either a simple but acceptable organization, or no organization at all.
Your essay demonstrates an appropriate use of language.	Your essay can be generally understood.
While your essay may contain some distracting errors, the errors do not interfere with a reader's understanding.	Your essay contains distracting errors that may interfere with a reader's understanding.

Writing Review

Follow these steps to write your best essay in the 30 minutes provided to you.

You will also find a comprehensive review of English skills and a full range of practice activities on pages 32–167. If the evaluation of your essay reveals specific difficulties with English skills, you should review the pages that address those concerns.

Step 1: Decode the Prompt

Your first step is to read the prompt. Make sure you understand the issue that is presented. Also think about the arguments that could be presented on either side of the issue.

Next, decide what position you are going to take on the issue. The prompt usually provides two perspectives on the issue, so you can choose one of those, or you can come up with your own unique point of view to discuss. When you're deciding what position to take, think about how you will support that position. In a time-limited situation like the ACT Writing Test, you probably want to choose the perspective that you can support most easily (this is usually, *but not always*, the perspective you agree with). Also think about what an opponent to your position could argue and how you could refute that opponent's points.

Step 2: Make a Plan

You won't have time to develop a full outline when you take the ACT Writing Test, but you should definitely still devise a plan for your essay. Spend no more than five minutes doing this.

Try to write a single sentence that sums up your position and put this in the introduction to your essay—think of it as your thesis statement.

Write down at least three ideas that support your main argument and think of specific examples to support those three ideas. These will be the points you discuss in the paragraphs that follow your introduction.

Also summarize the opposition's position, as well as points that refute that position. Decide whether you will address the opposing argument at different points throughout your essay or in a single paragraph near the end of your essay.

Lastly, think about what you will say to conclude the essay.

Step 3: Write Your Essay

You are not expected to write a strict five-paragraph essay for the ACT Writing Test. However, since this is a familiar form to most high school students, below is a summary of how you could structure an essay response in five paragraphs. Remember, you can use more or fewer paragraphs, but following the guidelines for each overall section of your essay will make for a coherent and effective writing product.

- Paragraph 1 (60–75 words; 3–5 sentences): Introduce the issue and clearly state your position.
- Paragraphs 2, 3, and 4 (100–150 words each; 4–7 sentences each): For each of these paragraphs, write a topic sentence that states a main point or reason in support of your position. Then provide specific details and examples that illustrate your point to the reader. Be sure to include transitions between sentences within paragraphs, as well as between full paragraphs.
- Paragraph 5 (60–75 words; 3–5 sentences): Summarize your argument in a final attempt to persuade the reader that your position is correct.

As you write the paragraphs of your essay, remember the five questions that ACT readers consider when scoring your essay.

1. How well do you explain your position on the issue?

    Clearly state your position in the first paragraph.

2. Do you maintain your focus on the issue throughout the essay?

    Avoid straying from your position, unless you choose to explain why an opposing position is inappropriate. In other words, resist the urge to digress.

3. Do you organize your ideas logically?

    Provide transitions between paragraphs, making sure that the second through the fifth paragraphs relate clearly to your first paragraph. Develop your ideas in a logical way.

4. How thoroughly do you support your position with evidence, details, and examples?

    Provide explanations and specific details to support the main point of each paragraph.

5. Do you use language appropriately, in a way that does not distract from or interfere with a reader's understanding?

Write clear sentences, avoid the passive voice (see pages 358–359), use appropriate vocabulary, and leave yourself time to correct grammatical errors, particularly those that might interfere with the reader's understanding.

Step 4: Reread Your Essay

A few minutes before the end of the ACT Writing Test, look over what you have written. Be sure that all the sentences make sense and that your ideas flow logically throughout the essay. Correct any spelling errors you notice and revise any words or phrases that seem out of place, are not formal enough, or don't convey your ideas clearly. Make all corrections neatly so that scorers will still be able to read your writing easily.

▬ General Guidelines

These tips will help you to write a higher-scoring essay.

Avoid the Passive Voice

Whenever possible, avoid writing in the passive voice. Although the passive voice is not always inappropriate, it is unlikely to enhance your short essay.

Passive Voice

The **passive voice** emphasizes the action rather than the actor. It often takes the long way around to explain something. Passive sentences usually include a form of the verb *to be* with a past participle.

Look at these examples of sentences in the passive voice and the active voice. Notice that the actor appears at the beginning of each corrected sentence, whereas it is either missing or placed toward the end of each passive sentence.

EXAMPLES

Passive (Incorrect):   The essay is completed.

Active (Corrected):   I completed the essay.

Passive (Incorrect):   The essay will be completed.

Active (Corrected):   I will complete the essay.

Passive (Incorrect):   The Writing Test was designed by ACT.

Active (Corrected):   ACT designed the Writing Test.

Passive (Incorrect):   The curfew was approved by the Town Council.

Active (Corrected):   The Town Council approved the curfew.

Passive (Incorrect):   The curfew is opposed by some students.

Active (Corrected):   Some students oppose the curfew.

The Past Tense Is Not the Passive Voice

Sometimes the past tense is mistaken for the passive voice, and vice versa. They are not the same thing. The past tense indicates that something happened in the past. The past tense can be expressed in both active and passive voices.

EXAMPLES

Past Tense—Passive Voice (Incorrect):   The ACT was taken yesterday.

Past Tense—Active Voice (Corrected):   I took the ACT yesterday.

Past Tense—Passive Voice (Incorrect):   The test was registered for by Ryan.

Past Tense—Active Voice (Corrected):   Ryan registered for the test.

Write Effective Transitions

Include transitions in your writing to guide the reader from one idea to the next, and from one paragraph to the next. The transition words and phrases that follow will help you write a coherent essay.

Transition Words

Cause and Effect: These transition words establish a cause-and-effect relationship.

and, so, as a result of, because, consequently, hence, therefore, thus

Continuation: Some transitions show that the same theme is continued or explained in more detail.

also, and, by the same token, further, in addition, in other words, that is, then

Difference: These transition words point out differences.

although, but, contrarily, despite, however, as opposed to, in contrast to, not, nevertheless, on the contrary, unlike

Example: These transition words signal an explanation.

for example, for instance, that is

Order: These transition words suggest that elements are being ordered.

first, primarily, then, last, before, after

Similarity: These transition words point out similarities.

alike, also, in common, similar to

Note:
Assume a confident tone when you are writing a formal persuasive essay like that required by the prompt on the ACT. Think of it this way: If someone were trying to convince you of something, you wouldn't take that person seriously if he or she were stammering or shaking. The same is true of persuasive writing: You need to come across as someone who believes the position you are arguing is the best possible way to solve an issue.

Use Formal Language

Remember that this is a persuasive essay. To be successful, you should sound intelligent so that those reading the essay will take your ideas seriously. Do not use slang or conversational language; rather, use formal words like those you see in your textbooks or the newspaper.

EXAMPLES

Informal: Uniforms help to keep kids looking nice.

Formal: Uniforms keep students looking neat and respectable.

Informal: A curfew is just a bad idea meant to kill all the fun for teenagers.

Formal: A curfew may be ill-conceived, as adolescents might perceive it as a tool intended to keep them from enjoying life.

Avoid Redundancies and Repetition

In the ACT English Test section of this book, you learned that good writing is not redundant—it doesn't say the same thing twice. Look at these examples to get a better idea of what redundancy looks like. You'll also see how easy it is to correct a sentence with a redundancy in your ACT Writing essay.

EXAMPLES

Redundant: Removing soda machines from school campuses will improve student health and be better for adolescents.

Corrected: Removing soda machines from school campuses will improve student health.

Redundant: The prevalence of billboards that are everywhere bombard people with advertisements.

Corrected: People are bombarded with advertisements because of the prevalence of billboards.

In the same way that you want to avoid redundancy in your individual sentences, you also want to make sure that you are not repeating ideas in the same paragraph or across paragraphs. When you write the plan for your essay, make sure your ideas are not too similar to each other. If you find you are having trouble coming up with enough ideas to support your position, consider switching your viewpoint to see if you can support a different perspective more effectively.

Note:
You can also prepare yourself for the ACT Writing Test by paying attention to media around you. Most news outlets like newspapers, Web sites, talk radio, and political opinion TV shows present current issues in the world and discuss them from various perspectives. Paying attention to these media will help you to get into the habit of forming an opinion and supporting it with evidence of various kinds. It will also show you how to present other sides of an issue and refute those standpoints.

ACT 6-Point Rating Scale

Readers award points based on this 6-point scale. They categorize an essay as upper third (5 or 6 points), middle third (3 or 4 points), or lower third (1 or 2 points). Then they decide whether the essay is in the upper part or the lower part of that third. Look over the following criteria for the different scores on the ACT Writing Test to get a better idea of exactly what scorers expect you to do.

ACT 6-Point Rating Scale
UPPER THIRD   Competent Writer
6: Outstanding. The essay takes a clear position on the issue in the prompt and provides complete, clear, and convincing support for the position. The essay is well organized, and it features a logical development and effective transitions. Sentences are clear and well written. The superior command of language and vocabulary in the essay help convince the reader of the essay's position. The few errors of grammar, usage, and punctuation in the essay do not distract the reader and do not interfere with the reader's understanding.
5: Advanced. The essay takes a clear position on the issue in the prompt and provides some convincing support for the position. The essay is organized, and it features some transitions. Sentences are usually clear and well written. Sound command of language and vocabulary help convince the reader of the essay's argument. The few errors of grammar, usage, and punctuation usually do not distract the reader and do not interfere with the reader's understanding.
MIDDLE THIRD   Developing Writer
4: Acceptable. The essay takes a position on the issue in the prompt and provides some support for the position. The essay is usually organized. Sentences are usually clear and well written. Acceptable command of language and vocabulary may help convince the reader of the essay's position. Although the few errors of grammar, usage, and punctuation do not interfere with the reader's understanding, they may distract the reader.
3: Marginal. The essay takes a position on the issue in the prompt but provides very little support for the position. The essay usually has some organization, but it may be difficult to follow. Uncertain command of language and limited vocabulary do not help to convince the reader of the essay's position. Frequent errors of grammar, usage, and punctuation may distract the reader and interfere with the reader's understanding.
LOWER THIRD   Emerging Writer
2: Poor. The essay is marked by significant errors. The essay may take a position on the issue in the prompt but provides almost no support for the position. The essay is unorganized and difficult to read. Sentences are often unclear and poorly written. The essay features poor command of language and vocabulary. Frequent errors of grammar, usage, and punctuation distract the reader and interfere with the reader's understanding.
1: Unacceptable. The essay is marked by significant errors. The essay may take no position on the issue in the prompt or provide no support for the position. The essay is unorganized and difficult to read. Sentences are unclear and poorly written. The essay features poor command of language and vocabulary. Frequent errors of grammar, usage, and punctuation interfere with the reader's understanding.

Developmental ACT Writing Test

This section will take you step-by-step through the process of writing an essay. Complete each step in order. Let's start with the prompt.

Prompt

School administrators frequently recommend that school boards adopt a strict attendance policy for high school seniors. This policy requires high school seniors to limit their absences in the last month of school in order to be eligible for participation in the graduation ceremonies. Some school board members support the policy because they believe it encourages seniors to attend school regularly and to act appropriately at the graduation exercises. Other school board members do not support the policy because they think it interferes with parents' prerogatives and with students' opportunity to visit colleges. In your view, should school boards adopt a strict attendance policy for high school seniors?

In your essay, state your position on the issue. Your essay may address either of the points of view above, or you may present your own point of view on the issue. Remember to support your position with reasons and examples.

---

1. Understand the prompt and write your position.

The issue is whether or not strict attendance should be a requirement for graduation participation. We can argue for the strict attendance policy, or we can argue against it. Or we can take another point of view altogether. I don't know about you, but I'm going to stick with one of the two points of view in the prompt.

Personally, I'm in favor of the strict attendance policy.

My position statement: *School boards should adopt a strict attendance policy as a requirement for graduation participation.*

What's your position on this issue? Don't just use the one above. Write your own position statement below.

Your position statement: _____

_____

Remember to include your position statement in the first paragraph. Next, move on to the plan.

2. Write a brief plan.

Take some time to think and plan. Once you start to write, you will need to concentrate on writing well. Here are draft topic sentences for five paragraphs written in response. They don't have to be perfect—you can revise them later.

A Plan

Position statement (notice it's been revised to make it clearer):

School boards should adopt a strict attendance policy as a requirement for graduation participation.

Three important points that support the position statement:

    1. Rules lead to appropriate behavior.

    2. Students who've been absent from school often disrupt graduation ceremonies.

    3. We must respect the rights of all students and all families.

A statement that will begin the summary paragraph (conclusion):

We must defend standards that benefit the entire school community.

Your Plan

Now write your own plan. Write one sentence for each of the five paragraphs.

_____

_____

_____

_____

_____

_____

_____

_____

3. Write the essay.

The first paragraph states your position. The second, third, and fourth paragraphs present points or reasons, along with explanations and details, that support your position. The fifth paragraph summarizes your position and makes one last attempt to convince the reader.

    Write your essay in the space provided.

_____

_____

_____

4. Reread and revise.

Leave at least two minutes to go over your essay and make any necessary changes and corrections. After you've finished, review the three model essays that follow.

Model Essays

MODEL ESSAY 1 — Lower Third

(121 words)

I am a high school senior who knows people who cut school a lot. This essay says that I think it is a good idea to have strict school attendance policy as a requirement to participate in the graduation ceremonies.

Our last graduation was a mess. Students were running around yelling and they interuptted things. Almost every problem was caused by those kids who were absent from school a lot. Students at the graduation should not be running around drunk or drugging and other things like that. I do not want my parents to see that kind of stuff. The people on the school board should be busy and do something before there is more problem and the police have to come.

MODEL ESSAY 2 — Middle Third

(320 words)

Even though I am a high school student I am in favor of a strict school attendance policy as a requirement to participate in the graduation ceremonies.

Our last graduation was a mess. Students were running around yelling and they interrupted things. That showed what can happen when high school seniors cut school and their parents just give them notes. How about students that forge their parents names on the office signature card and just write notes for themselves. A simple attendance policy will help solve a lot of problems.

I think students who are absent from school a lot are more likely to disrupt graduation ceremonies than those who have regular attendance. Students who are frequently absent often do not have as solid a connection to the school as other students. In previous years it has been the truant students who have interrupted speakers and embarassed their classmate and the school. When this happens we realize that we should have a strict attendance policy.

Each student family should be able to enjoy the graduation. These people should not have to put up with a lot of problems that were caused by a few students who think they can do whatever they want because their parents do not have any rules at home.

Students at the graduation should not be drunk or using drugs because that causes more problems. My parents should know that I am there because I followed the rules and that everyone there followed the rules.

I hope then when I graduate and some day I am on the school board that I know how to make rules that will help the graduation be better. But I hope I do not have to wait until that day to see the school board have rules that say a student must be in school or they will not be able to go to the graduation with their parents.

MODEL ESSAY 3 — Upper Third

(435 words)

It is very common for a board of education for the best high schools to adopt a strict attendance policy. Many students and some parents may not like the idea but it is a good one. My position is that schools boards should adopt a strict school attendance policy as a requirement to participate in the graduation ceremonies.

Rules lead to appropriate behavior. It is the very basis of our society that everyone must follow reasonable rules that are in the common good. Experience has taught us that without an attendance policy, without rules to follow, high school seniors will cut school and convince their parents to give them notes excusing them from school. It is an open secret that many students forged their parents names on the office signature card and these students will just write notes for themselves. A simple attendance policy will help solve a lot of problems.

Our school administrators say students who are absent from school a lot are more likely to disrupt graduation ceremonies than those who are attending school. Since college admissions decisions have already been made, there is no reason for a high school senior to visit a college on a school day during June. The students who are frequently absent often do not have as solid a connection to the school as other students. In previous years it has been the truant students who have interrupted speakers and embarrassed their classmate and the school. When this happens we realize that we should have a strict attendance policy. But by then its too late.

It is more important to respect the rights of a majority of the students and their parents than it is to respect the rights of students who want to skip school. The many should not have to sacrifice for the comfort of the few. I know that when my parents come to my graduation I don't want anyone interrupting anything. I want my parents to know that I am there because I followed the rules and that everyone there followed the rules. All of the student's families should be able to enjoy the ceremony.

The school board should take a stand now for standards. Students belong in school when school is in session, not at the mall or somewhere else. Attending graduation is a privilege and it is not a right. Students who do not show respect for the school and themselves should not be there. The board should implement this policy immediately and have an atmosphere that will encourage everyone to follow the rules and to want to be at the graduation.

5. Evaluate Your Essay

Work with your teacher to evaluate your essay. Remember that readers base their evaluation on an informed impression of your essay. They don't read the essay in detail. With this in mind, let's look at the similarities and differences among these three essays.

How are the essays similar?

Each essay takes a clear position on the issue.

Each essay is essentially free of significant grammatical and usage errors, although errors are more noticeable in the lowest-rated essay.

How are the essays different?

There is a single obvious difference. The higher-rated essays have more words. That means the higher-rated essays provide more evidence to back up the main points and reasons that support the position. The highest-rated essays provide at least three main points or reasons in support of the position and strengthen each of these points with examples and specific details. These essays feature smooth transitions between ideas, good sentence structure, parallel form, and a diverse vocabulary.

6. Rewrite Your Essay

If your essay is not in the upper third, you should write it again. Even if your essay falls within the upper third, it wouldn't hurt to rewrite it. Revision is one of the best ways to improve your writing skills. Do the extra practice now to get the score you want on the ACT.

Use the following guidelines:

- Respond to the same prompt.
- Take 30 minutes to rewrite your essay.
- Use the lessons you learned from writing and evaluating your first attempt.
- Incorporate your teacher's suggestions.

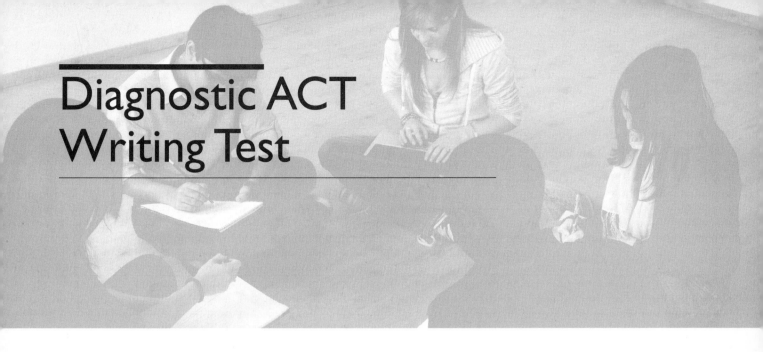

Diagnostic ACT Writing Test

Let's try an essay. This is the best way to find out how much work you have to do. After you write, look over the model essays that follow and review your essay with your teacher to determine whether it falls in the upper middle, or lower third of the rating scale.

Read the prompt, sketch a brief plan, and then write your essay on the lined pages that follow. Start now—you have exactly 30 minutes.

Diagnostic Prompt

Some parents asked the Town Council to impose a curfew that requires students under the age of 18 to be off the streets by 10 P.M. in order to reduce disciplinary problems and to help ensure children's safety. Other parents do not favor a curfew. They believe that imposing a curfew will not necessarily ensure children's safety and that it should be up to parents to decide what time their kids should be off the streets. In your opinion, should the Town Council impose a curfew for students under the age of 18?

In your essay, state your position on the issue. Your essay may address either of the positions above, or you may present your own point of view on the issue. Be sure to support your position with reasons and examples.

Review the model essays and their evaluations after you write your essay.

_____

_____

_____

_____

_____

_____

_____

_____

Model Essays

Here are two model essays. The first essay would receive a score in the middle third of the rating scale, and the second essay would receive a score in the upper third. Review each essay and consider the questions that follow.

MODEL ESSAY 1 | Middle Third

(211 words)

Some parents asked the Town Council to impose a curfew that requires students under the age of 18 to be off the streets by 10 P.M. in order to reduce disciplinary problems and to help ensure children's safety. Other parents do not favor a curfew. They believe that imposing a curfew will not necessarily ensure children's safety and it should be up to parents to decide what time their kids should be off the streets. In your opinion, should the Town Council impose a curfew for students under the age of 18? It is my opinion that the Town Council should vote for a curfew.

First off, if parents know there is a time a child should be home they will find the child if they are not. And second a child is probably going to be at a friends house if they are not on the streets and not home. They can always go there. Finally, a child is a child even if that person is in high school and they are their parents responsibility. The parents have a right to know where they are and that they are not on the street with drugs. Other they could end with a big drug problem.

The Town Council should vote for a curfew to have everyone who is under 18 off of the streets after 10 P.M.

Consider the five questions for Model Essay 1.

1. **How well is the position explained?**

   The position is fairly well explained, but almost the entire first paragraph is taken directly from the prompt.

2. **Is the focus maintained throughout the essay?**

   The focus is not consistent throughout the essay; it switches from one point of view to another.

3. **Are the ideas logically organized?**

   The strongest part of this essay is organization. There is a point of view and three associated ideas, but there are no clear transitions and no logical connections between paragraphs.

4. How thoroughly is the position supported with evidence, details, and examples?

This is the essay's main weakness. There is almost no support for any of the ideas mentioned in the essay.

5. Is language used appropriately, in a way that does not distract from or interfere with a reader's understanding?

The errors do distract the reader, but they do not interfere with the reader's understanding.

MODEL ESSAY 2 — Upper Third

(475 words)

The question of whether there should be a curfew for students under the age of 18 has been an issue over the years at many towns throughout America. People who support a curfew say it will help keep students off the streets and out of trouble. People who oppose a curfew think being off the streets will not keep students out of trouble, or think parents should decide how late their children are out. My view is the Town Council should vote for a curfew for students on school nights.

Some parents and other citizens in a town may believe that keeping students of the streets will not stop drug use and gang violence. That is not right. The reality is that the curfew will make enough of a difference to reduce these problems so that is well worth the effort, even if it saves only one child.

In the same way some parents think that they can control their children and keep them off the streets and off the street corners on their own. This is not right either. Students will always find some way to get to the street corner without their parents knowledge and we need rules the police can enforce to prevent these kinds of activities. No one says that a curfew all by itself will stop all these problems, but a curfew will be a first step to solving the problem.

A curfew will not only clear the streets of students it will also help solve other problems as well. With school children off the streets police will be able to concentrate on other problems. I remember a story about one town where crime was reduced overall once there was a curfew in place. That is what we need in this town, children off the streets, less crime and a safe place for everyone to live.

Perhaps the most important thing of all is that a curfew teaches responsibility. Students will know that being on the street after the curfew time will lead to consequences. The consequences might be a warning, punishment by parents, or in the very worst of cases some sort of detention. Parents will be responsible as well. They will face consequences if their minor children are on the street after the curfew. Over time both students and parents will have to learn that there is a right and a wrong.

Everyone in the town will be better off with a curfew. Minor children do not have the right to be wherever they want whenever they want. That is up to their parents and up to us the members of this a larger town who care about them and want what is best for everyone. The Town Council should vote for the curfew and we should all join in together with all of them to make it work.

Consider the five questions for Model Essay 2.

1. How well is the position explained?

The position is well explained.

2. Is the focus maintained throughout the essay?

The focus on the specific topic of the prompt is maintained throughout the essay.

3. Are the ideas logically organized?

The essay has a clear and logical organization, and the writer provides transitions between paragraphs.

4. How thoroughly is the position supported with evidence, details, and examples?

The writer provides support and details for each main point in the essay.

5. Is language used appropriately, in a way that does not distract from or interfere with a reader's understanding?

Some of the errors in the essay might distract a reader, but they are unlikely to interfere with a reader's understanding.

Evaluate Your Essay

Compare your essay to the model essays and decide whether it falls in the upper, middle, or lower third of the rating scale. It's a very rough estimate, but this exercise will help you identify what you need to work on in order to write a top-scoring ACT essay. With your teacher, go over your strengths and weaknesses, and determine the steps you should take to improve your writing.

ACT Writing Test I

In response to the following prompt, write an essay just like the one you will write for the ACT. That is, write an essay that will make the best impression on a reader. Clearly state your position on the issue. Include three main points or reasons in support of your position and back up each point or reason with details and examples. Compose a summary paragraph. Be sure to write at least between 450 and 600 useful words.

Use the model essays on pages 381–383 as you work with your teacher to evaluate your essay. The essays are rated as lower third, middle third, and upper third.

Write a persuasive essay for the prompt that follows. You have exactly 30 minutes.

▬ Prompt

A high school plans to construct a parking lot close to the campus. It will be used for either faculty parking or student parking. Those in favor of a faculty lot claim that faculty members often get to school earlier than students and that seniority entitles them to convenient parking. Those in favor of a student parking lot believe that students deserve to use the lot since their parents' tax money will be paying for its construction. In your view, should the parking lot be designated for faculty or student use?

In your essay, state your position on the issue. Your essay may address either of the positions above, or you may present your own point of view on the issue. Remember to support your position with reasons and examples.

Review the three model essays and evaluations after you write your essay.

_____

_____

_____

_____

_____

_____

Model Essays

MODEL ESSAY 1 | Lower Third

(78 words)

Currently our high school is building a parking lot. This lot is being bilt next to our school. Right now their is a lot of noise due to the tractors and trucks, coming and going. This is a distraction for students. This is why I think students should park in the new lot. Teachers aren't bothered as much by the noise. The students are under more stress which will be helped by not having to walk as far.

Model Essay 1 Evaluation

The paper represents an emerging writer. Its score would fall at the low end of the scale. Although the essay starts slightly off topic, the writer does take a position on the issue (that the new lot should be reserved for students since they suffer from stress) but fails to develop that idea. In addition, the writer provides no evidence to support the claim that teachers are less stressed than students. The organization of the response is unclear, lacking paragraph division. While the essay demonstrates a basic command of language, errors in spelling and punctuation are apparent. Sentence structure is simple and lacks variety.

MODEL ESSAY 2 | Middle Third

(131 words)

The proposed high school parking lot is a subject of much discussion. Some say the faculty should park in the new lot. Some say students should park in the new lot. All we know for sure is that both can't park there. I believe the new lot should be used for the faculty.

First and fore most is most teachers are way older than the students. They would have more trouble walking a big distance.

Second, students have more energy, especially after school, and need to burn of that energy before driving home or going into school.

Last, I've seen teachers carry boxes of work to and from their car. At most students only have a school bag and gym bag.

That's why teachers should park in the new parking lot.

Model Essay 2 Evaluation

The paper represents the work of a developing writer. It would score in the low middle of the scale. The writer provides several points in support of a position, but the ideas remain undeveloped.

The essay is sufficiently organized so that the introduction relates to points in each paragraph. However, the writer makes no apparent effort to link ideas, leaving the reader to make the necessary connections.

Although each of the main points has merit, the first and second points represent the same idea (that teachers' seniority should be respected).

Language and grammar are functional but simplistic. While sentence structure is generally repetitive, there is some evidence of advanced syntax.

MODEL ESSAY 3 — Upper Third

(470 words)

One of the landmark occasions of any teen's life is the acquisition of a driver's license. Cars symbolize a teenagers freedom and spirit. Conversely, cars are merely a functional tool to adults. This issue relates to the ongoing debate in our high school. At issue is who should park in the newly constructed lot; a lot that is mere feet from the front door. I believe the new lot should be for student use due to the following issues: economics, self-esteem, and logistics.

First the issue of economics must be examined. Teachers while not highly paid, make anywhere from fifteen to twenty times more than students. Economic solvency means teachers can afford nicer cars and the maintenance costs required for parking in older, smaller lots. Students, on the other hand, cannot always afford to pay for door dings from those who park too closer or tires shredded by potholes. The economic advantage afforded to teachers means they need not park in the newer, bigger lot, that privilege should be for the students.

The second reason students should be parking in the new lot is status and self-esteem. To a high school student, a nice car is a status symbol. Students spend time and what money they have making their vehicles look nice. When they succeed, they raise their social status and therefore their self-esteem. Low self-esteem is a problem that plagues high schools. While the new lot will not solve the issue completely, it will help some students. Teachers, the greatest advocates for students, must give up the new lot to help students feel better about themselves.

The third and final reason students should, indeed must be allowed to park in the new lot is simple logistics. When I arrive at school, the current faculty lot is full. In fact, I don't know if I have ever beaten a teacher to school. In that situation I am not alone. The teachers arrive early enough that they need not rush to their classrooms. Teachers are even required to arrive early, as much as twenty minutes before students. Yet students are often late due to lack of preparedness. A new lot will motivate students to be early in order to be in the prime spots. Early arriving students will cut down on tardies. In this case, as with the previously stated scenarios the greatest benefit is for students to park in the new lot.

Many people will argue that teachers are older or that they have more items to carry to the school, therefore they need closer spaces. But examining the situation rationally will lead anyone to see how the greatest benefit is for students to park in the new lot.

In conclusion there can only be one outcome for the current debate: students must park in the new lot.

Model Essay 3 Evaluation

The paper demonstrates solid writing and thinking ability. It would score near the top of the scale.

The essay has a strong thesis that provides the focal point of the paper. The thesis statement is preceded by an engaging introduction that captures the reader's attention. The essay stays on topic, and most ideas are well developed. One apparent weakness is the writer's assumption that the new lot would have larger parking spaces and no potholes.

While there isn't much variety in sentence structure, the essay demonstrates a sound command of language and vocabulary.

ACT Writing Test II

In response to the following prompt, write a response just like the one you will write for the ACT. That is, write an essay that will make the best impression on the reader. Clearly state your position on the issue. Include three main points or reasons in support of your position and back up each point or reason with details and examples. Compose a summary paragraph. Be sure to write at least between 450 and 600 useful words.

Use the model essays on pages 388–391 as you work with your teacher to evaluate your essay. The essays are rated as lower third, middle third, and upper third.

Write a persuasive letter for the prompt that follows. You have exactly 30 minutes.

▬▬ Prompt

A neighborhood association is trying to decide how to use an improvement grant. There is enough money to fund only one of two projects. The first project is upgrading underground water and sewer pipes, which will vastly improve water quality and sanitation. The second project is beautifying neighborhood streets and buildings, which will increase property values. Write a letter to the neighborhood association in which you argue for one of the projects, explaining how your choice will improve the neighborhood.

In your letter, state your position on the issue. Your letter may address either of the proposals above, or you may present your own point of view on the issue. Remember to support your proposal with reasons and examples.

Review the three model essays and evaluations after you write your essay.

Model Essays

MODEL ESSAY 1 | Lower Third

(117 words)

To whom it may concern,

I hear you have some extra money to buy more beautiful streets and buildings or new water pipes. Everyone knows the neighborhood looks real run down. If this is your choice I hope you know you need alot of money. We need the trash picked up and grass planted. Trees would help too. Some of the stores and houses look bad and need fixing. New water and sewer pipes are needed for better water quality and sanitation so we don't all get sick, like in Mexico when they tell you don't drink the water. But everybody drinks bottle water anyway. So you should take my advice and make the neighborhood more beautiful.

Model Essay 1 Evaluation

This response scores in the lower third of the scale.

The writer doesn't commit to a definite position until the last sentence. The few points made in the letter stand alone, without supporting details or examples. Organizational structure lacks paragraph divisions and transitions, making the ideas difficult to follow. The letter format is also incomplete, since the writer did not include a closing. Although the letter is comprehensible, there are numerous errors in vocabulary, usage, and sentence structure.

MODEL ESSAY 2 | Middle Third

(252 words)

Dear neighborhood association,

I am writing to tell you that you should use your improvement grant to beautify the neighborhood streets and building fronts. We have water and sewer pipes already, but we don't have a beautiful neighborhood!

What this neighborhood needs are sidewalks! We need a place for people to walk and ride their bikes without getting run over by the cars and making the drivers nervous!

Also what this neighborhood needs are flowers! The neighborhood would be more beautiful with colorful flowers, some shrubbery and trees, and bark chips around all the new plants. Better landscaping will give everything more curb appeal, and people would enjoy walking through the landscape on the new sidewalks.

We need paint too! Lots of the buildings and houses have peeling paint and faded paint. Also, some of the colors are tacky and clashing. We need to hire somebody to paint everything in nice colors that don't clash with the next door neighbor, like someone on my street who painted their house pink even though they say it's really just light brick. If everything was fixed up and looked nice, I think people would try harder to keep their yards cleaned up too.

There would be better moral if you could look around and like what you see. Especially now that its getting to be springtime, you want to go outside and enjoy the environment. Therefore the choice for more beautiful streets and buildings is the best decision for improving the neighborhood.

Sincerely,

Your neighbor

Model Essay 2 Evaluation

This response scores in the middle third of the scale.

The writer takes a clear position and supports it throughout the letter. Ideas are organized logically, and paragraph structure is appropriate. Examples are evident. Although there are some errors in sentence structure, word choice, and punctuation (such as the overuse of exclamation points), they do not distract the reader. The writer demonstrates a good command of language, usage, and vocabulary.

MODEL ESSAY 3 | Upper Third

(482 words)

Dear Neighborhood Association,

I am writing to let you know that the members of the neighborhood would prefer to see your improvement grant money used for the beautification project, rather than improved water and sewers. Beautifying the streets and building fronts would be a more noticeable use of the funds and increase property values.

The streets need the most immediate improvement. There are pot holes everywhere, especially on the side streets. It would be nice if curbs and grass could be added to the roadsides, so you could actually tell where the street edge is. Sidewalks would give pedestrians a great place to walk. If there are enough funds, I think a bike lane would be a very safe thing to have on the main streets. Another good safety feature would be to have "walk/don't walk" signs on the corners where the traffic lights are located. All of these improvements to the streets would enable people to get around town more safely and easily. Everyone in the neighborhood would appreciate this!

Improved fronts on all the buildings and houses would be another reason for the neighborhood to be appreciative to the association. I know the neighborhood association can't really control what the private property looks like for the business and home owners, but I think you can have people improve them in a fair way. You could let people write in to explain how they want to improve their store fronts and front yards, and distribute the money based on what each person wants to do. But, that would only improve some buildings. The ones that are the most run down are probably owned by people who don't care, so they wouldn't try to improve them anyway. The best way to improve the private property would be to have everyone do something. The worst ones could be given a list of repairs that need to be made, with a deadline to do it, and the association would pay for it. Places that already look nice could be given another tree to plant. That way, everyone would get something, and all the property would be improved. The entire neighborhood would be more beautiful, and everyone will have helped.

Beautifying the streets and building fronts will make everyone proud to live here, and proud of what the neighborhood association was able to get done. I know new water and sewer pipes are needed. However, I don't think this is the responsibility of the neighborhood association. Our water bill is paid to the city, so this is the city's responsibility. After the city earns more money from our neighborhood when our property taxes go up because of the added value the beautiful streets and buildings will bring, we will all have to sign a petition for the city to upgrade the water and sewer pipes!

Looking forward to a more beautiful neighborhood,

A concerned citizen

Model Essay 3 Evaluation

This response scores in the upper third of the scale.

The writer takes a strong position, maintains it throughout the letter, and refutes the opposing view. The letter is well organized, with appropriate transitions between ideas. Examples provide logical support for the ideas presented. The letter demonstrates excellent command of writing conventions, apparent in the variety of sentence structure, fluent word choice, and grammatical clarity.

Acknowledgements

Grateful acknowledgment is made to the following sources for having granted permission to reprint copyrighted materials. Every effort has been made to obtain permission to use previously published materials. Any errors or omissions are unintentional.

Martial arts passage. From *The American Martial Arts Film* by Ray Lott, McFarland and Company, Inc., 2004. Page 14.

"The Man Who Believed in Fairies" by Tom Huntington. *Smithsonian*, September 1997. Pages 142–143.

"The Sky Show in October" by Martin Ratcliff and Rick Shaffer. *Astronomy*, October, 1997. Pages 153–154.

"Thrills Every Minute" by Dick Victory. *The Washingtonian*, August, 1997. Pages 161–162.

From *Psychology: A Way to Grow* by Green and Sanford. © 2005 by Amsco School Publications, Inc. Pages 170–171.

From *Americans of Dream and Deed* by Robert J. and Lila Lowenherz. © 1993 by Amsco School Publications, Inc. Pages 173–174.

From *Western Civilization* by Antell and Harris. © 1983 by Amsco School Publications, Inc. Pages 174–176.

From *Science Fiction, Science Fact, and You* by Robert J. and Lila Lowenherz. © 1996 by Amsco School Publications, Inc. Pages 177–178.

From *Foliage House Plants* by James Crockett, Time-Life books, 1972. Pages 200–201.

From *Interpretation of Reading Materials in the Natural Sciences* by John T. Walsh, Cambridge and Coules, 1973. Page 200.

From *Walden* by Henry David Thoreau. Page 202.

From *Global Studies: Civilizations of the Past and Present* by Henry Brun. © 2003 by Amsco School Publications, Inc. Page 202.

From *World History* by Irving Gordon. © 2000 by Amsco School Publications, Inc. Page 202.

From *General Science* by Mould, Geffner, and Lesser. © 1991 by Amsco School Publications, Inc. Pages 202–203.

From *Global Studies: Civilizations of the Past and Present* by Henry Brun. © 2003 by Amsco School Publications, Inc. Page 203.

From "Flight" by John Steinbeck, in *The Long Valley*, Viking Press, 1938. Page 203.

From *Last of the Mohicans* by James Fenimore Cooper. Page 203.

From "The Open Boat" by Stephen Crane. Page 203.

From *The Bully, the Bullied, and the Bystander* by Barbara Coloroso, HarperResource, an imprint of HarperCollins Publishers, 2002. Page 203.

From "A Leader from the Start" by Kenneth T. Walsh in *US News and World Report*, June 2009. Page 203.

From *Invitation to Psychology* by Houston, Bee, Hatfied, and Rimm. © 1979 by Academic Press. Page 204.

From *Economics, Macroeconomics, and Issues* by James Cicarelli. © 1978 by Houghton Mifflin. Pages 204–205.

From "Bartleby the Scrivener" by Herman Melville. Page 205.

From "Crime and Punishment in Philadelphia" by John K. Alexander in *The Underside of American History*, Harcourt Brace Jovanovich, Inc., 1982. Page 205.

From *Touching Spirit Bear* by Ben Mikaelsen, HarperCollins Publishers, 2001. Page 213.

From *The American Martial Arts Film* by Ray Lott, McFarland and Company, Inc., 2004. Page 213.

From "Are Biopics History?" in *Newsweek*, February 2010. Page 214.

From *Forensic Science: An Introduction* by Richard Saferstein, Pearson Education, Inc., 2008. Page 214.

From *Psychology: A Way to Grow* by Green and Sanford. © 2005 by Amsco School Publications, Inc. Pages 216–217.

From *Call of the Wild* by Jack London. Pages 229–230.

From *Current Issues in American Democracy* by Antell, Harris, and Dobkin. © 2001 by Amsco School Publications, Inc. Pages 231–232.

From *Western Civilization* by Antell and Harris. © 1983 by Amsco School Publications, Inc. Pages 233–234.

From *Chemistry: A Contemporary Approach* by Paul S. Cohen. © 1996 by Amsco School Publications, Inc. Pages 235–236.

From *Science Fiction, Science Fact, and You* by Robert J. and Lila Lowenherz. © 1996 by Amsco School Publications, Inc. Pages 247–248.

From *Global Studies: Civilizations of the Past and Present* by Henry Brun. © 2003 by Amsco School Publications, Inc. Pages 249–250.

From *Psychology: A Way to Grow* by Green and Sanford. © 2005 by Amsco School Publications, Inc. Pages 252–253.

From *Western Civilization* by Antell and Harris. © 1983 by Amsco School Publications, Inc. Pages 254–255.

"A Tornado Struck" by Annie Dillard. Pages 256–257.

"Her First Ball" by Katherine Mansfield. Pages 259–260.

"G.I. Jane Stealthily Breaks the Combat Barrier" from *The New York Times*, © August 15, 2009. The New York Times. All rights reserved. Used by permission and protected by the Copyright Laws of the United States. The printing, copying, redistribution, or retransmission of the Material without express written permission is prohibited. Pages 261–262.

"Film Food, Ready for Its 'Bon Appétit' " from *The New York Times*, © July 28, 2009. *The New York Times*. All rights reserved. Used by permission and protected by the Copyright Laws of the United States. The printing, copying, redistribution, or retransmission of the Material without express written permission is prohibited. Pages 263–264.

"Is Time Travel Possible?" by Mark Davidson. © 1990 by the Society for the Advancement of Education. Pages 266–267.

From *Western Civilization* by Antell and Harris. © 1983 by Amsco School Publications, Inc. Pages 283–284.

From *Science Fiction, Science Fact, and You* by Robert J. and Lila Lowenherz. © 1996 by Amsco School Publications, Inc. Pages 286–287.

From *Global Studies: Civilizations of the Past and Present* by Henry Brun. © 2003 by Amsco School Publications, Inc. Pages 288–290.

From *Psychology: A Way to Grow* by Green and Sanford. © 2005 by Amsco School Publications, Inc. Pages 290–292.

"It's All in How You Say It" by Mickey Roberts. Pages 293–294.

"One Throw" by W.C. Heinz. Reprinted by permission of the William Morris Agency, Inc., on behalf of the author. © 1950 renewed 1978, by W. C. Heinz. Pages 296–297.

From *Psychology: A Way to Grow* by Green and Sanford. © 2005 by Amsco School Publications, Inc. Pages 298–299.

"Smart Skin" by Shawna Vogel. Reprinted by permission of the author. Pages 302–303.

"Just Desserts" by Dorie Greenspan. Reprinted by permission of Dorie Greenspan, food writer and cookbook author. Pages 323–324.

"Best Friends" by Caitlin and John Matthews. From *The Encyclopedia of Celtic Wisdom*. © 1994 by Caitlin and John Matthews. Pages 325–326.

"How Do You Say That . . ." *The Washingtonian*, August, 1997. Pages 328–329.

From *Nineteen Minutes* by Jodi Picoult. Reprinted with the permission of Atria, a Division of Simon and Schuster, Inc., from NINETEEN MINUTES by Jodi Picoult. Copyright © 1997 by Jodi Picoult. All rights reserved. Pages 331–332.

"Freeze Frame: Calais Remembered" by Gordon Marsden. *History Today*, August, 1997. Pages 333–334.

From *Madwoman in the Attic* by Sandra Gilbert and Susan Gubar. © 1979 by Yale University Press. Pages 335–336.

"The 'Mystery' of the Bermuda Triangle" by Sandrine Ceurstemont. From firstscience.com. Pages 337–338.

Index